Out of It

Out of It

A Cultural History of Intoxication

STUART WALTON

THREE RIVERS PRESS
NEW YORK

Published by Three Rivers Press, New York, New York. Member of the Crown
Publishing Group, a division of Random House, Inc.
www.crownpublishing.com

THREE RIVERS PRESS and the Tugboat design are registered
trademarks of Random House, Inc.

Published in hardcover by Harmony Books, a division of
Random House, Inc., New York, in 2002.

Originally published in slightly different form in Great Britain
by Hamish Hamilton Ltd., London, in 2001.

Printed in the United States of America

Design by Lenny Henderson

Library of Congress Cataloging-in-Publication Data
Walton, Stuart.
Out of it: a cultural history of intoxication / Stuart Walton.—1st ed.
Includes bibliographical references and index.
1. Alcoholism. 2. Narcotic habit. 3. Temperance. I. Title.
HV5020 .W35 2002
394.1—dc21   2002010961

ISBN 1-4000-4976-8

10 9 8 7 6 5 4 3 2

For Tim

Contents

Preface and Acknowledgments

The last ten years or so have seen the rapid accumulation of a body of work in an area usually given the name of the Drug Culture. Despite coming from a range of different disciplinary backgrounds, what this work has sought to do is to understand why certain groups of people within Western society use forbidden intoxicants. Much of the work has connected modern urban drug use to the ritual use of (usually hallucinogenic) intoxicants among the residual tribal cultures of South America, Africa and the South Pacific, and much of it has adopted a sympathetic tone toward cultural formations of this nature. We are learning more and more about the probable extent of the use of such profoundly mind-altering drugs as opium in contexts culturally a little too close to us for comfort, such as the ancient Greek. It now seems that opium almost certainly played a significant part in the everyday life of the Egyptian civilization.

This great socio-archaeological enterprise has further been accompanied from on high, somewhere in the political ether, by a developing debate about whether proscribed substances, or some of them at least (cannabis, generally, and perhaps ecstasy too) should be legalized, or at least decriminalized. Some have seized on the evidence that our ancestors had discovered and enthusiastically used psychotropic drugs, and that numerous preindustrial societies such as the Yanomani Indians of the Amazon basin still do, and sought to wave it in the faces of legislators in an attempt to crack their granite-faced refusal to consider relaxing the current prohibitions. With respect to much of the literature in this field, this is getting us nowhere.

This book is not another meditation on drug subcultures. Nor, with the exception of one passage of its argument in chapter 6, is it about tribal cultures. It is not intended to be another piece of special pleading on behalf of a drug-taking minority. It is, more radically than any of those enterprises, about intoxication itself, and the way it has formed an integral part of human cultural development since classical Greco-Roman times. To that extent, it is as much about the most widely used radical intoxicant in the world—alcohol—as it is about illegal substances. (Caffeine is more widely used still than alcohol, but doesn't provide anything like as profound an alteration of consciousness as alcohol does. Nonetheless, it is accorded its place in this study.) Intoxication plays, or has played, a part in the lives of virtually everybody who has ever lived, and yet throughout the entire Christian historical era in the West, it has been subject to a growing accretion of religious, legal and moral censure. These days, we are scarcely able to whisper its name for fear of falling foul of the law, of compromising ourselves in the eyes of others or of indicting ourselves as being part (however peripherally) of the multiple blight that has befallen our societies in the form of cigarette smoking, drunk driving, hooliganism, self-inflicted illness or drug-related crime.

My own intention in writing this book was to begin to rescue the universal human experience of intoxication from the clutches of politicians, health professionals and religious leaders, and to restore it to their beleaguered clients. This is not to say that those professional groups don't have a contribution to make in this field, but as the vast bulk of what they say tends to be prohibitive, admonitory or sternly judgmental, it is at last time that the other voice—the voice within ourselves—was heard. With the greatest respect to the Yanomani, they don't have to keep standing as a beatified example of intoxication for the purpose of legitimizing our own practices. That example occurs in our own everyday lives all the time. To seek to deny it is not only futile, it is a dereliction of an entirely constitutive part of who we are.

In researching this work, I have benefited hugely from the insights, experiences and practices of a great number of private individuals in the UK: in Southport, Manchester, Oxford, London and Brighton. Almost to a person, they have preferred, when asked, not to be acknowledged by name in these pages, for reasons that must be obvious from what follows. I hope they know who they are, and will be able eventually to award themselves the credit for the part they have played in helping me—like Pip in the house of Miss

Havisham—to tear down the moldering curtains that have shielded this subject from the bright, healthy daylight for so long.

At a procedural level, I do, however, insist on acknowledging the tireless attentions of my literary agents, Antony Harwood in London and Emma Parry in New York; the sensitive and constructive interventions of both my UK editor, Simon Prosser, and his American counterpart, Teryn Johnson, and the moral support I received from Clare Armstrong during a very tiresome sticky patch in the summer of 1999. The dedication is to my lifelong comrade-in-arms, for all the patient forbearance, the dialectical nights of music and symposium, not to mention the washed-out 9 A.M.s, and for being the only person in my life who finds Common Sense as overrated as I do.

Stuart Walton
Brighton, UK, 2002

Who will ever relate the whole history of nar-cotica? It is almost the history of "culture," of our so-called higher culture.

FRIEDRICH NIETZSCHE

(1 8 8 2)

Out of It

Introduction

Coming Up

Here is a modern recreational tale.

Three young men get together on a Saturday night. Their backgrounds are culturally diverse, but all reasonably comfortable. None of them has a criminal record, or comes from what sociologists used to call a broken home. They are of mixed ages (24–35), nationalities and sexualities; one is a mutual friend of the two others, who have not previously met. Two of them have come through a succession of relatively smart office jobs, but are now trying their hands at being self-employed. The third has held a responsible position in the catering industry, but is currently unemployed.

Two of them begin the evening in the apartment that one of them rents. They drink a bottle of sparkling wine and a bottle of white wine. While drinking, they also get through two grams of cocaine, snorting it in lines two at a time about every twenty minutes. They meet the third in a bar later on, and drink several rounds—perhaps half a dozen—of spirits with mixers. At around 2 A.M., they go on to another late bar, where one of them knows that drugs can be bought quite easily. Within minutes, they are offered ecstasy by a complete stranger. Following some gentle haggling over the price, they buy two tablets.

Outside the bar, a group of elderly bikers is selling amphetamine. They buy two grams of that as well. Back at the flat, they divide the tablets into six fragments and take two each. There is a further half gram of cocaine to finish, and the two grams of amphetamine. Whilst ingesting the drugs, they drink a further six bottles of sparkling wine between them over the course of the night. At 10 A.M., without having slept, they venture out into town again and, after lolling on

1

public benches for a while, go to a bar and embark on a round of bottled beers.

This is not exactly a typical weekend. It counts in the running narrative of their leisure time as something of a "blinder." None of them suffers much in the way of aftereffects. There is, to be sure, the sense of vacuumed-out listlessness that follows prolonged amphetamine intake. Two of them have acutely constricted sinuses, a compensation reaction to cocaine-snorting. None has an alcohol hangover. They are all fit and fully functioning again by Monday.

In a paneled room in the nether regions of one of Oxford University's more ancient colleges, a group of graduates and undergraduates that forms its illustrious debating society gathers. The room is lit solely by candlelight, lending the proceedings a vague air of masonic clandestinity, but only intended in the interest of a period feel, to evoke the time of the seventeenth-century poet-playwright after whom the society is named.

An oak cabinet, stained with age, and referred to as the Ark, is solemnly placed on the table around which the group is assembled. From it is drawn, with ecclesiastical reverence, a large two-handled pewter sconce. All eyes are trained on the president of the society as she fills this vessel to the brim with strong beer. Raising it above her head as if it were the Communion cup, she intones a Latin invocation of greeting to the foregathered company that ends with the solemn announcement, *"Nunc est bibendum"* ("Now is the time for drinking").

The sconce is then passed slowly around the table, each celebrant gripping it by both handles and uttering a Latin formula in honor of the household gods of the society's patron presence, before drinking a respectfully deep draught of the beer and handing it on.

Following this, a short talk on some agreeably nebulous moral theme is delivered—Honor, perhaps, or Forgiveness—and then the entire table sets to with a will, arguing over the points raised in convivial disarray, untrammeled by presidential intervention, and lubricated by copious quantities of wine and vintage port. At whatever time the room must be vacated, the members will totter away across the quadrangle, still disputing with each other in amiable inebriation, perhaps straggling into the nearest pub to continue their exchanges, assertions and refutations thickening the already smoke-dense air.

At such august institutions did many of Britain's parliamentarians once cut their debating teeth, thumping the drunken table to make their point about Pride or Altruism, quite as if it mattered. (In the mid-1980s, the group's president was herself the daughter of a Scottish member of the European Parliament.) But what particularly fascinated the parvenu guest, with his alternative haircut and redbrick degree, was the way in which drinking was not merely an incidental adjunct to make a lively evening the more commodious, but had been ceremonially incorporated into the ritual so integrally that teetotalers need not have applied. The Platonic dialogue flowed precisely from the sacred rite of intoxication, so that the meeting became a dialectical drinking-session, a far more dignified proceeding than colleagues getting slaughtered in the nearby Bull and Pennant were engaged in. Without alcohol, the society's disputations would have been aridly futile.

There are around two dozen subsidized bars in the British Houses of Parliament.

A pair of dining companions scrutinizes the menus in a smart, trend-setting restaurant in a European capital city. One has opted to begin with the tempura-battered strips of calf's liver with pomegranate cream dressing, and go on to herb-crusted rack of lamb with Provençale vegetables. For the other, it will be quail terrine with redcurrant relish and rocket, and to follow, poached perch with a sauce of lemon and capers. Now for the tricky business.

That dressing on the liver might present problems for a light white wine, and without knowing precisely how sharp it will be, the choice is something of a matter of stumbling in the dark. A crisp New Zealand Sauvignon might stand up to it, and cut any residual oiliness in the batter, but then, what of the quail terrine? Surely that needs a meatier white, even a light red? The merits of a sturdy white Burgundy are discussed, but the proposal is soon relinquished. An excess of oak would suit neither dish. Eventually, a compromise bottle is found. The weight and extract in a *grand cru* Gewurztraminer from Alsace will cope with the battered liver, and is a gastronomically unimpeachable match with any kind of terrine. The first bottle can safely be ordered.

How, though, to find a vinous chameleon to blend with both red meat and white fish? That way, gustatory madness lies. Pinot Noir might suit a densely textured fish like tuna, but could crush the delicacy of a river fish, while lacking the tannic heft required to stand up to lamb. The rich buttery sauce with the perch will happily negotiate the fleshiness of a Barossa Valley Chardonnay, but even that wine, with its layers of oak and alcohol, is just too *white* for rare red meat. An apposite half bottle each would be the obvious answer, were the list not so lamentably deficient in them. After much fretful chewing of bread, and flipping of pages back and forth, the issue is imperfectly resolved in favor of a bottle of *cru classé* Pauillac, the gameplan being that the fish-eater will be left the lion's share of the Gewurztraminer to go with the perch (which means drinking the same wine with two courses, alas), but will nonetheless be able to help finish the claret with some cheese. Now the logistics of it must be explained to the sommelier, so that he doesn't overserve the Gewurztraminer to the lamb-eater during the hors d'oeuvre.

In certain wine circles, food and wine matching has reached the status of an investigative science. A wine periodical convokes a bunch of journalists and wine-makers to pick wines to go with a succession of dishes, the linking theme of which is strawberries. There is goat cheese with strawberries, swordfish with strawberries, duck livers with strawberries in balsamic vinegar, and a strawberry and white chocolate gâteau. A forest of opened bottles clutters the table as the panel searches earnestly on behalf of the magazine's subscribers for the precise wine to marry with each dish. At the Fetzer winery in Mendocino County, California, there is a dedicated school devoted to this pursuit, where interested parties may enroll to spend studious days tasting and conferring. Is Sauvignon a better match than Chenin for the acid bite of sorrel, or is its up-front fruitiness more obviously suited to watercress? Then again, it depends on the dressing . . .

What all these scenarios are about is the alteration of consciousness. The use of illegal drugs, being a minority pursuit within society at large, is not subject to quite the same complex elaborations that drinking is; the various plant substances have been disconnected from their deep ritual histories by transplantation into Western economies and their quarantining by legal restrictions, while synthesized laboratory chemicals such as amphetamine have never had them. Alcohol, by contrast, has accrued over the millennia a rich and almost infinitely diverse set of symbolic contexts in which it may be taken, whether the aim be celebratory, consolatory, medicinal, scholastic, sacramental or gastronomic. What motivates our involvement with all intoxicants, however, is what they do to us. That may range across a spectrum from gentle tipsiness to stupefied collapse, from mild mood-heightening to gasping elation, from slight drowsiness to barely conscious narcosis, from faint dissociation to full-on hallucinogenic psychedelia. Sometimes the spectrums may be superimposed one on top of the other as substances are combined. The point is, nearly all of us will be somewhere along one of these spectrums for a significant part of our lives. And we always have been, depending on what was available, right back to Paleolithic times.

It is only in the last few years, however, that the subject of intoxication has come to be addressed in any systematic way. Part of the reason for this is that nobody is officially supposed to have any experience of the substances listed in the American Controlled Substances Act, the British Misuse of Drugs Act, or analogous legislation throughout the world. "What we cannot speak about," as Wittgenstein might have reminded us, "we must pass over in silence." Even in the case of the permitted intoxicants alcohol and tobacco, though, there was until not long ago very little explicit acknowledgment that their importance in human affairs derives primarily from their psychoactive impact in our systems. Where this was referred to, an uncanny decorum persisted, so that in some peculiar way, to have become even mildly inebriated in the course of partaking of intoxicating drinks had to be spoken of as though it were an accidental, embarrassing side-effect. Indeed, there is a sedimentary layer of apologetics, of bashful, tittering euphemism, at the bottom of all talk about alcohol as an intoxicant that was laid down in the nineteenth century, and that not even the liberal revolutions of the 1960s quite managed to dislodge. If anything, it is impacting and strengthening again, underpinned by the predatory mood of neo-Prohibitionism that the United States may well succeed in exporting to Europe, and by the proscriptiveness of professional bodies such as the British Medical Association. A hysterical editorial in *USA Today* calling for drink companies to be made to pay the medical expenses of cirrhosis patients may simply be the mood music of the new repression, but how to react to this introductory comment in a monumental history of wine-making by one of its most elegant chroniclers, Hugh Johnson?

> It was not the subtle bouquet of wine, or a lingering aftertaste of violets and raspberries, that first caught the attention of our ancestors. It was, I'm afraid, its effect.[1]

Quite so, but why the deprecatory mumble? What is there to be "afraid" of in acknowledging that wine's parentage lies in alcohol, that our ancestors were attracted to it because the ur-experience of inebriation was like nothing else in the phenomenal world? And what else in it attracts the oenophile of tomorrow in the first place, if not the fact that she found it a pleasant way of getting intoxicated today? Can we not say these things out loud, as if we were adults whose lives were already chock-full of sensory experience?

We can't. It is in many ways easier to be frank today about one's sexual habits than it is to talk about what intoxicants one uses. Illegality is its own form of straitjacket, of course, but the increasing requirement, even in quite irrelevant circumstances, to declare to doctors what the level of one's intake is, together with the concomitant imperative to cut it down or pack it in, quite as if such matters were invariably their concern, is rendering us all shamefaced inarticulates on the subject. Increasingly, corporate employers are awarding themselves the right to know what is in the bloodstreams of their staff. Decline the test, and you're out. A major psychological revolution was fomented in the early twentieth century when the infant science of psychoanalysis suggested, scandalously enough at the time, that we would be better off finding some honest way to acknowledge our sexual desires rather than continuing to stifle them. The same science might profitably direct many of its modern-day clients to be equally courageous in accepting the intoxication drive, which is at least as—if not more—peremptory in its demands on us. That task in any case lies before us all (Freudian analysands or not), I believe, as one of the challenges of the new century, and this book is an attempt to outline some of the most important historical reasons for our arrival at the present impasse. If we can see why we have come to be so embarrassed about the topic, then we will stand a chance of emerging from the long shadow of guilt that has been cast over that proportion of our lives for so many generations.

It isn't as though intoxication were evolving out of our history, after all. Tobacco-smoking may have declined in some Western countries as the health campaigns against it have gradually scared people off the habit, but we shouldn't simply rejoice at that tendency by pointing to the growing numbers in each generation who never so much as touch a single cigarette. There are many who, like the author, take it up in student years with the intention (successfully, as it transpired) to give it up a few years later, and they too count as part of the overall decline. No lasting harm may be done from a pattern of use like this, but that doesn't mean one can just edit the fact of it out of one's life. The fact is that I have been a user of tobacco— a temporary user, but a user nonetheless. And the propaganda may not be anyway quite as efficacious as its authors hope. An ex-smoker who professes to be baffled at the inability of others who want to stop, but can't, is disavowing the evidence of his own experience, while those who never started needn't feel obliged to weigh in. Temperance campaigners take a disproportionate amount of heart from antitobacco propaganda, in the sense that they believe that if they keep stressing, exaggerating and fabricating the health risks of alcohol, they will wean the next generations off that. This is a real hiding to nothing, though. A significant part of the impetus to stop smoking derives from the fact that the user becomes aware, relatively rapidly, of the physical consequences of the practice, an outcome not noticeably replicated by alcohol, where any demise through overuse is a much more gradual process.

Drinking, not least for that reason, is as pervasive as ever, with consumption by certain groups being explicitly about accelerating and enlarging the effects of it. The export-strength lagers that became conspicuously popular in the 1980s have been followed by ice-beers, in which a proportion of the water content of the drink is frozen off to concentrate the alcohol quotient in what remains, and then notoriously, in the 1990s, by alcopops, those brightly colored, fizzy fun-drinks that look and taste like children's pop and often come with cartoon labeling (anthropomorphized bubbles with scowling faces denoting the hyperaggressive blast of alcohol within them). The drink companies that produced alcopops—and once the commercial bandwagon was rolling, most of the major conglomerates did—were angrily denounced not just by temperance campaigners, but more surprisingly by some drink writers. There was an inevitable shudder of *dégoût* in this, the same spasm that goes through food journalists when they torment themselves by imagining the artery-furring cuisine of the proletariat. But what, I think, upset the wine writers more about the alcopop phenomenon was that it was targeted very effectively, whatever the drinks companies said, at those who were only just old enough to drink. Alcohol, we are asked to believe, is a dangerous gift that mustn't be allowed to fall into the eager hands of minors, for fear they should become initiated too soon into its potent mysteries. This attitude flies in the face of sound historical precedent. Boys as young as ten were once routinely given strong ale with breakfast to fortify them against the day ahead, while an extant photograph of a Victorian lady in a London pub holding a pint glass to the lips of her small daughter undermines at a stroke our cultural assumptions with regard to age, gender and alcohol in an era generally regarded as riddled with inhibition. To try to deny intoxication, even in private contexts, to those under the licensing age is to refuse an essential learning experience to them, and has no greater chance of success than any other prohibition. In any case, for most of the 1990s, alcohol has not necessarily been the drug of choice among young people.

We know that prohibitions, whether parental or legislative, don't work because virtually all other intoxicants are officially banned. Despite this ban, prosecuted worldwide by what I shall call "the enforcement industry," with ever more extravagant displays of force and fantastic budgetary resources at its disposal, the use of illegal drugs goes on relentlessly rising. I should state now that, far from seeing this as a troubling symptom of social breakdown, I consider it a heartening and positive phenomenon, a last tidal wave of mass defiance against institutional apparatuses whose power is now concerted on a global scale, and yet whose minatory efforts at dissua-

sion are being stubbornly brushed aside. When the Reagans resur-
rected the martial metaphors of their predecessor Richard Nixon in
the 1980s to inaugurate a fresh War on Drugs, this one intended like
all others to be the decisive assault, they could at least have no cause
for complaint that the challenge wasn't taken up. A war requires at
least two belligerent parties, and the latest skirmishes have been
going on for around fifteen years, and counting.

All that has happened is that more drugs have become more
widely available than at any time since the present drug laws began
to be formulated piecemeal out of the medical and moral panics of
the late nineteenth century. And not only are they more available,
but more people want them. In a gesture closely resembling despair,
the emphasis of the war changed in the latter half of the 1990s to
trying to reduce demand for them. TV campaigns, admonitory literature in schools, the stabbing fingers of politicians and health professionals, have all failed. When people want advice about what they
are taking, they will seek it out (and more often find it uselessly partial or else nonexistent). In the meantime, what they want is to be
able to take what they want without fear of legal harassment, and
without it necessarily becoming somebody else's business. Some may
argue that all drugs, legal or illegal, carry the risk of harm. This is
undeniable, but was dealt with briskly and philosophically by the
celebrated German toxicologist Louis Lewin writing in 1924:

> The force of the reactions with respect to the apparent obnox-
> iousness has at all times depended on the sensitiveness of the
> observer. This latter has extremely wide limits, from the most
> tolerant indulgence to the most severe condemnation . . . [Alco-
> holic excess] is the business of other persons just as little as the
> voluntary state of cocainism or morphinism, or the state of caf-
> feine inebriety produced by drinking large quantities of strong
> coffee, or excessive gambling, etc. Everybody has the right to do
> himself harm . . .
>
> An abstainer is not a superior being simply because he
> renounces alcohol, just as the person who has taken a vow of
> chastity may not consider himself better than another who obeys
> the normal impulses of his nature . . . Abstinence may be justi-
> fied as an individual conviction, but not a gospel. [I]ndividual

aversion to an agreeable sensation does not give a man the right
to measure his neighbour's peck by his own bushel.[2]

In Japan, the intensely toxic flesh of the puffer fish, fugu, is prized as
a fine seasonal delicacy. So dangerous is it that only tiny morsels
may be consumed under extremely controlled circumstances, and
fatalities arising from heart failure following an incautiously large
ingestion are by no means unheard of. We may find it unfathomable
that anybody should wish to take such a risk, but that is scarcely a
reason to prevent them from doing so. These arguments are developed further in chapter 5 of this book, but it will be useful to remind
ourselves at the outset of two uncontroversial but frequently forgotten points regarding illegal drugs.

The first is that we must learn to distinguish between substances.
Even the legal classifications permit some distinctions, crude and
unreliable though they are, between types of drugs, and the different
actions they have in the body. Some drugs carry a high potential for
dependency; others carry none. All that binds this entirely heterogeneous pharmacopoeia together is that all its elements have been
declared illegal. To accept that blanket classification without query
represents a failure of mental agility. Just because legislators have
voted to be part of that failure, enshrining its ignorance in the role of
the Drugs Tsar (whose unenviable task it is to bring about a reduction in consumption of these substances while simultaneously talking nonstop about them), does not mean that we have to accompany
them into the dark cloud of unknowing. It constitutes a laming of
the intellect to keep speaking of drugs as one amorphous, overweening category, as if the devil within it came forth and named its own
evil at the mere mention of that haunting monosyllable. "Drug" is
traceable back to the Old French *"drogue"*—the same as the modern French—before which its origin is swathed in uncertainty, but
for most of its career it has been a value-free shorthand for all phar-
maceuticals. Here is a sadly not atypical piece of maundering from a
review of twentieth-century cultural history—Peter Conrad's *Modern Times, Modern Places*—otherwise rightly praised for its intellectual grip:

> [I]n Los Angeles, Aldous Huxley experimented with psychedelic
> drugs, which he thought of as a chemical technology, a means of

instantaneous transport to nirvana. This was a seditious venture, because drugs challenge the imperatives of action and exertion which drive our history. They allow the user, immobilised during a trip which takes him nowhere, to slip out of time—to kill it by sitting still, rather than (like the Italian futurists in their sports cars) by frantic acceleration.[3]

A working mother of the 1960s, zipping through the ironing on prescription speed, might have been able to take issue with that last point, as might the superstar chef on cocaine, but it isn't simply that the hazed-out trance that was the paradigm state of "being on drugs" in the popular perception of the time won't serve as an emblem of all drug-taking now any more than it did then. It is also that it isn't especially serviceable as an account of the effect of hallucinogenic substances like Huxley's mescaline. (Huxley is actually anything but "immobilized" during his inaugural mescaline experience, as it is recorded for us in *The Doors of Perception*.) And then there is the familiar characterization of drugs as inimical to social functioning, as if a good deal of this "action and exertion" that has impelled our history hasn't in itself been brought about by individuals and classes whose awareness of reality was continually modified by intoxicants of all sorts. To posit the existence of a single, compendious substance called "drugs" is also to get away with the fiction that taking them is an eccentric pursuit found only in a deviant, dysfunctional subculture. But intoxicants in many forms have been an integral part of the lives of the mass of humanity both before and since many of them were declared off limits, and in the light of that fact, we must question what sort of agenda is served by such a malevolent act of synthesis.

Having created this menacing shibboleth by means of the law, it has been easier to convince those who have stayed within the bounds of the officially sanctioned intoxicants—caffeine, tobacco and alcohol—that use of any of the other substances is an enterprise fraught with peril. Two mythical notions have been brought to bear in all public discourse on the subject: (a) the addiction model, under which all illegal substances are invested with the power to enslave the curious should they venture anywhere near them, and (b) the slippery-slope narrative, which warns that the seemingly less dangerous drugs are really gateways to harder, more injurious substances, the process itself having a fatal inevitability about it that entraps even the most ironbound will in its tentacles. It will be seen that the two propositions can't both be true. Either all drugs are as addictively, corrosively bad as each other, in which case we may wonder what the derivation is of Schedule 1, Schedule 2 and so forth, or the truth is that there are some drugs that are not addictive. The latter is of course the case, but it is a truth that was only very reluctantly conceded by legislative authorities as recently as the 1970s, and it could only be apprehensively granted if it were tied to a mendacity that would prevent investigation of these so-called "soft" drugs. (A "soft" drug has always sounded to me about as exciting as a soft drink when what you want is a glass of beer, so the terminology may not have been an entirely fortunate one anyway.) There is no inevitable process that leads from cannabis to heroin, a point evinced by every single survey of illegal drug use; they all find that the vast majority of people who take proscribed substances take only cannabis, and have done so over many years. If the slippery slope does exist, it must be inclined at an extremely gentle gradient. In fact, as political administrators well know from their own commissioned research—much of it kept securely unpublished—it doesn't. It's just easier to lie.

This is the second point I would ask the reader to bear in mind. Only a small minority of drug use is what is currently termed "problematic," that is, leads to wrecked health, antisocial behavior and a drain on public finances. Most of it has no negative medical or social implications—nor should it, I believe, have legal implications. Saying this is not to deny the tragedy and squalor that dependency, particularly in the case of the opiates, can create. A lot of crime is committed in order to finance heroin addiction, and that, as I shall argue, is precisely a function of its illegality. I have heard of and personally witnessed hair-raising examples of the consequences of heroin addiction, as well as nightmare encounters with hallucinogenics. I have given assistance to people who have slithered into hypertensive panic after swallowing strong ecstasy in nightclubs. Most upsetting of all has been the helplessness I have felt at the sight of an old and valued colleague subsiding into the quicksand of alcoholism. This book, though, with respect, is not about them. Those hoping to hear recurring salutary tales of chronic illness and premature death will, in the main, be disappointed. It is rather about the broad, open field of intoxication in which most are able to disport themselves without sustaining anything more serious than the odd grazed knee or sprained ankle. Or thundering hangover.

A significant part of my research has consisted in talking to people who do use banned substances. Most of these take something every weekend, some (in the case of cannabis mainly) every day. Most of what I have gleaned has emerged in the course of ordinary social interaction. I have deliberately avoided the usual sociological fieldwork methods—questionnaires, interviews and so forth—because I strongly feel that as soon as research of this sort is cloaked with the trappings of official inquiry, you stop hearing the truth. Whenever I have allowed myself the sociological phrase "one of my respondents," I am using material that I personally know to be true, or that I have very strong circumstantial grounds for accepting. I am confident that the insights gained this way are more sturdily reliable than what results from sticking a micro-recorder under a teenager's nose, and asking, "Why do you take drugs?"

A strong clue as to the answer to this question is anyway supplied by the psychoanalytical theorist Slavoj Zizek in a collection of lectures on the theme of "enjoyment as a political factor," delivered in 1989–90. The immediate point concerns sexual passion, but speaks even more eloquently to the subject of these numberless and nameless "drugs" that bulk so large in many people's lives:

> [A] simple illicit love affair without risk concerns mere *pleasure*, whereas an affair which is experienced as a "challenge to the gallows"—as an act of transgression—procures *enjoyment*; enjoyment is the "surplus" that comes from our knowledge that our pleasure involves the thrill of entering a forbidden domain—that is to say, that our pleasure involves a certain *displeasure*.[4] [emphases original]

It may simply be that the displeasure of the criminal law incurred in intoxicating oneself with banned substances, and the excitement that that entails given that there seems to be no objective moral reason not to do so, is all that unites these incendiary materials called drugs. Drug-taking offers to all who have financial and social access to it the chance of breaking the temporal law without any cost in moral guilt, since nobody else is seemingly being hurt, deprived or incommoded in any way. It carries an innervating thrill all of its own, against which the officially sanctioned options—the roller-coaster rides, the gambling casinos, the aquaplaning and parachuting clubs—cannot begin to compete. Zizek goes on:

> The uncanny excess that perturbs the simple opposition between external social law and unwritten inner law is therefore the "short circuit" between desire and law—that is to say, a point at which desire itself becomes Law, a point at which insistence upon one's desire equates to fulfilling one's duty, a point at which Duty itself is marked by a stain of (surplus-) enjoyment.[5]

If the conflict between external and internal laws (the same conflict that is the essence of all human drama) motivates the first involvements with controlled substances, its excitement nonetheless fades away as the various intoxicated states become familiar. After that, one's choice of drug evolves into a matter of personal conviction. To some, the ever-present theoretical risk of confrontation with the law seems a tiresome burden to shoulder, and they will from then on make do with whiskey and espresso. To others, a particular banned substance is too enjoyable for itself to forgo. Still others will continually be open to new experiences, whatever the risks, costs or rules. The challenge to society, and to lawmakers (many of whom are themselves no strangers to intoxication), is to find a way of allowing individuals to fulfill those imperatives without either bleaching too much of the thrill out of them, or conversely threatening them with ever more furious and irrelevant penal tariffs.

The approach I have taken is a thematic one, and reflects the ways in which altered consciousness has been viewed within different contexts in Western culture. After an analysis of the attitudes to the subject that prevailed in the classical Greek and Roman periods, the focus is turned successively on the religious, social, legal, medical-biological and aesthetic facets of intoxication.

A copiously accumulating body of literature on this theme has been appearing in recent years, its contributors addressing it from different specialist angles, and this book is an attempt to synthesize and augment that literature. In chapter 1, I offer a selective overview of some of the more pertinent recent contributions to a field that I have called Intoxicology—the study of the alteration of consciousness by means of natural and synthetic chemical aids. Since the drive to achieve intoxicated states is a universal and abiding one, we may fairly conclude that it deserves to be studied in its own right. I draw an analogy with the surprisingly recent emergence of gastronomy as a serious aspect of cultural studies, and argue that intoxicology needs to be disentangled from its constricting associations with criminality, with the sociological study of deviancy, if we are to begin to understand its multiform appearances and its complex development.

Chapter 2 examines the ambivalence that existed within the classical cultures of Greece and Rome toward the question of intoxication, principally with regard to drinking. To the Greeks, wine played a double role. It was, on the one hand, the sacrament of the orgiastic worship of Dionysos, the antic god who was imported into the Greek pantheon from less socially developed, more oriental cultures, and who was only imperfectly house-trained by his translation to Mount Olympus. Then again, wine could be the social lubricant that played an undisguised, catalyzing part in the great postprandial philosophical debate known as the symposium. We shall look at the attitudes taken to drinking in religion, philosophy and social life, and at how these emphases began subtly shifting by the time of the Roman Empire's ascendancy. I believe this was the last period in Western history that intoxication was allowed this dual role, and all the antagonism that our cultural institutions have shown toward it in the Christian era stem from the willful repression of its hedonistic aspect in the interests of metaphysics and monotheism. Never again will being drunk have a dignified or serious side to it—until, that is, the nineteenth century starts to pathologize it. The classical era also saw the flourishing of an extraordinary religious rite given the name of the Eleusinian Mysteries, the sacrament at which was not alcohol but some sort of visionary substance of tantalizingly indeterminate identity. The chapter concludes with a description of these ceremonies, and of their eventual demise.

Picking up on the interdictive note sounded by the early Christian church with regard to Greek and Roman habits, chapter 3 looks

at the attitudes to drinking and drug-taking as they came to be codified in the three preeminent Western religious traditions—Judaism,
Christianity and Islam. We can trace a proscriptive trajectory among
these three from the relatively permissive stance of the Jewish faith,
through the moral ambiguities of the New Testament attitude to
drunkenness, arriving at the blanket ban that Mohammed throws
over the whole practice of intoxication for his followers. These
teachings and ordinances crucially cast the altered state of mind as a
less than perfect or even downright sinful state, and the sense of guilt
they encouraged their subjects to internalize has largely survived the
wholesale secularization that has taken place in non-Islamic societies. There is a moral aspect to the urgings of the modern-day
health lobbies on the question of intoxication that has replaced religion as the inculcator of guilt in the matter, and that may be read
everywhere from the gluing together of questions of moral and physical well-being in the work of temperance campaigners to the nebulous mystical authority—the Higher Power—who oversees the
operations of Alcoholics Anonymous.

In chapter 4, I address the question of whether intoxication is a
socially disruptive or destabilizing influence, in the light of the
inability of legislative authorities to resist the temptation to keep
throwing restrictions around it. Beginning with a consideration of
the findings of often dubious animal experiments on this theme, we
shall then turn to a catalogue of the principal intoxicating agents—
both permitted and proscribed—outlining something of the cultural
history of each, and describing the effects they have on those who
take them. Certain cultural (and subcultural) practices have evolved
around use of the various substances, and it is in the light of those
that we can best assess the question of whether intoxication is as
truly subversive—or antisocial, or solipsistic—as its detractors habitually claim. It is as agents of social corrosion, after all, that controlled drugs first came under the most exclusionary control of all:
their transformation into contraband.

Chapter 5 then traces the prohibitive enterprise from Mohammed
through to the contemporary drug laws to highlight the often violent
and extravagantly punitive deterrents that societies have devised
to warn people off them. The histories of the American and British

drug laws are most instructive because they have established the models by which most other governments have sought to fence off intoxication from their citizens' prying gaze. We shall look at the question of why bans don't work, paying particular attention to the doleful experience of national Prohibition in the United States, that social and legislative tragedy that not only blighted the lives of hundreds of thousands of its contemporary victims, but left a lingering residual stain of distrust in public office in the USA that stubbornly won't wash out. Notwithstanding that, the Drug Enforcement Administration (DEA) is the ringleader of an international enforcement industry that is fighting a losing battle, with both guns and dollars, to persuade people all over the world that intoxication must forever be denied to them. I have examined the arguments for and against drug legalization (that is, *relegalization*), taking as my text a richly detailed contribution to the debate from a sociologist who has been interested in this field for around thirty years, and who has concluded that relegalization is not the way forward.

If death threats, prison terms and fines won't persuade us to eschew our right to altered consciousness, then the agitation of the medical lobbies is the supplementary line of attack. Chapter 6 recounts how, in the mid-nineteenth century, there was a curious moment—more or less coinciding with the development of the first safe general anesthetics, chloroform, ether and nitrous oxide—when medicine briefly overlapped with the pursuit of pleasure, as scientists such as Sir Humphrey Davy discovered that there was more to these medical aids than had at first appeared. But as the altered states provided by opium, then morphine and cocaine, came to be seen to have medical implications, the recreational aspect of intoxicants was elbowed aside in favor of wholesale pathologization, which itself paved the way for the drug laws. I have cast a critical eye over the alcohol unit-counting system now advised by medical authorities in the USA, the UK, Japan and elsewhere, before moving on to a theoretical reflection on the eternally antagonistic concepts of moderation and excess. In order to establish why the use of intoxicants might be psychologically valuable, it is necessary to have some grasp of how each of the various classes of substances behaves in the body, which is to say, in the brain. I have tried to present this information as nontechnically as is consistent with gaining some insight into it, and I have incorporated some of the very latest findings about the action of drugs such as MDMA and cocaine, and what can be done to ameliorate the management of addiction. The chapter concludes with a philosophical investigation into why altered consciousness should be so important in the lives of most of us, and rejects the view that it is a dereliction of our better natures.

In chapter 7, I examine the question of whether intoxicants have the power to inspire the production of great art. This is the aspect of my theme that has perhaps received most attention of late, and so I am necessarily selective in the artists whose work I consider. A large volume of commentary has been produced on the opium ideology of Samuel Coleridge and others of the English Gothic-Romantic period, and the American Beat writers of the 1950s and 1960s have likewise received plenty of attention—more than most of their output perhaps merits. I acknowledge these examples, but I have also glanced at the careers of two singers—Janis Joplin and Billie Holiday—to see what impact personal drug use had on their work, and described the facilitating impact that unbridled drunkenness had on the precursor of Western philosophy, Socrates, as he is represented in Plato's texts. My contention is that intoxicants may perhaps animate the work of already gifted writers and performers, but that there is not within them some magic elixir that can inspire creativity at the push of a hypodermic plunger. After considering the question of why so many stars of the mass entertainment industries have succumbed to problematic, frequently fatal, drug and alcohol use, I draw a parallel between the view that ordinary mortals take of these exemplary excesses and the didactic tales of heroic ruin in classical drama.

It was only in the century recently ended that the name of intoxication was rescued from its etymological entrapment in malignity. Before that era, to be intoxicated was to be contaminated with some foreign substance that had a pejorative effect on the body and, perhaps, on the soul as well. From the seventeenth century, it implied stupefaction, a rendering senseless and incapable, a paralyzing and subjugating encroachment on the normal operation of the faculties. As a metaphor, it proved as easily susceptible as its inebriate victims of transference to another state, so that the faculties intoxicated might equally be the moral ones, as much as the mental. At its heart, and barely disguised by linguistic accretion, is the inescapable label *toxicum,* or poison—the lexical skull-and-crossbones that warned of its potency and peril. Then, in the early years of the eighteenth century, a new, more ambivalent usage arises that refers to "the action or power of highly exciting the mind; elation beyond the bounds of sobriety," and that allows it to qualify any headily exhilarating sensation, perhaps the intoxication of wealth and power. The contexts in which it is thus applied may still have some morally tendentious resonances (to be drunk with power and money is assuredly not to be in a state of grace), but suddenly there has been artfully imported into it these notions of excitement and elation. How did they get in there? And how can they be reconciled with the stupefying action of alcoholic liquor, or the mortifying consequence of poisons? By the time Wordsworth uses the participular adjectival form to invoke "the mind intoxicate/With present objects," we are not sure whether he means stupefied or excited, so befuddled have we become with intoxication's Janus-faced character.

In the Gillespie and Coots lyric of the interwar years, "You Go to My Head," the experience is now thought sublimated enough to account for the wholly benign impact of love on the helplessly enamored, whose very soul is intoxicated by the lustrous eyes of the beloved. We should not run away with the idea that this is a metaphor cut loose from its literal analogue, however. The whole lyric is a play on the business of drinking, with its references to champagne, to sparkling Burgundy and to the spirituous kick of a julep, so that we may be sure that the singer's rising temperature is something to do with alcohol hypertension, as much as the hot flush of carnal obsession. Its finest deliverer came when Billie Holiday recorded it, in the winsome bloom of youth in 1938 and then, even better, with the careful, measured tread of the seasoned drinker in 1952. On the latter recording, the song's metaphoric scheme is reconnected unequivocally to its real-life model by the singer's own evident drunkenness, in the double plosion of "bubbles" and the paradoxical collapsing swoop of pitch just as the lyric says "rise."

"Will you be writing about all forms of intoxication?" asked someone, on hearing of my project. "Such as?" "The intoxication of love!" Well no, but I am content to record that the word has all but thrown off its noxious implication in poisoning, and is now thought fit to supply the sign of love's force. This marks some sort of coming-of-age. If, following our linguistic habits, we can learn to love intoxication itself as well, instead of approaching it in bitter dread and reviling, we will be fit to face its own very literal force with the stoutest minds and boldest hearts.

1

Intoxicology

The website editor locks the door behind her in the lavatory of an expensive New York restaurant. Working quickly so as not to arouse suspicion, she opens a small paper envelope of white powder on top of the cistern. Having mashed it a few times with the edge of a credit card to remove potentially troublesome lumps, she tries her nasal passageways by emitting sharp outward breaths through them. Finding them unobstructed, she produces a ready-rolled ten-dollar bill from her jacket pocket, and inhales a plentiful dose of the powder up each nostril. By the time she has gathered everything up, flushed the toilet for the sake of credibility, washed her hands and returned to the table to join her colleagues, the cocaine will be hammering around her system, setting bells jangling in her head and lending a spasmodic, gasping quality to her breathing. As swallowing is now something of an effort, she might wish she hadn't ordered the roast quail to start.

The Yanomani Indians of Venezuela are practiced snorters too, although they inhale the dried and powdered bark of the virola tree, which is rich in the potent hallucinogenic compound 5-DMT (dimethyltryptamine). They have fashioned special vessels for its administration, essentially small bowls with a long spout on one side and a shorter one on the other. Each tribesman inserts the long tube into a nostril, while another blows down the opposite side in a steady crescendo, sending rather more material than our website editor has just taken into her nose through his companion's nasal membrane. The effect is reportedly agonizing, but the recipient somehow copes and goes into an explosive dance, oblivious to the long mucal strings that now begin to trickle viscously from his nostrils. Eventually, he enters an intense hallucinatory state, in which he will likely see his gods massing in the fevered sky to greet him.

In city nightclubs, they wait on the edges of dance floors for the ecstasy (or whatever else was in the pills) to take effect, an initial flutter of butterflies in the stomach and a flashbulb aftereffect on looking up at the lights announcing its earliest tentative onset. In coffee bars in Amsterdam, they stuff little pipes with loose cannabis, take lengthy inhalations and hold the sweetly pungent smoke in their lungs as long as they can, letting its dreamlike swathes unfurl through the brain. A hilltop café in the Alentejo in southern Portugal fills up with vineyard workers in the afternoon swelter of September, eating jointed lamb that comes to table in the roasting dish, lubricating its digestion with copious quantities of scented, soupy red wine. The commuter emerging at the suburban end of the Underground line stops on the pavement outside the station to light the cigarette he has been fantasizing about for the last twenty minutes. Massaging the temples of a hungover head, the journalist hears the happy spurt of the espresso machine delivering the day's first reason to live.

Intoxication is a universal human theme. There are no recorded instances of fully formed societies anywhere in history that have lived without the use of psychoactive substances. In fact, the only one ever known to anthropology is the Inuit (the people known to less enlightened generations as the Eskimos), for the very good reason that they were the only culture unable to grow anything. When the first European explorers discovered them, they introduced the Inuit people to alcohol, and a conspicuous biological anomaly in our species was forever erased. Whatever role intoxicants have played, whether it be as an integral part of religious ritual or spiritual enlightenment, as a social fixative binding a group of people together, as aids to endurance in periods of duress or as the preferred means of livening up a Saturday night, they are an inescapable feature of the way we spend a significant part of our waking (and even sleeping) hours. It may seem unusual, then, that the proper study of psychoactive substances in their various cultural contexts has not,

until very recently and provisionally, been accorded its own dignified status, but its neglect is not entirely unexpected.

The instructive comparison is with food history. Nothing could
be more universal than the need to eat and drink, and yet a global
history of the gastronomic development of our species was still a
novelty as late as 1973. There were microhistories of habitation and
of dress, of weaponry and of body adornment—such inquiries
helped to map out the territory of the newly emergent science of
anthropology at the end of the nineteenth century—but it is almost
as if something as absolutely biologically indispensable as eating and
drinking was thought too humdrum to be worthy of transhistorical
study. One might as well write a comparative history of urination
techniques. Nobody now, however, questions the scholarly validity
of food studies. Similarly, it should be possible to examine the uses
of intoxication—whether they take place with official approval or
not—in the light of their boundless persistence in all human cultures
throughout time.

One of the early academic pathfinders in the intoxication field,
Andrew Weil, was able to note in 1973, "The ubiquity of drug use is
so striking that it must represent a basic human appetite."[1] One of
the purposes of this book is to argue for the value of this field of
inquiry, and to introduce an enterprising band of pioneers who have,
in their sharply heterogeneous ways, all contributed to the founda-
tion of an emergent strand of cultural history that one might call
intoxicology—the comparative study of altered states of consciousness, the social contexts in which they are practiced and their implications for public policy.

Academic study in this field has been limited for two reasons.
Firstly, intoxication is not perceived to be quite as indispensable to
human existence as, say, the consumption of food and drink. Physical addiction may carry its own kind of imperative, and we shall see
in chapter 6 that there is a biological predisposition to intoxicated
states in all of us, but nonetheless, the prospect of a month without
intoxicants is considerably less drastic than a month without food.
Secondly, and more obstructively, because of the course that social
policy has taken in most Western societies, intoxicology must
struggle to free itself from criminology. Nearly all the substances

discussed in this book are illegal, and became so during the course of the twentieth century. Thus we are dealing with an area that does not officially exist as a legitimate cultural practice, but only as a matter of intractable social recalcitrance.

No topographical study of Andalucía would be worth the paper it was printed on if its author had described it solely from snapshots. And yet the writer on intoxication is driven to suggest that his only experience of the subject was the time he had a few too many glasses of punch at a party. This gives many otherwise highly pertinent contributions to the subject so far a kind of spurious coyness, or else— where more honesty is forthcoming—a thrilling samizdat character. The problem is well described by one of our most important recent contributors to this field, the literary academic David Lenson, who speaks of the way in which official attitudes to the subject matter coerce him into reinventing himself

> as a disinterested and disembodied philosopher taking up an unpleasant matter against my will, doing a dirty job that someone has to do, my self-effacement necessitated by an ongoing social crisis that must enlist everyone, even reluctant metaphysicians.[2]

However, there is no chance of arriving at an intelligent, adult appraisal of drug-taking if it is wrapped in layers of misplaced discretion. I have taken illegal drugs both recreationally and in the interests of research, and I daresay that I shall take them again on both counts, not out of some willful desire to court confrontation with the civil authorities, but because we shall never understand this subject if we leave all the direct experience of drug-taking to people who are incapable of or uninterested in illuminating it in this way.

Although intoxicology is not yet considered a formal discipline, it is already possible to classify the types of work that have been written in this area. There is the ethnographic work of writers such as Terence McKenna and Richard Rudgley, in which the use of intoxicants in tribal societies is seen as superior to what they hold to be debased and secularized recreational drug practices in Western society. Then there are locally grounded historical studies of the use of intoxicants at specific stages in history, and the ways they shaped a particular society's view of itself. Peter Thompson's work on tavern life in eighteenth-century Philadelphia and Marek Kohn's study of cocaine during the Great War period in London are both striking contributions of this kind. Polemical works such as Lenson's *On Drugs* (1995), or Scottish publishing editor Kevin Williamson's *Drugs and the Party Line* (1997), in which a sustained argument against the prevalent conservative orthodoxy is mounted, are becoming more numerous, as are reference guides such as *Buzzed* (1998) by a team from the Duke University Medical Center or Andrew Tyler's compendious *Street Drugs* (1995) that, in filling in the historical background and describing the current use of each substance within an encyclopedic framework, aim a little higher than the medical or pharmacological textbooks they otherwise resemble. One would probably have to include the mass of specialized clinical literature, sociological studies such as Alan Dean's *Chaos and Intoxication* (1997), confessional personal accounts that span the range from Thomas de Quincey's *Confessions of an English Opium-Eater* of 1821 to Jerry Stahl's *Permanent Midnight* (1996), not to mention films and works of art that take altered states as their subject matter. This book aims to draw something from all these disciplines in order to bring the subject of intoxication into focus as a unified cultural entity. My argument doesn't demand wide-ranging technical understanding of specialisms such as botanical classification or brain chemistry, but it does make use of the published expertise in different fields to illustrate and support the argument at the heart of it— that intoxication is an integral part of Western civilization, and that we would do better to accept and celebrate that fact instead of making it a matter of criminal sanctions and repression.

Much has been written on the possible source of the impulse toward intoxication. Some anthropological studies of the phenomenon accord it a crucial place in their accounts of human evolution, many of them dense with provocative and persuasive findings. A California ethnobotanist, Terence McKenna, has written one of the more challenging contributions in this area. *Food of the Gods: The Search for the Original Tree of Knowledge* (1992) attempts to strike a new path by making intoxication the fulcrum of the long-running debate about exactly where, why and how tree-dwelling apes came to make the transition to early hominid life. Evolutionary theorists have not yet ascertained what the precise trigger must have been that led to certain anthropoid species developing a capacity for self-reflective consciousness and subsequently linguistic aptitude. The missing link, suggests McKenna, is *Stropharia cubensis,* a mushroom native to tropical regions and perhaps first encountered by our ancestors in the dung of wild cattle on the African grasslands. *Stropharia*'s active constituent is psilocybin, the intensely hallucinogenic component of various mushroom species. When swallowed, either eaten whole or infused in tea, the effects range from a mildly amusing sense of derealization to full-blown auditory, visual and tactile hallucinations, accompanied by radical disruption of normal cognitive faculties. (Many users claim that psilocybin affords them an extended conceptual grasp of their surroundings, and that communication with others in the same state is deepened and enhanced by the experience.)

McKenna argues that prolonged willed exposure to such mental states would have produced over a relatively short evolutionary span a far-reaching alteration in the brain's synaptic structure, encouraging the formation of a mental capacity not simply geared to recognizing and remembering external stimuli in the most primal instinctual way, but elaborated into systems of logic based on the postulation and connection of ideas. A dog may know that a flung stick is meant for chasing, but it is not able to question the point of such behavior or modify its rules. We can. Succinctly put, consciousness is "the awareness of awareness." Since it had to come from somewhere, could it be that the psilocybin mushroom was the catalyst?

However resistant orthodox science might be to the proposition that the whole human show, from shamanism to Schopenhauer to shopping malls, owes its existence to a bunch of African apes tripping on magic mushrooms, the idea is not wholly unconvincing. The question is rather whether the emergence of consciousness may be ascribed to a single cause, and one would have to ask why the process should appear to have stopped there. Indeed, those tribal societies in which hallucinogenic intoxication has been a constant, ritualized practice should by now be several centuries ahead, by many measures, of their postindustrial counterparts, whose only response to the chance of self-improvement has been to issue health warnings against it. But this is McKenna's whole argument. While the Native Americans became proficient psychonauts, we ended up in a self-torturing dystopia. A simplistic hypothesis such as this seems a little insufficient to plug a major gap in evolutionary theory. Furthermore, McKenna is profoundly selective in the matter of those forms of intoxication he considers valuable and those he doesn't. For example, a significant cultural setback for him is marked by the beginning of the systematic production of alcohol, against which he fulminates as lustily as any nineteenth-century Salvationist. All succeeding Western intoxication practices, according to McKenna, are infected with the postlapsarian sickness and futility of the "dominator world," with the synthesizing of morphine from the opium poppy in 1805 initiating another vertiginous descent in the Fall from Eden. He sees a momentary respite in the countercultural discovery of hallucinogenics during the psychedelic sixties, but then it's on down the chain to crack-smoking, butane and glue—and ultimately the collapse of civilization, if we don't mend our ways.

Intoxicology has to free itself from this sort of millenarian anxiety if it is to be taken seriously, but McKenna is a writer for whom no type of drug experience is nobler than the hallucinogenic, and one of the cumulative side-effects of such substances is often a deep dissatisfaction with the drear reality that the user always has to return to. Much of his argument reads as if it is sympathetically as averse to that reality as the sixties student was when, coming down off LSD, she found it seeping back into her consciousness. (Pharmacologist Alexander Shulgin notes, with an approving chortle, a T-shirt slogan that reads, "Reality is for people who can't handle drugs.") A broad paradigm of recreational drug use in the West, at least since the sixties, has been that—just as drinkers divide into aficionados of the grape or of the grain—drug consumers are classifiable according to whether they prefer hypnotics and hallucinogens or stimulants (although the advent of ecstasy did a great deal to disrupt this typology, as its effects combine elements of both sorts of experience). McKenna's work, while methodologically rigorous in many ways, is squarely situated in the hypnotic/hallucinogenic camp.

On this reading, LSD was a potent elixir to the sixties counterculture not because it scrambled the perception of reality for its users so radically that they felt they were now cut loose from any obligation to participate, but more pertinently because it facilitated an alternative and better perception:

> The sudden introduction of a powerful deconditioning agent such as LSD had the effect of creating a mass defection from community values, especially values based on a dominator hierarchy accustomed to suppressing consciousness and awareness.[3]

But the confrontational impetus in this argument is thrown into relief when he considers the properties of cannabis. Here a distinctly more acquiescent and conciliatory note is sounded, as we are told that

> [n]o other drug can compete with cannabis for its ability to satisfy the innate yearnings for Archaic boundary dissolution and yet leave intact the structures of ordinary society. If every alcoholic were a pothead, if every crack user were a pothead, if every smoker smoked only cannabis, the social consequences of the "drug problem" would be transformed.[4]

His highest praises are reserved for dimethyltryptamine (DMT), active alkaloid in the smoked and snuffed bark of virola trees, as well as the ground and toasted seeds of another tree found in the Amazon basin, *Anadenanthera peregrina*. As their native users have known for millennia, the DMT experience is a profound and ecstatic one. For McKenna,

> [u]nder the influence of DMT the world becomes an Arabian labyrinth, a palace, a more than possible Martian jewel, vast with motifs that flood the gaping mind with complex and wordless awe . . . The tryptamine entities offer the gift of new language; they sing in pearly voices that rain down as coloured petals and flow through the air like hot metal to become toys and such gifts as gods would give their children . . . The Mysteries revealed are real and if ever fully told will leave no stone upon another in the small world we have gone so ill in.[5]

It is all too easy to satirize this sort of writing, but it is notoriously difficult to verbalize about hallucinogenic experiences. The oversensualized descriptions are no more assured of direct intelligibility than the mimosa-and-nectarine descants of the wine writer are, and yet the point is forcefully made that there is a whole other world of submerged consciousness awaiting any courageous investigators who can lay their hands on these substances. We may wish McKenna would make up his mind whether he wants to disrupt the ill, small, dominator world he apostrophizes with such regularity, or is content that—under the influence of cannabis—we should leave its structures intact. Either way, though, we are left in no doubt that these latter substances, rather than alcohol or crack, are where our only hopes for redemption lie.

In a less apocalyptic vein, the British anthropologist Richard Rudgley has outlined a useful chronology of intoxication's cultural trek from Stone Age hallucinogenic practices to contemporary Western nicotine addiction. In *The Alchemy of Culture: Intoxicants in Society* (1993), he suggests that Paleolithic existence almost certainly allowed humankind more unoccupied time than had commonly been supposed by early anthropologists. Not until the development of agricultural systems with the Neolithic era, around 10,000 B.C., did more intensive and therefore time-consuming labor patterns arise. The most inchoate prehistoric societies had evidently discovered the use of hallucinogenic mushrooms, and did not lack the time to establish rituals based on taking them. Franco-Cantabrian cave art is characterized by the juxtaposition of pictorial representations of animals alongside apparently abstract markings. The latter are compared with the so-called "entoptic phenomena" to be observed under the influence of hallucinogens, luminescent geometric patterns that float and dance before the user's gaze. Wiggly lines may indeed recall the onset of psilocybin intoxication, although they could equally be indicative of the visual disturbance caused by severe fatigue or migraine.

By the time of the Middle Neolithic (6000–5000 B.C.), there is much firmer evidence, in the numerous findings of poppy seeds at burial sites, that opium was being systematically cultivated at locations throughout Europe from the western Mediterranean—where it may well have originated—up to southern Britain and Poland. Where its ritual use as an intoxicant may have begun remains unclear, but an archaeological find in a cave at Albuñol near Granada in southern Spain in the mid-nineteenth century marked a break-through. Among the artifacts buried with the dead were spherical bags of esparto grass, which were found to contain a number of opium-poppy capsules, the part of the plant from which the psychoactive resin is tapped. The Albuñol capsules have been carbon-dated to around 4200 B.C.

In his Conclusion to *The Alchemy of Culture,* Rudgley contends that Western secularization has led to a loss of mystical awareness so that, divorced from any relation to the spiritual, intoxication becomes merely recreational and hence of no intrinsic value to modern ideals of personal advancement. What does, however, survive from tribal culture is the hierarchical division not only between the licit and the illicit, but between those who may be privileged to partake of the available intoxicants and those who may not. The struggle over access is nothing less than "a political, and sometimes spiritual, conflict over the nature of consciousness itself." As David Lenson more polemically puts it in *On Drugs,* the regulation of controlled substances has recently expanded from customs checks at international borders to the micro-surveillance of what is passing through the bloodstreams of private citizens. Random drug-tests in the workplace, in which every last trainee accounts clerk will get his chance to be treated like an Olympic athlete, are already upon us. The argument about access to altered consciousness, however, remains unexplored by Rudgley, who concludes with a fairly familiar ecological analysis of tribal societies as untainted by the corruption of the postindustrial world. This, he insists, makes them capable in their "poetic approaches to truth" of shedding light on the benighted chaos of self-restriction and alienation that is the contrasting late Western condition.

The polemical force that impels many of the more recent contributions on the subject frequently comes from the notion that there is a biological predisposition in many life-forms (and by no means exclusively mammals) toward periodic intoxicated states. We shall hear more in chapters 4 and 6 about the pioneering work of Ronald K. Siegel, a psychopharmacologist who has not hesitated to throw himself into the path of an enraged inebriated elephant to stop it from charging a rhino during one especially hectic experiment in a California game park, but we know from his and numerous other studies that intoxication exists as an abiding drive throughout the animal kingdom. There are laboratory experiments in which rabbits, rats or monkeys are given the opportunity to avail themselves of unlimited supplies of food, water and cocaine by means of pressing a range of levers. Their appetite for the drug is frequently so inexhaustible that they will continue to ingest it to the apparent exclusion of any instinct for sustenance, only stopping when physical exhaustion calls a halt. It would therefore appear that there is a heedlessly self-destructive side to the inclination toward intoxicated states that may be more obviously seen in the case of the destitute alcoholic who spends her last five dollars on a bottle of wine or the intravenous drug-user who spikes himself in the foot once the veins in both arms have collapsed. How does this contradictory instinct arise, short of the dictates of simple addiction?

In the relatively early days of research into intoxication, Andrew Weil argued in *The Natural Mind* that the desire to disrupt everyday perception arises in very early infancy. Children as young as three and four years old who discover the mind-altering effects of inhaling domestic products such as dry-cleaning fluid or strong fixative often repeat the experience, however repellent the consequent nausea may be. Toluene, the active constituent in many such substances, is a particularly destructive compound, and may cause liver and kidney damage as well as neurological disorders. Yet the vomiting and severe dizziness that may arise from inhalation of solvents over a protracted period does not often appear to act as a sufficiently powerful warning against further investigation. The pleasure centers of the brain are extraordinarily adept at overriding whatever signals it may be receiving about the risks of particular habits. Many are the adolescents who have vowed after an initiatory episode of heavy vomiting and an incapacitating hangover that they will never touch alcohol again, but the numbers that do remain abstinent will be insignificantly few. (One of the latter, a student colleague recalling his own teenage nightmare, told me, "I remember lying on my bed the next morning and promising whoever made the world that if they would take this feeling away, I wouldn't do it again." He had indeed remained teetotal ever since, crediting the Creator with the gradual recovery effected by his own shocked metabolism. For the rest of us, learning to forgo that third Jack Daniel's after the evening's half gallon of Special Brew amounted to acknowledgment enough that there were lessons to be absorbed.) Peer pressure plays a strong part too, of course, in reorientating the beginner to a toleration of alcohol, but clearly won't stand as an explanation for the toddler who returns to the Tippex thinner. What happens, though, if access to intoxicants is effectively barred to children until the onset of adolescence? If the urge to subvert normal consciousness is instinctually deeply driven, how else would it manifest itself?

The answer to that, suggests Weil, lies in the near-universal occurrence in infancy of spinning games and experiments with oxygen deprivation. Small children quickly learn that whirling around rapidly on the spot induces a brief but intense sensation of pleasurable giddiness. Many work at extending the duration of spinning for as long as physically possible, and savor the result by dropping to the ground in order to watch the world go careering wildly about overhead. Others discover that holding their breath for a prolonged period produces a similar light-headedness. Parents and teachers encountering such behavior invariably attempt to forbid it as potentially dangerous, handily habituating the child to the descant of disapproval that will attend a lifetime's intoxication, but the ban will have as much dissuasive power as the liquor laws have on the 16-year-old in the bar.

The question of this predisposition to altered states is tantalizingly skirted in the opening sections of a deconstructive text, *Crack Wars: Literature, Addiction, Mania* (1992), by the literary academic Avital Ronell. Her book argues for the existence of a "toxic drive" that is not simply about the physical compulsion at work in addiction to certain drugs, but functions as an animating impulse in consciousness itself. She cites the German existentialist philosopher Martin Heidegger who, in his defining work, *Being and Time,* argued that inasmuch as there is in human beings an irresistible will to *live,* as distinct from merely existing, then there is also a motivating force in them that drives them on to intervene in reality and seek to change it for the better. This is what constitutes people's concern for the life they have to live, a concern that every now and then replaces the shrug of resignation. However,

[t]he average everydayness of concern becomes blind to its possibilities, and tranquillises itself with that which is merely

"actual." This tranquillising does not rule out a high degree of diligence in one's own concern, but arouses it. In this case no positive new possibilities are willed, but that which is at one's disposal becomes tactically "altered" in such a way that there is a semblance of something happening.[6]

Translated from the abstract, the point he is trying to make is that the shopper in the bus line who might find herself wishing she were in a beach bar on St. Lucia copes with the unavoidability of her plight by trying to see it more positively. Heidegger argues that all addictive behavior arises from care for one's own psychic welfare. It is precisely this "semblance of something happening" that is most conspicuously provided by intoxication for most individuals. As some form of universal psychosomatic urge, it is a function of the "urge to live" itself. And because it concerns the *modification* of sensate existence, as opposed to the simple sustaining of it through eating, drinking and breathing, the process of becoming intoxicated just feels more like living than feeding oneself does. Perhaps, indeed, a caged rabbit senses more point in getting blasted on coke than unassumingly nibbling lettuce leaves in order to keep a featureless existence going.

McKenna, in one of his imaginative reconstructions of the tribesman's experience of hallucinogenic bliss, puts the same point somewhat more feverishly:

He had a sense of flinging himself happily into death, a kind of wild orgasmic paroxysm of self-affirmation. A previously inarticulate bubble of emotive intent came to his lips. Tears were running down his cheeks. He had said the words before. But he had never said and understood them in this way before. *Ta vodos! Ta vodos! I am! I am!*[7]

A consciousness of one's own presence in the world, achieved by means of a deliriously heightened apperception of it, is the beatific result of much experience of intoxication. The onset effects of MDMA, originally the principal component of the pills sold in nightclubs as ecstasy, is a hurtling, head-cleansing sensation of scarcely containable happiness, like coming back to a richly nuanced appreciation of the surrounding world that had been tragically neutered by the treadmill of one's daily routines. Less dramatically, the nightly drinker may derive the same sense of growing back into oneself again at the end of another demanding day, as the external world starts softening at the edges halfway through the evening's second glass of wine.

For a writer like McKenna, the presence of the toxic drive is so insistent that society, he argues, must find safer and more natural ways of supplying the need it engenders than the currently permitted options. The availability on the street of devastating substances such as crack and crystal meth, highly concentrated syntheses of the more traditional stimulants, could only arise in a culture that has long since shunned the creative use of plant hallucinogens. Having to acknowledge that drug-induced visionary experiences may be biologically indispensable to our species, so that deprivation from them can be seen as having caused the deformities of late Western civilization, requires a shift in perspective no less radical than those that accompanied the birth pangs of the twentieth century:

> We are discovering that human beings are creatures of chemical habit with the same horrified disbelief as when the Victorians discovered that humans are creatures of sexual fantasy and obsession. This process of facing ourselves as a species is a necessary precondition of a more humane social and natural order. It is important to remember that the adventure of facing who we are did not begin or end with Freud and Jung.[8]

Indeed not, although the task of facing up to who we are and what we want to do might conceivably involve accepting that there is no possibility of disinventing alcohol. Meanwhile, it is equally impractical to separate the efflorescence of Western culture from the intoxication practices in which it is partly rooted, either in classical antiquity or in the raves of today. The various types of altered consciousness—drunkenness, ecstatic hallucinogenic states and acute neural stimulation—represent ways in which rational individuals exercise an impact on the realities in which they are anchored, as opposed to quiescently accepting their circumstances. It might be argued in the light of this that they are therefore comparable to artistic creativity. Furthermore, in that they decorate and dynamize the world around us just when it has come to be perceived as bleached and static, these intoxicated states may also activate a critical faculty in us that prompts us to make judgments about the everyday world, and ask ourselves why it is we should wish to alter it so regularly. Ronell, at the outset of her study, thinks the previously unthinkable:

> What if "drugs" named a special mode of addiction . . . or the structure that is philosophically and metaphysically at the basis of our culture?[9]

Rudgley too is convinced by his own ethnographic findings of the "active role [that] altered states of consciousness play in the shaping of culture."[10] From this perspective, the will to intoxication is a primal, universal, civilizing and overwhelmingly beneficial human impulse, integral to the development of our higher selves. How, then, did we ever find ourselves reduced to the mantra of "Just Say No" and the trench-bound hostilities of the War on Drugs?

In the UK, at least, the answer lies principally in the early years of the twentieth century, in the attempt to stamp out cocaine and opium use among the demimonde of Soho. Marek Kohn has written, in *Dope Girls*, an instructive and meticulously researched study of the period between the Great War and the mid-twenties, when the wartime regulations against possession of cocaine and opium that were introduced in ad hoc fashion solidified into statute, and became the basis for the later Misuse of Drugs Act (1971). Until 1916, drugs were not in any meaningful sense illegal, the only statutory provision against their sale to civilians being the Poisons and Pharmacy Act of 1868, which was aimed at regulating the pharmacists rather than street dealers. The dealers were able to obtain supplies of cocaine and opium, which were both in general medical use, from licensed chemists, and in the West End of London, a roaring trade was done in sales of little boxes of coke to the prostitutes and actresses who frequented the racier bars and clubs of the district. Soldiers on leave who consorted with them would be introduced to the drug, which to an Army prosecuting a grinding war of attrition on the Continent with only volunteer forces at its disposal could only be cause for alarm. Calls for sterner regulation than the law then provided for began to grow. In April 1916, two police sergeants observed a former porter from the Ambassadors' Café on West Street, W1—one Willy Johnson—stopping young women in the street and unsuccessfully trying to sell them something. As the policemen approached him, he made a futile attempt to escape, in the process jettisoning a woollen bag that was found to contain eleven boxes of cocaine. He was tried under the provision of the 1868 Act, but since he hadn't actually succeeded in selling anything, the court could only reluctantly acquit him. Not only was Johnson the first street dealer ever to be arrested in London, but the impotence of the law in dealing with his case was the major catalyst that led to the framing of Defence of the Realm Regulation 40B. Under the umbrella of emergency wartime provisions, and despite the fact that it was acknowledged in the Home Office that such measures would be too controversial to be dealt with in normal legislative terms, the two drugs most prevalent in café and club society at the time—cocaine and opium—were made illegal. That is to say, it wasn't just the traffic in them that was forbidden, but the substances themselves were given the status of contraband. Mere possession of them by ordinary private citizens was henceforth an offense.

Like many another piece of emergency legislation, the Regulation that became law on 28 July 1916 has long survived the circumstances in which it was formulated. The control of pub opening hours, introduced to increase the output of workers in wartime munitions factories, did not begin to be abandoned until the 1980s, fully 70 years later, and then only by very cautious, piecemeal initiatives. Once any state apparatus has invested itself with certain powers, it seems inevitably to prove jealously unwilling to surrender them, no matter what unabashed invocations of personal liberty successive administrations claim to govern by. Without the Defence of the Realm Regulations, the Misuse of Drugs Act—which classified the forbidden substances in three categories of risk—could not have been framed. We shall return in detail to the debate on decriminalization in chapter 5, but it is a case that certain writers on intoxication are increasingly bold in making.

A foretaste of the kinds of argument now deployed may be seen in the early 1990s in the work of writers such as Thomas Szasz, the free-market economic theorist who contends that the untrammeled operations of the nonregulatory economy he supports ought to make control of personal drug use an affront. "Let the market decide!" is the cry of followers of Milton Friedman, and indeed Szasz cowrote a pamphlet with the monetarist guru in 1992 outlining precisely this thesis. Just as the government should abstain from intervening in the workings of the market, so should it also preside over a libertarian social dispensation. The individual should have the right to buy what any trader wishes to sell him, and any harm he incurs from subsequent use of the commodity is his business and his alone. There is no want of prescriptive boldness in this work, but it is essentially an argument about economics rather than a contribution to the drug debate. Szasz's central argument is that the market will solve the drug "problem" without the need for law enforcement, suggesting that there is still a coercive agenda at work here, even if the personal profit motive has replaced the narcotics officer. What this argument curiously lacks is any acknowledgment that, ever since the legal restrictions began to be formulated, the market in narcotics has never been anything other than free. The response of the state may be to exert itself ever more strenuously to try to prevent a trade from taking place, but meanwhile the lucrative global trade that does exist, however illicitly, is wholly unregulated. The boy in his bedroom unwittingly vacuuming baby laxative up his nose, when what he thought he had paid for was speed, is an exemplary beneficiary of deregulated free-market economics.

Terence McKenna too has a prescriptive answer. *Food of the Gods* ends with a ten-point manifesto for legislative reform in the United States, running the gamut from punitive federal taxation and sterner health warnings on alcohol and tobacco (and sugar), through a blackmail system operated by the IMF and the World Bank to wipe out cocaine and opium production by withholding funding until the crops are eradicated, to the extension of private health insurance to include therapeutic access to hallucinogenic drugs. The use of capitalist institutions as a blunt instrument to dictate to Third World countries what they may and may not grow might raise the odd eyebrow of those who thought this was an argument for blissed-out personal freedom, and an excruciating contradiction arises when—that principle having been established in point 3—point 5 offers the ringing declaration, "The legality of nature must be recognized, so that all plants are legal to grow and possess."[11] (Except, of course, if you are a Bolivian coca farmer.) Such apparent inconsistencies do a good deal to undermine the persuasiveness of McKenna's work.

David Lenson's contribution, on the other hand, represents a major advance in thinking on these issues. He takes as his starting point the "Just Say No" campaign of the 1980s (he calls it "Just Say Nothing") and proceeds to ask precisely what it is about drugtaking that is considered so inimical to mainstream society. In the assault on intoxication, the rhetoric of the drug war must posit a default state of nonintoxication that it presumes is the happy condition of its more conformist citizens. "But what," asks Lenson, "would sobriety mean if there were no such thing as intoxication?"[12] Being in a drug-free condition can hardly have any special significance if one is never otherwise, and it is precisely in order to avoid having to relativize, and thereby undermine, the concept of sobriety that the catchall category of Drugs is so tenaciously retained. Despite the fact that American legislation follows the same classification structure as British law (Schedules 1 to 5 being reflected across the Atlantic as Classes A, B and C), the rhetoric of the War on Drugs allows no such typological niceties. A TV advertising campaign that ran on the US networks in 1998 was in many ways a classic of the genre: it consisted solely of a frantic young woman smashing up a kitchen with a frying pan. The implicit message was not, as it first appeared, "Drugs will make you act like this, kids." Rather, at several linguistic structures lower, it was saying, "This is what drugs do to your brain—they smash it up rather like a hysterical woman with a frying pan might if you let her loose in your kitchen." In this climate, drugs have become as much of an undifferentiated enemy as Communism once was, and the same kinds of paranoia are attendant upon their pursuit. In the same year that the frying-pan campaign was broadcast, a professor of criminology at Utah State University wrote a pamphlet warning parents of the telltale signs of the drug-addicted teenager. The victim may "avoid the family while at home," and display an "excessive preoccupation with social causes, race relations, environmental issues, etc." No more luminous illustration of Lenson's opening thesis could be wished for:

"'[S]obriety' is a cultural construction created for the furtherance of a political and economic agenda."[13]

Lenson goes on to argue that one of the reasons that Western societies feel so uneasy about intoxication in their citizens is that, in altered states of consciousness, we are least accessible to the forces of consumerism that otherwise reach so pervasively into our psyches. Put simply, a population at peace before the television, soaking up the commercial breaks, is a population docilely receiving the messages that corporate culture wants to transmit to them. But who, coming up on ecstasy or buzzing with the night's first line of speed, has either the concentration or the patience to take in the advice of the middle-aged couple shown gloating about their pension plans? In fact, they probably wouldn't even have turned it on. The argument might at first glance appear crudely paranoid, but it makes a valid economic point. Drug-taking disrupts the operations of the postindustrial economy. It is about the acquisition of states of mind, of feelings, rather than of material goods. That is not, of course, to suggest that the drug trade is without its own particularly vicious economic laws; nobody paying £60 for a gram of white powder that turns out to be two-thirds crushed-up caffeine tablets has opted out of capitalism. And yet the variant choices, the reordered priorities, even the revivification of human relations typical of the use of at least some of the proscribed substances, do not make the lives of advertisers and marketing departments any easier. One only has to look at the wholesale panic the drink industry went into in the late 1980s and early 1990s in the US as a generation of clubbers discovering ecstasy found their requirement for alcohol reduced to near zero. The aggressive promotion of wine coolers, and such concoctions as "hard" lemonade and iced tea, in the 1990s had as much to do with sugaring the alcohol pill for those whose central nervous systems were frequently stimulated by real pills as it did with initiating naive young tastebuds to a lifelong affinity for drink.

At the close of his book, Lenson proposes a concerted political campaign that goes beyond the localized efforts of the Legalize Cannabis movement or the more general pleading for an end to jail terms for possession. His analogy is the continuing battle for lesbian and gay equality, in which the case is pressed that homosexuality "has existed from the dawn of time, and all efforts to eradicate it are based on an incomplete understanding of human nature."[14] Exactly the same assertion might be made, he argues, about "the practice of getting high," and the efforts that liberal politics has made in the United States to ensure respect for social diversity can be harnessed on behalf of "a diversity of consciousness" too. Not only would decriminalization boost the Western economy and terminate the careers of the drug overlords (or at least force them to diversify), it would also roll back the repressive frontiers of the surveillance state, which would once more have to learn to care for its citizens instead of stigmatizing them for life for engaging in victimless "crime."

A more recent British contribution to this strand of argument comes from Kevin Williamson. Williamson's book *Drugs and the Party Line,* supplemented by a website providing a constant monitoring of the drug debate, addresses head-on the public policy issues involved in any proposals for reform of the legislation. It is an agenda for change that is methodical in the order of its suggestions. Heroin and cannabis are seen as the priority substances for decriminalization, the former because of the potential for ruthless criminal exploitation that physical dependency creates, the latter because it is arguably so harmless and yet accounts for the lion's share of police seizures and prosecutions. In time, he suggests, other substances would follow them out of the jungle of repression, until we were left wondering finally why it took us so long to see our way out of the present impasse. Williamson emphasizes that he is not proposing a free-for-all, and cites the provisional legal relaxations tried out by the Dutch authorities since the 1970s as an example of what can be achieved by enlightened public policy. These may be the most obviously practical recommendations for change to be found in any of the writers discussed here.

The field of intoxication is complex and varied territory. While so many intoxicants remain fenced off by legal restrictions and penalties, there will always be a prescriptive side to the discussion of it. Beyond that, however, lies a fertile, productive terrain in which cultural and anthropological explorations of human development can be carried out. We shall look first at how intoxication was treated in the classical civilizations of Greece and Rome, the religious rituals and philosophical systems that were built around them then and the ways in which those traditions influenced later Western societies. It is an eternal verity of gastronomic history that we are what we eat. I shall argue throughout this work that, to at least the same extent and perhaps even more so, we are what we become intoxicated by.

2

The Ridiculous and the Sublime

A lcohol has always lived a double life, which is to say that those
who drink it have. On the one hand, it is invested with an
almost sacred significance. It is the free-flowing blood of Christ in
the Transubstantiation, the elusive elixir of eternal life to the
alchemists trying to isolate its soul or spirit (and thus giving the
name of "spirits" to their earliest rudimentary distillates), the offering of a bountiful nature spilling forth its annual cornucopia of
berries gravid with fermentable juices. It is implicated through and
through in religious ritual—indeed is one of the primary motivating
forces for such ritual, as we shall see—from the polytheistic carnivals of the Egyptians and the Greco-Roman cults to the benignly
providing Yahweh of the Old Testament, who in one of his better
tempers, as the Psalmist tells us, created wine "to gladden the heart
of man." The churchly reverence with which wine in particular is
approached may be observed at such events as the first showing for
the London wine press each year of the newly released vintage of
Burgundy's Domaine de la Romanée-Conti estate: the reds ascend in
opulence to the majesty of *grand cru* Romanée-Conti itself, so awe-
inspiringly expensive that members of the press who haven't arrived
at 9:30 sharp may not taste it but only sniff at what remains in a single communal glass, while the estate's sole white wine, Le Montra-
chet, is produced in such limited quantities that it is not shown at all,
but merely hovers somewhere unseen, as numinously present in its
absence as the Holy Ghost.

But there is another alcohol too, one that doesn't mind what company it keeps, one not confined to a privileged band of initiates, but happy to slum it in the bloodstreams of the hoi polloi. This is the alcohol of the taverns and back alleys, the dangerously exhilarating potion that produces raucous laughter and embarrassing scrapes, indiscretions, the staggers and poisoned livers, a thudding head in the overindulgent and a riptide of sentimental drivel from the lips of the incautious. It was for this side of its nature that Islam, around the turn of the seventh century, became the only one of the world's major religions to forbid it on pain of severe chastisement. If alcohol was a sacrament to the Dionysian worshipers, and to communicants in the early Christian church, it was also an agent of social corrosion, too readily available to the mass of humanity to remain exclusively the property of cult followers and priests. Increasingly, as classical antiquity gave way to the early medieval period in Europe, the double life of alcohol became untenable. To be under its influence was either to be in a state of ecstatic spiritual union with the gods (or symbolic contact with the one God), or it was to be in a befuddled, squalid fog of inebriation. It couldn't, however, be both.

The Greco-Roman era is the historical turning point of this ambiguity. Whatever spiritual associations alcohol still retains today are the fossil evidence that there was once another way of feeling its effects and responding to its ministrations. Few now would seriously advance the claim that being falling-down drunk was a sacred mental state. Before the question was resolved in this way, however, classical society was much exercised by the dilemma presented by the dual face of drinking. Not only does the achievement of drunkenness animate certain cultic practices in the antique religions, as well as furnishing the descriptive framework for many accounts of the afterlife, but it is one of the organizing principles of much Greek philosophy, indeed is often itself the wellspring from which the act of philosophizing pours forth. In the midst of these elevated endeavors, though, may be heard the tut-tutting of the sages at the riotous behavior in the wineshops and taverns, at the gluttonous indulgence of the feasts hosted by the ostentatiously well-to-do and at what came to be seen as the abuse of the symposium—those wine-fueled debating societies whose name literally means "drinking together." Traditionally, wine was genteelly taken in a fairly dilute form, the host watering it before passing it around, but certain headstrong youths (the spiritual ancestors of the boys in the off-license comparing ABV numbers on the beer cans before stocking up for the night) and, perhaps surprisingly, many women became notorious for drinking it unwatered. Such behavior may have been unspeakably vulgar to refined Platonic sensibilities, but the real threat that lay in it was that it was, by a process of attrition, slowly but surely prizing alcohol away from its theological context and resituating it squarely within the social.

In this chapter, I shall look successively at these three aspects of ancient drunkenness—the religious, the philosophical and the social—and explain in each case how the Greeks and then the Romans viewed them. Some of the attitudes of the classical writers will strike an uncannily familiar chord to the modern reader, for all that the ceremonial forms of cultic worship are by now generally quite alien.

That drunkenness should once have had a spiritual facet at all may be hard to understand in a climate in which moderation is sternly counseled via the counting of one's weekly intake of alcohol units. In polite society today, to become inebriated in the course of social drinking is a faintly embarrassing side-effect of an evening's conviviality; only the immature, or the seriously addicted, drink with the sole aim of getting (or staying) drunk. We have, as I shall show, progressively devalued such states of transformed consciousness from the end of the classical period on, allowing first ecclesiastical and then medical authorities to warn us away from intoxication. Once, though, there was another authority, a sublimated, permissive authority responsible not just for intoxication, but for all the dynamic aspects of the natural world, such as springtime growth and rebirth, and the harvests and vintages of autumn. Through his pervasive influence, nature was not merely supplemented, but actually set in motion, by the intoxication impulse, his various forms—the verdant tree, the rampant bull—elemental indications of his unity with natural forces. The Greeks knew him as Dionysos.

The complex, endlessly mutable figure of Dionysos is the gate-crasher in the august pantheon of classical Greek divinities. With his entourage of hysterical women followers, the Maenads, he is a late arrival, a foreign or immigrant deity who came to civilized Athenian society from the remote north, from Thrace or Phrygia. There is a distinct touch of the Asiatic about him too, perhaps garnered when Thracian tribes migrated eastward into Asia Minor and encountered orgiastic cults of oriental origin. Foremost among the rude northern tribes of Thrace was an unconquered people called the Satrae, who by linguistic osmosis become the horned, dwarfish satyrs numbered among Dionysos' regular attendants, and an even more ferocious brigand band known as the Bessi, much feared for their murderous rampages on and around Mount Haemus. To the historian Herodotus, the Bessi were seemingly the priesthood among the Satrae, those charged with interpretations of the oracle of the savage god who lived in the mountain peaks, but it seems likely they were simply a rival hill-tribe, albeit an even more martial and untameable rabble than the Satrae themselves. The worship of Dionysos originated among such peoples.

From around the turn of the sixth and fifth centuries B.C., the Dionysian cult gradually inveigled its way into classical Greek cosmology. Its Asiatic borrowings were emphasized over the Thracian, so that Athenians need not feel that such a feral form of worship could have arisen in too close proximity to them, and the preferred intoxicant—which, in the inhospitable north, had been a cereal beer—became the wine with which the god was to become exclusively associated. To the Athenians, beer was an alien drink that never became rooted in their society. The form of intoxication it delivered was simply the muddle-headed, nodding-off type, whereas wine was seen as belonging to a higher stage of culture, as the source of intellectual and spiritual inspiration. (Something of this climatically based hierarchy can still be felt today, where the wine-producing peoples of southern Europe tend to look pityingly on those dank northern cultures where the vine can't perform, reserving an especial sympathy for those—like the British—who, in defiance of grim metereological reality, seek to deny their cereal inheritances by trying to ripen Cabernet Sauvignon grapes under tunnels of polythene sheeting.) What proved less susceptible to the theological house-training of Athenian religion was the form the Dionysian rituals took. Quite apart from the fact that to have restrained the orgiastic impulse in them would have denuded them of their significance, there was also the inescapable biochemical fact that the wine with which the demotic Thracian beer was substituted in the rituals was an appreciably stronger intoxicant.

For those reasons, the Dionysian celebration was an exuberant, uninhibited affair in which, following an offering of food at his shrine, the god's worshipers would perform frenetic masked dances to the accompaniment of clashing percussion instruments. Wine was taken in liberal quantities, often for days at a time, and one of the more potent symbols of the abandonment of traditional civility that it provoked lay in the eating of raw meat (omophagy). By this, the celebrants acknowledged that, whatever the refinements of civil society, they were themselves nonetheless inextricably part of the rude nature that Dionysos presided over. The chorus of Maenads in Euripides' late drama *The Bacchae* celebrates the delight of the worshiper on the mountains, where "he hunts for blood, and rapturously/Eats the raw flesh of the slaughtered goat."[1] Indeed, the ritual had once involved the gnawing of bleeding sections hacked from a *living* rather than freshly slaughtered goat, the central significance of streaming blood indicating that its origins lay almost certainly in ritual human sacrifice. Although Dionysianism was a late addition to the Greek cults, it became a formidably widespread and influential one. By the time of the great post-Socratic philosophers Plato and Aristotle, the period that denoted the high-water mark of classical Greek culture in the fourth century B.C., the cult of Dionysos was the most widely practiced of all Hellenistic religious observances.

All the intoxication cults of antiquity must inevitably recall, however faintly, the earliest protohuman encounters with alcohol. Whether the original hangover of primeval history was produced by rotting fruit, festering palm-sap or spoiled honey will never be known, but its effects must have been dramatic. To a consciousness unprepared for the perceptual shifts, not to mention the glow of mammalian contentment that fermented liquids induced, drunkenness must have seemed both fascinating and profoundly welcoming. By the time early societies had learned how to control fermentation, and an alcoholic drink was being systematically manufactured (probably in the form of a wheat or barley beer rather than a fruit-based product, although researchers still disagree about this), alcohol had its obvious ritual uses.

The Egyptians, who had possibly learned to make beer before they invented bread, went on to develop viticulture too, and the respective drinks soon had their proprietorial deities. Hathor, the wine god, was generally represented as a bull, as Dionysos would later be in one of his northern Greek incarnations, and the Egyptians dedicated a monthly Day of Intoxication to him in their ritual calendar. There would appear to have been two sides to the practice of ritual intoxication by the time it takes the form of the Dionysian celebrations: in one sense, the altered state of consciousness was held to elevate the practitioner into temporary access to the godliness within, but there was also, and perhaps more crucially, the emollient aspect of it. Wine is a gift from the god to soothe the hearts of a troubled humankind, to smooth its passage over the storm-lashed seas that Fate prescribes for it in this world. It is this latter character that opens the door of the Athenian pantheon to Dionysos, and will later prove of use to the Fathers of the early Christian church as they begin trying to wean European society away from the old cultic beliefs and on to the monotheistic new one.

The consoling power of drunkenness is expressed with striking pathos at the end of the Herdsman's speech in *The Bacchae*. Against the prohibitive wishes of King Pentheus of Thebes who, exasperated by mad Dionysian women leading nude extravagances on the mountains, has set out to suppress the ritual once and for all, the Herdsman—one of those extras indispensable to the Greek drama who arrives breathless with tales of outrage or lubricity happening just offstage—offers the humblest explanation for the popularity of the god:

> *His powers are manifold,*
> *But chiefly, as I hear, he gave to men the vine*
> *To cure their sorrows; and without wine, neither love*
> *Nor any other pleasure would be left for us.*[2]

Wine is the gift that even Zeus, in his overweening pomp, refuses to deny to suffering humanity. It is the outstanding contribution of Dionysos to life in this world, and for that alone, the Father of the gods adopts him as his own—shrieking Maenads, hooligan satyrs and all. The God of the Old Testament appears to take much the same view, and even in the Christian era, we encounter St. Paul advising the sorely tried, "Take a little wine for thy stomach's sake, and thine often infirmities." To be sure, this is a rather medicinalized version of the principle, but the comforting role of drink is still evident. To a later Christian tradition, the expectation of being redeemed in the hereafter is intended to provide the solace for the tribulations of our earthly existence, but even this has its demonstrable roots in Greek religion. As the Dionysian ritual came to be subsumed by the Orphic, which many hold to be the prototype of Christian doctrine (indeed, there is hardly a theme in Christian cosmology that isn't anticipated in Orphism, with its stress on the striving for immortality and the privileging of spiritual ecstasy over physical intoxication), the image of an afterlife fit for heroes came to be institutionalized. Not the least reward for the noble individual who had passed through corporeal existence without incurring the fractious wrath of the gods was the survival of his soul in a state of "eternal drunkenness."

If intoxication had been simply a comfort blanket, however, it would be inconceivable that the worship of Dionysos would have assumed such orgiastic and profoundly ambiguous forms as it did. In fact, of course, it was more. It wasn't just analgesic, it was hugely liberating too. The savagery that appears to be implicated in much of the ritual, and that Euripides depicts with such horrifying force, stems from its importantly disinhibiting character. In *The Bacchae*, Pentheus is torn literally limb from limb by his mother and aunts, becoming to their inflamed appetites the sacrificial goat of the old ritual. This is very much the kind of behavior he had in mind when he tried to stamp out the Dionysian cult, but—with his remains being delicately jigsawed back together again in the final scene as his mother curses herself—he is scarcely in a position to feel vindicated. To its defenders, though, the drunkenness and sexual celebrations, the gnashing of raw meat and throwing off of clothes, are what keeps society healthy all the rest of the time. The Dionysian rites were an outlet, a safety valve, for the forces repressed in human beings in the day-to-day conduct of their civic lives, a point not lost—several centuries later—on either Freud or Nietzsche.

To the follower of Dionysos (or Bacchus, Bromios, Sabazius or any other of his multifarious aliases), the precious state of intoxication was one of possession. Indeed, all extreme mental states, across the whole spectrum from abjection to ecstasy, were seen as divinely borne. Precisely because such moods marked a radical departure from the common emotional round, they could not but derive from higher powers working through the individual, and taking up temporary residence in his or her being. Intoxication, for all that it had an obvious physical trigger in the drinking of wine or beer, represented the supreme version of this principle. This is a theme seen in cultic intoxication rituals down to the present day, among those South and Central American Indian and South Pacific tribes whose ritual observances involve the ingestion of psychotropic drugs. One is literally out of one's head on this reading of the experience, evicted for a spell from the premises of one's own consciousness while a god, or even indeed a whole boisterous gang of gods, goes on the rampage there.

Whatever factors the worship of Dionysos shares with that of other deities, such as the celebration of the natural cycle, intoxication is his and his alone. The gifts of other gods in the form of successful harvests, victory in war and so forth may have been revered as equally indispensable, but none other had quite the instant tangible impact on the true believer as Dionysos' sacred substances had. As a result, his cult had become—even more so than the cult of the love goddess Aphrodite—the most popular of all Greek belief systems in Periclean Athens (the latter half of the fifth century B.C.). Shrines to Dionysos arose all over the country, and the forms the celebrations took became increasingly unbridled and outrageous. Nocturnal revels were a particular hallmark, as was the involvement of women, unusual in an essentially patriarchal society. And while cultured civic society tried to circumscribe the use of alcohol, even within the philosophical discussions of the symposia, by means of diluting the wine and drinking it from effetely shallow cups, the Dionysian rituals encouraged no such restraint. If wine was good, and intoxication a sacrament, why should not more of it be even better?

That the Dionysian form of drinking was at first utterly divorced from the culture of the symposia may be seen in the vessels from which wine was taken. The preferred vessel for refined social imbibing had a flat, saucerlike bowl that required frequent replenishing, and was generally filled with wine that had been watered down in a ratio of as much as four to one. A deeper, larger cup was the trademark of Dionysos (he is often depicted on vase-paintings holding just such a cup), sometimes the *kantharos,* a capacious goblet with protuberant handles on either side, sometimes the rhyton or horn, a huge vessel with a possible capacity of upward of seven liters. Not only did these cups contain more heroic quantities of drink, they tended to be filled with less diluted—or even wholly unmixed—wine, which was gulped down greedily rather than being occasionally sipped at. And there were other designs, as James Davidson explains:

> The *kumbion* was a deep vessel shaped like a boat, a favourite shape of one notorious drinker in the fourth century [B.C.], known as Euripides. Another deep cup called *lepaste* was associated with the verb *lapto,* which Athanaeus glosses as "to drink in one go" . . . One of these deep cups is actually called a "breathless cup," because its contents were drunk down without a breath.[3]

In time, these larger vessels made their way into the symposia too, occasioning some fastidious disapproval from the likes of Socrates and, later, Plato. Originally, however, the brutally instrumental version of drinking, in which the swiftest route to inebriation was the goal, was confined to the worship of the wine god. Classical Athens was not a particularly alcoholic society otherwise, and tended to be nonplussed and alienated by the more thoroughgoing habits of northern peoples like the Thracians. Even Plato, however, the arch metaphysician whose own *Symposium* is all too rudely interrupted by the untimely arrival of the swaggering general Alcibiades, roaring drunk and game for disputation, allows that the Dionysian festivals were the one time when deliberate drunkenness was acceptable.

This form of ritual survived—as did much else from Greek culture—into the Roman Empire. Just as the agenda of the banquets imitated Greek tradition, with the main business of eating succeeded by a clearing of the tables in preparation for the drinking and debating that were to follow, so the Bacchic festivals survived virtually unmodified. The celebration of Bacchus/Sabazius (the twofold nature of the god as the deity of both wine and beer is also preserved) was popular because it evoked unambiguously happy associations as opposed to apprehension at the doings of the temperamental gods, and was inextricably about initiation into sexual pleasures as much as it honored the sacred act of intoxication. Among the proliferating cults and confraternities of Roman religious life, the Bacchic groups were inevitably the most louche and disorderly. They held their noisy devotions at night, often to the chagrin of more abstemious neighbors, and the same blend of devotional piety and personal gratification may be observed in them as is the case in the earlier Athenian period. The difference is that Roman society was considerably more gender-repressive than the Greek. Women were absolutely forbidden alcohol because drunkenness was held to be unbecoming to their sex, to the extent that a nobleman who beat his wife to death for drinking wine from a barrel could be cheerfully exonerated for his actions. (At the other end of the scale of permissiveness in classical times were the Etruscans, whose civilization fizzled out around 200 B.C., but who had been so relaxed about the idea of women drinking that it was they who often led the toasts at banquets.)

In the period of political and social instability that followed the Punic Wars and the consequent creation of large itinerant populations that brought Dionysian practices with them into the Roman city-state, the Bacchic form of worship created particular upheavals and underwent a certain amount of modification. From being an essentially seasonal festival centered on the grape harvest, the Bacchanalia became a much more movable, and repeatable, feast. As the various confraternities multiplied, the imperial authorities sought to contain the more obviously riotous manifestations of Bacchic worship, so that they were driven out of the public and officially sanctioned forms of religious observance and into more private and familial contexts. At last, following a largely stage-managed public scandal in 186 B.C., the Bacchanalia was officially banished from Rome. The repressive measures taken lacked nothing in imperial thoroughness, as the French classical historian Robert Turcan outlines:

> The Senate was convened as a matter of urgency, public opinion terrorised, the town put on a state of alert, if not siege, and combed by the police of the *tresviri capitales* . . . Comings and goings at the gates of Rome were strictly controlled. Many initiates managed to flee, while others who were subjected to

searches and interrogations chose to kill themselves rather than break the rule of silence about the mysteries.[4]

By the time the emergent Christian church started attempting to establish itself by currying favor with the imperial authorities, it was only too happy to acquiesce in the public disavowal of intoxication rituals, claiming that it was the baneful influence of Sabazius the beer god and his oenophile relative Bacchus that had contributed to the moral pollution of the Roman Empire.

Notwithstanding the eventual interdiction on Bacchic worship, the eschatology of the wine god proved extremely durable. Sarcophagi in the form of grape vats are thought to have intended the transformation of the plucked fruit of the physical body into the intoxicating sacrament of wine (this theme will have its echo in the extensive use to which Christian doctrine will put the metaphor of vinification), and the inscriptions on tombs often had a defiantly hedonistic character. Just as an afterlife of "eternal drunkenness" was seen as the only possible fit fate for the Greek hero or nobleman, so the Roman paradise was envisioned as an unbridled continuation of the sensory pleasures of this world—but now untrammeled by guilt, the depredations of state authorities or the whinging of the neighbors. The inscription on the sarcophagus of a Sabazian priest, Vincentius, speaks heartwarmingly from beyond the grave to his remaining coreligionists:

> *Eat, drink, enjoy thyself and come to me. As long as thou livest have*
> *a good time: thou wilt carry it with thee!*
> *Here lies Vincentius, priest of the god Sabazius, who with pious heart*
> *hath celebrated the divine holy ceremonies.*[5]

With the exemplary mass convictions that ensued in the years following the Roman ban on the Bacchanalia, ecstatic and debauched forms of cultic worship were effectively suffocated. Whatever hedonism the priest's tomb might have enjoined among the living, it had to find purely social forms, in the taverns or within the family home. Dancing around fires in the middle of the night was no longer an option. The Christian church, into which the Roman Empire was finally baptized under Constantine in the fourth century, while not encouraging its adherents to abjure alcohol, nonetheless left them in no doubt that there were higher spiritual callings than ritual intoxication. When wine became the saving blood of Christ in the Eucharist, its sanctifying power could be ingested in the tiniest of sips.

More than anything, though, what enabled the early church to see off the challenge of the Dionysian cults so unanswerably was its monolithic, single-deitied unity. It quickly spawned theological councils and committees, first for the compilation of the New Testament and subsequently for interpretation of the Scriptures, so that a seamless body of fixed doctrine issued from it. Compared to the fluid forms and content of such cultic rituals as the Dionysian, it was able to unify its adherents under one unquestionable dogma, and thus offer stability in a spiritually unstable world. Shrewdly enough, it incorporated many of the elements of cultic belief that it deemed inoffensive to the new, more forgiving, post-Judaic God. Among these was the belief in an ameliorating afterlife of bliss that it largely lifted from Orphic cosmology, the genius of the gesture lying in its positing of a nether world that was unimaginably more exciting than this one, rather than being a mere uninterrupted prolongation of its better moments. Furthermore, Christianity opportunistically sited many of its own festivals (most notably Christmas) in the religious calendar to coincide with the old pagan celebrations. In place of the vernal tree that was the occasional incarnation of Dionysos, son of the bountiful Earth Mother Semele, it offered the Tree of Life, the Holy Cross on which God himself, born into humanity by the miraculous fecundity of a Virgin Mother, was sacrificed in order to put an end to sacrifices. And of the gift of alcohol, there remained only the consoling therapeutic side mentioned by the Apostle. Perhaps not quite only: Christ's debut as miraculist, the transformation of several enormous purification jars of water into enough wine to keep the average wedding, such as the one at Cana, going for around two months, suggested that the church he founded was not entirely antipathetic to intoxication.

Surviving outposts of paganism endured for as long as four centuries into the Christian era. While the full-undress version of

Dionysian hysterics, the drunken orgies and the Bacchanalia, became a favored theme in literature and the decorative arts, safely distanced from the societies of late antiquity both theologically and historically, some of the clandestine cells intent on keeping the flame alive moved out of the cities (Pompeii was their last great urban redoubt, and we know what happened to that) into the suburbs, and then into the countryside that had always been the natural habitat of the cultists anyway. For a while, the Christianized authorities tolerated a diluted ceremonial version of Bacchic observance residually acknowledged by certain Roman senators, but it went no further than their assumption of honorific titles in furtive meetings of rather well-behaved underground clubs. These groups by then had about the same institutional status as the latter-day wine confréries of Burgundy, whose members garb themselves in beribboned cloaks from time to time in order to induct into their number another visiting journalist on a freebie. The ban of 186 B.C. had resulted in the destruction of many of the Bacchic shrines, and now—toward the close of the fourth century A.D.—idolatrous forms of worship were prohibited by law. Statuettes and small altars were salvaged from private homes in order to furnish the ritual observances under cover of a few secret societies, but these were increasingly unearthed and forcibly disbanded. Sporadic survivals of quasi-Dionysian behavior, often centered on the wine harvest, were permitted only because they seemed to have no discernible focus. Indeed, some of these may still be seen today in festivals like La Tomatina, which takes place every August in the town of Buñol near Valencia, when the people gather in the streets to pelt each other with pulpy ripe tomatoes. The church has never had much difficulty in absorbing the lineaments of pagan worship once belief in them is no longer literal. Westminster Abbey may be forested with Christmas trees in December, but only because the cultic homage to a coming spring they once announced has been lost to collective memory.

Christian proselytizers were still destroying the occasional makeshift shrine to Dionysos or Sabazius in isolated parts of Gaul (France) as late as the middle of the fifth century, but the considerable literary energy that the theologians still devoted to condemning cultic practices was by now very largely wasted on their urban constituencies.

Nobody knew anybody who attended screaming wine-powered orgies in the dead of night, or at least they hoped they didn't. Gregory of Tours, in his sixth-century *History of the Franks,* refers to the contemporary case of a Provençal peasant who, evidently stung rather literally into action by a cloud of wasps, went raving mad, threw off his clothes and arrayed himself in animal hides instead. He went running through forests in the south of France in the company of gangs of naked followers, profanely proclaiming himself to be the risen Christ. The Bishop of Le Puy, whose forces finally caught up with him and arrested him, had him put to death for his blasphemous outrages. Was he the last Dionysian?

It is anthropologically tempting to see in the nighttime raves of the 1980s and 1990s in Britain the popular survival of the Dionysian instinct. Liberated for a night from the exigencies of straight society, entering another mental dimension by means of thrashing Techno music and brain-scrambling MDMA, these events must often have resembled the ecstatic communal rites of the Dionysian worshipers, but with one crucial difference. The ravers didn't by and large believe they were being filled with the inspirational presence of a deity. They knew the source of their bliss was purely chemical. It may have induced the kinds of reflections not available to undrugged consciousness, but there were no shrines to the supreme presence (the German pharmaceutical company Merck, as it happens) that bestowed the gift of E on a suffering humanity. If we look for the tangible evidence of Dionysos, or one of his chemical descendants, in the nocturnal rites of the ravers, we find only a blank space. But then, even in ancient times, the mischievous god who started the party was as devoid of singular identity as a trick of the light. In his multiform manifestations—now gnarled oak, now snorting bull, now the bearded incorrigible old roué, now the beautiful glowing-skinned boy—he has always already vanished.

Because wine played a role in the day-to-day social life of classical society, as well as being a religious sacrament, it also became a key theme in the discourses of philosophy. To the skeptical intelligences of the Greek and Roman philosophers, dramatists and poets, a belief in the literal presence of Dionysos was not a sine qua non, and yet they were much exercised by the whole question of the sensory life, as arguably no other branch of Western philosophy would be until the efflorescence of the left-wing Hegelians led by the young Karl Marx. Philosophy and the material world were still very much intertwined in the classical period, at least until Plato declared that the proper currency of philosophical reflection was the Idea. Inquiries now thought proper to biology or physics sat alongside musings on the just life or the nature of love. Democritus proposed that all matter was made up of tiny particles called atoms, Aristotle came within an ace of discovering distillation by observing the strange "water" that formed when wine was subjected to intense heat, while the largest extant text of Epicurus, whose name was to become misleadingly synonymous with gourmandizing and self-indulgence, is a metereological treatise that hazards a methodical series of guesses at everything from the origin of lightning to a beautifully concise explanation of the causes of rainbows that a modern encyclopedia would be hard put to improve.

The central metaphysical concepts in much philosophizing, however, were pleasure and suffering. Since the largest portion of human life seemed to be unhappiness, many thinkers addressed the question of whether such travails were the natural condition of humanity, against which resistance was not only futile but somehow heretical too, or whether the smart life was the one that was lived in determined avoidance of as much misery as possible. Riches and celebrity may be hard to come across, fame a chimera and romantic fulfillment an often thankless quest, but there were more reliable ways of achieving gratification. There was sex (courtesy of the hetaeras, courtesans, concubines and boys whose lives and livelihoods revolved around the bestowal of sexual attentions), there was food and there was wine. The problem was what, if any, limits should be imposed on their consumption. To the more metaphysical temper, as exemplified in Plato's text *Phaedo,* which concludes with an account of the execution of Socrates by poisoning, there is a constant conflict within each individual between the lures of sensual pleasure and the higher life of the mind. With Plato, we are left in no doubt as to which way this conflict should best be resolved. Physical pleasures are mere distractions. The contemplative life is the noblest, and death the great release from the incriminating appetites. He has

Socrates, the condemned man, assure his colleague Simmias of the necessity of separating the physical and the spiritual:

> We must not infect ourselves with the body's nature, but keep ourselves in a state of purity from it, until god himself sets us free. This is the way we can be pure, and freed from the body's foolishness. We shall be with others who are pure, in all probability, and we shall know through ourselves everything that is untainted. And that perhaps is truth.[6]

There is, though, an alternative tradition within Greek and Roman philosophy that eschews such semidetached mentalism in favor of a more direct ministering to the demands of the body. If it was never quite entirely forgotten by the Western philosophical tradition, it was nonetheless ruthlessly marginalized—not least at the behest of the Christian influence that came to predominate in speculative literature for several centuries. It lived on through this as a sort of after-hours comic relief, the satyr play that followed the dignified tragic drama of ponderous metaphysics. English philosophy after the Reformation, with its idiosyncratically commonsensical bent, its disputatious insistence on the empirical against the airy abstractions of the Catholic scholastics, is noticeably more hospitable to it than the likes of Descartes or Spinoza were to prove. Shakespeare is steeped in it, its most visible personification in his oeuvre, the enormous, bibulous old philanderer Falstaff, permanently farting drunk and up to no good, an embarrassment finally but one whose passing leaves the world a grayer and tediously quieter place. "Eat, drink and be merry, for tomorrow we die" is by no means the last hurrah of this tradition, but it does grow fainter after the Jacobean era and the ascendancy of the Puritan program, which included the shutting down of the English theater. By the time of Robert Herrick's famous lyric, it has acquired an edge of desperation, has become a mere matter of gathering rosebuds while ye may under the shadow of universal doom—a little like the atmosphere of the early 1980s, when popular music retreated into a fantasy world of swashbuckling Romanticism just as the threat of nuclear conflagration was hustling its way to the top of the protest agenda.

Among the Socratics of classical Athens, the hedonistic attitude is most defiantly represented by Aristippus (circa 435–366 B.C.). Almost every story about him concerns feasting or fornication, his single-minded indulgence in them or his dialectical defense of them. While others tried to balance the contemplative and the sensual aspects of existence, for Aristippus there was no third way. There was no point to life other than maximizing the intake of pleasurable experience available from day to day. Accused of gluttony by the ever-censorious Plato while returning laden from a shopping spree in the fish market, his reply was that he had beaten the fishmonger down to a bargain price. When Plato remarked that even he might have been tempted to buy at such a pittance, Aristippus replied, "Well then—it isn't me who's the glutton, but you who are the cheapskate." When challenged by anybody who dared to criticize his sumptuary lifestyle, his riposte would be "If it's wrong to live like this, why do people celebrate the festivals of the gods this way?" The conundrum posed by this question marks the beginning of the gradual disengagement of sensory pleasure from the exclusive realm of religious ritual. If it's good enough for Dionysos, it must be good enough for us, is the strength of the argument.

Not only did philosophy attempt this transition of sybaritic eating and drinking from ritual observance into daily life, but gastronomy was anyway developing in accordance with its own internal dynamic. In the early fourth century B.C., Archestratus wrote a long gastronomic treatise entitled *The Life of Luxury,* some of which survives, and which was much cited by later authors. To be sure, judging from the surviving proportion, the work was not the apologia for unconstrained hedonism the title seems to promise; the recommendations for correct table-setting have an almost Victorian persnicketiness, while the painstaking catalogue of the best types of fish and at precisely which markets to buy them are laid out in all the fastidious earnest of the Sunday supplement food writer. Nonetheless, it is interesting that the work gained that reputation almost immediately after it appeared, and retained it into the next century while it remained intact. It did so for the very reason that it accorded to food and wine the same exhaustive taxonomic labor as was assigned to agriculture or the law. Among the catalogue of endorsements, notes Andrew Dalby, Archestratus

approves the eels of Lake Copais, the bread and cakes of the
Athenian market, the small fry of the Bay of Phalerum, the con-
ger eels of Sicyon, the wines of Thasos and Lesbos.[7]

Where once the cook devoted his art to the preparation of offertory
food for the gods, which it was forbidden to mortal beings to touch,
now he brought his skills to bear on the cooking of dishes for human
enjoyment. Similarly, when wine was purely and simply the medium
of intoxication in the Dionysian rituals, it scarcely mattered what
its gustatory characteristics were as long as it performed its function. But once the wines of particular regions—and even particular vintages—came to be valued, and the idea of aging wine to
improve it gained currency, then not only did a full-scale wine trade
come into being, but drinking itself was well on the way to complete
desacralization.

More than either Aristippus or Archestratus, however, one name
alone resonates through later epochs as a byword for the philosophy
of high living: that of Epicurus. Today, the epicurean is one supposedly dedicated to the delights of the table and (to a lesser extent) the
pleasures of the flesh, not indeed in vulgar concupiscence but with
discriminating objectivity. To drink a bottle of white wine with the
lobster salad and a bottle of red with the *carré d'agneau* may be
thought hedonistic in a grimly appetitive way; to insist on there
being an impeccably chilled young Condrieu and the '82 Gruaud-
Larose, carefully decanted and properly *chambré,* is epicurean.
When we come to examine what remains of Epicurus' output, however, considered alongside the contemporary biographical accounts
written by members of his school, the picture often turns out to be
far more complexly nuanced. In fact, in the surviving letter to
Menoeceus, the sentiment is forcibly expressed that it is paradoxically only by living frugally that true sensual fulfillment can be had,
because in so doing one comes to enjoy the extravagant times the
more. This is nothing other than "Blunteth not the fine edge of seldom pleasure" in classical garb, and is still wearing well in the mid-
twentieth century when, during the privations of the Second World
War, the American gastronomic writer M.F.K. Fisher ends her book
How to Cook a Wolf—a digest of advice on stretching budgets
and making do—with a recipe called "Fruits aux Sept Liqueurs,"

in which the reader is invited lubriciously to envisage the less-straitened times to come when pouring kümmel and champagne and so forth over a plentiful bowl of fruits will exhaust the mildewed concept of "luxury" at a stroke. For the rest of the time, the mere avoidance of physical pain and spiritual disturbance, and not the continual pampering of the corporeal self with drinking bouts and boys, are in themselves the indispensable conditions for pleasurable living. In this, Epicureanism reveals itself to be far more a philosophy of humility than that spouted by the Aristippean "I want it all, and I want it now."

> For it is not [says Epicurus] drinking-bouts and continuous partying and enjoying boys and women, or consuming fish and the other dainties of an extravagant table, which produce the pleasant life, but sober calculation which searches out the reasons for every choice and avoidance and drives out the opinions which are the source of the greatest turmoil for men's souls.[8]

And yet one suspects that the staggering success rate at which the Epicurean academy recruited new converts and pupils could not have been accounted for solely by its being founded on just another espousal of self-abnegation. There was quite enough of that around already. In an earlier passage of the letter already cited, Epicurus states, in what may sound to us like an early counterblast to Marx, that to announce that the time for philosophy has passed is like saying the time for happiness is past. It can't have passed because it has never truly arrived. "Therefore," he goes on, "we must practise the things which produce happiness, since if that is present we have everything and if it is absent we do everything in order to have it."[9] The point is that teaching oneself to wait for the next major drinking session, and the next disrobing boy, ineffably heightens the very pleasure that is dissipated by an unrelieved diet of such treats. On the other hand, to have to wait too long is what casts a cold gray pall over life. In the *Vatican Collection of Epicurean Sayings,* a posthumous compilation of aphorisms that is considered to be reasonably well-attested, Epicurus is quoted as saying assertively, "Life is ruined by delay." A certain sicklied overfamiliarity may indeed set in if each evening brings another willing body and another brimming *kantharos,* but the indefinite postponement of reward makes life a still drearier treadmill. This is an argument incontrovertibly put in modern times by the German philosopher Theodor Adorno. In the course of a long essay on astrology of 1952–3, he highlights its animating principle of deferred gratification:

> If the satisfaction of instinctual urges is denied or postponed, they are rarely kept under reliable control, but are most of the time ready to break through if they find a chance. This readiness to break through is enhanced by the problematic nature of the rationality that recommends postponement of immediate wish-fulfilment for the sake of later permanent and complete gratifications. One is taught to give up immediate pleasures for the sake of a future which only too often fails to compensate for the pleasures one has renounced. Thus rationality does not always seem as rational as it claims to be.[10]

If Epicureanism was not quite the headlong plunge into hedonistic excess that later ages have hoped to discover in it, its libertarian and ameliorative temper made an indelible contribution to the development of philosophy. The fact that such experiences as intoxication with wine were unflinchingly brought within its ambit not only unleashed them from cultic practices that would eventually come to be frowned on very heavily, but saved them for the time being from exclusive confinement to the frivolous margins of life, the seedier purlieus of town and the kind of company that didn't care two obols for speculative reasoning or its somber gurus.

The impulse lived on, perhaps burned the more brightly indeed, in Imperial Rome from the first century A.D. onward. While the general attitude of Athenian society had been "Nothing too much," the more characteristic Roman proverb was "Bathing, wine and Venus exhaust the body but are what life's about." Here too there is ample evidence of the live-for-today theme in philosophy, and again it appears on tombstone inscriptions and engravings. The depiction of banqueting is a not uncommon theme, signifying as it does the belated counsel of the grave's inhabitant: "This is the way to live, for life is short." And in the unforgettable figure of Trimalchio, lording it over a preposterously lavish feast in the *Satyricon* of Petronius, Western literature is given its most ineradicable image of the pleasure-seeking life. Here we see the crafting of sensual gratification through food and wine made obscenely meticulous, as colossal pies are cut open to release flocks of live songbirds, roast birds are stuffed one inside the other like Russian dolls, fermented fish sauces and unimaginable offals succeed one another in demented profusion and the copious libations go round and round without cease. The portrait is a tour de force of comic exaggeration, and yet the implied sentiment is, "Who *wouldn't* live like this, given a glimmer of a chance?"

Of drunkenness, the gift of the outsider god consecrated in the doomed confraternities of the faithful, there is now only the rank absurdity of befuddlement, the reclining diner yodeling vulgar songs to his long-suffering but equally sozzled guests, guzzling down half-diluted wine and chucking it up again as the boys go on patiently refilling the jugs. The Roman comic drama teemed with helpless drunks, just as the Greek satyr plays had done, inebriated confusion being the stock device by which amorous indelicacies and all manner of infractions against authority could be introduced and optimistically explained away. Slaves in particular were an easy vehicle; since their lives were deemed to be one long round of onerous duty and unearned beatings, they could readily be portrayed as anything from hilariously tipsy to virtually comatose, the scrapes they then fell into forming the comic impetus of the plots. This is the fag-end of the Dionysian line, intoxication not as a transport into regions of the sublime, but as a ridiculous stripping away of the veneer of respectability on every civic individual, from the dignified tribune of the people to the well-trained, obedient slave.

If the ritualistic use of intoxication was designed as a means of controlling the madness that potentially raged within even the most civilized breast, by letting it out cathartically in a ceremony of worship, the social uses of wine in classical Athens were more to do with unleashing the intellect. The symposium was the most sublimated form of this process. Here groups of like-minded male friends would gather at the house of one of them, in a room specifically dedicated to the purpose and, recumbent on couches arranged in a square around the four walls, would engage in postprandial disquisitions on the preoccupying themes of human existence. The wine was generally served in shallow cups and carefully watered down to a conservative alcohol level, since this was thought to be the refined and properly respectful way of taking it. Rough-hewn northerners might take it nearly neat, but Athenians prided themselves on a culture of moderation in such matters, in which inebriation set in at a genteelly leisurely pace. (The one exception to the dilution rule came with the initial toast that set the party off; here the taking of a measure of unmixed wine was a fitting gesture of homage to the gods, and perhaps also served to remind the symposiasts of the dangerous power that lurked within the cup.) Poetry and songs punctuated the flow of discourse, the themes typically romantic or venereal, the contributions proceeding around the gathering in circular order. Toasts, those handy pretexts for ceremonializing the ingestion of drink, were offered at regular intervals. The amount and frequency of the libations was usually strictly controlled. It was often decided at the outset how many krater, or bowls, were to be consumed. The wine was mixed in these bowls, sometimes with warmed water, sometimes chilled with snow, before being ladled into the jugs from which individual cups were to be filled. At the end of the evening, the symposiasts were expected to disperse in an orderly fashion, thanking the host for his hospitality and promising to meet again soon. The structures and rituals of gentility that attended the symposium have their descendants in the modern dinner-party, in which a further bottle or two are opened as plates are cleared away and the conversation flows on, becomes competitive, perhaps slightly controversial.

It is clear, however, that the Greek symposia did not always proceed along such securely patrolled lines. Often, the predetermined number of bowls became elastic as the evening wore on. Gatecrashers would arrive and have to be catered for, and the odd guest—notorious perhaps for unruliness while under the influence—might grab the jug from the servant boy's hands in order to top himself up, while at the most riotous assemblies, it was by no means unheard of for the proceedings to descend to something like the chaos of Alice's banquet at the end of *Through the Looking-Glass*, with couches being overturned, tables being thrown about and guests greedily swigging undiluted wine directly from the cooling-jugs. Davidson quotes an entertaining story from an account by Timaeus of Taormina:

In Agrigentum there is a house called "the trireme" for the following reason. Some young men were getting drunk in it, and became feverish with intoxication, off their heads to such an extent that they supposed they were in a trireme, sailing through a dangerous tempest; they became so befuddled as to throw all the furniture and fittings out of the house as though at sea, thinking that the pilot had told them to lighten the ship because of the storm. A great many people, meanwhile, were gathering at the scene and started to carry off the discarded property, but even then the youths did not pause from their lunacy. On the following day the generals turned up at the house, and charges were brought against them. Still sea-sick, they answered to the officials' questioning that in their anxiety over the storm they had been compelled to jettison their superfluous cargo by throwing it into the sea.[11]

Such an outcome was not officially approved of, but was philosophically accepted by most as the realistic risk inherent in a drinking party. If nothing else, it made for a few good stories in the days following.

Unbridled inebriation was not thought desirable mainly because what the symposium was about first and foremost was sociality. Conversation, meaningful human interaction, was its raison d'être, and drink—whilst initially serving to make the participants loquacious—could soon gum up the works if taken in excess. The problem was that excess slowly but surely became the norm. Many must have been the offended sensibilities that attended such a soiree in hopes of an evening of highbrow reflection, only to see it degenerate before their eyes into raucous anarchy. Plato's own *Symposium* shows the drunken Alcibiades at first disrupting the gently competitive atmosphere of the gathering, but then allowing himself to be beguiled by the elevated tone of the dialecticians. In reality, this may only have happened very seldom. Once intellects had taken off on the wings of intoxication, it was not thought appropriate to attempt to tether them down again with chairmanly calls for order, and so they carried on flying in opposing directions to each other as the debate spun out of control, until the inevitable crash-landing of alcoholic collapse supervened. Nonetheless, despite the unseemly affray that so many of these occasions turned into, the symposia held on to their reputation as meetings of the cultured elite, largely because they were private institutions. The average symposiast had nothing but supercilious disdain for the world of public drinking that might be going on not far down the street, for all that the resultant behavior there might have been indistinguishable to the untutored eye. In this unblushing hypocrisy was born the durable belief that intoxicants are too hazardous to be allowed to fall into the hands of the lower orders. (One is reminded of the situation at British football grounds in the 1980s when the alcohol that flowed freely in the hermetic cocoon of the directors' box was denied as an incendiary poison to the rabble they saw in the stands.)

The public drinking that went on in the wineshops or taverns was not necessarily more rowdy—indeed, it was probably typically less so—than that of the symposia. Watered wine was the standard fare here too, and certain establishments prided themselves on exemplary wine lists. It was by no means unusual for the elite to eat and drink there too, often first thing in the morning; the noisier debates in the Areopagus were very likely attributable to some members of the Assembly having popped in for a swift jugful on the way to the session. Where the distinction was drawn between symposium drinking and that of the taverns was in the fact that the latter were open to those strata of society to whom the symposia were characteristically barred: slaves, foreigners, even women. Additionally, of course, there was no pretense about drinking being an adjunct to intellectual exercise. Drinking here was about getting drunk, pure and simple. To be sure, there were different grades of tavern, from the relatively refined to the honest-to-goodness drinking den, but the attitude to alcohol consumption within them was consistent across the board. Since what was taking place here was more obviously a commercial transaction, correspondingly greater attention was paid to the quality—and especially the quantity—of what was served. Short measures (or overdilution) excited something approaching the degree of paranoid indignation that they would assume in Tudor England, when humiliating exemplary punishments were instituted for those found guilty of cheating Crown subjects of their due. Unscrupulous taverners often tried to stretch their stock-in-trade as methodically as contemporary drug-dealers do, while those who dispensed full and honest measures became local heroes. Everybody's favorite barman, as now, was the one who knew exactly what mixture of wine and water you liked, who didn't need to be reminded each time you happened in, but who just got on with the blending to your remembered specifications. Though he makes an honorary appearance in a speech in Aristophanes' comedy *Wealth* of the late fifth century B.C., the cultural archetype of the set-'em-up-Joe barman—dependable trusty, discreet confidant, Father Confessor—was just making his debut in Western iconography.

To the Romans too, the life of the taverns, and public drinking in general, was felt to have a slightly louche character. Many of the taverns, or *cauponae,* doubled as restaurants, and even offered the service of boiling or warming up brought-in food for those who had no means of cooking it at home. For this reason, because they didn't discriminate against the poorer classes, it was thought a little infra dig for a nobleman to be spotted dining there—and social death to make a habit of it. To the instinctively repressive cast of mind of the imperial authorities, the conviviality of the taverns placed them under the same rubric of suspiciousness as the religious confraternities. They were meeting-places of the like-minded where political sedition might well be brewing as soon as officialdom's back was turned, and serial attempts were made over centuries to close them down, or at least curtail the range of facilities they provided so that they became less of a magnet. The implication was that it was somehow less salubrious to eat and drink in public, that the private home was the more reputable context for these activities.

By the time of the Christianization of the Roman Empire in the fourth century, the idea of intoxication as a higher state of consciousness was looking pretty shop-soiled. Drunkenness was funny, or it was squalid, but it was more readily interpretable as evidence of moral decline or self-indulgence than it was as sympathetic contact with the divine.

Alcohol is not, though, and never has been, the whole story. There was another version of ritualized intoxication that spanned a two-thousand-year period from around 1500 B.C. through the zenith of classical Athens to the time of Constantine and the ascendancy of the Christian church in the eastern Mediterranean that followed the

Roman emperor's conversion in the fourth century A.D. Even more than the spectacular ceremonial savageries of Dionysian worship, it exerted a powerful, positively life-changing impact on its participants, and its forcible eradication by Christianity—newly ensconced in government and flexing its muscles for the first time on an imperial scale—represents the beginning of systematic repression of the intoxication impulse in the lives of Western citizens.

The Eleusinian Mysteries were a vast ten-day ritualistic celebration, attended by thousands every year in the temple at Eleusis, to the west of the city of Athens. They were held only once a year in September, in honor of Demeter, goddess of agriculture, to acknowledge her providence at another bountiful harvest-time, but the effect of them appears to have been not merely exhilarating but soul-stirring. The festival climaxed with a daylong procession from Athens to the temple, culminating in a nocturnal ritual in which new initiates would be enrolled into the cult. A sacramental cup was shared, some sacred brew imbibed from it, but what was it? The question has been the focus of much academic examination, but remains tantalizingly unsettled. It was called *kykeon,* and descriptions of the ritual in both Greek and Roman writers, Homer and Cicero among them, leave us in no doubt that the celebrants underwent a hallucinatory experience, seeing astonishing visions and entering a benign state of ecstatic consciousness, the memory of which persisted indestructibly. The participants felt they had left the quotidian world of travails far behind them, had been reminded of the notion that a joyful life was not an elusive chimera but a real and present possibility. Many of the principal philosophers and writers of classical Athens, as well as Roman royalty during the imperial era, had at least one taste of the Mysteries, including the great tragedians Aeschylus and Sophocles, the poet Pindar, Aristotle and even the metaphysical Plato, who perhaps found himself more attuned to hallucinogenic intoxication than to the base corporeality of the alcoholic kind.

The favored theory is that they were ingesting ergot, a fungus that parasitically attacks cereal grasses—rye in particular, but also wheat and barley. It forms hard little bruise-purple nodules that invisibly take the place of the seeds in these plants, and are massively toxic if regularly swallowed. Their stupefying disorientating effects would doubtless first have been observed in cattle or sheep that had unwittingly eaten them. Sustained use causes traumatic obstruction of the bloodstream, with the result that entire limbs become useless, insensate and finally rotten with gangrene. Outbreaks of ergot poisoning have bedeviled farming communities from time to time over the centuries, usually because the unnoticed fungus will have been consumed in grain used for bread. If Demeter was the goddess of grain, then the sacrament taken at the Eleusinian ceremonies would certainly have been grain-based, rather than a wine preparation, which in any case was specifically forbidden. And if the intoxication that proceeded from it really was as psychotropic as the written accounts insist, some form of ergotized beer—or possibly simply a mixture of infected grain with water, and maybe handfuls of mint to make it more palatable—seems the likeliest candidate.

Some cultural historians have rigorously tried, and are still trying, to undermine this theory on the not unreasonable grounds that if ergot had been systematically used in this way, we would expect there also—certainly over 2,000 years—to have been recorded outbreaks of mass toxicity. And yet there are none. One recent source suggests that a probable explanation for the hallucinatory quality of the experience lies in the fact that celebrants traditionally fasted for several days before the night of the Mystery. In this state, and perhaps mesmerized by the nature of the mass spectacle (a phenomenon more familiar to twentieth-century citizens from the pioneering work on crowd psychosis by Wilhelm Reich), the first taste of alcohol, even if it were only normal beer, would have been relatively dramatic. This is an undeniably practical possibility, and yet it seems a pitifully milk-and-water proposition to account for the reactions of so august a figure as Cicero, who candidly says that what happened to the communicants at Eleusis provided them with a means for living in unalloyed happiness. That would seem a bit strong as a description of the well-known effects of drinking on an empty stomach.

At the conclusion of the Mystery night, after much ecstatic dancing and celebration had gone on under the influence of the *kykeon*, the Eleusinians assembled in an internal enclosure within the huge temple complex. At the bidding of the officiating priest, a burst of fire would pour forth from behind the enclosure's one great door and, as it swung open, the purple-clad apparition of Demeter herself would be made manifest to the gathering. It is scarcely possible to imagine the effect a materialization of the divine presence would have had to sensibilities far less skeptical than those of Plato or Sophocles. Fainting fits, helplessly surging joy, outbreaks of gibbering hysteria must all have been common, and as the goddess withdrew, the spectacle ended with the priest didactically presenting a single cereal grain to the blissed gaze of the new initiates. The Mysteries were theirs too now.

So how to explain the evidently nontoxic effects of ergot if it did indeed lie behind the Mystery? Some have argued that in low concentrations, and used only very occasionally, it need not be particularly dangerous. This seems to me a triumph of hope over probability. Somewhere along the line, over two millennia, there would have been at least one large-scale disaster, if not several. An outbreak of ergotism from poisoned rye bread killed 40,000 people in the French district of Aquitaine toward the close of the first millennium A.D. There is seemingly no such thing as a slight case of ergotic poisoning. In most instances, its constrictive effect on the blood vessels leads to the limbs literally dying on the body and dropping off like withered leaves—and that within days. Alternatively, it produces convulsive seizures like epilepsy that lead to total delirium. In either event, the chances of survival are vanishingly small. Two more persuasive theories have been advanced. Firstly, we know that the grain that went into the cups at Eleusis was specifically barley rather than rye, and that the strain of ergot that barley plays host to is significantly lower in toxins than rye ergot. Secondly—and this point may well compound the first—soaking the grains in water would effectively separate the hydro-soluble psychotropic alkaloids from the lipo-soluble toxic ones. The preparation of the sacrament was presumably done to a strict, and closely guarded, recipe.

A decade before the ergot theory was first advanced by R. Gordon Wasson, Carl Ruck and Albert Hofmann (the last the true progenitor of the ergot-related synthetic hallucinogen LSD), the English poet and sometime cultural historian Robert Graves had suggested that the key ingredient in the Eleusinian sacrament may have been a hallucinogenic mushroom gathered from the damp autumnal earth—perhaps the *Stropharia* variety that contains psilocybin. The Wasson-Hofmann-Ruck proposal has found greater favor since its publication. The roots of the Eleusinian ritual would appear to lie in the visionary rites of the ancient Minoan civilization on the island of Crete, to the south of the Greek mainland, in which some form of ergotized beer (and indeed opium) is known to have been ritually used. Furthermore, it surely makes more sense to envisage the goddess of grain being celebrated with a grain-based intoxicant than a mushroom one, and the point is suggestively put that the traditional color of Demeter's garments, a deep, rich purple, is the precise color of the ergot spores.

The *longue durée* of Eleusis, its continual modification over the centuries and the fact that—in keeping with a true mystery cult—its intimates jealously guarded the innermost secrets of its operations (frustratingly enough for later anthropologists) combine to leave us with an impression both of awe and of pathos. Awe because the mass nature of the ritual and the degree of refinement brought to its theatrical elements, the smoke and fire of it albeit vaguely reminiscent to us of the Wizard's bogus pyrotechnics in the Emerald City of Oz, represents an extraordinarily advanced level of ritual intoxication. But the pathos of the Eleusinian Mysteries, seen through the long refracting prism of history, is that they were to be the only institutionalized form of hallucinogenic initiation rite that the West would ever permit itself. To Christianity, with its motivating concern for personal salvation through altruism and abstinent piety, the Mysteries could only prosaically be seen as diabolic, a profane distraction from the only mystery that now mattered: the intervention of God in human affairs by means of his incarnation, sacrifice and resurrection. When the temple was destroyed (its ruins survive today amid the housing projects and industrial estates outside Athens), the sacramental use of psychotropic materials was buried in the rubble.

The historical period covered by the Eleusinian Mysteries is arguably the one time in Western history that the two views of intoxication—the sublime and the secular—coexist in more or less equal strength with each other. Earlier societies, such as those of the Egyptian dynasties and the Minoan-Maecenean civilization on Crete, are known to have made much ritualistic use of intoxication practices in their ceremonials, consecrating the experiences of inebriation and hallucination to their respective multiple deities, but it took the Athenians to conceive of the symposium and to bring the sensuous impact of alcohol within the ambit of a worldly philosophy. Later societies in Christianized Europe and the colonized New World would develop whole mythologies and social rituals around the use of intoxicants, preeminently alcohol. But, aside from the symbolism of the Holy Communion, there was no meaningful space within these cultures for the spiritual reading of the intoxicated state. The classical period is the authentic time of transition from the one version to the other.

To the citizen of Periclean Athens, wine was a gift to humanity from the one god in the pantheon who, despite his chameleon nature, seemed the most sympathetically semi-human of the lot. It was also part of the very fabric of life, inextricable from the vision of fulfillment held out to human beings by the philosophers and orators whose reasoned arguments endeavored to make sense of it all. There may have been counsels of moderation in their discourses, but rarely counsels of complete abstinence. Certainly, there was an ascetic temper in certain strains of philosophy, by means of which it was held that stripping away the needless fripperies of material life enabled one to concentrate on the issues that were presumed truly to matter. (Socrates is very largely responsible for this: he is said to have once remarked, on gazing upon a market-stall laden with commodities, "What a lot of things I don't need.") However, the Stoics and Cynics, generally held to be the temperamental others of the adherents of Epicureanism, turn out not to be substantially different from them in their assumption that a way had to be found to survive this earthly life, even if that meant through the rigor of mental exercises in their case, as opposed to the Epicureans' preference for voiding the self of unnecessary desires.

It is the apotheosis of metaphysics in the thinking of the members of Plato's Academy from the fourth century B.C. onward that begins to set the tone for the antimaterialist bias that was to invest all Western philosophy until at least Schopenhauer. For Plato himself, it was vital to the existential health of the individual that the three constitutive aspects of his or her being—namely, reason, will and the appetites—be brought into harmonious balance with each other, if a fulfilled and right life was to be attained. Inevitably, this meant rigorous curtailment of the last faculty, tellingly sited, so it was thought, in the nether abdominal region, below the valiant chest that housed the will and the head from which cerebral glories—such as Platonic philosophy, for example—flowed. In Plato's view, the world experienced by the senses was a poor, slipshod, evanescent thing, an occasionally sublime but fleeting illusion that should fool nobody. He wished to make humanity wake up to the true and unchanging world of Ideas that lay behind all the forces of nature, to go beyond the surface froth to the eternal verities beneath. To the refined intellect, toiling away at these Ideas in a ceaseless labor of luxuriously idle contemplation, there was no higher reward than the theoretical breakthrough, no more enlightening human interaction than the company of other *bien-pensants,* and it was their insights that could and should be the touchstones not just for the thoughtful individual but for the whole of society. Philosophers should be the rulers of human affairs, virtual monarchs in a well-tuned and supremely ordered polis in which appetitive excess and all unnecessary gilding of existence would be banished by intellectual fiat. In his most notorious bit of sensual repression, he declares in the *Republic* that poets would be among the irrelevant nuisances to be dispensed with.

I am by no means the first to detect in Plato's austerely mentalist philosophy the icy blast of fascist authoritarianism. In its sublimated pursuit of the life of the mind, it disastrously presumes that the corporeal being is a mere husk that can be blown off at will, an attitude that will find an easy passage into the precepts of the early Christian church, where mortification and self-denying ordinances will quickly become the mood music of the exemplary spiritual life. By the time it finds its rock bottom, the antimaterialist temper issues in the corpse heaps of the extermination camps, so much tangible evidence of the expendability of the physical individual. If Aristippean gratification had emerged as the predominant theme of Western philosophy, it may be conceded, we should certainly have paid the price in terms of not just speculative, but scientific advancement too. And it must be allowed that Plato believed as an article of faith in the civilizing influence of education, so that the masses could progress at least a little further toward the privileged intellectual enlightenment of their political masters. However, given the evident unpleasantness that we can't all turn out to be Platos, however early the prescribed education starts (and he did advocate preschooling as fervently as any modern Social Democrat), the Platonist state would inevitably be strictly stratified, with everybody down to the humblest slave understanding and accepting his or her station within it.

There is precious little space for the consoling operations of intoxication here, scarcely a murmur of Euripidean compassion for the troubled lives of blameless individuals for whom the solace of wine and the chance of love are interwoven inextricably. Intoxication is the common currency of the laboring folk who will keep the Platonist apparatus in business, just as they will throughout the entire period of entrepreneurial capitalism, when it will play for them the same unsavory role as chemical comforter while the philosopher-kings of the Temperance movement urge them to aspire to a loftier state. Temperance to Plato at least still means what it says, rather than the total abstinence that Victorian Salvationists fraudulently urged on the benighted poor in its name. If the grand narrative of Western philosophy has found so little room to accommodate the physical needs of the beings on whose behalf it presumes to speak, we cannot avoid tracing the source of this heartbreaking lacuna to Plato, to whose work it is all famously footnotes anyway.

If further proof were needed that, despite Plato, classical antiquity was the period when the sacred and profane views of intoxication sat unremarkably side by side, a well-attested story concerning Alcibiades the general might serve to emphasize the point. In 415 B.C., he was the center of a public embarrassment when he was charged with, and subsequently fined for, having in his house a substance that turned out to be nothing less than a sample of the Eleusinian sacrament. He had evidently purloined it to use in private parties at home as a more entertaining alternative, or perhaps adjunct, to the customary wine. Whatever the substance was (and the case, incidentally, certainly dispenses with the alcohol-on-empty-stomachs theory of Eleusinian hallucinations), whether it was a bag of dried mushrooms or a bunch of ergotized cereal, Alcibiades was evidently very fond of it. The audacity of his actions neither undermined the ritual of Eleusis nor ruined him. But caught in possession with intent to supply, he was the first drug criminal.

3

The Fourth Deadly Sin

If intoxication as a cultural practice has, through Western history, often been hidden behind dense veils of censure, it is because ever since the worship of Dionysos fell from favor, it has been consistently seen as wrong. Definitions of "wrong" may be subject to more or less subtle modulations—at various times and in various contexts, it may mean sinful, or immoral, or just plain irresponsible—but there is always at least a sense of discomfort with the idea that turns, at its most rabidly censorious, to righteous condemnation.

Its career as a sin has survived the Reformation of the Christian church, the revolutionary politics of the great social upheavals from 1789 on, the pervasively searching gaze of psychoanalysis and even—to a surprising extent—the agnosticization of Western societies in the postwar period. When we hear an old Fundamentalist preacher like Dr. Jerry Falwell declare with unruffled conviction that "drunkenness destroys the morals and integrity of our nation," we may smile at the gorgeous anachronism of it, as if this were the authentic voice of one of the last old-time Salvationists in captivity. But when Britain's Royal College of Physicians publishes a report on drink-related diseases entitled "A Great and Growing Evil," as it did in 1987, we are inclined to accept the stigmatization without demur, scarcely noticing the incongruity of the white-coated doctor donning General Booth's battle cap. Drunkenness must be a sin if its agent, alcohol, is a force for evil. To allow it into the body can only be the reckless action of one who has turned his face away from God. Once in there, it is held to provoke all manner of devilish behavior, from impure and lustful thoughts to breaking into the liquor store to get more of it. "I done a few crimes," said the boy on day-release from a reformatory, sitting next to me on a daytime TV debate about alcohol, "but it was drink what made me do it."

If intoxication is wrong, it is in large part these days because it is perceived to be guilty of inciting criminality and other antisocial activities in too many of those who regularly take intoxicants. We shall return to this notion of diminished moral responsibility later in the chapter, but what needs to be addressed first is the question of whether the altered state itself—regardless of whether we mean drunkenness, tranquilization, hyperstimulation or hallucinogenic trance—is a transgression. There are many aspects of the ecclesiastical view of morality that persisted down the centuries right up to the threshold of our own era. Suicide remained illegal in the United Kingdom until the mid-twentieth century, with the ghastly result that a botched attempt with too few aspirins could easily mean a stretch in jail. In the field of sexual morality, masturbation, the mother of all self-indulgences, was counseled and cautioned against by priest and teacher as likely to make its practitioner sluggish, vituperative or not very good at contact sports. And yet these have passed beyond ethical censure now as a more sympathetic view of personal morality has dawned upon society. Suicide may be tragic or enraging but scarcely in itself an evil act, while autoeroticism is positively urged on us as beneficial to health. And yet intoxication can't be persuaded into the light. It remains, even in the face of its virtual universality, something that we have to pretend we don't do, or at least not deliberately, or at least not very often, or at least only after we have done a decent day's work. When a sick hangover or clattering comedown then follows a night's partaking, we feel—as David Lenson has accurately shown—that we are now receiving our just deserts.

For the citizens of classical times, as we saw in chapter 2, intoxication held a privileged place in certain sacred rituals. Certainly, there was a suggestion, inscribed in the Athenian motto "Nothing too much" and in the urgings of the more cerebral philosophers, that excessive indulgence was not an ideal, largely because it offended against the crucial concept of balance that was deemed to be the organizing principle of the best way to live, but wine itself and the drinking of it weren't demonized. That process sets in with the arrival of Christianity in the middle of Imperial Rome.

In the Jewish faith, the question of drinking did not particularly excite any great moral concern. There are passages in the Talmud that actually ordain not just the taking of wine, but the attainment of a state of unequivocal inebriation. The general observation that there is "no celebration without wine" may be taken as cheerily proverbial, but at the festival of Purim it is required of Jews that they should get to the stage of not quite knowing "whether you are blessing Mordechai or cursing Haman." To the Christian temper, the idea of celebrating any of God's festivals by drinking to the extent of not knowing what you were talking about has an almost profane ring, and yet for many Jews—the Hasidic branch of the faith in particular—the use of alcohol was thought to have a liberating effect on the spirit. By partially displacing everyday consciousness, the believer could perhaps feel his or her soul more freely communicating with the Creator. This did not absolve individuals from maintaining the correct degree of respect for the body, nor indeed from accepting the law of the land if exile had taken them into societies where alcohol was forbidden or its use heavily circumscribed, but to the Jew, wine is one of God's gifts to humanity, a point emphasized by the fact that the man who is entrusted with salvaging life on earth at the time of the Flood is also responsible for establishing the first vineyard. But here, at the outset of the new world that supervenes after the receding of the waters, just as God is promising to deliver no more punitive inundations to the world since human beings (his own faulty creation, after all) are incapable of anything other than recalcitrant behavior, there arises an all too typical indiscretion:

> And Noah began to be an husbandman, and he planted a vineyard: And he drank of the wine, and was drunken; and he was uncovered within his tent. And Ham, the father of Canaan, saw the nakedness of his father, and told his two brethren without. And Shem and Japheth took a garment, and laid it upon both their shoulders, and went backward and, covered the nakedness of their father; and their faces were backward, and they saw not their father's nakedness. And Noah awoke from his wine, and knew what his younger son had done unto him. And he said,

Cursed be Canaan; a servant of servants shall he be unto his brethren. And he said, Blessed be the Lord God of Shem; and Canaan shall be his servant. God shall enlarge Japheth, and he shall dwell in the tents of Shem; and Canaan shall be his servant. (Genesis 9.20–27)

Reducing his grandson to a state of servitude is very much in keeping with the idea of visiting the sins of the fathers on the children through the generations, the example that God sets in the second commandment that Moses receives on Mount Sinai ("I the Lord thy God am a jealous God, visiting the iniquity of the fathers upon the children unto the third and fourth generation of them that hate me"—Exodus 20.5). The compelling aspect of this story, though, is not so much the irascible edict of an old man with a hangover, but the fact that being drunk made Noah incriminatingly indiscreet before one of his sons. In the non-canonical Hebrew tradition of the tale, he has first discovered the intoxicating effect of the juice of overripe grapes when happening upon a frolicking goat that had evidently drunk its fill. In that version, the inebriated Noah again sheds his clothes on the way home to invent viticulture. But in the naked state, man becomes a beast, which wasn't what God had in mind for him at all, and by this shameful metamorphosis—passed on to the luckless son who happens in on him in his abandonment—the business of drinking is indelibly stigmatized.

The intoxication historian Ronald K. Siegel cites a Romanian variant of the story in which the goat again appears. This time, the founding of the primeval vineyard is witnessed by the Devil as well, who slaughters the goat and uses its blood to nourish the vine's roots. A second libation of blood from a slaughtered lion, and then a third from a pig, are added for good measure. Thus does the Devil determine the bestial pattern that constitutes the three stages of the drinking man. The first stage is the innocent gamboling of the goat (the extent to which Jews celebrating Purim are permitted to go perhaps). The second is alcohol rage like the roaring of the lion, in which formerly rational people turn on their fellows for no evident reason, and the final stage is the shameless, squalid wallowing of the swine.

Noah's story may resonate with a skeptical audience today, if at all, as a paradigm of the hero whose fame is founded on some grandiose feat such as saving the planet, but who then—resting on his laurels—becomes a shambolic embarrassment, living on far too long (another three and a half centuries, in fact) and undermining his own achievement. What his downfall taught the exegetical tradition, however, was that drinking wine, for all that it may be a divine gift, is fraught with risk. In reducing a wise old patriarch to the status of a swine, and upsetting the natural order of paternal authority and filial respect, it exposes the soul of man to danger and the wrath of God. There clearly must be a certain level of intoxication that the Creator is prepared to countenance in human beings, since the means for it are provided as some kind of reward for preserving life on earth, but equally obviously there is an implicit "so far and no further" inscribed within it, a point beyond which the blameless merriment of the spirit becomes vulgar concupiscence stained with guilt. With the early Christian writers, most notably Paul, the question takes on a significantly more urgent spiritual note, even though the precise boundary-line between the innocent and the culpable remains as elusive as ever.

The new church that emerged in the aftermath of the judicial execution of Jesus Christ was composed of many conflicting strands. It was of course primarily a Jewish church, its founder a recognizably Semitic teacher in the rabbinical tradition, even though one who came somewhat out of left field, wandering through Galilee, preaching a radical gospel of forgiveness against the retributive temper of the established church, and advocating a concern for personal salvation through the sanctified ideal of neighborly love. The vision of moral transformation that it held up to a society riven by tribal divisions and laboring under the yoke of a brutally repressive Roman hegemony was one that was once thought the proper preserve of philosophy. Religious observance was considered a matter of worship and of presiding over ceremonies such as marriages, comings of age and burials, but it wasn't expected to try to change the world. Jesus, with his reported miracle-working and his occasional act of civil defiance such as the overturning of the money-changers' tables, marked a sharp departure from this view. Urging a new code of ethical conduct on his Jewish followers, he absolved them from observation of the dietary laws and prescriptions set forth in the Torah (the first five books of the Old Testament), and recommended to them a complete moral shift, in which careful stewardship of the soul was the prerequisite for admission to the kingdom of eternal bliss that awaited the pure.

Sections of the nascent church interpreted the Messiah's teachings in this regard to imply a wholesale rejection of the lineaments of the material world as intrinsically evil. The body, on this reading, was a mere vehicle for transition to the state of bliss, but also the locus classicus of temptation. Its yearnings for sensual gratification had to be sternly, even cruelly, resisted, and the phenomenal world it was doomed to wander for the allotted span of three-score years and ten was a teeming cesspit of the means to such gratification. The Gnostic sect that flourished during the first couple of centuries of the new faith was the prime exemplar of this tenet. One of its principal extant texts, the lost Gospel of Thomas, recovered with the discovery of the Dead Sea Scrolls in 1947, expounds this view very clearly. The writer describes the Christ figure as appearing in the world, but managing to escape its taint. In this sense, he is truly—as the canonical gospels will posit—"with us but not of us."

The Gnostics thus lived in hermetic communities, rejecting all congress with the polluting world of material display to be found in the towns and cities, and humbly, ascetically awaited the enlightenment that they believed would in due course dawn upon them, obviating the need for following exemplary teachers like Jesus. While the Gnostic tradition was decisively excluded from the earliest Christian councils, and works like that of Thomas cast out of the synoptic mainstream when the New Testament was being compiled, some of its enshrinement of self-denial did survive within the new faith. It is viscerally present in the late Gospel of John, and forms part of the practice of those communities, known as Johannine, that took his scripture, together with the Apocalypse text (the Book of Revelation) that bears his name, as their chief inspiration. Based in Asia Minor, though with their roots in the Palestine of Jesus' milieu, the Johannine communities were the ones that broke most irreparably with the established Jewish tradition, becoming alienated from the fallen world of human society as it was and urgently anticipating the coming of the dreadful day when it would all be swept aside. The same millenarian mood is luridly evoked in the epistle of James, who reminds his readers, with the bleak certitude mobilized so strikingly centuries later by Samuel Beckett, that human life is a mere exhalation, blown away on the passing wind. Devoting our time here to sensual pleasures is therefore as grotesquely inappropriate as fattening ourselves up for the abattoir: "Ye have lived in pleasure on the earth, and been wanton; ye have nourished your hearts, as in a day of slaughter" (5.5).

Certain branches of the church came, over the ensuing centuries, to raise the standard of asceticism as the optimal route to paradise. It is an impulse at large in the stripped-down contemplative life of the monastic orders, in the fulminating of the Puritans against the licentiousness of the social life of Jacobean England, in every flagellating Catholic zealot who, in the name of the risen Lord, redirected the scourge from self-mortification to the thrashing of defenseless children in the Jesuit and convent schools, despite the fact that nothing in Jesus' own teachings appears to condone such practices. The Salvation Army may require teetotalism of its enthusiasts, but it is not a scriptural demand. The Gospel text that is thought above all to recommend asceticism to the adherents of the new church is the highly mythicized account in Matthew 4, of Jesus defying the blandishments of the Devil during his sojourn in the wilderness. Not "all the kingdoms of the world, and the glory of them" can persuade him to accede to Satanic authority, but nor will he even be tempted to use his own transformative power to turn a handful of stones to the bread that might assuage his howling hunger: "Man shall not live by bread alone, but by every word that proceedeth out of the mouth of God" (4.4). To this formidable statement of spiritual piety will eventually be offered the modern riposte of Bertolt Brecht, "Bread first, then morals!" but in the early Christian era, the example of the Messiah transcended any argument over social provision.

We are still no nearer, however, to answering the question as to whether there is a theological stricture within Christianity against the state of intoxication. If no precise position can be fixed, it is to a large degree because the Christian church is not concerned with such strictures. Whether to take intoxicating drink or not is, after Jesus, at the same level of prescriptive specificity as the decrees in Leviticus that permit to Jews the eating of the bald locust or the grasshopper, but not of the cormorant or the camel. His first miracle is the transformation of water into copious quantities of wine during the wedding at Cana, in order to bail out a host who had underprovided or indeed been faced with a bunch of unexpectedly ravenous guests, so we can assume Jesus is not averse to the idea of drinking to celebrate. And if we search the writings of Christianity's first and most diligent exegeticist, St. Paul, for guidance, we come upon a number of conflicting signals.

The overall force of Paul's recommendations is in favor of the ascetic life that he himself lived. He acknowledges that in its liberation from Mosaic and Levitican legalism, Christianity is not a narrowly doctrinal faith, and yet he is keen to counsel against any lapse into a laissez-faire opportunism of the will, insisting that that is just as much, if not more of, a state of bondage. True, Jesus' sacrifice, according to chapter 2 of the epistle to the Colossians, blots out the sum of written ordinances against the faithful, "nailing it to his cross" instead. The apostle then continues:

> Let no man therefore judge you in meat, or in drink, or in respect of an holyday, or of the new moon, or of the sabbath days: Which are a shadow of things to come; but the body is of Christ. (2.16–17)

It seemingly doesn't really matter, according to this text at least, whether Christians partake of intoxicating drink, because there are considerably more important issues to concern them.

However, elsewhere, Paul appears more determined to encourage his readers to abjure the dangers of drink. The first epistle to the Corinthians sternly includes "drunkards" among its blacklist of thieves, extortioners and so on who can't possibly hope to inherit the kingdom of God (6.10). By the time of the letter to the Galatians, the warning is couched in the weary tones of a schoolteacher chastising an unruly class for the same monotonous infractions: "Envyings, murders, drunkenness, revelings, and such like: of the which I tell you before, as I have also told you in time past, that they which do such things shall not inherit the kingdom of God" (5.21).

Furthermore, inebriation is identified in 1 Corinthians 11.21 as one of the subversive factors upsetting the proper conduct of Christian fellowship at mealtimes: "For in eating every one taketh before other his own supper: and one is hungry, and another is drunken."

Alcohol's power in excess to make us forget the decorum that is expected of us in the shared meal is why Christians would come to be asked by the church to see that it may also lead them to neglect their deeper spiritual observances such as prayer.

In the letter to the Romans, a prolonged disquisition on the business of living "after the flesh" is offered. Mortification of the flesh in the interests of the health of the spirit is advised. The two cannot ultimately be reconciled, for only those who are led by the spirit of God to revile corporeal deeds—denying their bodies the solace of intoxicants, together with the sexual relief the flesh may cry out for in the night—will be considered God's children. Those looking for a suitable role model of the right life are modestly offered the example of Paul himself in the letter to the Philippians (3.17), as against those "whose God is their belly, and whose glory is in their shame, who mind earthly things" (3.19).

At other points, the apostle is persuaded of the bountiful mercy of a God who let his own son die to redeem humanity. "Who shall lay anything to the charge of God's elect?" he postulates in Romans 8.33. "It is God that justifieth." This is the Paul who believes that the Creator can work for good in all human experience, regardless of how improbable the site of the divine grace may turn out to be, a more beneficent figure than the moralist counting off on his fingers the inventory of the damned (the covetous, the revilers, the adulterers, the fornicators—oh, and don't forget the effeminate, and so despairingly forth). The second chapter of Colossians, cited above, also ridicules the pettifogging rules—"Touch not; taste not; handle not"—that can't begin to matter to those who have trained their sights on the higher life to come. In this mood at least, Paul can see that God wants us to move on to more vital concerns than whether we have correctly drained the blood from the slaughtered fowl before we eat it, or perhaps whether the wine we drink momentarily befuddles the senses.

In what are known as the Pastoral letters, Paul is at his most permissive, dialectically balancing a benevolent belief in the good intentions of the first Christian communities with the need for responsible self-husbandry. The letter to Titus suggests that "denying ungodliness and worldly lusts, we should live soberly, righteously, and godly, in this present world" (2.12). Certainly, there is no ambiguity about that "soberly," and yet the injunction ends with the recognition that it is "this present world" that we have to come to a finely judged accommodation with, as opposed to seeking ways of evading it altogether by donning hair shirts and retreating to the hills.

The first letter to Timothy goes further in explicitly abjuring asceticism, pointing out that God "giveth us richly all things to enjoy" (6.17), and enjoining the long-suffering reader, "Drink no longer water, but use a little wine for thy stomach's sake and thine often infirmities" (5.23). In this, he has rediscovered the distant wisdom of the Psalmist, whose own pre-Christian version of the Creator (104.14–15) is a portrait of the beneficent Father showering comforts and blessings on the wayward progeny he can't help but love:

> He causeth the grass to grow for the cattle, and herb for the service of man: that he may bring forth food out of the earth;
> And wine that maketh glad the heart of man, and oil to make his face to shine, and bread which strengtheneth man's heart.

Other evangelists will ply the more prohibitive line. The writer of the first epistle of Peter counts "excess of wine," and indeed "revelings" and "banquetings," among the checklist of iniquities that the Christian communities have now turned their backs on, blandly equating the behavior of the wedding guests at Cana, for example, with such offenses as "abominable idolatries" (4.3). But stretching over the whole field of moral debate is the undeniable conviction, common to all branches of the first Christian church, that the terrible Day of Judgment was imminent.

In a postmodern world where all kinds of arcana have flourished, pronouncements of impending apocalypse have become a bit ten-a-penny. There always seems to be someone warning us that, come the third Thursday of August 2008, the game will be up, whether in the form of mighty deluges, global conflagration or alien landings in the Atacama. The earliest adherents to believe in the Resurrection of Christ, however, felt the imminence of apocalypse as an honest article of faith. Indeed, Jesus himself would almost certainly have accepted that view. If God's Judgment was hastening near, then, it scarcely made sense to waste the short remaining time one had for proving one's spiritual mettle in carousing and inebriation. What if the Final Judgment arrived in the middle of a riotous party, just as you and your friends were embarking on a second amphora of wine? It might look a bit incriminating. All effort had better be directed toward demonstrating to the adventitious God that you were a suitable candidate for his kingdom, for when he came, it was chillingly warned, it would be as a thief in the night, at the time he was least expected.

At the heart of the unease that Western religions feel toward the practices of intoxication is the notion that our bodies do not belong to us, but are merely mortgaged from their Creator. In some versions, they are described as a gift, but this is clearly not a serviceable metaphor, since a gift is after all one's own possession and may be used accordingly. The theological emphasis has more usually tended to be on the physical being as belonging to God, on loan to us for the temporary term of our passage through the earthly life. On this reading, the use of intoxicants is always potentially an abuse of what is not our property. This would imply, though, that all intoxication practices are physically damaging, which is manifestly not the case. To fall into a cycle of addiction to opiates or wear one's nasal membrane away with cocaine are indisputably cases of damage, but then, so is clogging one's lungs with nicotine tar or furring the arteries with reckless intake of saturated fats, and Christians are not expected to seek forgiveness for the sin of smoking or having a penchant for creamcakes. Evidently, the question of self-damage is something of a red herring, or at least is only being interpreted very selectively. The biblical authority, in any case, comes once again from Paul:

> What? know ye not that your body is the temple of the Holy Ghost which is in you, which ye have of God, and ye are not your own? For ye are bought with a price: therefore glorify God in your body, and in your spirit, which are God's. (1 Cor. 6.19–20)

This is certainly unequivocal, and must give pause to every adherent who has ever gone on a drinking binge to celebrate a promotion or can't quite kick that 20-a-day habit that even the doctor—let alone the priest—is warning against. (To the Jews too, placing the body in any form of needless physical danger, getting into harm's way, is inherently transgressive.) Then there is the evident duty of Christians, as expressed in 1996 by Anglican priest and educationalist Trevor Shannon, to prevent others not even of the faith from indulging:

> A Christian response to the drug situation would reject the attitude that it is people's own concern whether they drink, smoke or take drugs, not the concern of anyone else. In the first place even passive smoking . . . is known to be harmful while people's addiction to alcohol or illegal drugs often leads to terrible unhappiness, the breakdown of family life and sometimes to crime.[1]

The passive-smoking issue is rather a boon to this argument, which would be trickier to put if the long-awaited smoke-free cigarette were one day to be invented, but otherwise we are being offered a lazy equation that insists that all intoxication practices inevitably lead to social problems. One might have thought that Christians might prioritize their pastoral efforts in the direction of those who actually have fallen into a state of "terrible unhappiness," as opposed to presuming that addiction is the universal fate of everybody who enjoys a bottle of Chardonnay with dinner or unwinds in the evenings with cannabis. And what of the luxurious happiness that unadulterated MDMA once brought to a generation of nightclub bers? To reinterpret the glowing sense of empathy that the drug induced in all manner of individuals as the infernal misery of addiction could be accounted shoddy logic in an outraged letter to *The Times*. From someone who has been involved in children's education, it is nothing short of malevolent. "But beyond the effects on others," the warning goes on, ". . . our bodies are not our own to use or misuse as we please."[2] The writer harks back to an era, the late Victorian and Edwardian, in which "the dangers and evils of alcohol were well known." Surely this can't be the same substance that Jesus provided for those wedding guests?

Turning his attention to illegal drugs, Shannon mobilizes another classic anti-intoxicant argument, that "people experiment with drugs because their lives are empty and they are bored."[3] To this mind-set, intoxication always has to be seen as a desperate remedy, a last-chance throw of the dice to counteract a life gone dreary through, in this case, a deficiency of religious dogma. "Taking drugs is a poor substitute for religious experience," is the bald assertion. Since the varieties of religious experience are always intensely personal and internal, and cover a multitude of graces anyway, from the weeping effigies of Our Lady to the lonely prayers that go unanswered for some unfathomable reason, this statement is not one that can easily be tested. But however tempting it may be to be drawn into a prolonged scholastic inquiry into Reverend Shannon's claim, it only suffices to respond to its deaf self-assurance with the query, "And how would you know?"

An elaborate mechanical contrivance once persuaded the inhabitants of the Irish village of Knock in County Mayo that the Blessed Virgin in the company of saints had appeared to them to warn them of their backsliding ways. Church attendances soared again, and piety was restored. So successful was the trick that there is now an international airport there, filtering multitudes of pilgrims to the place each year from all corners of the world. Such mass deception, the Catholic church asks us to believe, is better than having a drink, for all that there are hostelries on hand in the town to refresh the weary planeloads. But why is it not deemed possible to reconcile the enjoyment of intoxication with doing God's work in the world? Being clinically alcoholic, or intravenously dependent on heroin, may not have been his purpose for us, one might accept, but that was never the whole story about either alcohol or even heroin. Stealing to fund an addiction, or stealing the drugs themselves from pharmacies, is incontestably morally wrong, but arise at least partly because the drugs addicts need are illegal, and as long as the church continues to acquiesce in that disastrous proscription, it must be understandingly but firmly deprived of the drugs-means-crimes credo. This is a point we shall return to in chapter 5.

We would, in any case, be reducing theology to a mere matter of consulting the rule-book—the preferred habit of certain fundamentalist branches of the evangelical church, though not of the more evolutionary Catholic and Protestant mainstream—were we to focus exclusively in our search for spiritual guidance on what the

Bible has to say. Church authority has installed drunkenness as a sin under the general rubric of "Intemperance," which also takes in gluttony, ever since the idea of the Seven Deadly Sins was first formulated. (The earliest surviving written reference to the Sins appears in the writings of a fifth-century English monk, John Cassian.) The notion of a sevenfold blacklist of particularly heinous offenses came to stand theologically as Christianity's answer to the ten Mosaic Thou-shalt-nots of the Commandments. Whilst their precise formulation varied from one author to another, they survived through the edicts of Gregory the Great (who reigned as Pope Gregory I from 590 to 604), and on into Thomas Aquinas in the twelfth century. A theological writer in the time of Queen Anne calls these principles "The Seven curs'd deadly Sins," and gives "Intemp'rance" as the fourth.

That an excess of drinking was considered undesirable by the faithful seems clear enough, but again, it is just what precise state constitutes inebriation that remains ill-defined in these schemas. Certainly, ecclesiastical history shows that the church did not at all remain aloof from involvement with alcohol. The Holy Communion itself involves the drinking of wine, in which the fermented juice of the grape is transformed (as a matter of literal belief in the Catholic Mass) into the Blood of the Lord. That can't be sinful, then, and indeed many monasteries in the medieval period had vineyards planted in the surrounding land, some of the wine they yielded providing the sacramental offering and its surplus going on sale to the outside world to fund the work of the church. There are vineyards under monastic ownership to this day in the Rhinelands and the Franken region of Germany, in Austria, in northern Italy and in Spain. All are run as charitable foundations, and are not seemingly concerned that they may be pouring an evil substance down the throats of their customers.

The European discovery of distillation around 1100 at the celebrated medical school at Salerno in Italy paved the way for monks to produce aromatized spirit drinks—the precursors of the traditional liqueurs—which were popularly and professionally held to have various therapeutic properties. Bénédictine, the honeyed herbal liqueur, was once made by that particular monastic order at Fécamp in Normandy (its bottle today still bears the gold imprint DOM,

Deo Optimo Maximo, after the apocryphal exclamation of its inventor on first tasting it in 1510). The Revolution did for the Fécamp monastery, and the liqueur was only revived, by a descendant of the order's lawyers, in the late nineteenth century. In contrast to the secularization of Bénédictine, Chartreuse is still made by monks at a site outside Grenoble not far from their monastery. The Carthusian brothers don't actually taste their products during manufacture (nor can they discuss them since the order is a silent one), but are content to smear a little of the infusion on the back of the hand, sniffing to see whether the aromatic balance seems right. While yellow Chartreuse is bottled at the standard spirit strength of 40 percent by volume, the green version achieves a mighty 55 percent—and there is even an Elixir Végétale sold in 10cl bottles at a palate-blasting 71 percent, the same strength as Polish Pure Spirit or the absinthe that became newly available in Europe in the late 1990s. There may well be a point beyond which God would like us to stop drinking, but it seems the strength of the drink itself is not an issue.

The development of monastic vinification and distillation is reflected in the fact that much of the drink manufactured was consumed in-house. A sixth-century biography records that the abbot of the monastery on Caldey Island off the north Wales coast met his doom by falling down a well while stumbling about the grounds one night in an advanced state of drunkenness. This level of indulgence led to the formulation of ecclesiastical rulings intended to apply to the monks and their superiors, with the sanctions against misbehavior rising in accordance with the superiority of the offender. Thus, the eighth-century *Penitential* attributed to Theodore, Archbishop of Canterbury, opens with a disquisition "On Intoxication and Drunkenness," prescribing thirty days' hard penance for a monk who drinks himself into an emetic state, rising to forty days for priests and deacons. Here, evidently, vomiting—or at the least a heavy dose of morning-after syndrome—is the trigger for punitive action, although the miscreant is absolved of any offense if he has become drunk on the instructions of a bishop or in the course of celebrating one of the festivals. So saints' days, Easter and Christmas were fair game, much as the Jews are commanded to partake at

Purim, to celebrate the salvation of their Persian community 2,500 years ago. When St. Wilfrid, seventh-century Bishop of York, marked the founding of a new church in Ripon with an almost Saturnalian festival of bibulous excess that continued for three days, the monks and priests who took part in it would have done so with the redeeming excuse, much tried on by malefactors down the centuries, that they were only obeying orders.

Nor could the bishops themselves necessarily be trusted to set a sober example to their subordinates. The French theologian Gregory of Tours writes that his fellow bishop Cautinus of Clermont was in the unseemly habit of getting so drunk during banquets that it took no fewer than four monks to lift him eventually, slumped and engorged, from his piggery. Despite the apparent hypocrisy, the illuminating aspect of Gregory's tittle-tattle is that it shows that intoxication was not felt to be such a shamingly mortal sin that its effects couldn't be displayed before assemblies of the pious, nor frankly acknowledged in an honest monograph, however unfriendly the intention of the writer may have been.

As the numbers of church buildings proliferated throughout the England of the Middle Ages, the matter of their upkeep was never far from the minds of the priests. A certain amount of social licentiousness was happily tolerated, even encouraged, if it brought in funds, and rumbustious village fetes were an abidingly popular means of raising cash. These events, known as "church ales," are the less decorous ancestors of the coffee mornings, jumble sales and cheese-and-wine evenings that have crucially underwritten Anglican finances in recent times, but whereas a sip of Bulgarian Merlot may now be the norm, drinking to disintegration was far more the thirteenth-century habit, as Christopher Hibbert elaborates:

> These events, at which villagers were encouraged to drink as much as they could, were usually held in the churchyard or in a building known as the church house nearby. The ale-wife was generally asked to suspend her brewing for as long as they lasted. Some went on for three days. At the Deverills in Wiltshire in the thirteenth century, bachelors who could still stand up were allowed to go on drinking for nothing.[4]

Perhaps those church elders who have simultaneously bemoaned the indisciplined behavior of inner-city beer-boys, while worrying about how the church might play a more relevant role in their lives, have missed a rather fruitful opportunity here, one sanctioned by the precedent of history. At any rate, the English Puritan view of sensuous pleasures was still a long way off in the future, and if Christians honestly disporting themselves were pouring valuable pennies into the church coffers as they did so, would not God overlook the beer-sodden tantrums and lascivious fumblings that might attend the ales?

What helped to sustain a benevolent view of inebriation, in the English context at least, was the fact that what was being drunk was beer, the rough-and-ready peasant brew that—before modern clarification techniques—would have been hazy with yeast cells in suspension and of rude alcoholic strength. That marked it out from the Communion wine that was central to the Eucharist, in which the bread and wine that Jesus consumed with the disciples at the Last Supper becomes thenceforth transubstantiated into his own flesh and blood. This wine is not for reveling and drinking competitions, but is the tangible means by which Christ's spirit enters the bodies of his followers. Nonetheless, the Christian churches came to worry about the presence of alcohol in their services, and as the Protestant churches after the Reformation reinterpreted the Eucharist as more symbolic than literal in its operations, so the path was cleared for certain church reformers (notably the Methodists, though not their founder John Wesley) to deplore the involvement of intoxicating liquors at all in the worship of God.

At the same time, the Roman church, more for practical reasons such as hygiene as any other, required only the officiating priest to partake of both bread and wine, while the laity could cheerfully make do (an unfortunate resonance, this) with the bread alone. It wasn't until the Second Vatican Council of 1963 that it was ordained that individual bishops could authorize, if they so chose, Communion with both materials within their dioceses. The Catholic church became exercised enough in the 1970s over the question of alcoholism among the priesthood to consider permitting reformed alcoholics within their number to take in the blood of Christ in the form of unfermented red grape juice, as many of the Methodists had done for the past hundred years. The dispensation was temporarily granted from 1974 until 1983, when lingering theological doubts about writing an opt-out clause into a ceremony of such profundity as the Eucharist brought about its formal revocation. Intinction—lightly moistening the bread with wine by dunking it—is now the recommended solution.

Elsewhere in Europe, it was precisely the sight of rural peasants in a habitual state of wine-driven drunkenness that led some Christian church authorities to include intoxication among the sins that required confession. When wine was the daily means of the peasant's befuddlement, it perhaps felt too much like an abuse of the sacrament, and anyway diverted him from the straight and narrow path prescribed by the Lord. The Frankish peoples in particular, we are told by contemporary writers evangelizing in the region, were particularly tenacious in their attachment to wine. (In fact, virtually every European race has been characterized at some stage as drunken sots. The early Germanic peoples had a reputation as brutish drinkers of undiluted wine, an image transmuted into a disappointing sober-sidedness in more recent history. The Italians, like their Roman forebears, have long been seen as heedless indulgers, not least since, for most of the last century, they have produced more wine than any other nation, a vast proportion of it never leaving their shores. To the nobility of prerevolutionary Europe essaying the Grand Tour in reverse, the British—cultural cynosures in so many other respects—turned out to be revoltingly given to drinking, tolerating public displays of intoxication squalor unthinkable in the ordered green spaces of the Tuileries and the Tiergarten. Holland in the seventeenth century was a den of beer-soaked vulgarity to the oenophile French, while the legendary capacity of the Irish to put it away has been one of the hardiest Western cultural axioms of the lot. It seems that, even more than the alien foods they eat, foreigners are always readily definable by the immoderation of their drinking habits, so unlike one's own temperate maturity. The unabashed relativism of it all recalls W. C. Fields' celebrated definition of an alcoholic as "anybody who drinks more than I do.")

At least drink had its recognizable place in social and religious life, though. Other substances, very often the psychotropic herbs associated with witchcraft, were seen as far more dangerous, and if the early church could come to recommend excommunication for anyone engaging in any ritual that smelled of Dionysianism, however apologetically dilute such practices had become at the onset of the Christian era, then herbalism and its related doings must be absolutely reviled. Medicinal folk remedies were not the problem, so much as the ecstatic and ritualized use of certain plants in divination, prophecies and maledictions. The attempt to stamp out these practices led, from the medieval period on, to some of the most rapacious cruelties ever to darken the church's record. They were largely directed against women, fallen daughters of Eve the temptress who were held to be more easily drawn to witchcraft and necromancy because of their inferior powers of reason and their more lustful fleshly appetites (a woman fallen into witchcraft, it was believed, had performed for the Devil the profane service of inserting her tongue in his rectum), but there were male victims too. Hibbert cites the case of an innocent who had been vicar in a Suffolk parish for 50 years, but found himself arraigned for witchcraft. He was ducked until he confessed, and was then hanged at Framlingham, having been granted the last dignity of reading out his own Order of Burial.

Witchcraft was nothing without its magic potions. Love philters to be slipped by stealth to the object of one's erotic obsession were, not surprisingly, much in demand, but it was the "flying ointments" that the witches applied to themselves that were held to be the most incriminating preparations. They were assumed to be rubbed into the skin, but were probably more effectively administered vaginally and perhaps anally, and once under the influence, the witch would fly (by broomstick, classically) to her sabbat—the hideous nocturnal ceremonies at which they commingled, sexually of course, with imps and demons from the underworld. The precise compositions of the ointments remains as elusive as one would expect from such arcane and severely punishable activities, but alongside the Shakespearean taxonomy of fur of this and blood of that was a range of common European psychotropic plants whose use was kept alive from pre-Christian times. Henbane (*Hyoscyamus niger* and related species), belladonna (*Solanum loethale,* or deadly nightshade) and mandrake (*Mandragora officinarum*) were the three principal agents, but there were other equally potent psychoactives, apparently including on occasion opium or cannabis. The dried venomous exudations of toads, now known to contain the hallucinogenic alkaloid bufotenine, may well have been a prime constituent of many ointments, sealing the image of that unlovely creature as one of the witch's constant familiars, while the fungi deemed to be among its excreta—i.e., the toad's stool that turns out not in fact to be an item of reptilian domestic furniture but the fly agaric mushroom—will also have played an integral part in many recipes.

Richard Rudgley has pointed out that proximate explanations of the effects of these mixtures, and the subsequent mythological belief in the witches' sabbats, were being proposed as early as the fifteenth century in works by not only medical writers but leading theologians such as Alfonso Tostado, Bishop of Avila. It was the latter who suggested—correctly, did he but know it—that the whole delirious ambience of the sabbat was a drug-induced fantasy. Others posited the ointments as the true sources of the flying sensations experienced by the Devil's aficionados, while the belief that they had sexual congress with his Satanic Majesty, who was reported to have a penis of monstrously bestial dimensions that felt soul-chillingly cold as it entered you, was attributed—correctly again—to the temperature-lowering effects of some hallucinogenic plants. The fly agaric mushroom, in common with its psilocybin counterpart, does indeed often induce a sensation of deep shivering cold, notably during the initial onset of its effects.

These theories, enunciated as they are at the threshold of the Enlightenment, are all the more impressive because, as well as being put to experimental validation, they offered the church a means of denying the power of the Devil as it was mythologized in the beliefs and practices of the witches. As so often in its history, however, the church declined the helping hand of science, preferring to cling to its own bluntly doctrinal view of truth and falsehood, in the process granting that solemn credence to the witches that it infamously denied to Galileo. All the plants used in the ointments were officially classified as diabolical, although we know from a tenth-century Anglo-Saxon medical text that henbane had for a while been a permitted ingredient in an ointment applied during Christian exorcisms. The salve was at this time rubbed into the eyelids and foreheads of "women with whom the devil hath carnal commerce," but by the time of Tostado, such practices seemed to have been reoriented toward achieving precisely that profane aim.

In the succeeding centuries, the Christian churches have taken the view that the use of proscribed substances is sinful precisely because they are against the law in most countries. This is why the Catholic catechism forbids the taking of illegal drugs, but not tobacco smoking or drinking alcohol. The churches require of their adherents, just as Judaism does, that they submit to present-day governmental decree and avoid becoming criminals; thus does ecclesiastical authority accommodate itself with the temporal powers. Thus also is obviated a lot of tiresome theological energy that might have to be spent in deciding why some drugs, such as wine, are accepted as divine gifts, while others with a comparable range of effects, such as cannabis, are to be reviled as contaminants of spiritual purity. One would be interested to tease out the Catholic church's position on a substance such as gamma-hydroxy-butyrate (GHB), a sedative anesthetic used on the club scene to produce a mild state of dissociative euphoria, now proscribed in the USA but not, at the time of writing, illegal in the UK. Do Americans wallow in sinfulness where the British enjoy immunity? How can that be theologically consistent? Or would God prefer us all not to swallow GHB, in which case why does he not mind wine? It doesn't make a scrap of sense, either to the adept or the agnostic. But then, for true consistency, we must turn to the third great faith of Western history, Islam.

Only the followers of Mohammed, among mainstream Western religions, are absolutely forbidden any contact with intoxicants. There may be "dry" branches of Christianity, such as many of the Baptist sects of the United States, or the British Salvation Army, but they do not generally claim that they hold the title deeds to Christian authority in the matter. Adherence to their tenets is a matter of personal choice. For Islam's faithful, the import of one solitary verse of the Qur'an is sufficient to demand—on pain of thrashing, as it later came to be enforced—complete abstinence. But this position evolved from an originally liberal tolerance.

Early on in the Qur'an, the view of Allah's compassionate concern for his people, expounded to Mohammed by his angel and relayed in turn by the Prophet to his followers, is strikingly similar to that suggested by the Old Testament Book of Psalms we recalled earlier. Along with water, and the milk and honey with which the fertile lands of the favored will forever proverbially flow in both Judaic and Qur'anic traditions, it is stated that "We give you the fruits of the palm and the vine, from which you derive intoxicants and wholesome food." At this stage, the function of intoxication is not dissimilar to that suggested by the Psalmist; it is one of the provisions that a merciful God has made for human solace during our earthbound, physical plight. Then, much as the cautionary undertone begins to creep into the epistles of Paul, a warning is sounded: "They will ask you concerning wine and gambling. Answer, in both there is great sin and also some things of use unto men: but their sinfulness is greater than their use." A more prohibitive note is certainly discernible in this, but as long as there are "some things of use" in drinking, it cannot yet be quite beyond the pale, nor was it considered so. The outright ban arose as a result of a fracas that broke out among Mohammed's disciples one night after dinner.

The incident occurred during the eight-year period of exile that the Prophet spent in Medina, a city some 250 miles to the north of his native Mecca, across the barren expanse of the Hijaz. Rivalry between the two ethnic groups was not always entirely amicable, as may be appreciated from the story. In the course of drinking after their evening meal, one of Mohammed's Meccan contingent sought to entertain his comrades by reciting an insulting bit of verse about the Medinites. We are not, understandably, quoted this embarrassing doggerel verbatim, but suffice to say, it occasioned such offense that one of the Prophet's rival followers felt moved to defend Medina's honor by giving the idiot a clout on the head with a large meat-bone left over from dinner. The blow was sufficient to cause a wound to the offender, who had violated not just the courtesies of the dinner table but, more culpably, the hospitality that his exiled tribe was being offered by the Medinites. Mohammed was horrified, and sought guidance from Allah as to how he might better keep these contentious groups in order. The response was to have world-historical impact:

> Believers, wine and games of chance, idols and divining arrows, are abominations devised by Satan. Avoid them, so that you may prosper. Satan seeks to stir up enmity and hatred among you by means of wine and gambling, and to keep you from the

remembrance of Allah and from your prayers. Will you not abstain from them?[5]

Virtually as soon as the pronouncement was uttered, every jug of wine in the city was emptied out into the gutters, much as the wine cellars of hotels and restaurants the length and breadth of America were sacked after the enactment of Prohibition. So zealously sure was he of the intentions of Allah in this regard that Mohammed himself set the example during his lifetime by sentencing wine drinkers to 40 lashes. The tariff was doubled by his second successor as leader of Islam, Umar, on the grounds that wine not only caused enmity and hatred among men, but also loosened their tongues to a degree whereby they were quite likely to impugn the chasteness of women.

Not all of Mohammed's devotees accepted the interpretation of the revelation as being wholly prohibitive (one of his wives, Ayesha, was later to insist, less than convincingly, that the Prophet had been heard to say, "You may drink, but do not get drunk"), but any such exegetical niceties were soon drowned among the cries of the scourged. Skeptical critics of Islam who are enjoined to accept that it is at heart a peaceful faith are constantly dismayed that it nonetheless harbors within itself this harsh, retributive temper that it won't quite relinquish, and with the interdiction on alcohol, the pattern was set.

As Islam spread into regions where viticulture was central to the life of the people, such as the Mediterranean islands and the Iberian peninsula, it arrived at a precarious compromise with local customs. It permitted Jews and Christians within its administrative ambit to carry on consuming and trading in wine, not least because it extracted valuable fiscal revenues from them. For this reason alone, some of the oldest established vineyards were preserved from destruction, and the viticultural tradition in some areas was never interrupted.

Then again, not all Muslims observed the proscription. In Persia, Syria and Mesopotamia (now Iraq), it was quite common for certain wealthy families, caliphs and so forth, to serve exceptionally fine wines at opulent banquets that may well have continued for up to three days. In doing so, they perhaps had in mind the visions of sensual splendor that the Qur'an holds forth as the heavenly reward for righteous males. Their afterlife will be an eternity of luxurious pampering, in which, recumbent on squashy sofas, they will have their fill of exquisite fruits and exquisite girls, and what's more: "They shall drink of a pure wine, securely sealed, whose very dregs are musk." This strikingly terrestrial-sounding paradise is in sharp contrast to the Christian version of the afterlife, about which the New Testament is as light on detail as Marx disappointingly is when gesturing toward the postcapitalist paradise to come.

The image of a paradisal wine that will surpass all previous vintages, though, does link the two faiths, as—in a sense—does the self-denying ordinance of their founders. The meticulously attested words of Jesus during the Last Supper, given in all three of the synoptic gospels, hold out the hope of a deferred intoxication. This is Matthew:

> But I say unto you, I will not drink henceforth of this fruit of the vine, until that day when I drink it new with you in my Father's kingdom. (26.29)

Note that it is the "new" wine specifically that is promised. In an era before corked bottles and refrigeration, old wine was not generally, as now, the triumphant finished article of maturity, but would more likely have been ruined and stale, spoiled with gradual exposure to the air. The best of wine was frequently the sweetly ripe new vintage, exuberant with fizz perhaps from its recent fermentation, or certainly in no more than its first year, so that the deposits in it had had time to settle out and it could be poured bright and clear, but still full of what is today referred to as its primary fruit. In the Qur'anic version, the assurance that the paradisal vintage has been "securely sealed" offers a guarantee of its quality to the faithful. Oxidation hasn't spoiled it, and it is fragrant right down to the lees. The difference arises in the fact that Jesus' statement that he won't be drinking wine in this life again is more a prediction than a manifesto—he knows the authorities are closing in on him, and there isn't long to go—but to Mohammed, the abjuration of alcohol is an ideology.

How to reconcile the castigation of wine as Satan's abominable brew with the rather specific promise of it in the afterlife was to exercise early Muslim scholars to an almost obsessive degree, as they sought a way around the colossal stop sign of Mohammed's example. That it is still not resolved is perhaps most obviously exemplified in the fact that some Muslim societies today, the Turks, the Iraqis and the Arab Emirates, for instance, are happy to rub along with alcohol, while others, such as the extended dynastic monarchy of Saudi Arabia and the Shi'ite theocracy in Iran, still absolutely forbid it, on pain of chastisements as cruelly severe as anything seen in the Prophet's day.

It is not only alcohol that the Islamic faith prohibits, however. Dr. Mashuq ibn Ally, an Islamic academic and trustee of the Birmingham Central Mosque in England, summarizes the Muslim position for us:

> In Islam, drugs such as marijuana, cocaine, opium and the like are definitely prohibited because their use produces illusions and hallucinations, which impairs the faculty of reason and decision-making. Such drugs are taken as a means of escape from the inner reality of one's feelings . . . In addition, there are serious moral consequences—moral insensitivity, weakening of will power, and neglect of responsibilities. Eventually, addiction to drugs renders a person a diseased member of society, which may result in the destruction of the family or even in a life of crime.[6]

The same simplistic certitudes that informed Reverend Shannon's exposition of the Christian viewpoint on drugs underpin this model too, in which we proceed with indecent haste from dope smoking through the myth of drugs as a means of craven escape, then on to the unquestioned inexorability of the addiction paradigm, to arrive at family breakdown and crime in one breathless paragraph. It does appear, as with the Christian stance, that if the spiritual authorities were ever actually to address the infinitely more nuanced realities of most actual drug use, in which one's inner feelings are not evaded but allowed full voice, in which addiction never raises its head, one continues to play a full role in society and never so much as comes near a court of law (*Deo volente*), the whole purblind theology on this matter would have to be rewritten. In fact, Islam has not always been so antipathetic to the other drugs, any more than it was toward wine in certain regions. When viticulture fell into decline in Asia Minor, more as a result of the destructions wrought by the Mongol incursions of the thirteenth century and the consequent economic collapse of the area than of the Mohammedan prohibition, an intoxicant about which the Qur'an has nothing to say—hashish—became the drug of choice.

It was at precisely this time that there flourished within the Persian sector of Islam a notorious cult, described by several European explorers, including, in 1273, Marco Polo. This was the Ismaili sect, a mystical branch of Shi'a Islam that held that Mohammed was the sixth of seven great prophets, the last of whom was the eighth-century Imam Ismail, who—returning to earth from paradise—would revoke Islamic law. It was an initiatory sect, very much in the manner of tribal societies, in which one passed into the ranks of the adepts through a hierarchically ordered series of stages of enlightenment. Unlike tribal cosmologies, however, it was highly intellectualized, its spiritual efficacy centered on the sacred work of interpretation of the prophets' utterances. More controversially than this, it believed in eliminating its enemies by carefully planned and selective murder as opposed to any form of general crusade, to which end it trained certain of its followers as expert killers. The theory has persisted down the centuries that hashish, better known in western Europe as cannabis, was the agent with which the killers were primed, earning them the nickname of the Hashishins. This is the etymological derivation of the word "assassins" to mean trained killers.

The cult's leader, Hasan ibn Sabah, became known to Western legend as the Old Man of the Mountains. He built a huge impregnable fortress at Alamut to guard the entrance to a mysterious valley, which could only be reached by a secret passage within it. Within the valley, so the story went, he had created a garden paradise, replete with palaces full of gold artifacts, furniture draped in gorgeous silks and ingenious hydraulic systems along some of which streamed sparkling-clean water, while others carried fresh milk, luxuriously oozing honey or fragrant wine. Furthermore, the palaces were staffed with obliging houris, who could sing and dance and play music, and who were well versed in the erotic arts as well.

If it all sounds somewhat familiar, it was meant to, for this was an artfully contrived version of the afterlife as set forth in the Qur'an.

The drill seems to have been that, after Hasan had hand-selected each new batch of raw recruits, teenage boys whose build and spirit seemed auspicious enough to make them formidable Assassins, they were given unawares a potion that lulled them off to sleep. While drugged, they would be transported to the garden palaces they had never set eyes on, and upon waking would believe they had some-how arrived in paradise. After several days of disporting themselves with the girls and the wine and the honey, no doubt believing they must have been heroically good lads in the last life to have earned all this, they would be drugged again and transported back to the fortress.

Their heartbreak on reawakening back in the tawdry world of Hasan can only be guessed at, but this unorthodox military training seems to have left them willing to carry out whatever orders they were given, if it meant a chance of returning to the paradise they had had the merest tantalizing taste of. Some were as young as 12, and must have found the experience shattering. Nonetheless, they became trustworthy killers in the name of Ismail, and if they should run the risk of being killed themselves in the course of their assassi-nations, then that only guaranteed their return to the heavenly gar-dens the quicker.

An Arabist scholar of the early nineteenth century, Silvestre de Sacy, was the first to uncover the lexicographical root of the cult's name in the intoxicating herb hashish. From his researches, it came to be generally accepted that the sleeping draught administered to the young recruits was based on cannabis. When swallowed, the range of the drug's effects is nothing like the mildly hypnotic relax-ation induced by smoking it. It is a strongly disorientated, even hal-lucinogenic state that lasts for considerably longer than inhalation of the smoke, so the postulate certainly holds water. Richard Rudg-ley, noting that subsequent research has questioned this interpreta-tion of the Assassins' name, attempts to warn us off this theory:

> Hashish was widely known throughout the Middle East, and the dubbing of the Ismailis with the epithet "hashish-users" is more likely to have been an empty term of abuse: the use of the drug is mentioned neither in Ismaili sources nor in the more reliable of the Sunni accounts.[7]

This does not convince. It is no more surprising that mention of the drug does not appear in Ismaili sources than that the European witches didn't write down the recipes for their ointments for posterity. Not only was the use of hashish disreputable within mainstream Islam but, as historian of religion Ninian Smart points out, the Ismaili faith was critically dependent on the notion of an arcanum of privileged knowledge, by which interpretation of the sayings of the prophets was the exclusive preserve of certain "silent ones." Indeed, he goes on to say that "the whole Ismaili system was based on secret knowledge"[8]—not therefore the climate in which the formulation of the Assassins' hypnotic draughts would be divulged. As to the name being meaningless abuse, it would be hard to think of any other example of a sectarian nickname being "empty." They are invariably witheringly precise, as was the seventeenth-century term "dippers" to refer to Anabaptists who believed in baptism by total immersion, or as is the contemporary characterization of those Evangelicals who appear to like nothing more than a vacuously smiley singsong as "happy clappers." Elsewhere, Siegel demolishes the proposition that the killers were primed with hashish before going out on their missions, which is persuasive enough, since dope intoxication is typically a markedly nonaggressive state in which concentration is distinctly impaired. In other words, it would be a positive liability in a boy who had been commissioned to plunge a dagger into somebody's heart. Whether the composition of the sleeping draughts will ever be known seems doubtful, but after all, the story of the Assassins says more about the chicaneries to which organized religion is prepared to stoop than it does about cannabis.

Meanwhile, we may expect the mainstream Islamic tradition to remain silent about the matter. At the very moment that the Ismaili sect was flourishing in Persia, one of the preeminent Muslim scholars of the period, Shaikh al-Islam ibn Taymiyyah, was laying down for the devout the only correct attitude toward hashish:

> This solid grass is prohibited, whether or not it produces intoxication. Sinful people smoke it because they find it produces rapture and delight, an effect similar to drunkenness. While wine makes the one who drinks it active and quarrelsome, hashish produces dullness and lethargy; furthermore, smoking it disturbs

the mind and temperament, excites sexual desire, and leads to shameless promiscuity, and these are greater evils than those caused by drinking.[9]

If the Christian looking to biblical authority, or to that of the church, for that matter, for guidance on how much is too much when it comes to intoxication, is doomed to nebulous ambiguity, the Muslim has no such alibi, according to this text. That "whether or not" in the opening declaration sounds the stentorian warning. It is forbidden. Even a single inhalation is an offense, and more may result in those soul-corroding conditions, "rapture and delight." These too are forbidden, at least in this earthbound existence.

What the positions of the three mainstream faiths of Western history would appear to have in common on the question of intoxication is that its danger lies in its capacity to deflect the attention of the believer from his or her God. If you have to satisfy this one preeminent God by means of adherence to a fixed set of beliefs that permit little or no flexibility, and your ultimate salvation depends on such good behavior, then you'd better stay sober enough to know what you're doing. This impulse represents a clear and obvious turn away from the notion, alive throughout the Egyptian, Assyrian, Babylonian, Greek and Roman variants of religious belief, that intoxicated states may in themselves be spiritual, or at least constitute a means of access to the spiritual. They have become, and have remained ever since, an unacceptable risk factor to the health of the soul, obscuring its awareness of the God who nonetheless sees into the remotest recesses of the individual being.

Given that the intoxication instinct manifests itself in such multifarious and innumerable ways in human affairs, the achievement of the religions in stigmatizing it was a formidable one indeed. It could only have happened with the widespread transition to monotheistic modes of belief ushered in by the Christian revolution. True, the Jewish Yahweh already insisted, "Thou shalt have no other gods before me," but he was very much at odds with prevailing traditions in doing so. In other systems, a committee of gods each had their departmental portfolios (Agriculture, War, Fire and so forth), and although they eventually came to represent philosophical principles more than geophysical ones, they were still nonetheless a collective. With the extraordinary spread of Christianity into quite diverse parts of the Roman Empire and the Near East, theological authority was consolidated. Not only did the new faith establish the singularity of God once and for all (albeit in the mysterious form of an interdependent trinity of divine presences), its constitutional forms allowed it to dispense ecclesiastical authority by simple ukase. The Councils and Commissions of the early church, ancestors of the Congregations and Synods of today, reserved to themselves the right to prescribe correct interpretations of the scriptures as well as establish the modus operandi of the church itself, and once they had spoken, there was to be no further appeal. In this way was religious belief made simultaneously more opaque and more transparent: more transparent because the old pagan ceremonials, in all their ecstatic but unfocused spontaneity, were reoriented to more specific observances derived from the details of Christ's life and mission, but more opaque because an authoritarian clique—far removed from the lives of the downtrodden sinners in whose names it governed— now held sway where democratic diversity once flourished. The arrival of Islam, with its punishment codes and its irreconcilable opposition to all forms of consciousness other than absolute sobriety, then carried the prohibitive proclivity to its logical religious conclusion.

Over the course of the ensuing centuries, the church in the Christian countries came to adopt a more or less benign view of drinking among its adherents. It couldn't counsel complete abstinence while one of its central rituals involved the use of wine, and so it confined its interest in the issue to discouraging that perennially indefinable problem, excess. If the consequences of an individual's intake of drink were disorderly conduct, domestic affray or uneven chapel attendance, then it spoke up, but the parsons and priests were not denied their wine cellars, nor infants their fortifying breakfast draughts of ale, nor the laird his hip flask on the hunt. When spirit-drinking among the urban poor reached pandemic proportions in the mid-eighteenth century, the English churches added their voices to those campaigners for social reform who wanted to see such corrosive beverages made unaffordable to them, but the more compassionate saw in the miserable economic condition of working people under entrepreneurial capitalism the true cause of recourse to the bottle. Nonetheless, the feeling began to take hold that if the church (the reformed churches, specifically) could persuade working people to give up alcohol altogether, then not only would their socioeconomic lot be immeasurably ameliorated, but the tricky question of deciding how much was too much would once and for all be given the slip.

The Temperance movements that arose in very different circumstances in the United States and Britain in the early nineteenth century are interesting in the present context for two reasons: firstly, because they established a means by which the Christian churches could, in the name of God, finally forbid alcohol in a way that hadn't been dared before, and secondly, because they managed to shift the moral emphasis away from the individual's culpability for his own actions while under the influence and onto the substance itself. A drunken laborer who frittered his family's income on boozing through his leisure time was a wayward soul in need of pastoral guidance. The deal the Temperance campaigners effectively offered him was absolution from his sinfulness on the grounds that he had innocently fallen under the diabolic possession of an evil potion, and that, assuming he could summon—with the assistance of the Almighty—the willpower to forswear it henceforth, he would nevermore stumble into such wicked ways. To persuade adults who had taken alcohol all their lives hitherto to give it up forever for the love of the Lord meant relentlessly investing the stuff with negative moral value, often in terms so patronizingly lurid that the laborers must have wondered whether their souls could ever now be saved. Thus was born a concept brand-new to theology: the Demon Drink.

The founding text of the Temperance and Prohibitionist movements in the United States was a medical work of 1784 by Dr. Benjamin Rush, *An Inquiry Into the Effects of Spirituous Liquors on the Human Body,* to which was added in the edition of 1790, a chart described as "a moral and physical thermometer," in which the gradations of moral decline attendant upon the habitual use of hard liquor were painstakingly calibrated. Dr. Rush was no fire-eating cracker-barrel snake-oil merchant, but a distinguished Philadelphia physician, signatory of the Constitution and adviser to governments on public health, whose patrician physiognomy is depicted in silhouette to this day on the insignia of the American Psychiatric Association. But his medical thought was rooted firmly in the tradition that equated physical well-being with moral health in a mutually dependent relation. Indeed, there is an innovative energy in many of Rush's pronouncements that helped to extend and develop the ways in which this hypothesis might be made to apply. The Moral and Physical Thermometer is its most elegantly refined codification.

The table purports to identify the cumulative effects both on the body and, concomitantly, on the behavior of the individual of all the types of drinks commonly in use. It should be noted, against the thrust of subsequent temperance campaigns, that the audit does not entirely show a deficit account. The calibrations on the thermometer range from 0 up to 70 in the upper half of the table, and down to –70 in the lower. At the top, with a maximum spiritual efficacy rating, is water, the consumption of which evidently guarantees "health and wealth." At the 60 mark is milk-and-water (although why that should be slightly less beneficial than unadulterated water seems unclear—perhaps it has something to do with the dangers of lactic fat). At 50, we might be permitted a stifled hurrah at the appearance of "small beer," a thin potation that would have been no more than around 2.5 percent alcohol, and on which later American medical opinion would insist it was impossible to get drunk. So far, the moral column is still in credit, showing "Serenity of Mind, Reputation, Long Life, & Happiness." Cider and perry are pegged at 40, which may be slightly surprising, as the cider that was consumed in riotous quantities by early immigrants to America, who had imported the taste for it from southwest England, was as potent as farmhouse cider still is today in the UK. Then comes wine at 30, which presumably included—along with light table wines—the fortified article such as Madeira, of which President Jefferson was inordinately fond, porter at 20, and strong beer, a stiffer proposition than wine seemingly, at 10. Against these last four categories, though, we may still anticipate "Cheerfulness, Strength, and Nourishment," but with the caveat "when taken only in small quantities, and at meals." To the homiletic continuum thus far, the modern sensible-drinking guru would doubtless raise no murmur of emendation.

On the liabilities side of the balance sheet, however, the problems start. Now the consequences of ingestion of each drink are subdivided into the moral vices, physical diseases and punishments the heedless indulger can confidently expect from them. At –10 comes punch, the recipes for which were as varied as were the households that possessed a punch bowl, but which could be presumed to be spirit-based as opposed to wine-based. "Idleness" is the risk there, accompanied by an unhelpfully nonspecific "sickness," the punishment for which is generally "Debt." "Toddy and egg rum," which to some might have had a deceptively health-sustaining allure, appear at –20. Beware warming yourself up on a wintry night with a hot, honeyed draught, for that way lies "Gaming, peevishness and quarrelling," resulting in symptoms more familiar from a far heavier intake—"Tremors of the hands in the morning, puking, bloatedness."

It would be a bit of a milksop who threw up the morning after a hot toddy, but there it is, and the likely punishment for it is "Jail," presumably for getting into a maladroit twiddle putting on one's nightshirt. At –30 comes grog, defined here as "brandy and water" rather than the resented rum-and-water of the British naval issue instituted by Admiral Vernon earlier in the century. The risk of quarreling has now stiffened into "Fighting," hand-to-hand combat no less, with the boozer's lineaments of "Inflamed eyes, red nose and face" the physical symptoms, but the punishments bemusingly rising to nothing more vigorous than "Black eyes, and Bags." That baggy eyes should be a more severe retribution than a jail term might make them seem a risk worth incurring for a spot of grog, especially when the less incriminating fare is rum with an egg in it. Egg drinks pop up again at –40 in the form of "Flip and Shrub," the former a mixture of perhaps whiskey, brandy, port or sherry (though not, it would seem, rum, since that was accounted for at –10) with sugar and a beaten egg, the latter an infusion of a large quantity of spirit with loaf sugar and citrus juice that is sealed in a bottle for anything up to several weeks. Indulgence in such infernal brews will issue in a predilection for "Horse-racing," we are told, with its inevitable consequences of "Sore and swelled legs" (perhaps from standing all day at the racecourse), and institutionalization in a "Hospital or Poor House." At –50, the drinks are taking on a cocktail-lounge particularity, as "Bitters infused in Spirits and Cordials" raise their ugly heads. "Lying and Swearing" are the vices occasioned here, with "jaundice" likely among the physical indicators.

Below this, the table becomes befuddled, as the categories start spilling drunkenly into each other, the ghastly lubricants of −60 and −70 status taking in "Drams of Gin, Brandy, and Rum, in the morning," then "The same morning and evening," or worse, "The same during day & night." These can only lead to "Stealing & Swindling, Perjury, Burglary, Murder" committed by a helpless sot afflicted by "Pains in the hands, burning in the hands, and feet, Dropsy, Epilepsy, Melancholy, palsy, appoplexy [sic], Madness, Despair"— all the ills that flesh is heir to, in other words. For this agonized, quivering remnant of human existence is reserved only "Bridewell" or "State Prison for Life," and at the last—inescapably— "Gallows."

Despite what to us seems the taxonomic absurdity of Dr. Rush's schema, what lay behind it was an unimpeachable professional concern for the regularly encountered plight of patients suffering from what a later era would term "chronic alcoholism," a condition indubitably aggravated by the consumption of harder forms of drink than the wine and beer to which Rush is quite happy to accord beneficial status. It wasn't medical compassion that set the tone for what followed it, however, but its disastrous a priori attribution of moral disorder to such spiritual pollutants as flip and shrub. To be sure, there is in its descent to the innermost circles of alcohol Hades an acknowledgment that it is the rate and quantity of intake that determines the baleful consequences he outlines, the "day & night" treadmill of alcoholic dependency, but such niceties were quickly drowned out by the luminaries of the Temperance movement, who in their clarion call to total abstinence made Rush's alarmist invocation of life imprisonment and the death penalty carry all before it. A nip of whiskey might seem a commodious digestive now, but look where it led: to the gallows. This model of intoxication behavior— the slippery-slope paradigm—has served prohibitionist campaigners very durably in the two centuries since Rush's treatise was published. Although it has largely failed in the alcohol arena since the discrediting of the Temperance project, it has been unquestioningly aired during every defense of the drug laws mounted in the last hundred years. Start on cannabis, and you soon graduate through stimulants to habit-forming opiates, in an attritional slither from smoking to sniffing to spiking up in public toilets, accompanied by the whole dismal narrative of alienated friends, broken family, petty crime and uncertain personal hygiene.

It had all been so different once. Before the eighteenth century started exercising itself about the links between spirits and moral perdition, the products of distillation had been virtually beyond reproach. Like most new food and drink products, they had been welcomed as having medicinal properties. Extracting the alcohol principle out of wine was seen as exactly analogous to the long-running but doomed project of turning base metals into gold. Indeed, distillation was explicitly considered a branch of alchemy, by which the soul or "spirit" of the wine was retrieved from the base materials that enveloped it. The potent drinks that resulted from these procedures, which would have smelled and tasted fairly foul because the means to rectify (purify) them lay centuries ahead, were nonetheless prescribed by physicians as specifics against all manner of ailments. Their rankness masked with botanical elements that themselves had curative potential, the earliest spirits were the fore-runners of the aromatized vodkas of today. Gin is a notable case in point. Originating as a diuretic tonic in the Netherlands, its pungent juniper scent is as strange and apothecarial to the uninitiated today as it must have been to its first consumers. Common to many European languages down the centuries are regional variations of the Latin phrase "aqua vitae" (water of life) that denoted the hopes invested by the continent's medical profession in what was universally seen as a panacea. The Gaelic word is "usquebaugh," or in its Scots variant "uisge beatha," which are the precursors of the Anglicized "whiskey." In the Scandinavian countries it becomes "aqua-vit" or "akvavit," and to the French, "eau-de-vie." In each case, the nomenclature refers to a basic distillate of either grain or fruits, the archetypal form in each region of an ardent spirit valued precisely for its vital sustenance.

The findings of Dr. Rush, and his fellow Edinburgh alumnus, Thomas Trotter, working on the opposite side of the Atlantic, were to explode that view of distilled spirits, perhaps forever. How much longer could society be hoaxed that the caustic substance in these bottles was a life-improver? The "water of life" had been found to be exactly the reverse, a noxious swill that led innocent souls to moral incontinence and the scaffold.

Perhaps it was precisely this sense that society had been duped that inaugurated the Temperance movement with the denunciatory fury in which it was to prosecute nearly a century and a half of campaigning. With God enlisted to the colors, it descended on village and town the length and breadth of Britain, Ireland and America, waving placards outside saloon bars, preaching and fulminating in the parks and gardens, singing soul-saving hymns to Sunday strollers, setting up camp outside workplaces and public houses, urging all to sign up to the Pledge—its very own initiates' code, formulated in language as sententious and solemn as any military oath of honor. It published pamphlets full of the most garish productions of Victorian eschatology, awash with the fire and brimstone of St. John's Revelation, the travails and eternal torments that surely awaited those whose pickled brains were impervious to God's redemptive presence. It blasted from the Sunday pulpits with vindictive fervor, fixing on the reddening gaze of the hapless cobbler who had a bit of a reputation for the bottle of a Friday night, or the contemptible scullery maid whose babe in arms was innocently suckling the polluted milk of a beer-swilling mother. It managed to create surveillance societies in some communities, in which neighbors were prepared to report on each other if they thought they smelled alcohol on somebody's breath, or heard so much as the popping of a cork in next door's back parlor. In the USA, where the Temperance movement created the most rabidly inquisitorial abstinence regime ever seen outside the Islamic world, whole new towns were established on the temperance (i.e., teetotalist) principle. One such was Harvey, Illinois, founded in 1891 by Turlington Harvey, a Sabbatarian mill-owner who was president of the Chicago YMCA in the 1870s. The town's real estate was purchased in the name of the Harvey Land Association, and sold to prospective residents with the following clause written into each set of title deeds:

> If the purchaser uses any part of the property for the purpose
> of permitting any intoxicating drink to be manufactured, sold
> or given away upon said premises, or permits gambling to be

carried on therein, or creates any house or other place of lewd and immoral practice thereupon, he, his heirs, executors, administrators and his assigns shall be divested of the entire estate and it shall revert to the party of the first part.[10]

Even in the UK, where a certain residual libertarian contrariness always threatened to cough the temperance pill back up again, the Pledge enjoyed fairly widespread dissemination. Not everyone could be persuaded, however, that the pubs and taverns were dens of mindless cupidity. Indeed, for many, they were the focus of the only form of intellectual life working people would ever regularly know. Marianna Adler records the mid-nineteenth century case of a pair of Bolton laborers who, when asked by their vicar why they had not been seen at church on the previous Sunday, replied that they had been detained at the pub by a discussion about the existence of God.

Until well into the postwar period, though, the British Temperance Society still toured the schools—infant schools, at that—in order to spread the gospel. I dimly remember, as a small boy, sitting through an inordinately long presentation that involved much in the way of abstruse medical information, together with a film in which a man was seen attempting and failing to walk steadily along a straight white line. We laughed as he toppled about, without knowing why it was funny.

It is all too easy to ridicule the efforts of Temperance campaigners in an era when we have been told that little and often is good for our hearts. At its core, though, was a genuine concern over the fate of working families that were impoverished by the heavy drinking of the wage-earner, and of the wife and children whom he assaulted in his rancorous inebriation. In the vanguard of the movement was the Women's Christian Temperance Union (WCTU), whose indefatigable activists were often all that stood between women and their drunken husbands and fathers. If there is a stridency of tone, and an unforgiving quality to many of their pronouncements on the Demon Drink, the explanation only has to be sought in the catalogue of avoidable domestic suffering that they continually encountered in the course of their missionary work.

Although, at one level, it is true to suggest that the Temperance movement was very largely about making working-class families more willing participants in the capitalist economy by encouraging them to manage their time in ways more conducive to productivity (at considerable cost to their established patterns of sociality, it should be added), at another the WCTU deployed trenchant criticisms of the double standards that obtained in legal treatment of the sexes. It had a keen internationalist sense of the comparative lack of liberty women suffered in foreign cultures, and pointed out that the law on prostitution provided for penalties against women that were not equitably applied to their male customers.

The depiction of a home fractured by drink was a favorite trope of cautionary postcards and booklets of the period that the WCTU and others produced. In a typical image of 1900, a man staggering about in the middle of the family parlor grimly raises a smashed stool above his head. It is aimed at the back of the seated huddled figure of his wife, whose body is bent over a baby, paradoxically fast asleep in her arms. While an elder daughter turns her weeping face toward a cupboard so as not to see, her younger brother, barefoot and schooled in masculine valor at a pitiably early age, raises his arms vainly to try to stem his father's inebriate wrath. Behind them on the table is the empty bottle that is the author of this dismaying cruelty.

There was undeniably a certain nobility in a life of abstinence against this background. It represented a determined turning away from an aspect of social and cultural life that had been ingrained for generations. But the Temperance movement ultimately failed in its mission to put intoxication beyond the pale. Too few of its clients were prepared to accept that it was God's will that we should all abstain, because too many drank without beating their wives or relapsing into prostitution or neglecting their children. When the movement failed in the UK, it withdrew to the margins of society, intermittently buoyed by restrictive legislation like the licensing laws, but evidently content to remain a pressure group. In America, failure turned it vicious, and faced with its inability to persuade significant numbers to take on its self-denying ordinance, it reached for the demagogue's megaphone to achieve by statutory amendment to the Constitution what it couldn't achieve with tambourines and pamphlets. To today's Prohibitionists, still agitating for drinking to be made as publicly disgraceful as cigarette smoking now is, the

established news that steady alcohol intake is decisively more beneficial to overall health than complete abstinence must have seemed as
much a body blow as it was a relief to every liverish old soak.

Campaigns against alcohol have never been solely motivated by
concern for the physical well-being of its aficionados. Even today,
in a theoretically more secular age, the shrill alarums of the neo-
Prohibitionist caucus in the USA are inscribed through and through
with the moral indignation of nineteenth-century revivalism. Not
only does this tendency survive, though, but it is also strengthening.
Where once the movement was confined to urging teetotalism on its
target audience, it now underscores that with a vituperative attack
on the liquor industry itself. These are the evil corporations that
have grown rich and fat on poisoning the systems of successive generations of unsuspecting Americans, and not just the big corporations, but every bar, every restaurant and hotel, every liquor store,
every winery in the country is complicit in the monstrous conspiracy
to pour Satan's nectar down the throats, into the stomachs and
through the livers of a Christian nation.

In a culture that has long been hospitable to religious fundamen-
talism of the most freebooting kind, it shouldn't seem strange that
the antialcohol lobby should be driven by such righteous fervor, and
yet what does bemuse the outsider is the degree to which it has been
able to gain admittance to national political discourse, to the broadcast media and even to otherwise rational sections of the press. A
campaign to impose swingeing taxes on the drink industry to pay for
the huge collateral damage their trade is accused of causing in terms
of auto wrecks, industrial accidents, absenteeism from work and
personal health problems has the editorial support of state newspa-
pers across the nation, most unquestioningly of all from USA Today.
If it is true that a culture of blame is now sweeping America, in
which everybody who trips over a broken paving-stone must have
somebody to sue, then it is entirely consistent that those with alcohol difficulties should be able to take the bourbon distillery to the
cleaners. One day Homer Simpson will sue the Duff brewery for
making him fat.

It is all particularly hard to understand when one considers that,
in the last 20 years, alcohol consumption has fallen in the United
States by 40 percent. But then, to the teetotalists, this is a heartening

sign that their propaganda is sinking in. It would be foolish therefore to stop now when, if they only redouble their exertions, they
may be able to accelerate that decline. The Federal Bureau of Alcohol, Tobacco and Firearms, perpetually fearful of the Prohibitionists
to the extent that they yielded to the pressure to label all alcohol
products with a health warning, now turns a deaf ear to the findings
on wine and health, in which American studies have replicated the
results of the European ones. When the wine industry lobbied for
the right to add information on health benefits to the labels of wine
bottles, the phrase "health benefits" in the alcohol context was too
much for the Bureau to swallow. It would rather the nation believed,
against the force of medical evidence, that alcohol can never be beneficial. In any case, it would mean neutralizing the Surgeon General's existing warning, which concludes that what's in the bottle
"may cause health problems."

In the UK, meanwhile, rumblings about national drinking habits
tend to be much more noises off, although there is an identifiable
fringe within the antialcohol movement that shows signs of being
influenced by the American trend to litigation. When I suggested
during the course of a TV debate on antisocial alcohol behavior, to a
woman who blamed it all on the breweries, that there was such a
thing as taking responsibility for one's own actions, her reply was,
"Yes, and when are the drinks companies going to take responsibility for theirs?" It was once deemed the fault of the parents, then it
was trendy teachers in hock to silly progressive teaching theories,
now it's the likes of Anheuser Busch that makes young men go
shouting along the street at night when others have gone to bed.

If the searchlight of blame can be turned on an individual industry, then the teetotalists may yet have their day in court. How could
sloppy parents ever be sued? Underpinning it all is the same moralistic impulse that motivated the Salvationists. It may have got a little
bleached in the wash in Britain, but the accusing tone is still readily
discernible. There is a better way than self-indulgence, it insists. In
this context, a pressure group such as Alcohol Concern, whose
proper concern was once with problem drinkers, now reserves to
itself the right to comment on pub opening hours. When it was
announced at the beginning of 1999 that there would be extended
licensing time for the millennium weekend, the nagging response

that the government seemed to be suggesting we all drink ourselves to oblivion was instantaneous. This too is the counsel of the British Medical Association, which was reduced to near apoplexy when the safe-drinking limits were liberalized shortly before Christmas 1996. Nothing must muffle the moralizing drumbeat of professional concern. We shall return to the medical aspects of intoxication in chapter 6.

Once theological guidance has become a matter of mere morality, God has usually quietly left the scene. Since morals are a much more readily privatizable commodity than the doctrine of the faith, his voice grows fainter than it was when it boomed through ecclesiastical edicts and the injunctions of scripture. But one version of God lived to fight another day among intoxication's casualties. He is the God of the twelve steps of Alcoholics Anonymous and of all the recovery groups, including Narcotics Anonymous, Cocaine Anonymous and so forth, that are made in its image. The Twelve Steps, AA's Nicene creed, opens with an acknowledgment of his reality:

1. We admitted to ourselves that we were powerless over alcohol—that our lives had become unmanageable.
2. Came to believe that a Power greater than ourselves could restore us to sanity.
3. Made a decision to turn our will and our lives over to the care of God *as we understood Him.* [emphasis original]

Whichever way each individual chooses to understand this solicitous "Power" invoked in step 2—who by step 3 is already named as none other than God—his reappearance here is a testament to his hardy durability. Hovering above the heads of those whose lives fell to bits because they couldn't see when enough was too much, his presence at these gatherings of the convalescent reflects his abiding interest in the effect he had on us when he chose to fill our worldly home with drugs.

4

From Gin Lane to Crack City

Are drugs a menace to society? We know that drug-related crime is a major nuisance, that alcoholic transients can quickly lower the tone of the new shopping mall as they loll about drinking cheap cider and that the restaurant dinners that will be ruined tonight by the hovering fogs of smokers are legion. But does the intoxicated individual in his or her own person actually threaten to corrode the social fabric on which we all depend?

When most of the major intoxicants were made illegal in the Western world in the early years of the twentieth century, an image of drug-users as the enemy within came to be cemented. High-profile opiate and cocaine casualties, cases of severe addiction in the theater world and elsewhere in society, not to mention the spectacle of a self-indulgent demimonde sniffing happy powder while the Great Powers were fighting each other to a standstill on the Western Front: all these combined to produce the impetus for a body of legislation that is still with us today. Once the mass of intoxication behavior had been criminalized in this way, it was a short step to seeing dope-takers as no more responsible participants in society than housebreakers were. Even though it wasn't entirely clear who the innocent victim was supposed to be if a well-to-do hostess offered her consenting guests morphine along with the afternoon tea, nonetheless the fact that such practices came to be outlawed made those who still wished to indulge in them opponents of the social consensus, potential disrupters of social harmony. This view has always been heavily dependent on what I have called the "addiction paradigm," the idea that all substances are eventually habit-forming, and that all episodes of use are either the consequence of some irresistible chemical slavery, or at least a staging post on the way to that condition. In the light of this, the numbers of genuine cases of abject dependency are ruthlessly seized on as being the raison d'être for the legislation. Only now, nearly one hundred years after the laws were first formulated, is that distorting view being undermined throughout society, not because of any polemical onslaught by interested parties, but as a result of direct or reported personal experience. Eventually, the addiction paradigm will be so threadbare that it will come to be the subject of near-universal derision, and will no longer serve the purposes of apologists for the legal status quo, but what may just survive it is the notion that, however they are treated officially, intoxicant-users are alienating themselves from or withdrawing from the social structure. Being stoned, in this view, is ipso facto to be apart from society. To the temperance (i.e., abstinence) campaigners of the Victorian era, alcohol too, while not illegal, carried within it the same hidden power to enslave as the criminalized substances are now held to possess.

To see whether this view holds water will necessitate looking at all the major intoxicants—legal and illegal—in turn, to see whether their effects are inevitably and ultimately antisocial or not. First, however, it is as well to cast a glance at the findings of the copious animal research (not all of it impeccably ethical, one should warn) that has been done in this area.

Hardly any social group in the animal world is as perceptibly, touchingly close-knit as a shoal of neon tetra. In the jungle-shrouded waters of the Amazon rain forest, or in their tank at the City Aquarium, they flash about in phosphorescent packs, their ultramarine-striped flanks darting and weaving through the water in one great constellation, driven seemingly by a unified collective mind. The distance between them, which looks uncannily like the precise length of the average adult fish, never alters, no matter the rate at which they swim. They negotiate obstacles and other fish with relentless singularity of purpose, undulating up and swerving around in mesmerically perfect formation. Like Oscar and Bosie, they do *everything* together.

Ronald K. Siegel, who has experimentally drugged everything from hornets to the higher primates in the pursuit of understanding intoxication behavior, once administered LSD to a small batch of neon tetra, and then inveigled them into a larger group. Although the tripping tetras formed only 10 percent of the school, their disruptive influence on the group was out of all proportion to their numbers. If they had space to do so, they obligingly split themselves off from the main group, which carried on moving in synchrony, evidently doing its best to ignore the dropouts. Interestingly, the dropouts themselves did not form an alternatively cohesive group, but just meandered aimlessly about, one or two going completely off on their own tangents, floating in an unnatural vertical position apart from the others. When the experiment was repeated in a smaller tank, where there was no room for the acid-doped fish to ostracize themselves, unseemly confusion reigned. The drugged fish continually collided with the undrugged, snagging the seamless movement of the group. So great an irritant did they eventually become, like shambling drunks among a rush-hour subway crowd, that the straight fish (and it is normally an irreproachably placid species) fell to taking the odd surreptitious snap at those that were off their heads, nipping lumps out of their fins in protest at their silly behavior.

The experiment has been successfully repeated with pigeons in a loft, and with rats, mice and monkeys. Once under the influence—and the findings hold good for alcohol as much as for hallucinogenic drugs like LSD and mescaline—the target animals will separate themselves off from their peers until such time as the effects of the drug wear off. What they appear to be doing is not so much isolating themselves as a consequence of not functioning normally, as protecting themselves from the investigative, and frequently hostile, behavior of their undrugged colleagues. Note that in the experiment with the neon tetra, it is the fish that haven't been given LSD that start behaving aggressively, for all that they have the defense of being sorely provoked. Similarly, stoned mice will retreat to the far corners of a spacious cage to be away from those that want to get on with feeding, grooming and mating. In more cramped conditions, the sober ones will often set upon a drugged animal, even when it isn't

doing anything immediately disruptive to the others, with potentially dire consequences, as Siegel explains:

> When a fight breaks out, animals still under the influence are at
> risk of being abused because they may be too sleepy or immobile
> to fight well. And even if they are capable of moving but are
> clumsy and wobbly, the uncoordinated behavior may trigger a
> pathological attack by a sober animal . . . [1]

It is as if the sight of a fellow creature in a state of clearly altered
consciousness is constitutionally intolerable to those who haven't
partaken. The impulse in intoxicated creatures to get away from
their sober mates is particularly pronounced in monkeys, which will
resort to hurling themselves against the bars of their cages in the
effort to do so. Transfer them to the wild, though, where the spaced-
out can truly space themselves out from the straight ones, and the
dysfunctional behavior disappears. (The exception to these findings
would appear to occur with cannabis, which drives monkeys chronically habituated to a daily dose of it to develop aggressive tenden-
cies toward their non-stoned mates, although this effect is only
noted after tolerance develops—i.e., after two or three months of
sustained daily dosing. Perhaps this explains why, despite the widely
canvassed relaxant properties of cannabis, those who have a nightly
spliff or three as a matter of routine are quite as capable of flaring up
over which TV channel to watch as the rest of us.)

Siegel's research findings obviously vary according to the nature
of the intoxicant used. Relatively transparent drug states, such as
amphetamine or cocaine stimulation, cause social isolation for different reasons to the more appreciably mind-changing substances.
Obsessive but pointless behavior, such as objectless searching and
physical self-examination, are the hallmarks of these states, but the
same desire to be left to one's own devices while engaged in it are
repeatedly seen. The chattering of an infant wanting attention is
wholly uninteresting to the mother primate on amphetamine, and
neither can the mewling of its kittens distract the coked-up cat from
its pointless stalking. Not even catnip can tempt it.

The enlightened social anthropologist might pay respectful attention to all this, and note the interesting and provocative parallels to

be observed between the responses of laboratory animals and those of human beings. To be dosed with speed and shut in a box with too many other people might well be the cause of some truculence. We don't care to have the faces of others in suffocating proximity to us on the overcrowded commuter train as it is, let alone want to be on mind-altering drugs in such conditions. Hallucinogenic agents commonly confer a sudden deep desire to be outside in the open air, rather than confined in a dimly lit room, when their effects first come up, and so the news that the neon tetra turn on each other when some of them are on LSD, in a tank where there isn't room to swing a sprat, wouldn't seem to add greatly to the sum of enlightenment.

The real problem, though, with the laboratory studies carried out by Siegel (by methods he has since renounced) lies in the interpretation of isolation reflexes as antisocial. We can accept that excessively stoned monkeys who attack the unstoned are engaging in conduct disruptive to the cohesion of a group. But those who go off on their own, or just stick with others in the same state, are not necessarily acting antisocially. It may be precisely because they know they are functioning in a different way from normal that they absent themselves from their peers. This, Siegel has in fact acknowledged in his gloss on the neon tetra experiment. "The drugged fish tend to group together and apart from the rest. This division is actually a benefit to the school, which can now swim independent of the drugged subgroup."[2]

An even more obvious fault seems evident to me, moreover, in the interpretation of these findings. The difference between a laboratory rat on a huge administration of amphetamine and the Friday-night clubber on an equally heroic dose is that the rat doesn't *know* it's speeding. It might sense that something has changed about the way it is now reacting to everything, but it can't understand the change, and nor—crucially—does it know when or whether it will stop. It is certainly incontrovertible that the higher primates are intelligent enough to be able to recognize an experience repeated to the point of predictability, but the individual still can't understand what causes the effect if the drug is clandestinely administered to it. This is not, barring the odd idiot who imagines it would be funny to spike an introverted friend's beer with speed to see how he reacts, the way that humans take drugs. It is all but impossible to imagine how one might react on falling unexpectedly under the influence of some major hallucinogenic without knowing how it had got into one's system, but then—unlike the hapless fish in the laboratory tank—we don't have to. And more to the point, without wishing to be needlessly controversial, we are not neon tetra.

If experiments on unsuspecting animals in artificial conditions do not conclusively prove that drug-taking is antisocial, however, we are left with the question as to whether there are any drugs whose effects are always in themselves desocializing, whatever the intentions of the user. Some might suggest heroin or any of the other opiates as clear-cut candidates for this definition, since the stupefying effect they have on the cerebral function is scarcely conducive to conviviality. Certainly, the intravenous addict may have long since ceased to be a social being in any readily apprehensible meaning of the phrase, but a mild degree of opiate sedation does not preclude rational intercourse, by any means, and it is clear that opium-smoking communities are still recognizably communities, however little their mores may appeal to those whose drugs of choice are less habit-forming. That said, though, drugs that have a sedative or tranquilizing effect on the system are obviously the least social of substances. The implied objective of taking such intoxicants is to go into a beatific drowse or slip into actual unconsciousness, an urge not so much to alter the phenomenal world perceptually as to draw a veil of narcosis over the whole tawdry spectacle. In this way, prescription tranquilizers such as diazepam, together with the more rarely prescribed barbiturates, represent the preferred escape routes of those who have largely given up on sociality anyway. Those who can't persuade their doctors to prescribe them, and do not wish to become involved in the black market, may often resort to alcohol, an arguably much more corrosive recourse for the individual bent on real oblivion.

The only other substance that has worked its way into popular use in recent years that may on the face of it seem antisocial in its effects is ketamine, known to the club culture as Special K. It is possible to buy it on the street in the form of a white powder for snorting, but most ketamine is probably unwittingly ingested by clients of the ecstasy dealers, since many of the pills that are sold in clubs and bars contain a noticeable admixture of it. (In a UK survey undertaken by *The Face* magazine in June 1998, in which street samples of various drugs were laboratory-tested to discover their level of purity, and what adulterants they had been cut with, the ecstasy pill procured contained no other active ingredient than ketamine.) The first sign of it kicking in is a sudden jerking-awake feeling, very similar to what happens when, on a long car journey, the drowsy passenger is suddenly jolted back to consciousness by a bump in the road. You may not have been aware of nodding off, and yet here you are suddenly waking up. A glass may have smashed on the floor as it slipped through your numbing fingers. Those who do notice the onset effects, perhaps with the next wave of somnolence, are often aware of a disquieting separation of mental perceptions from the body, so that the torso and limbs one looks down on are not immediately recognizable as having anything to do with the blurring consciousness that sees them. As the next jolt back to awareness occurs, one isn't even able to tell whether one's eyes had closed or not. A kind of automatic-pilot effect can take over, so that one may go into a ketamine trance (or "K-hole," to give it its vernacular name) in the middle of a dance floor and apparently continue to dance, even though the sensate body is momentarily out of commission.

One man I spoke to reported taking a pill with his boyfriend as they left a club at 5 A.M. to go home. As he remembers it, they were leaving the place one minute and turning up outside their house the next, with nothing apparently having happened in between. They knew they hadn't been conscious, and yet they had found their way home, and crossed at least one main road on the way back. Although they hadn't themselves identified it as such, this is a classic ketamine state. None of this is surprising, in fact, because ketamine is used medically as a general anesthetic. (A myth persists on the drug scene that it is specifically a veterinary drug—I have heard it referred to as both "horse tranquilizer" and "cat Valium"—but it is also used in a minority of human surgical patients, particularly children and those with critically low blood pressure, since it is the only general anesthetic available that doesn't depress the heart rate.) And yet, as so often with unofficial intoxicants, there is another side to the story, as Siegel reports:

The drug literally knocks people down with ecstatic visions . . .
I have given the drug to many human volunteers, who report

being unable to move while mesmerised by feelings of harmony and joy in all that they see.[3]

He goes on to recount the story of a wild bear that was shot with a ketamine dart intended to knock it out. It retreated, still conscious, to a high mountain ledge, where it seemed to sit in dazed contemplation of the landscape, swinging its head from side to side in a state of serene ursine contentment. Perhaps it was having "ecstatic visions," or perhaps it was just relieved to have escaped its would-be captors, but either way, neither the bear's nor the volunteers' experiences of ketamine seem to accord with the warning note sounded by Andrew Tyler in his otherwise impeccably dispassionate guide to street drugs. He assures us that "few who have tried it have any favourable words on the subject," and reports the case of a man who said he felt as if he had been raped by it, although—saliently, perhaps—he had taken it unintentionally, possibly in the form of an adulterated E.[4] Taken intranasally in minutely measured doses, it can be an entertaining enough excursion into mild derealization, but there is a very definite trip-wire point in it, and once past that, a considerably more startling state of hallucinating immobilization comes over the user. Attempting to move the body in this condition is quite hazardous, and the drug's effects, which had been coming and going in a couple of minutes, now linger on nauseously for half an hour or more. Perhaps this explains the feeling of having been violated that Tyler's respondent mentions. If ketamine only ever made the user nod off, it could be classed with the benzodiazepine tranquilizers as an essentially solipsistic experience, but it may be that the appropriate use of the drug, under the tutelage of somebody as knowledgeable as Professor Siegel, may indicate its potential for a more outward-looking range of effects.

Certainly, the story of one American adept of the drug, reported in *The Face* in 1997, brings whole new meaning to the concept of solipsism. He checked into a hotel room with a sizeable stash of ketamine, hung the "Do not disturb" sign on the doorknob and made a sort of tent out of the bedclothes, within which he proceeded to indulge himself to the full. It was only when a housekeeper tentatively tapped on the door three days later to see whether the minibar needed replenishing that his solitary indulgence came to light. He had spent the time luxuriating in a K-hole so deep it was practically a bottomless pit, and the society of others was most definitely unwelcome.

An even more gruesomely solipsistic experience is to be had from phencyclidine, otherwise known as PCP or "angel dust." First formulated in 1958 (therefore predating ketamine by seven years), it too was initially used as a general anesthetic, until awareness of its disturbing hallucinogenic properties consigned it, unlike ketamine, to the veterinary repertoire. After a brief flicker of interest in the late sixties, it became a serious, fairly widely used street drug in the 1970s and '80s, when it was often sold in America under some other guise. Smoking a cigarette that had been dipped in or sprayed with the liquid form of the drug was the preferred means of administering it, as is quite extensively documented in Edmund White's autobiographical novels. The drug has an uncommonly complex range of effects, usually combining a clenched state of amphetaminelike stimulation, allied to total disorientation and hallucinogenic tripping. As with ketamine, the tripping tends to feel rather squalid, less a dance of the liberated unconscious than a scraping up of psychic muck from the bottom of the mental tank. Cautiously small doses can be pleasantly dreamy, but in extreme concentrations, it has led to many notorious outcomes, in which individuals have committed brutal murders or acts of self-mutilation, but appear to recall nothing about these episodes afterward. Accounts of phencyclidine trauma are as close to the truth as tabloid alarmism about drugs tends to get. Somewhat surprisingly, PCP has failed—so far at least—to catch on in the UK.

Notwithstanding the examples of heroin dependency, ketamine and phencyclidine, it is my firm contention that intoxication practices are not inevitably antisocial at all, but in many cases amplify the opportunities for sociality, creating their own forms of it, or serving to structure and reinforce the existing ones. This chapter will look in turn at the different ways in which different intoxicants have helped to achieve these results, beginning with the most sociable psychoactive substance of them all.

CAFFEINE

Caffeine is the most widely used legal drug in the world. The forms in which it is sold range from the jar of freeze-dried instant coffee and the box of teabags through cans of cola, isotonic sports drinks and bars of chocolate to guarana capsules and linctuses, tubes of wake-up pills, analgesics and cold remedies. It is an immensely popular drug for much the same reasons that amphetamine would be if it were available to anyone other than the chronically obese: it is a reliable and almost instantly effective stimulant. In certain patent painkilling recipes, its function is to contrict the blood vessels surrounding the brain, alleviating the throbbing feeling of some headaches, as well as speed the principal analgesic components (aspirin and acetaminophen) into the bloodstream, a relief for which the disastrously hungover will give much thanks on many a bilious Sunday morning. In purer form, as Magnum or NoDoz, it is sold to sustain wakefulness and alertness for those who have to work long hours or stay up all night. The manufacturers may have in mind security guards or junior doctors, but many caffeine tablets are swallowed by students cramming for exams and those just starting out on their intoxicant careers, for whom caffeine tablets are a crudely legal kind of beginner's speed. (The latter will rapidly discover that caffeine is not a nice thing to take to excess in this form, since it irritates the stomach woefully, and almost invariably leads to episodes of vomiting.) Most of the caffeine we take, however, is absorbed in liquid form.

The buzz that is expected from commercial fizzy drinks is now derived largely from caffeine. That uplifting effect is traceable historically to the nineteenth-century tonic drinks that were vigorously marketed as cure-alls to societies on both sides of the Atlantic becoming obsessed with self-medication. It took the form of coca leaves and kola nuts in John Pemberton's 1886 patent recipe, Coca-Cola, and did so until 1906, when coca was removed from the recipe—not long before trading in cocaine itself was made illegal. A new generation of soft drinks that came on to the market in the 1990s was explicitly positioned in this way. Known as energy drinks, they were aimed officially at those engaged in vigorous contact sports, but nonetheless contained a scarcely subliminal appeal to clubgoers whose intake of intoxicants was not likely to include alcohol, but who wanted to rehydrate themselves with something a touch more exotic than water. Sometimes the energy content in these drinks was derived entirely from natural sugars such as glucose and fructose, as was disappointingly the case with a product called Red Card made by the Britvic company in the UK, the logo on which, promisingly, was a furious referee dismissing a footballer over the slogan "Keeps you going till you're sent off," but mostly it was from some caffeine source, notably the increasingly popular guarana.

Guarana is a ligneous vine (*Paullinia cupana*) native to the central Amazon, where it has found its way, in conjunction with certain hallucinogenic plants, into some shamanistic rituals, but is also widely used to aid hunting, since the caffeine in it maintains alertness and endurance. It is now being cultivated commercially for use in fizzy drinks—but also in phials of honeyed syrup, chewing gum and capsules of the finely ground seeds—as a more powerful, and seemingly more gently absorbed, source of caffeine than is available from coffee, tea or chocolate. The boost to be had from guarana in these forms is quite an appreciable one. One gram swallowed in the absence of any other intoxicant delivers a mild but appreciable feeling of lightly jittery cheerfulness after about 45 minutes. When you then begin your circuit-training, or road-racing, or dancing, the level of potential energy in the muscles feels correspondingly maximized. Guarana's essential oil is also held, in its native region, to have aphrodisiac properties, which its Western promoters have not failed to point out.

Most of our caffeine intake comes from tea or coffee, though, where its stimulant effects may be enhanced, as they are with chocolate, by the addition of refined sugar. Given the quantities in which these drinks are commonly taken daily in widely divergent societies all over the globe, it is certain that the greater part of humanity has caffeine in its bloodstream at any given moment. Caffeine certainly has its side-effects. It is intensely diuretic, as are its related compounds theophylline and theobromine, in the company of which it is often found, meaning that intensive users will find themselves needing to urinate to an inordinate degree, and it tends to create peaks and troughs of energy so that an alert period may be followed in due course by relapse into yawning lethargy. But we go on drinking it in the quantities we do, and considering it a daily staple that can create a minor domestic crisis if we suddenly find ourselves out of it after the nearest shop has closed, because it is also seriously addictive. Anybody who has ever unwisely tried to switch from drinking real coffee (by which I mean anything from regular Nescafé to freshly ground Blue Mountain beans) to the filthily chemical-tasting decaffeinated article for the good of their health will have found the experience deeply startling. After a couple of days' deprivation, it becomes almost impossible to cross a room without pausing to rest on the way, and drifting into deep mid-afternoon sleep at the office desk is a real risk. These adjustment effects wear off, of course, leaving the abstainer free for a lifetime of coffee that has been denatured by means of chemicals more commonly used in paint-stripper and cleaning fluids, but those for whom that presents a less than alluring prospect can at least comfort themselves with the thought that the next *cafetière* of thick black full-on French roast is going to be scarcely less dramatic than crystal meth.

What we become dependent on is the stimulant effect that can be measured in increased neural activity in the central nervous system, augmented heart rate and the turbulent churning of stomach fluids that speeds up the digestive process. The day's first hit of caffeine is responsible (in alliance with the first cigarette for many) for the day's first evacuation of the bowels, and for the kick-start that our daily routines require in us. Caffeine keeps us mentally alert, accelerates our cognitive functions and—to some extent—keeps our moods buoyant through the day, although an excess of it may make us irritable as well as vaguely nauseous. Taken too late in the evening, it disrupts the ability of the brain to shut down in preparation for sleep, an effect that is frequently exacerbated by those who, tossing and turning and finally getting up again in despair, then drink a mug of hot milky coffee to help them sleep.

Presumably because of the assonance between the words "coffee" (or its European variants, *café*, *Kaffee*, *caffè* and so forth) and "caffeine," it is popularly believed that coffee contains more of the stuff than anything else does. Tea is mostly, however, quite as rich a source of the drug as instant coffee, as is chocolate, which may be considerably higher in it if the chocolate is particularly rich in cocoa solids. When the stimulant effect insinuates itself into our systems, the effects may be pleasant enough, but sometimes an immediate and energizing rush is what's required, in which case premium chocolate (with a cocoa-solids quotient at around 70 percent) will answer the call. The high level of theobromine in chocolate can produce both the pounding heart and brimming bladder effects very quickly, as my panel and I discovered when undertaking a comparative tasting of specialty chocolate for a food magazine. It isn't hard to see why the cup of neat black espresso in the coffee shop is often accompanied by a slab of black bitter chocolate—or, as has become the vogue in recent years, chocolate-coated coffee beans. Then there are the versions of Italian coffee that are even stronger than standard espresso. Ristretto, which is made by the same method as espresso but with a proportionately smaller quantity of water forced through the compressed ground coffee, has a virtually instantaneous impact on the heart rate. Swallowing it in one on an empty stomach can leave the recipient literally breathless. If the Americans and the British typically drank their coffee as it is taken in Italy, Portugal and the Arab countries, the endless stream of anemic filter coffee that sustains offices all over the Western world would rapidly become obsolete.

The social and cultural transformations that were wrought by the arrival of caffeine in western Europe in the seventeenth century were immense. No drug has ever established itself so quickly and so ineradicably in any culture or group of cultures, nor had such pervasive effects on the nature of the society that flourished on it. Before it began its triumphal sweep through European capitals, borne along by the three thoroughbred stimulants of coffee, tea and chocolate, nothing quite like it had ever been in the bloodstreams of citizens of the civilized world. Certainly, the stimulant properties of particular herbs and spices such as peppermint, ginger, mustard and pepper were well enough known, but their effect was considerably more subliminal and they were not anyway being taken continually. Sugar was confined to the well-off, and even fresh fruits—which might have given an appreciable shot of energy in the form of fructose—were not much eaten, since in England at least it was commonly believed that they carried the risk of inducing fever, just as vegetables were felt, more accurately in some instances, to be harbingers of flatulence. The caffeine beverages caught on so speedily, they made the heads of the intelligentsia spin. Venues devoted to each of them sprang up in the cities, preeminently London, where more coffee was drunk in this initial fanatic period than anywhere else in the world, although the first commercial coffeehouse in England was established in Oxford. Soon, the coffeehouses were joined by chocolate-houses, such as White's and the Cocoa Tree, the former still going strong today as one of London's more venerable gentlemen's clubs. It wasn't merely the craze for the drinks themselves that made these places so culturally cataclysmic, but the behavior that went on in them.

Caffeine brought a democratic political consciousness to whole classes that had never before troubled themselves with such matters. The coffeehouses came to be seen as hotbeds of sedition, much as had the wine taverns of classical Athens, because there—wreathed in the smoke of boiling urns and of fashionable tobacco pipes—the great constitutional questions of the day might well be thrashed out as they had not been in anybody's living memory—i.e., stone-cold sober.

The currents of unrest that led in England to the period of the kingless Commonwealth (1649–60) and the Civil War were seen as having been aggravated by the plentiful availability of cheap alcohol, always preferable to the alternatives of milk or water, which were only of very unreliable freshness. Milk in particular was nearly always halfway to rancid by the time it reached the city-dwelling consumer, fruit-based drinks were unknown and an unrelieved regimen of water was enough to drive anybody to alcohol relief. Not only did the caffeine drinks provide a novel and fascinating stimulant lift, but they also contributed to a wholesale sobering-up of the upper strata of society, in which political debate, under the sporadic influence of whatever philosophical speculations filtered through to them, enjoyed an unprecedented efflorescence. The coffeehouse culture made possible the Glorious Revolution of 1688, and much in the way of political upheaval across the Continent thereafter. Not for nothing did Charles II make an attempt to suppress the coffeehouses in December 1675, the reasons given in the bill laid before Parliament being that they had become magnets for the worst sort of social dissident, had encouraged idleness among tradesmen,

> but also for that in such houses . . . divers, false, malitious [sic], and scandalous reports are devised and spread abroad to the defamation of His Majesty's Government, and to the disturbance of the Peace and Quiet of the Realm.[5]

It was perhaps fitting testimony to the overweening constitutional power the King realized was brewing within the coffeehouses that his edict stood for a mere 17 days before the supposedly dissolute mobs it was aimed at forced its ignominious revocation.

Circles of social disaffection have been quite as often fueled by alcohol over the centuries. Behind every gate-storming canaille in pre-Revolutionary Paris, at the root of the Gordon anti-popery riots in London in 1780, lurked the specter of inebriation, spurring the disgruntled on to uninhibited acts of gratuitous vandalism. The dissidence of the coffeehouses, however, was of a totally different order. For all its babble of voices, and the pre-Hogarthian melee of slopping coffee dishes, the sneezes of snuff-takers and the disputations that often came to fisticuffs, the dissent here was intellectually grounded. Those who couldn't have summoned the phrases to condemn the rotten constitution in a month of Sundays found themselves exposed to the declaiming of those who could, and thus the seeds were sown. No wonder that the King was persuaded it was all getting out of hand. Some have been moved to wonder during the course of the recent drug debate why governments who might well prefer their citizens placid with dope don't just let them get on with it, instead of locking them up.

In an era of protest marches and rioting, the argument undoubtedly had force. In a more apathetic time, when proliferating TV channels and the globe-hugging tentacles of the Internet have induced sedentary indifference in millions, the need for dope seems even less apparent. But what always stood in the way of drug legalization was not the addictiveness of opiates, but the awful hyperactivity that the stimulant drugs might unleash. The influx of caffeine in the system of seventeenth-century Europe remains the cautionary tale in this regard. It made everybody just that little bit brighter, in both senses of the word: more intelligent by stimulating cerebral activity, and more cheerful about the prospect of changing the world. The intellectual tradition of the coffeehouse survived in Europe, even as it fizzled to nothing in England. Parisian surrealism would have been nothing without it in the 1930s (the formal expulsions from its ranks of the raving dramatic theorist Antonin Artaud, as well as the stubbornly unmalleable Dalí, both took place in cafés), and twenty years later, the heyday of Sartrean existentialism was played out in the coffee bars of the Left Bank and Montmartre. In 1998, the philosophical coffee-bar made a much-trumpeted come-back to the French capital, with the opening of a venue explicitly designed for bickering the afternoon away under a Gauloise-scented fug of half-digested Derrida.

In southeast Europe too, in Greece and Turkey, the coffeehouse has always played a focal role in the life of small communities, neighborly disputes being settled over the bubbling pot of thick black arabica. We can perhaps, not entirely facetiously, trace the decline of the English tradition to a concomitant decline in the caffeine levels of what was being served. By the postwar period, the Lyons Corner Houses and Kardomah Cafés that represented the most visible form of public coffee-drinking had become places where solitary ladies might eat a slice of lemon cake or a chocolate biscuit while waiting for the rain to ease off. The coffee might have frothed exuberantly (the steam-pressured milky coffee known as "expresso" stored up terminological bewilderment for a later era when real Italian espresso arrived), but of the steam of political ferment, not a wisp remained.

Coffee has had a somewhat troubled career within the Islamic tradition. It is one of the gifts of Allah to the prophet Mohammed, sent via his messenger Gabriel to buoy him up during a period of fatigue. The Islamic cultures embraced coffee-drinking as a social habit about 200 years before the Europeans did—it was transported along the desert trade routes from its native East Africa, across the Red Sea and into Arabia—and it was prized precisely because it demonstrably encouraged the sort of animated scholarly dialogues on which early Islam thrived.

A backlash with strikingly similar overtones to the London fracas occurred in 1511 when a newly appointed governor of Mecca found his fastidious pieties the subject of satirical burlesquing in the coffeehouses. An edict was promptly issued, à la Charles II, to close down these seedbeds of dissension on the official grounds that they engendered rowdiness and staying up all night, and so resembled the forbidden wine taverns too closely for theological comfort. Responding even more vigorously than their London successors, the Meccans broke out in spontaneous rioting in defense of their coffeehouses, as a result of which the governor now banned coffee itself. To a culture with no other obvious intoxicant, making coffee a Class A substance was bound to be unenforceable, as was perhaps recognized in the luridly ridiculous punishment that was instituted for anyone caught consuming it. The miscreant was to be tied to the back of an ass with his face at the rear end, and paraded around the streets, while being lashed to ribbons. Although the governor had clearly given of his best imaginative exertions in formulating the punishment, when it came to seeking official ratification of the edict, his Sultan in Cairo overruled him in the matter, gently pointing out that there was no Qu'ranic authority for prohibiting coffee. The coffeehouses were reinstated, and grateful Muslims given back their only permitted drug.

In the seventeenth century, further attempts to abolish the institution of the coffeehouse in Constantinople were made by successive Ottoman sultans. In 1633, Murad IV blamed them for fomenting the murderous mutiny among his imperial guards, the Janissaries, that had led to the assassination of his brother Osman II, and closed them down on spurious public safety grounds. This interdiction stood for ten years before being repealed, but was reenacted in 1656 by Grand Vizier Mehmed Köprülü, acting on behalf of the teenage Sultan Mehmed IV, who had gone about the city in disguise and had his worst fears confirmed on discovering the coffeehouses were full of malcontent Janissaries criticizing the Empire's conduct of its war with Venice. Anybody presiding over or attending a coffeehouse was now to be beaten senseless and, if caught again, was to be stitched up in a sack and hurled into the sea. As if in acknowledgment of the comparative subversive potential of caffeine over alcohol, the wine taverns (which were also officially forbidden in the Ottoman Empire) were left alone. The Grand Vizier discovered that all alcohol seemed to do was to make the tavern patrons sing and tell tall stories of military or erotic exploits. Only caffeine made them politically articulate. This was of course exactly the conclusion that the London government was to arrive at less than twenty years later.

Today, we use caffeine more unassumingly than was the case in the coffeehouses of the 1600s. It gets us going in the morning rather than fuels acts of political dissent. The church coffee-morning is not a hotbed of ecclesiastical schism, nor does the fecundating list of novelty flavors on offer in Seattle and Soho betoken radical nonconformity (it is more about turning coffee into what it was never meant to be—a *soft* drink), but there is one sense in which it may still save us. Much comment is excited about the trancelike passivity of the young today, as they gape at garbage information on the Internet or play round after round of computer games. All that stands between this generation and cyber-stoned apathy, it would seem, is caffeine, bubbling into their systems in streams of Coca-Cola, supplemented by a formidable annual tonnage of commercial chocolate. Be it ever so costly in dental enamel, the caffeine will nourish their brains.

TOBACCO

While they sit tapping away in the computer room, however, some of their teachers may well be skulking on the fire escape inhaling another stimulant, having been prevented by majority vote from doing so in the staff room. The communities of the ostracized created by smoking bans are the huddled masses of legitimate drug use in the Western world, held less at arm's than at barge-pole's length from the nonparticipant majority to force them to recognize their status as the untouchables of a health-conscious society. Were the exchequers of postindustrial countries ever to find it within their economic will to cut off the lucrative revenues that smokers contribute to the public finances every year, and were the health departments willing to pick up the pieces in terms of the numbers that would face traumatic withdrawal as a consequence, it would be understandable for the alien anthropologist to conclude that this was a drug that was gradually being made illegal in our societies, much as opium and cocaine were in the period leading up to the Great War. Nonetheless, tobacco remains available, the most acutely addictive substance (legal or illegal) in general use.

The swingeing increases in excise duty imposed each year on its clients are not, despite the protestations of all governments, intended to discourage its use, but represent a particularly efficacious way of exploiting dependency. If tobacco addiction was unambiguously considered to be a public health disaster requiring amelioration, it would be grotesque for the Treasury to be seen to profit from it, quite as if an annually inflated excise take could be applied to the insulin that diabetics need. And yet tobacco addiction is treated as an indispensable revenue stream. A durable urban myth of the post-sixties era has been that of the evil pusher who, offering some nameless white powder or candy-colored capsule to an ingenue at a party, assures her that it will make her feel "real good." Then, 24 hours later, once she is hooked for life, the extortion process begins. Applying hyperinflationary excise increases to tobacco every year is to do nothing other than this.

Tobacco has always had a rough ride, for one very obvious reason. It is the only psychoactive substance, in most Western countries, that may with legal impunity be smoked, and all smoke annoys the nonsmokers. Smoke inhalation is not quite the most historically recent method of ingesting intoxicants, the hypodermic syringe having only been invented in the mid-nineteenth century, but it is still a relative newcomer to Western societies. Columbus' sailors were the first Europeans to witness native Indian peoples smoking tobacco, although the first plants were not brought back to Spain until Oviedo's expedition to Mexico in 1519. By the close of the sixteenth century, pipe smoking was quite the rage, celebrated in the pentameters of philosophical poets as the fit pursuit of delicate and cultured sensibilities, and valued for its medicinal properties as virtually every new substance was on arrival. (When the Great Plague swept through Europe in the following century, tobacco was so highly valued as a specific against the Black Death that boys at Eton were severely chastised for not taking their morning pipes.) Tobacco had its detractors from the beginning, though, and for much the same reasons that the antismoking lobby of today regularly enunciates. The territory was most famously staked out by James I as early as 1604 in a pamphlet entitled "A Counterblast to Tobacco." There, he indicts the latest craze as

> a custome lathsome to the eye, hateful to the nose, harmeful to the braine, dangerous to the lungs, and the blacke stinking fume thereof, nearest resembling the horrible Stigian smoke of the pit that is bottomlesse.[6]

Modern antitobacco agitation can add little to this. What is curious is that it set a tone that has scarcely abated over the centuries. There is a feverishly enraged quality to much of the argument about controls on smoking that reaches apoplexy more rapidly than any indignation about illegal drug-use ever does. Heroin addicts may be poor fools, but tobacco addicts are inconsiderate slobs who must be ruthlessly pilloried for their weak-willed cravings. To some extent, this may be explained by the numbers of people tobacco addiction has caught in its legally sanctioned grip compared with opiates, and yet that doesn't quite fully account for the news stories of have-a-go train travelers who, finding that verbal haranguing is a pygmy's straw against the lone gasper defying the smoking ban, then resort to the fire extinguisher. A TV humorist who fell into the most notoriously virulent class of antismoking campaigners, the ex-smoker, once called for smokers at private functions to be imprisoned within a kind of giant bell-jar whenever they lit up until their noxious fumes had dispersed entirely within their own poisoned airspace. It isn't the influence on the user that is so violently objected to—smokers are much nicer people with nicotine in their systems than without—as the by-product of its use, now accused not merely of making everybody else's clothes smell rank, but of bequeathing emphysema, asthma and lung cancer to others in the form of exhaled smoke alive with hypertoxic free radicals.

Tobacco is a very old intoxicant, known to have been cultivated in South America since the early Neolithic period, up to 8,000 years ago. The native American strains of it have been used in shamanistic rituals more or less ever since (these indigenous forms being much more potent, indeed hallucinogenically so, than the contents of what the cigarette companies offer their customers), and it is now thought that the first cultivation of tobacco may have had no other purpose than as a drug crop, which would make it the earliest cultivated intoxicant of all. It was intuited very early on in its career that burning the plant released considerably greater concentrations of its active alkaloids, harman and norharman, in the form of smoke than were naturally available in the leaf. Thus did inhalation eventually take precedence over the multifarious other ways of ingesting it. These included chewing the leaves, drinking the expressed juice of the plant, which could also be boiled down to a syrup and molded into a paste that could then be licked or chewed or administered as a suppository.

The only alternatives to smoking tobacco that were translated to European societies with the first importation, and where they are both now all but extinct, were chewing it (which enjoyed more prolonged favor in the United States, as may be witnessed in the figure of the tirelessly ruminant Mayor in the Marlene Dietrich and James Stewart Wild West comedy *Destry Rides Again*) and snorting it. In Regency England, snuff—ground tobacco leaf that was sniffed into the nasal passages—was as finely calibrated an indicator of social standing as which club one belonged to or whom one knew. Exotically scented snuffs were used alongside an entire paraphernalia of little implements in a ritual to rival the precision of a Japanese tea ceremony, and yet for all its associations of rubicund old gents spluttering into silk handkerchiefs, snuff was not especially classbound. Cheap snuffs were used in great quantity by the laboring classes. When the habit all but disappeared in the twentieth century, it took with it the last visible vestiges of one of the most effective ways of taking dry powdered intoxicants. The reason that cocaine snorting is scarcely acceptable today even in noncensorious company is that nobody legally consumes any other solid substance by snuffling it into the nose.

More than with any other intoxicant, the prevalent ways of taking tobacco have always proved irritating and dirty to those who don't indulge. If it wasn't stale smoke hanging in the air, it was the sight of tobacco-chewers expectorating copiously into spittoons (or onto the floors of London buses) or it was snuff takers sneezing eruptively into their handkerchiefs. Tobacco can't ever seem to extricate itself from spit and snot and gurgling phlegm, the wrenching coughing-up of black blobs and the stained fingers and teeth of a lifetime's use. Its best chance to do so, the nicotine patch, has not proved conspicuously popular other than for smokers who have to grin and bear their way through some interminable nonsmoking function or arduous train journey. When used, as intended, as an aid to giving up, it is often felt to administer an infuriatingly gradual, low-level dose so that, in a nonprohibitive environment, the addict may find himself lighting up anyway to supplement the patch on his arm. The melancholy truth about tobacco is that, while it is not in its modest effects an antisocial drug, the ways of taking it are as toxic to social harmony as its alkaloids are in the user's respiratory system.

CANNABIS (dope |weed |hash |grass |puff |blow |draw |shit)

If the allure of the illicit substances is directly related, as a certain branch of tabloid thinking insists, to their being proscribed, so that—like contrary children drawn toward the cliff edge by a sign that says "Do not go too near the cliff edge"—we just can't stop ourselves from investigating them, then cannabis is of all of them the least likely drug to deliver the promised thrill of the forbidden. The last twenty years have seen it move inexorably into a legal twilight-zone of begrudging tolerance, especially in Europe. While recent British governments of officially divergent political tempers have adopted identically repressive attitudes to it (at least until 2001), increasing the maximum fine for possession by fivefold at a stroke, for example, the policy of the enforcement agencies on the streets has in some areas become so benign as to be almost Dutch in its rational permissiveness. (This is by no means the universal experience, however. In the smaller towns, it is still quite typical to have the book thrown at you for even a first count of possession, and school students may well have their records blotted for life.) Dope is openly smoked not just at cannabis legalization rallies, but at all sorts of less polemical gatherings. The liberal intelligentsia rallying in the city park for al fresco Haydn and a summer picnic have no qualms about skinning up for a digestive drag, while patrons of a social club just off London's Charing Cross Road were able, until a risibly overdone police swoop in 1998 put a stop to it, to buy bags of high-grade hydroponic skunk from a cashier at a hatchway on the top floor. It was just still possible to characterize cannabis in the 1960s as being the exclusive preserve of students and hippies, although the reality was already a deal more complex than that, as was shown by the all-walks-of-life nature of the list of signatories to the famous *Times* letter of 1967 that called for legal reform.

These days, though, dope is everywhere, not quite in your face perhaps but certainly not skulking behind society's bike sheds any longer. Its use is candidly referred to in the mass media, and the emerging evidence of its manifold medical applications—known to medical science for years, and to folk medicine for centuries—has inveigled it onto the news agenda in a way that simple arguments for the legalization of a relatively benign intoxicant never could have done. Even the lexicon has begun to seep through to mainstream discourse, so that those of an earlier generation to whom being "stoned" was another of the protean synonyms for alcohol inebriation are vaguely aware that it now has another, more specific meaning. If the appeal of drugs lies in their prohibited status, then we must expect that cannabis will soon be about as fascinating as a new set of tax guidelines.

The wild plant originated in central Asia, in the barren steppes of southern Siberia, at the paleobotanists' best current guess. Its thick-stemmed girth meant that it was cultivated for hemp fiber from a very early period, perhaps as far back as the Mesolithic, or Middle Stone Age, and records of such cultivation are found in China, India and western Asia, and eventually in Europe, where it probably arrived with silk along the Middle-Eastern trade routes. So versatile and reliable a fiber was hemp that it found itself pressed into service for everything from ships' rigging (an edict passed under Henry VIII demanded of English arable farmers that part of their land be set aside for the production of hemp to supply the needs of a prodigiously expanding naval power) to the noose that the hangman slipped around the necks of the condemned. In addition to this industrial use, cannabis was extensively used in all its regions of cultivation as a medicine. The earliest written record, dating from the third millennium B.C., appears in a medical encyclopedia compiled for the Chinese emperor Shen Nung. Culpeper's seventeenth-century herbal compendium cites cannabis as a specific against inflammations and all manner of unspecified aches and pains, knowledge he had almost certainly gleaned from the medicinal practices of country witches, and the plant was by then widely used in apothecarial preparations. George Washington is known to have grown some for his own personal medicinal use, while Queen Victoria's physician, John Reynolds, prescribed it to Her Majesty for the relief of menstrual discomfort. To medical science in the late Victorian era, cannabis—particularly its notably potent Indian species, *Cannabis indica*—was an indispensable cure-all, a view not uncommon among habitual recreational users today.

The leaves of the most common species, *Cannabis sativa,* which flourishes in the humid climates of southeast Asia, are widely used in the cooking of Thailand, Cambodia and Laos, imparting not only pungent flavor to green curries and soups, but a mild intoxicant effect as well. In classical Greece, the seeds were popularly nibbled after a banquet to counteract postprandial flatulence. Centuries earlier, the Chinese had pressed the oil from them for use as a cooking medium. The recipe for hash brownies given by Gertrude Stein's companion Alice B. Toklas in her celebrated cookbook have spawned a million space cakes and dope biscuits, eating the resin being the most spectacularly psychoactive method of ingesting the drug.

Much as with opium and tobacco, the psychoactive properties of cannabis were discovered and systematically exploited from a very early stage in human affairs. Archaeological investigations at two early Bronze Age sites in eastern Europe have identified the charred remains of hemp seeds in pipes made expressly for smoking it, showing that ritual use of cannabis as an intoxicant dates back at least as far as the third millennium B.C. in Europe, and presumably to even earlier in its Asian heartlands. For a long time, it was the Scythians, a nomadic people of the Black Sea area, who were credited with bringing cannabis to Europe (a superseded theory still propagated by Terence McKenna in *Food of the Gods*). Their claim for this achievement rested on the vivid account given by classical Greece's preeminent historian, Herodotus, in the fifth century B.C. He witnessed a rudimentary form of pipeless cannabis smoking among the Scythian people, and describes it with all the transfixed fascination of an ecotourist vacationing in a foreign culture:

> On a framework of tree sticks, meeting at the top, they stretch pieces of woollen cloth. Inside this tent they put a dish with hot stones on it. Then they take some hemp seed, creep into the tent, and throw the seed on the hot stones. At once it begins to smoke, giving off a vapour unsurpassed by any vapour bath one could find in Greece. The Scythians enjoy it so much they howl with pleasure.[7]

We may assume he was sorely tempted.

Precisely for the very reason that the plant is so adaptable, it is one of the most widely used illicit substances in the world, playing a fully legitimized role as ghanja in the Rastafarian religion of Jamaica, while fueling first the Black jazz culture of Prohibition-era America and then the Beat movement of the 1950s. It was the drug of choice for sixties dropouts until LSD steamed into view, and has made an unpredictable return to favor among sections of youth culture who in the late 1970s, when punk rock officially reviled it as the zombifying elixir of hippie slobs, had previously shunned it in favor of more pertinently aggressive stimulants. One of my respondents had a cannabis plant growing on the windowsill of his Civil Service office in the 1970s, unremarked on by his supervisor but for its charmlessly scrawny look. If current research succeeds, as expected, in establishing once and for all its efficacy in the symptomatic relief of glaucoma, multiple sclerosis, arthritis and the depredations of AIDS, so that to continue to deny it to sufferers from those conditions will be tantamount to administrative cruelty, then cannabis is clearly likely to return to the medical mainstream, for all that—as a Schedule 1 drug—it exercises in politicians a potential for superstitious terror that would have mystified Mr. Culpeper. It is, famously, the one proscribed drug that is demonstrably less physically damaging than the permitted ones, tobacco and alcohol.

Years of research have so far produced only the suggestions that it increases the heart rate, which may in certain cases be dangerous, has a mildly obstructive effect on the respiratory function, though to nothing like the extent that tobacco smoke does, and more recently, that it may depress the functioning of the immune system. This last finding is still at a highly speculative stage, but if borne out, may well have implications for cannabis users who already have impaired immunity levels. Despite its relatively benign toxicological status, though, the legislative hue-and-cry over cannabis that was provoked as a toxic by-product of the international conferences on the opium trade in the 1910s and 1920s managed to cast it in an extraordinarily disfiguring light.

Part of the problem in deciding the likely social effects of permitting cannabis intoxication is the multiform methodology of its use over the years. Eating the resin is a profoundly mind-altering experience, less of a roller coaster than hallucinogens like LSD or psilocybin are prone to be, but powerfully hypnotic and disorientating nonetheless. The impact of smoking it depends heavily on the type and quantity of material used, and the implements with which the smoke is administered. Inhaling it through water cools and softens its entry into the throat, thus permitting deeper ingestion, and paraphernalia designed for this method range from simple small pipes with a water chamber—the hubbly-bubbly pipe of many a sixties dope den—to elaborate contrivances that are the true heirs of the nineteenth-century hookah. An especially sensual delivery is given by a friend or sexual partner blowing a mouthful of inhaled smoke down your own throat, while a "blowback" involves inhaling the smoke deeply from a joint that is held back to front in the partner's mouth. Anyone offered a "hot knife" at a civilized gathering will be treated to a bottleful of smoke created by sizzling a pellet of dope resin between a pair of red-hot knives. The smoke is gulped down in one fell swoop like an oyster. All these techniques are about maximizing the uptake of mellow swimmy-headedness that cannabis is chiefly about. To an unlucky few, the effect instantly produces the kind of nausea suffered during travel sickness, and it can be lethally emetic if mixed with too much alcohol. To the great majority of those who use it, dope is a deeply relaxing unwinder, more immediately efficient in the task than alcohol, productive of sensuous calm and arousing a hunger that must be satisfied like an itch crying out to be scratched. Although it is theoretically a peaceable experience, it does excite the most acute opprobrium in its detractors. In what was for some years the official text (long since disowned by both its authors) of the then defunct punk movement, it is confidently stated by Julie Burchill and Tony Parsons that

> Dope-smoking produces sluggishness, silliness, a mouth that tastes like a Turk's turd, and increases the appetite to such proportions that prolonged smoking results in gross obesity.[8]

Gross obesity, for Terence McKenna, would seem a risk worth taking in light of its other properties:

> It diminishes the power of ego, has a mitigating effect on competitiveness, causes one to question authority, and reinforces the notion of the merely relative importance of social values.[9]

It will be seen that these assessments are not necessarily mutually exclusive, for all that the obituarists of punk might have enjoyed a laugh at the idea that dope-smokers are in a fit state to question any-thing more adversarial than the speaking clock, let alone authority. McKenna's argument about the "merely relative importance of social values" is a provocative one, though. He also credits cannabis with the socially enlightening trend to long hair for men in the 1960s, as the drug released a flow of planet-saving femininity in them. His point is that cannabis has the power to subvert the entrenched and tragically restricting social forms that bind us all too tight, which is why the authorities therefore feel they must deny it to us. My own view is that this is a distinctly overheated estimate of the drug's normal capabilities. Far from calling forth the kind of rest-lessly questioning intelligence that caffeine did in the seventeenth century, cannabis seems instead to pour a honeyed salve over one's dissatisfactions, smoothing down ruffled feathers to make it all seem more bearable again. It is not in its effects an antisocial drug, but ingested in quantity, it is a *de*socializing one. On my last visit to Amsterdam, in the autumn of 1997, I was struck by just how little meaningful communication goes on in the coffee shops of the War-moesstraat. A sense of bland contentment hovered in the air with the thickening smoke, the viscerally familiar ambient low-down dub of Portishead's *Dummy* album played on an endless loop, and the man who had opened the Sunday paper on the table in front of him pretty soon couldn't be bothered reading the food reviews. The eyes drift out of focus as the Acapulco Gold kicks in. "Every little thing," as Bob Marley once insisted, "is gonna be all right."

To the nonparticipant, the state of being stoned looks merely like bombed-out apathy, which creates its own sorts of friction. Nonetheless, if any of the controlled substances is ever relegalized, this will be the one. When the enforcement authorities have been weaned away from their article-of-faith belief that the use of so-called soft drugs soon creates a fearful craving for the harder variety, it will be relatively easy to countenance cannabis intoxication as a perennial state among their client populations. Of all drug scare-stories, that surrounding cannabis was always the least readily cred-ible. In 1952, an intrepid barrister called Donald Johnson went undercover into a London bebop club to investigate for a Sunday newspaper the reputedly salacious goings-on among users of what he called Indian hemp. Scarcely had he got through the door and been assailed by the arhythmic caterwauling of the saxophones, it seems, than his worst fears were confirmed. The scene that met his eyes was a nightmare of miscegenation, as Black males—anthropologized as "colored" in the vocabulary of the period—were seen gyrating lubriciously with white girls rendered malleable and drooling-daft with hemp:

> In a corner five coloured musicians with their brows perspiring played bebop music with extraordinary fervour. Girls and coloured partners danced with an abandon—a savagery almost— which was both fascinating and embarrassing. From a doorway came a coloured man, flinging away the end of a strange cigarette. He danced peculiar convulsions of his own, then bounced on to a table and held out shimmering arms to a girl. My contact indicated photographs on the wall. They were of girls in the flimsiest drapings. I had seen my first bebop club, its coloured peddlers, its half-crazed, uncaring girls.[10]

And lived to tell the tale. The Presbyterian indignation that suppurates from every pore of this account is by no means a dead language in the West even as the new century dawns, but the terror intended to be invoked by the prospect of drug-crazed Negroes making free with our girls has resonances of the opium panics of the Edwardian period. It isn't just garbage now, it was garbage then, as its author would have known perfectly well. To those familiar now with the foggy tranquillity of being stoned, the disappointing truth is that cannabis just isn't as exciting as that.

AMPHETAMINE (speed \whizz \Billy \sulphate \bombers \bennies \blueys \dexies \pep pills)

For excitability, one has to turn to stimulants, as many did in the early 1960s, having discovered in amphetamine a drug that had demonstrable functional applicability in the way they lived their lives. Among commonly used street drugs, amphetamine is most obviously the diametrical antithesis of cannabis. Where the weed is a natural plant substance, a source of mellow contentment to the habitual user, and imbued with a range of therapeutic benefits, speed is a synthetic chemical invented in a laboratory, a dirty white powder full of noxious adulterants that makes the user aggressive and obsessive, leaves a feeling of deflating, miserable fatigue in its wake and has only a decidedly ambiguous repertoire of medical indications. It also imparts, at its best, an exhilarating onrush of yappy, happy stimulation, and as its street name promises, it speeds up a life that has crawled along through the five drear days of the working week into a fast-forwarding, breathless thrill. To urban youths balancing the demands of gainful employment with the lure of a weekend on the town, speed fulfilled something of the function that ecstasy was to deliver to their eighties' and nineties' descendants. It was a way of capitalizing fully on what little leisure time their normal routines permitted them. Later, it was to be the house drug of the punk period, partly because it revved up the spiky-haired masses into the apt level of righteous impatience with the torpor of a music industry in the shameful throes of middle-aged spread, and partly because it supposedly made you aggressive, which is what the Sex Pistols sounded like they were. Its self-evident appeal to a teenager starting out on illicit substances was that it apparently did the opposite of what all the familiar intoxicants (including that first queasy drag on someone else's joint) tended to do—i.e., knock you out. To the depressed housewife stuck at home in a world of dirty laundry, it made the treadmill suddenly fly round.

Amphetamine was first synthesized in Germany in 1887, but the first serious research into its possible medical applications didn't take place for another forty years. As soon as it was discovered that it appeared to imitate the action of the body's own natural stimulant norepinephrine in the brain, leading to heightened mental activity and a powerful surge of physical energy, it was used in the treatment of narcolepsy. Before too long, it was being dispensed in lower doses as a general pick-me-up or as an endurance pill for those who had to work long hours. Sir Anthony Eden, British Prime Minister of the early 1950s, confessed after his fall from office that the only thing that had kept him going in 1952 during the Suez crisis that was the unmaking of him was a constant supply of Benzedrine. Nearly all the major combatants in the Second World War issued it to their troops to give them stamina, but also just to keep up their morale. Hitler himself subsisted on several daily injections of methylamphetamine, with extra pills to fill the spaces in between shots (a gruesome regimen for a man with probable Parkinson's disease), but British soldiers in the field also consumed a reported 72 million tablets during the hostilities. The American Army was to outdo even this rate of intake during the Vietnam period. No fighting force in military history has ever been so freely provided with controlled substances. Rumors persisted at the time that the injections that Chinese government troops were given immediately prior to the 1989 massacre of pro-democracy demonstrators in Tiananmen Square were of amphetamine.

When the troops were demobilized after the war, they brought the taste for pep pills back home with them. Until the 1960s, amphetamine was fairly freely prescribed by doctors for anything from mild depression to obesity. As well as being a stimulant and an appetite suppressant, the drug also has the effect of dilating the bronchial sacs in the lungs, meaning that anybody suffering from bronchial congestion, whether through asthma, hay fever or just a heavy cold, found that it helped to clear the airways. Patented amphetamine inhalers could be bought over the counter in pharmacies and also in corner-store groceries. If you couldn't get hold of a ready supply of black-market amphetamine pills for the weekend, such as Benzedrine, Dexedrine, Durophet or, best of all, Drinamyl—an ingenious 50–50 mix of amphetamine and barbiturate known on the streets as purple hearts—the next best thing was to buy a benzedrine inhaler. It could be opened by taking a fretsaw to it, and inside was a rolled-up wad of what looked like blotting-paper that was saturated with a massive concentration of the drug. Caution was advised: to soak a whole one of these in a drink was a colossal overdose.

The speed mania of the fifties and sixties was the first and, until the advent of ecstasy in the late 1980s, the most dynamic drug craze of the postwar years. Everybody wanted it. When doctors were finally encouraged to stop prescribing it so freely, they were told that official thinking now insisted it was a highly dangerous drug with addictive potential. The genie, however, was out of the bottle and flying around. When the pills were no longer available and even the inhaler was banned, street dealers took to either breaking into pharmacies or, even more straightforwardly, making it themselves. It isn't an especially difficult drug to manufacture, and there are other amphetamine substitutes, such as diethylproprion and duromine, in general circulation that can be used in the preparation of bathtub speed.

In a particularly unfathomable move in the 1960s, the British government stopped GPs from prescribing heroin and methadone to registered addicts, the suggested alternative being methylamphetamine or Methedrine, the awesomely powerful version of speed that had helped to make Hitler so sweetly reasonable. In a TV drug documentary of 1998, surviving opiate addicts of the period who were briefly switched to Methedrine for a few months while it was the recommended experimental dose recalled its searing intravenous assault on the system with evocative shudders. It was all set to become a social disaster of horrible magnitude when it was itself withdrawn, and is thought to have been the only drug with abuse potential that has ever been therapeutically disseminated into the community, and then successfully retracted without having left an eternal black market in its wake.

In the UK, speed is still the second most popular illegal drug on the streets after cannabis (in America, by contrast, it is held in contempt as a peculiarly crude affectation of the Brits). Doctors still prescribe it, or its chemical analogues, in fairly heroic quantities to tackle obesity, and one of my respondents told me that he has the only legitimate amphetamine prescription in his county—not for obesity or narcolepsy, but because he went to the GP and said, "I can't live without speed." A new generation seems to have arisen that is surprisingly squeamish about the idea of snorting, which was the classic method of taking the powdered form, assuming you were too sensible to get mixed up with needles. The preferred route of administration now is to wrap a quarter gram or so in a bit of cigarette paper and swallow it. This is known as "doing a bomb," or "bombing it," and is certainly a more discreet strategy in a public place, but is considerably less efficient in terms of delivery since it means the drug has to be metabolized through the digestive system rather than being introduced more or less directly into the bloodstream.

The Controlled Substances Act of 1970 made amphetamine a Schedule II drug, in recognition of the fact that it had some limited medical applications (and it correspondingly appears in Class B of the British drug legislation, unless it is prepared for injection, in which case it becomes Class A, recognizing perhaps, however crudely, that almost any drug becomes potentially addictive when administered intravenously). Amphetamine is not in itself a physically addictive drug in the sense that the opiates are, but the delivery of big shouty happiness, even euphoria, that it offers about ten minutes after snorting it is so gorgeously removed from mundane everyday consciousness that the urge to maximize it even further is strong indeed. Ultrarefined examples, such as base speed, ice or southeast Asian yabba, produce a stimulant jolt that initially appears to crush the diaphragm with its intensity before gasping elation sets in.

Speed is a sociable drug for the very obvious reason that it makes the user immensely cheerful and chatty. It is profoundly unsociable when it wears off, and the body begins the tiresome process of restoring its depleted energy reserves. To the novice, the comedown can be pitiful, a lethal, haunted combination of sleeplessness and depression, aching and complete immobilization. Taken to excess, which is the measure that all medical authorities insist on using when assessing the social impact of any drug, it induces over time a jittering state of paranoia known as amphetamine psychosis. In low doses, it can apparently be tolerated by the body on a more or less daily basis. To decide whether amphetamine is socially disruptive involves deciding whether it is undesirable for people to be in a state of energetic alertness, as opposed to unruffled quiescence. The culture of speed is not alternative because the drug itself is illegal; it is so because, short of engaging in competitive athletics, to be bursting with combative, restless energy is not considered our natural estate.

COCAINE (coke |Charlie |snow |toot |nose candy |Bolivian marching powder)

Of all the commonly used street drugs in the West, cocaine is the one that has had perhaps the most colorfully varied career. Its cultural positioning has been subject to continual transformation during the course of the twentieth century, and the client groups it has found itself attached to in society have been more fascinatingly heterogeneous than is the case for any other mainstream illicit substance. While officially viewed as being on the same level of hideous rapacity as heroin in its psychological and physiological fallout, it is used by increasing numbers as if it were of no more consequence than smoking dope. Its street price, together with the fact that, as a white powder, it is as easy to adulterate as any other white powder, mean that poor-quality cocaine is the worst-value drug in the world, and yet it came back to social prominence in the 1990s on both sides of the Atlantic with a far greater social reach than would have been thought possible a generation ago. There is, I believe, one overriding reason for the broadly based appeal of cocaine, quite apart from the economics of the drug market and the cultural politics of drugs as status symbols. It is that, of all the substances discussed in this chapter, the sensations offered by snorting cocaine are the most modestly tame of any.

Cocaine is derived from two principal species of the coca plant, *Erythroxylum coca* and *E. novagranatense,* which grow wild in the tropical rain-forests of northern South America—Bolivia, Peru, Colombia and Ecuador. It has been used by native Indian peoples for centuries, by chewing wads of the leaves mixed with some alkaline ash in order to release the active compound. It is an endurance drug, aiding physical labor in the unforgiving heat of the tropical day, and it is also, like the synthetic amphetamine, a vasodilator, expanding the air sacs in the lungs and facilitating easy breathing in the rarefied sky-high atmosphere in which these mountain communities live. Ronald K. Siegel once found a pottery shard on an archaeological dig in the environs of Lake Titicaca in Peru that appeared to depict the origins of the native discovery of coca, attributed in their folk narratives to a sacred llama, Napa, that acquainted humans with its benefits. The pottery fragment evidently depicted an awestruck Indian observing the bulging-cheeked llama feeding at the branches of what was recognizably coca, himself reaching out toward the plant in astonished imitation. The shard was never properly dated before it was spirited away by a mercurial museum curator whom Siegel consulted, but it was certainly several centuries old, and is believed to have commemorated an event that took place as far back as pre-Inca times, perhaps 7,000 years ago.

It is known that coffee was effectively discovered when an Abyssinian farmer noticed his animals becoming frolicsome after eating the berries of the *Coffea* plant, and the stimulant properties of *qat,* the Middle-Eastern shrub that is also chewed in its region of origin to promote physical stamina and mental alertness, were similarly stumbled upon when a Yemeni goatherd saw his goats romping about on it. Even Noah, in one version of his story, finds out the intoxicating properties of fermented grapes by watching the crazy behavior of an inebriated goat. Wherever there is an intoxicant to be discovered in antiquity, it would seem, there is a possessed goat to point the way. Siegel's shard may just have been the missing link that established once and for all that intoxication behavior was learned by humanity from the animals in distant prehistory.

When the Spanish conquistadores arrived in South America, their first instinct as European colonists was to try to stamp out the use of coca among their latest subject populations, but they rapidly discovered they had shot themselves in the foot when they realized that depriving the Inca mine-worker of his staple stimulant impaired his productivity in the gold and silver mines. Coca was swiftly reinstated. The Spanish brought it back to Europe with them, but whereas many other of their imports, such as tomatoes, chilli peppers, chocolate and tobacco, caught on like the hot new fashions they were, coca never did, largely because the psychoactivity of the leaves rapidly breaks down once they dry out.

It was not until the mid-nineteenth century in Germany that the alkaloid in the leaves was isolated, and the process for refining it perfected by a Göttingen University chemist, Albert Niemann. In 1880, its potential as a powerful local anesthetic was discovered by a Russian doctor, von Anrep, and it entered the pharmacopoeia. Its first and greatest medical champion was Sigmund Freud, who published a paper in 1884, "On Coca," in which he argued that, while there was an identifiable danger of physical wastage and "moral depravity" in excessive use of the drug, its benefits far outweighed this peripheral risk. He used it enthusiastically himself, perhaps partly because he viewed it as an aphrodisiac, among other things, and believed that it would prove useful in treating cases of morphine addiction that had reached critical levels over the preceding 30 years, following the invention of the hypodermic syringe. Freud began dispensing it freely, both intravenously and orally, and within the year had created the first European cocaine addict out of his colleague Dr. von Fleischl, who had previously been hooked on morphine. Nothing daunted, Freud continued to prescribe cocaine, although he moved discreetly away from intravenous administration after confidently announcing that there was no such thing as a cocaine overdose and then promptly killing one of his patients with one.

Barely two years after the publication of "On Coca," Freud stood accused by another colleague, Dr. Erlenmeyer, of having single-handedly invented a new type of addiction in adding to the existing dual typology of opiate dependency and alcoholism the previously unknown phenomenon of cocainism. Freud reluctantly retracted some of the basis of his original arguments, but continued to believe that cocaine could still prove the Holy Grail in curing other forms of addiction. In a statement that now reverberates with world-historical significance, he avowed in a paper of 1887 that cocaine addiction was to be attributed not to "the direct result of imbibing a noxious drug, but to some peculiarity in the patient." This was the twinkle in the eye that would become psychoanalysis, the pseudo-science that made the reputation of a mediocre Viennese medical researcher, where cocaine and the hunt for addiction cures so spectacularly failed.

As cocaine's reputation as a pick-me-up spread abroad, it became hugely fashionable in a number of forms. We have already noted its inclusion, at least for the first 17 years of the patent recipe, in Coca-Cola, and there was an adults-only French product that rose to international ascendancy even quicker than Coke. Vin Mariani was a wine-based drink that contained an infusion of graded coca leaves. Launched in 1863, it was the invention of a Corsican chemist, Angelo Mariani, who promoted it as a health-giving tonic drink that refreshed the weary body and nourished the mind. By the close of the century, it was being drunk and wholeheartedly endorsed by political leaders, popes and royalty the world over. William McKinley, the last American president to be assassinated before Kennedy, adored it, as did Queen Victoria and Pope Leo XIII, who awarded Mariani a papal medal in honor of the wine's achievements as a "benefactor of humanity." The product's endorsement book, which is now in the British Library, runs to some thirteen volumes of rhapsodic tribute, most couched in terms that seem astonishing for a product that has since been totally forgotten. A French cardinal, Lavigerie, wrote of Vin Mariani, "Your coca from America gave my

European priests the strength to civilise Asia and Africa." It must have been good stuff, then. It fell foul, however, of the developing mood of prohibition in the USA. Cocaine itself was at this time quite legal, and was sold in dissolved form in medicines and as little bottles of white powder for snorting. Some of these "cold snuffs" were pure cocaine, explicitly advertised as being up to 200 times stronger than coca leaf.

One such American product, Birney's Catarrh Remedy, containing a high proportion of cocaine, became the downfall of Annie C. Meyers, Chicago arts patron, wealthy widow and author of the first drug confessional work to be written by a woman, *Eight Years in Cocaine Hell* (1902). Mrs. Meyers became so dependent on Birney's that she emptied her bank account, became a shoplifter and forged checks in order to obtain an interminable supply of it. She had to talk her way out of several arrests, on one occasion fleeing to a roof and only agreeing to come down when the police officer sent up a bottle of cocaine tied to the end of a length of string. At the height of her addiction, she was snorting about every five minutes, scarcely eating or sleeping but devoting all her mental energies to working out ways of raising money for the next batch. She sold stolen jewelry and furs for a fraction of their retail value. She yanked a gold tooth out of her mouth and sold that.

When she was arrested for the final time in the course of ineptly trying to dynamite a safe, she writes, "It would be hard to conceive of a more repulsive sight" than cocaine had reduced her to. Her teeth had gone, she was virtually bald, her upper jaw was gangrenous and her face and large tracts of her body had ulcerated, while her gaze had the persecuted, ghostly pallor of classic stimulant psychosis. She was down to about five and a half stones. Extraordinarily enough, she was to recover, in a sanatorium where the medical treatment was interspersed with religious exhortation. Her book established a literary genre, and her case helped to outlaw cocaine.

Not long after it was published, Coca-Cola removed the coca from its product, and Mariani retired hurt from the American market. He died in 1914, believing to the last that the world was deluded, that coca—unlike refined cocaine—was a wholesome panacea and not the villain of the piece at all. He was of course right, but that year the federal government enacted the Harrison Narcotics Act that made a start on curbing the availability of the major intoxicants, and America, seduced by the tantalizing prospect of total prohibition now hovering in the middle distance, was no longer in the mood to listen to reason.

Cocaine scandals also came to London at this time. The grisly suicides of two struggling stage actresses, Edith and Ida Yeoland, in 1901 from brain-rupturing overdoses of cocaine brought the drug question into the public eye as never before, but—as in the USA—over-the-counter sales of heroin, morphine and cocaine were subject to license but still perfectly legal. One of the chief ramifications of the Yeolands' case was that it focused attention on the degree to which impressionable girls in the theatrical profession were being seduced into dabbling in lives of vice by associating with the louche West End underground, in which organized crime was as much a feature of the alternative lifestyle as a taste for exotic intoxicants was. The opium dens of the Chinese community in the Limehouse area of east London, together with the cocaine-sniffing decadence of the Soho clubs, were thought to be sapping the moral integrity of girls who worked in a theater world that was changing beyond recognition from the genteel Shakespearean elegances of Mrs. Patrick Campbell's heyday.

When the Great War broke out, such fripperies were considered the more tasteless, and the enactment of paragraph 40B of the Defence of the Realm Act, universally known as DORA 40B, in 1916 became the first piece of UK legislation to make mere possession of controlled substances a criminal offense. Cocaine in particular, for all that Conan Doyle had Sherlock Holmes injecting himself with the stuff in order to oil the wheels of cogitation in more than one of his stories, was seen as the drug of silly overpaid girls with too much time on their hands. Just as it would shortly become in the nascent days of Hollywood, it was portrayed as the lure by which unscrupulous fixers could bend the tittering starlets to their will, and the scandal sheets soon had their most incandescent sacrificial victim in the beautiful young stage star Billie Carleton. Carleton had enjoyed a rocketlike rise to fame, was the youngest and one of the most highly paid leading ladies on the West End stage and was poised to go into the movies when she died alone, age 22, apparently of a cocaine overdose in her apartment in the Savoy buildings. Her story is meticulously and eloquently related by Marek Kohn, who surmises, convincingly, that not the least malodorous aspect of the investigations following her death was the confiscation of a box containing the barbiturate veronal by a infatuated doctor friend of hers, Frederick Stuart, who had supplied it to her. Stuart had unethically appointed himself Carleton's financial manager, and may well have feared that if her death were to be attributed to a barbiturate overdose rather than cocaine, he might find himself arraigned for manslaughter. Kohn's suggestion is that Carleton overdosed herself with veronal attempting to get to sleep after a long, excitable, coked-up day that had culminated in her going to the lavish society Victory Ball at the Albert Hall, held two weeks after the Armistice.

The autopsy was inconclusive and resulted in a prolonged court-room clash between conflicting medical theories, as a result of which the truth almost certainly slipped through the net. By then, the showbiz press and the popular prints had already run away with the story that Carleton was the tormented victim of evil drug-pushers, who had crushed her in the relentless tentacles of cocaine. The story ran and ran, enduring well into the post–Second World War period as a cautionary tale of how getting mixed up with drugs could only end in tragedy, long after anybody who absorbed this propaganda would have been able to say who on earth she was.

What did in cocaine in Britain after the emergency wartime regulations solidified into the Dangerous Drugs Act of 1920 was partly the restricted availability of the drug (which wasn't in itself wholly effective because the world's leading cocaine industry, Germany, refused to accept many of the American-sponsored international controls on it), but more appositely the sudden medical championing of amphetamine in the 1930s. Those who could remember the cocaine rush must have been quite struck by the harder, more jagged but indubitably more sustained lift that the new pep-pills delivered.

Cocaine's comeback in the 1970s, after the hippie era had been outlived, was very much a class-based affair. Its aura of elite unaffordability made it the drug of choice among semiretired West Coast rock musicians and their associates, and a fashion for expensive paraphernalia with which to ingest it became the norm. If you didn't have a jewel-encrusted coke spoon to shovel it up, you rolled up a hundred-dollar bill. Thus did the drug look like being the exclusive last redoubt of those who felt too sedately middle-aged to tolerate anything else. In the 1980s, it found its way into the financial world, amid reports that the fortunes that were being made in frenetic futures trading on Wall Street and in the City of London were fueled by brains rendered hyperactive by mounds of snorted cocaine. Then, like all commodities that become plentifully available, it began overflowing from the pockets of the well-to-do and spilled out onto the street. Soon, every working-class kid who'd been suckled on speed had now traded up to Charlie. The street price moderated, then dropped a bit, and the purity started weakening. Exactly the same thing happened at exactly the same time to champagne. Bumper vintages in the early eighties led to a juddering price plunge, and the world's most expensive sparkling wine started flowing down throats that had previously only ever encountered it at weddings.

The fruits of overindulgence in cocaine are as ghastly as Annie C. Meyers could attest. Even moderate continual use over a period of years has the excruciating effect of eroding the nasal septum, with the result that the stories, long thought to be mere legend, of cocaine users sneezing long trails of frazzled cartilage out of their noses one day are quite true. The drug mixes very uneasily with other substances: it reduces the aftereffects of ecstasy to a sort of jumpy paranoia, and it combines particularly toxically with alcohol to form a by-product called coca-ethanol that leaves a vile feeling of nervy melancholy when the two primary intoxicants recede. None of this has the power to deter, however, because the drug itself seems so unassumingly mild in its effects. The first hit of the evening can deliver a cozy low-voltage buzz of electricity that the second one might enhance. Its cycle of duration, though, is pitifully short, so that more is required far earlier than is the case with amphetamine. It is a perfect capitalist construct in this sense, delivering tormentingly brief satisfaction that requires further lavish expenditure to sustain it. Eventually, its effect is virtually undetectable, the snorted lines merely producing copious mucal evacuation and a fine film of stale sweat all over the body. But just because of its price and its newfound cross-class ubiquity, it has become one of the most effort-lessly saleable drugs in common use. If cocaine were ever relegalized, PR companies would kill each other for the account.

HEROIN (smack |skag |horse |junk |shit |China white |brown)

If cocaine is an easily promotable commodity, heroin has for most of its time as a street drug been at the opposite end of the attractiveness spectrum, at least to those who have not hitherto come into contact with it. Almost superstitiously shunned for its associations of rank addictiveness and diseased squalor, it occupies an intoxicological category all its own, standing as the permanently irreducible sign of a dangerous drug. When concerned authorities talked about Drugs, the Drug Menace or the War on Drugs, these collective, hypostatized Drugs they were talking about had until very recently the lineaments of heroin alone. To be "hooked on drugs" meant being addicted to heroin, to be "hopped up to the eyeballs on drugs" was to be in the grip of heroin's opiate stupor, to be experiencing the trauma of "coming off drugs" was to be going through the agonies of heroin withdrawal. Although ecstasy and, to a lesser extent, cocaine have now elbowed their way onto the news agenda, subtly altering that crudely undifferentiated model, the resurgence of heroin use among working-class youth in the early eighties, and again (though less vis-ibly) in the late nineties, meant that the terror of the Drug Menace was still inextricably bound up with the spectacle of heroin depend-ency. What could be more antisocial than dirty needles, flattened lives orientated solely toward satisfying cravings that refuse to go away, and—most appositely—the cycle of crime that it generates as the requirement for greater and greater financial outlay to sustain the habit acquires its own relentless momentum?

Heroin is derived from the opium poppy, *Papaver somniferum,* which seems to have originated somewhere along the northern shores of the Mediterranean. Archaeological evidence of its ritual use in Europe as far back as the Neolithic—perhaps even as early as 8000 B.C.—is plentiful and persuasive. Not only was it used medici-nally for its potent analgesic properties, but the dreamlike state induced by inhaling the smoke of its congealed and dried sap appears to have been among the very earliest examples of systematic intoxication in human history, almost certainly predating alcohol. The discovery of opium poppy capsules at a Spanish site have been dated to around 4200 B.C., and later finds have included charred pipes of fairly elaborate construction and decoration from the late Bronze Age (circa 1200 B.C.) on Cyprus. By the classical period, the use of opium was familiar enough to be described in pharmacological detail by the third-century B.C. Greek naturalist Theophrastus. Not only were its medicinal powers known by this time, but its potential for creating dependency had been warned against two centuries earlier by a medical theorist, Erasistratus.

The next great development was the invention of laudanum, a tincture of opium in alcohol, by the sixteenth-century medical writer Paracelsus. Laudanum (its name is Latin for "praiseworthy") was optimistically held to be effective in the relief of mania among psychologically disturbed individuals, but only worked in this context in the sense that the patient became too stupefied to throw fits. In the relief of all sorts of physical anguish from dental pain to neuralgia and the yowling of distressed babies, laudanum reigned supreme until well after the Great War. (At the time of writing, it is still technically available for prescribing by British doctors.) Its use was widespread as a recreational drug and stimulant to the aesthetic faculty by the English Romantic poets of the early nineteenth century, Coleridge, Shelley, Byron and Keats all being aficionados. The classic text of this period, to which we shall return in chapter 7, is Thomas de Quincey's *Confessions of an English Opium-Eater,* a candid account of personal disintegration through addiction that set the tone for drug confessions right up to the present day. As well as the physical ravages his weakness for the tincture wrought in him, de Quincey also frankly tells us what a warmly reassuring part it played in his months of seclusion in the Lake District in 1816. Inviting his artist addressee to sketch a homey picture of his idealized interior there, replete with tea-tray set by the fireside, he enjoins the painter not to leave out the all-important tipple:

> As to the opium, I have no objection to see a picture of *that,* though I would rather see the original: you may paint it, if you choose; but I apprize you, that no "little" receptacle would, even in 1816, answer *my* purpose . . . No: you may as well paint the

real receptacle, which was not of gold, but of glass, and as much like a wine-decanter as possible. Into this you may put a quart of ruby-colored laudanum: that, and a book of German metaphysics placed by its side, will sufficiently attest my being in the neighborhood . . .[11] [his emphases]

What de Quincey achieved in this, his most celebrated work, was a retrospective glance at the dissolution he has now survived, but one that doesn't feel constrained to abominate his earlier life as incomprehensibly alien to him. There is a distinct tone of wistful pining for the simplicities of it all, and that stands in the place of the older, sadder and wiser mode that we expect from today's outpourings.

Opium was at the root of what remains one of the most scandalous episodes in British colonial history, when the Royal Navy was used to protect the illicit trade in opium from occupied India to China by the East India Company. Two naval wars were fought, 1839–42 and 1856–60, in order to keep opium flowing into China by the hundredweight in defiance of Chinese imperial decree, the first ending in the Treaty of Nanking that ceded Hong Kong to the UK on lease until 1997. It wasn't as if the British thought they were engaged in the innocent trafficking of a harmless commodity. The very opium they were selling to the Chinese, 1 percent of whose population was thought to have been addicted to it by this stage, was denied as a pernicious toxin to Britain's own subject peoples in India. The shop-soiled argument used by traders in all dubious commodities down the centuries—that if we don't sell it to them, somebody else will, so we may as well clean up—was the homily used to justify the opium trade by the East India Company. As drug-runners jealous of their markets to the extent of killing to defend them, their tenacity in keeping the trade going was unparalleled until the advent of the Colombian cocaine cartels. The Chinese tried everything to disrupt it, including staging barbaric exemplary executions of opium dealers in full view of Western merchants and their families taking the air in Canton, but they were not to be deterred. The international conferences aimed at stemming the trade in drugs such as opium and cocaine in the early years of the twentieth century eventually put paid to the opium trade, but the habit had now become so firmly rooted in Chinese society that when immigrants started moving to the USA and then Britain in search of a more lucrative life in the West, they took the opium habit with them. It has never gone home.

What complicated the picture further was the isolation of opium's active principle, morphine, and its further synthetic refinement into heroin. Morphine was first separated out of opium in 1805 by a German chemist, Sertürner. In the strange logic of nineteenth-century pharmacology, it was proposed that morphine treatment might be the answer to addiction to laudanum, much as cocaine was later to be promoted as the antidote to morphine addiction. Morphine was at first swallowed in the form of medicinal syrups, but the perfection of the hypodermic syringe in 1853 by Alexander Wood of Edinburgh opened up a whole new method of administration. So enthusiastically was the new technology taken up by all and sundry that Wood's own wife became the first recorded fatality from an intravenous overdose.

Nor was injection confined to medical contexts. Within the circles of the novelty-hungry beau monde in France and Britain, self-administered injection became quite the thing. Ladies particularly, for whom riotous drinking was not a social option, had customized syringes made, with which they might whack themselves up with morphine during an interval at the ballet. If pressure of circumstance meant they couldn't get away for a moment's privacy, they became adept—if such a thing can be imagined—at surreptitiously injecting themselves in the hands while appearing to be merely toying with some bejeweled trinket. An item from a popular weekly magazine cited in 1902 in a report in the British Medical Journal referred to the craze for morphine tea parties, at which a society hostess would invite acquaintances around for tea at 4 P.M., after the service of which the ladies would be invited to draw up their sleeves and receive an adorably divine injection of morphine from their hostess, who—one may assume—was scrupulous to a nicety in observing the hygienic imperatives demanded by needle-sharing. This sort of behavior had been all but invisible up to that point, but once the chorus girls got wise to it, and morphine slithered down the social scale, it ceased to be considered the eccentric preserve of ladies of leisure panting for the shock of the new, and became the depraved recourse of the heedless hoi polloi who'd picked it up from East End coolies. In the USA, the morphine habit was disseminated into society following the cessation of hostilities in the American Civil War in 1866. It had been used extensively to treat the wounded during the bloodiest fighting, and doctors were happy to go on prescribing it for the returning combatants who found in many cases that it served to soothe their shredded nerves.

The opiate stakes were further raised when, in 1874, a research chemist named C. R. Alder Wright, working at St. Mary's Hospital in the Paddington district of London, created a new substance by boiling morphine down with an acidic agent. A little experimentation was done in London and Manchester on the new substance, briefly christened diacetylmorphine, but the breakthrough was only made in 1898 by a German pharmaceutical company, Bayer, who perfected a way of making it more fat-soluble. In so refining it, they renamed the substance after a German word meaning heroically strong and powerful, "heroisch." Pharmaceutical heroin had seen the light of day. One of its earliest suggested applications was to cure morphine addiction, which was itself the result of an attempt to cure opium addiction. It took less than twenty years for this formidably potent new analgesic to become a street drug, although interestingly, when the voracious Billie Carleton, who took anything put in front of her, tried it, she turned up her nose at it on the grounds that it didn't seem to do very much compared to the effects of opium and cocaine.

This may at first seem an extraordinary verdict, but to a system unhabituated to it, heroin isn't basically very exciting, especially if it is ingested by one of the alternative methods to injection, snorting the powder or inhaling the smoke that comes off a cooked line of it (the latter technique famously known, in a bit of oriental kitschery, as "chasing the dragon"). Taken alone, it induces merely a feeling of heavy-headed, perhaps slightly seasick lethargy. Speech becomes slurred and vacuous, the eyelids droop and a pervasive sense of can't-be-bothered-ness comes over the user. A modest introductory dose of pure pharmaceutical material slops around in the system for around an hour or so before the fug begins gradually to clear, while an administration of adulterated street smack may have scarcely any noticeable druglike effect at all, save for a dulling of the attention, a little like the effect of having had one too many pints or joints. Contrary to the drug-panic view, it is not instantly, or even particularly quickly, addictive, but determined daily use over a period of a couple of weeks will in due course create dependency.

While heroin has been unequivocally illegal in the United States since 1924, and continues to be unavailable to the American medical profession, the treatment of intravenous opiate addiction has gone through more bureaucratic somersaults in the UK than anywhere else in the Western world. Once trailblazers in the field, the British medical lobby believed until the late 1950s in a policy called maintenance, by which registered addicts were prescribed the drug by their GPs in order to keep them out of the black market. Virtually no heroin prescriber was more heroic than Lady Frankau, a London GP who in the late fifties was singly responsible for prescribing nearly 20 percent of all the heroin in circulation in the country. She viewed her role with missionary fervor. By dispensing heroin legally, she would kill the street trade in it. In the event, she unwittingly became one of its major sources of supply, because her prescriptions, once redeemed, were being sold on by addicts who would then return to the surgery for another consignment. To a medical establishment desperate to strangle the drug problem at its source, suppressing the official supply seemed the only morally justifiable course, and GPs were forbidden to prescribe it. The chosen alternative, methadone, has been in its own ways disastrous. Addicts by and large hate it, and it is now anyway commonly thought to be actually more addictive than heroin. Half a hardened addict's daily dose brings the unhabituated user very gradually indeed to the brink of unconsciousness, speech is reduced to the faintest mumble, followed by interminable convulsive vomiting. Many of those on prescription methadone use street heroin alongside it. Thus has the wheel come full circle.

No drug interdiction is more corrosive to social cohesion than the criminalization of opiates. Addiction craving does not go away simply because it is not officially permitted, with the result that the crime generated by addicts desperate for funds to keep themselves out of withdrawal has become one of the most intractable social problems of recent times. The dependable provision of safe equipment, clean drugs and sympathetic clinical advice is the only way of managing this problem, as has been admirably shown by the systems operated in Switzerland and the Netherlands.

Opiate addicts do not have to become social pariahs if they are given what they need, instead of being enjoined to give it all up in favor of an even emptier life. They can hold down responsible jobs if they are the sort of people to want responsible jobs in the first place, and once infections from filthy needles and the insane economics of the street trade are removed from the equation, heroin dependency turns out not to be a particularly damaging physical state. Increasingly, there are numbers of young people, perhaps even the majority of users of the drug—hidden from view in the drug polemics—who do heroin occasionally without ever becoming pathetically enslaved to it, a pattern of intake known as "chipping." And as if we needed any more heartwarming reassurance, Martin Booth, opium's historian, cites the case of a Hebridean woman, close kin to all those doughty souls who have smoked two packs of cigarettes a day since the age of twelve and never had a hint of respiratory disease, who in her mid-eighties had been an intravenous heroin user for six decades.

ECSTASY (E |Adam |doves |disco biscuits |pills)

The revolution in drug consumption occasioned by the arrival of MDMA and its various secondary analogues on the club scene in America, and subsequently the UK, in the 1980s was the greatest upheaval in the realm of intoxication since the dissemination of hallucinogenics in the 1960s. So absolutely pervasive had the use of E become within a few years that it was being used more regularly and more often by tens of thousands than the supposedly less heinous drugs, cannabis and amphetamine. Ecstasy changed the way people communicated with each other, both on and off the drug, it revivified a club culture gone clichéd and static, partly by inventing in the rave a wholly innovative way of partying, and it altered relations between the sexes and between the sexualities in ways that could not otherwise have arisen. As the 1990s ended, it had become a victim of its own success, so hugely and indiscriminately in demand that what was being sold in its name bore no relation whatsoever to the real thing, as the first generation to take it could readily attest. As one contributor to a TV drug documentary appositely commented, there is an entire generation of clubbers and party-goers out there who have never taken ecstasy. That is to say, they may have bought pills on a Saturday night out that imparted a vague feeling of spaciness, but they would have been no more related to MDMA than were the pills swallowed the following morning to blank out a headache.

As with many another synthetic drug, the origins of ecstasy, or MDMA (3,4-methylene-dioxy-methylamphetamine) lie in a German chemical research laboratory, in this case that of E. Merck and Company in 1912. Its antecedent drug, MDA, had been formulated two years earlier by chemists working on amphetamine, itself a German invention, in order to investigate its powers as an appetite suppressant. When the drug was first marketed, it was sold as a slimming pill, but appears not to have found favor. Not much research was subsequently done on it, except that in the 1950s the US Army, forever on the lookout in the paranoid era of the Cold War for a drug that might be useful in counterespionage or even chemical warfare, undertook some inconclusive trials with it.

Its contemporary career really began with the pioneering work in the mid-1960s of the Russian-born California pharmacologist Alexander Shulgin. More than any other figure in modern intoxicology, Shulgin and his wife, Ann, have contributed hugely to the understanding of mind-altering intoxicants through their work on two classes of drugs, phenethylamines and tryptamines. As well as researching with MDMA, the Shulgins have helped to create, by minutely detailed molecular interventions, an entire family of 179 psychotropic drugs, many of them previously unknown to chemical science, testing them all out on themselves. In the cases of dozens of these drugs, Shulgin's own bloodstream has represented their first introduction to humanity, even as he has entered his eighth decade, and his frank and fascinating notes, published in two vast volumes in the 1990s, are a moving as well as deeply enlightening account of professional devotion to a subject all but taboo on either side of the Atlantic. Shulgin's work on ecstasy in the sixties led groups of psychotherapists to prescribe MDMA to patients suffering from classic anxiety and depression syndromes. So efficacious was it to prove that, by the early eighties, in parts of the USA, notably the big cities of Texas, the streets and bars were awash with pills being sold on, much as Lady Frankau's heroin had been in Britain in the fifties. It was but a short hop from Texas to California, the spiritual home of American drug culture for the past thirty years, and the emergence of MDMA as a purely recreational drug. It was here that it gained its street alias, ecstasy, although the story has it that its pioneer distributor at this time had wanted to give it a more reflective sobriquet, empathy. As in: "Oh man, I was out of my head last night on empathy."

By the late seventies, it had entered the club culture, most notably in New York, and within a few years had acquired its own style of simplistically beat-driven dance music known as House, after a Chicago venue called the Warehouse. It arrived in the UK in the 1980s in an initial trickle, imported, according to one version, by disciples of the Bhagwan Shree Rajneesh, a self-invented Indian religious con-merchant with a penchant for luxury cars and a gospel of get-down-on-it sexual freedom. The earliest users, unsure quite what to do on it, reverted to a sixties hippie archetype and lay around on soft furnishings gasping in wonderment at the phenomenal beauty of their living rooms. It was quickly intuited, however, that its real strength lay in the unprecedented combination of hallucinogenic bliss and almost hyperventilating energy the onset effects delivered.

The gold rush, however, only really began in 1988. En route from the East Coast of America before that, it had stopped over in the beach bars and nightclubs of Ibiza, young Britain's favorite holiday island, and coupled with subtle modulations in the structure of the dance music being played, it became the house drug of Acid House. So extensive had the reach of the new culture become in London by the summer of 1988 that the existing club scene was blown to smithereens practically overnight. Long grown self-obsessed and joyless at the behest of a style culture that insisted on dictating, via the pages of proliferating glossy magazines all competing for the same market, what its clients should wear, drink, listen to and think, it found itself overrun by the same sort of tidal wave that punk rock had represented a little over a decade earlier. Aging punks were left a little nauseous at the apparent return of unreconstructed hippie iconography, but what couldn't be ignored was the transformative energy of it all, and whereas punk, which had briefly short-circuited the economics of the youth industry by releasing the work of untutored wannabe bands on tiny independent record labels, had also doomed itself by not realizing that the stream of screaming fury with which it began couldn't possibly be sustained, the acid-house movement was brimming over with jiggy, clappy happiness.

Before long, the clubs were too small to contain it and most still closed at 2 A.M. anyway. Thus were the great raves conceived, massive clandestinely planned nocturnal gatherings at which the increasingly electronic beats of what was now being called Techno thumped out all night in some forgotten field somewhere off the London orbital road. The government of the day formulated legislation to prevent such gatherings, as much in response to the vigorous protests of those who lived in the vicinity of the racket as because they were the foremost context for the sale and use of ecstasy.

When the rave scene began to decline at the dawn of the nineties, the drug migrated back into the clubs, which had themselves now changed beyond recognition. On the gay scene in particular, the music grew relentlessly harder and faster, as the tearing off of shirts necessitated by soaring body temperatures conveniently doubled as sexual display. It had been felt by the straight ravers that E, while making you feel incomparably sensual, nonetheless crowded sex itself into the background. Boys and girls could be tactile and "loved up" with each other without the girls needing to feel they were being pursued. The gay scene put the sex back into ecstasy, however unpredictable the erectile function became under its influence. Relations between the sexes, and between gay and straight, at last became as unrecognizably fluid as sixties youth culture had promised, so that a seafront club on the south coast of England where the E was on tap from an in-house dealer advertised itself without irony as "a gender-free zone."

What was left of ecstasy by the end of the nineties was an avalanche of noxiously suspect pills, many containing grudging amounts of one of MDMA's analogues, such as MDEA, or the anesthetizing ketamine, together perhaps with a tantalizing flash of the genuine article as if in residual acknowledgment of what all the fuss had once been about. The street price had fallen to about 20 percent of its original level. Vomiting and episodes of diarrhea were by no means uncommon as more and more of these pills had to be taken in order to approximate the desired effects. Any enterprising supplier with a reasonably pure source of E might now clean up, before the last devotees who can remember what it ought to be like lose interest altogether.

And what ought it to be like? Here is Shulgin in his book *PIHKAL: A Chemical Love Story,* tottering out into the garden on 120mg of pure MDMA:

> I felt that I wanted to go back, but I knew there was no turning back. Then the fear started to leave me, and I could try taking little baby steps, like taking first steps after being reborn. The woodpile is so beautiful, about all the joy and beauty that I can stand. I am afraid to turn around and face the mountains, for fear they will overpower me. But I did look, and I am astounded. Everyone must get to experience a profound state like this. I feel totally peaceful. I have lived all my life to get here, and I feel I have come home. I am complete.[12]

And on another 120mg, just to double-check:

> I feel absolutely clean inside, and there is nothing but pure euphoria. I have never felt so great, or believed this to be possible. The cleanliness, clarity, and marvellous feeling of solid inner strength continued throughout the rest of the day, and evening, and through the next day.[13]

These testimonials may sound tiresomely trippy to the uninitiated, but they do grasp at something of the extraordinary serotonin rush that real ecstasy delivers. And while other hallucinogenic drugs may make the user focus inward on what is happening inside a profoundly disturbed consciousness, MDMA made its clients start talking to and embracing people they might otherwise have ignored. It is, in that sense, probably the most socially constructive intoxicant in this book. With exhilarating music churning around you, the jumping lights sparkling like fireworks, and your nipples being teased by somebody you hadn't yet met, it was possible to believe at last that happiness existed.

D-LYSERGIC ACID DIETHYLAMIDE (LSD |acid |tabs |trips |A)

Much as heroin did too, LSD as a street drug looked like an idea whose time had gone by the mid-1970s. It had been the source of visionary inspiration (and much in the way of cod-surrealist banality) during the hippie high tide of the late sixties, the period in which it was made illegal. Stories of acid-heads who rode its wave of hallucinogenic enlightenment too hard and too long, and ended as driveling idiots, began to proliferate (the salutary case was that of Pink Floyd founder Syd Barrett, diagnosed as incurable by none other than the late R. D. Laing). The return to amphetamine in the youth culture of the economic crisis of the late seventies betokened a renewed urge to aggressive excitement in the drugs used, and the mesmerized infant state that acid seemed to reduce its devotees to was hardly the mood of the moment. Since then, the rave movement that arose around ecstasy has proved sufficiently hospitable to LSD as well for it to make something of a comeback, although—as has happened over a much shorter span with ecstasy itself—what is currently in circulation would appear to be considerably tamer than the throngs at Woodstock and Monterey were on. The term "psychedelic," the etymology of which means "mind-revealing," was coined in this period specifically to denote the effects of LSD on the cerebral cortex, and more mystical verbiage has since been spouted about the drug than about any other illicit substance. The consequence is that the jury is still very much out as to whether acid is a mentally liberating truth serum or whether, like the natural plant hallucinogens to many of which it is structurally related, it is simply a fascinating, disorienting drug that has as many multifarious outcomes as there are individuals who use it.

The father of LSD is Dr. Albert Hofmann, a Swiss research chemist who had worked in the laboratories of Sandoz Ltd. in Basel since the 1920s. In the course of investigating the vaso-constricting properties of ergot, the cereal fungus we encountered in the ancient Greek Mysteries at Eleusis in chapter 2, Hofmann prepared a series of synthetic compounds based on its alkaloid, ergotamine. This had itself been isolated at the same laboratory by his colleague and mentor, Dr. Stoll, in 1918. Twenty years later, one of Hofmann's new compounds was to be LSD, which he catalogued as LSD-25 because it was the twenty-fifth member of the series. A modest amount of animal experimentation yielded nothing of any apparent significance, and the new substance was put in storage and almost forgotten about as war broke out.

In 1943, however, whilst preparing another batch of it (he was later to insist, with the advantage of hindsight perhaps, that he had always had a "peculiar presentiment" that there was to be more to it than he at first supposed), he found himself becoming vaguely light-headed and nauseous and, concluding that he must be coming down with a cold, left work early. By the time he arrived home, he was feeling most peculiar indeed and took to his bed. Unable to sleep, he gradually found himself in an intense hallucinatory state, with shifting patterns of brilliant color swaying to and fro before his vision. With nothing in his experience to attribute the sensations to, he feared he was losing his mind. In fact, did he but know it, the hallucinogenic drug experience, all but forgotten in Western history since the Christian church suppressed the Eleusinian rituals, had returned to European consciousness.

It didn't take Hofmann long to surmise that it must have been the substance he had been handling in the laboratory that was responsible for this first-ever acid trip. What struck him dumb was the realization that the only way it could have got into his bloodstream was through traces absorbed by his fingertips, and the minutely residual quantities that implied meant that LSD must be of terrifying strength. Three days later, he took it again, this time swallowing a monster dose of one four-thousandth of a gram. Within about forty minutes, it was coming up like thunder and, as many were to do after him, he went into a wholesale acid panic. An assistant accompanied him home. They rode bicycles, Hofmann complaining that, as in a nightmare, his exertions seemed not to be getting him anywhere. Once home, he collapsed on a sofa, the entire room one dancing mass of hallucinated forms, a kindly neighbor who popped in with a comforting glass of milk appearing to him as an evil old witch. He became convinced he was going to die, and had an out-of-body sensation, in which he floated above the sofa looking down on his own corpse. A doctor was called, but by the time he arrived, the experience had leveled, and as the doctor pronounced that there seemed to be nothing physically wrong with him, Hofmann at last calmed down and the visual and auditory distortions began to take on a sublime nature. By the time the trip faded off, he was convinced he had had a profound spiritual experience. The rest is mythical history.

LSD passed quickly into psychiatric use in the 1950s, being prescribed in ludicrous dosages to alcoholics, schizoprenics, homosexuals and the terminally ill. At best, around half of any target group of the mentally ill seemed to benefit from it, with the rest undergoing severe psychotic disturbance and one or two eventually committing suicide. To the US military establishment, this sounded mouthwateringly promising, and they began experiments in the fifties designed to see whether LSD could be used as a debriefing drug or, better still, as a brainwashing agent that might conceivably win them the Cold War.

Although some of the truth of what the CIA did to unsuspecting "volunteers" during this period emerged in the mid-seventies when a Freedom of Information lawsuit forced the federal government and the then President Gerald Ford into shamefaced apologies to the surviving victims, as well as the family of one of the suicides, the complete truth about the LSD experiments will possibly never be known. Irresponsible, shocking dosages were given to people who had no idea what was going to happen to them, often over a period of days on end until the drug's psychoactive impact was all but deadened. Then it would be withheld for just long enough so that the cerebral cortex was cleared of its residue and another colossal administration would be given. The CIA was not merely giving the drug orally, but injecting it into the victims too, so that the onset effects, alarming enough when gradual, were immediate and shattering. Some were given it as a Mickey Finn, dissolved in a drink when they were unaware that any test was being carried out.

The decision was eventually taken to stockpile it for military use in nuclear-weapon quantities, and bulk orders were put in to Sandoz in Basel, the company that still owned the patent. Peering into the abyss that the CIA was cheerfully digging, Sandoz declined to supply them, and so the American government simply co-opted one of its own pharmaceutical companies, Eli Lilly of Indiana (producers today of the universal antidepressant drug Prozac), to produce the material instead. This was in flagrant contravention of international patent agreements, but to a government bent on finding the weapon that might finally trump the Russians in the arms race, legal niceties like that were of no account. When government authorities fulminate against the international drug trade of the present, they should perhaps remind themselves that they were history's first manufacturers of contraband acid.

While the CIA was stuffing it into the veins of nonconsenting adults, the acid gurus Al Hubbard and Timothy Leary did their level best to bring the drug to the streets. Ironically, what probably put paid to further medical (and perhaps even military) experimentation was the sight of this supposedly awesome substance being used recreationally by longhaired dropouts at pop festivals. Suddenly, acid was everywhere, and the authorities reacted predictably by making it illegal. The inextricable association of acid with a social sector as tawdry as the rock industry at least had the effect of throwing into relief some of the more lapidary utterances of the acid gurus. Hubbard was a mega-rich business mogul and the head of the Vancouver Uranium Corporation, who tried acid in 1951 and, four years later, was buying it in industrial quantities from Basel, insisting that everybody should take it for its spiritually liberating potential. He seemingly supplied a wide variety of individuals with it, from radical priests to business tycoons, who claimed to have seen God while under the influence. Cary Grant loved it, claiming that its mind-expanding effect had cured him of a fit of the glums.

Timothy Leary was a Harvard psychology lecturer who, during a visit to Mexico in 1960, took psilocybin mushrooms and declared he had had a religious epiphany. In 1961, in the atmosphere of feverish curiosity fomented by Hubbard, he took LSD and had another. He too now began insisting that everybody should take it, much to the disquiet of his employers. Leary got away with this increasingly obsessive campaign for two years before Harvard, fearful that its psychology department was being brought into disrepute, finally dismissed him. Wondering just what had taken them so long, he embarked on his self-styled career as the High Priest of LSD, enjoying the role of dropout academic consultant to the hippie movement to its utmost. His literary output during this period is now of no consequence whatsoever, for the reason that he himself later recanted the acid faith, disowning virtually all the subversive pronouncements of his post-Harvard career (the most famous of which—"Turn on, tune in and drop out"—was the "Come on in, the water's lovely" of its day). He is reliably reputed to have grassed on several former associates, and happily provided information that led to the arrest of those who had helped him escape from prison while serving a term for possession of cannabis. When he died in 1997, having written a final book on the subject of dying, his last wish was for his ashes to be sent into extraterrestrial orbit. Leary was no guru, but a man of strikingly mediocre intellect whose career stands as a salutary caution against the fake appropriation of tribal cosmology in societies long grown out of it, and who—to borrow Lenin's famous sneer at the bourgeois Western Marxist—was more likely viewed by the mud-caked crowds at Woodstock as a useful idiot.

Acid is a very easily smuggled drug as a result of its being active in such minuscule concentrations. A fragment of blotting paper invisibly impregnated with a powerful dose of it need be no more than the size of a pinhead. Fifty micrograms, which is the average strength of the single-measure acid blotter of today (that is, fifty *millionths* of one gram), is enough to impart a transfixing state of gently hallucinatory tripping, considerably less dramatic than the heroic potency of the acid of the sixties and seventies, which was about five times that. When I asked a respondent who vividly remembers it what the LSD of the earlier period had been like, I was told, "You hadn't a clue where you were when it came up. Everything went haywire. It was like being in a cartoon."

More than any other type of drug experience, the phenomenon of hallucinogenic tripping stretches one's descriptive powers to the limits. All five senses are radically subverted, with their functions repeatedly interchanging in an effect known as synesthesia. The apprehension of perspective becomes dizzyingly fluid, so that the other side of the room may suddenly leer up in unexpected close-up, while something being said by people several yards away sounds as amplified as if it were being murmured directly into one's ear. Unintelligible mental concepts appear to acquire physical attributes, so that chains of words repeating in one's head take on the metallic jingling of real chains as they flow through, and one's sense of self becomes bewitchingly, even upsettingly, acute. The caricature of acid-tripping believed by nonparticipants—that the hallucinations have a sort of Disney surface-quality to them, so that one briefly sees the armchair as a pink elephant—is nothing like the actual experience, in which the distortions are instantaneously rooted in the mind of the perceiver, implicitly believed for a second before normal consciousness breaks back in again and exposes the madness of the perception. Most difficult of all to cope with can be the phenomenon of time appearing to slow to a standstill, so that what feels like it must have been another hour has in fact been two minutes. To those not quite enjoying it, this leads to a sort of acid fatigue, in which one grows sick at heart of the nonsense consciousness and earnestly wishes to come out of the other end of the tunnel. The distress of full-blown acid panic can be pitiful, and it behooves those who are with somebody in this state to offer a constant stream of verbal reassurance, however tiresome they might find it.

Siegel contends that the effects are paradoxically much less startling in the dark, perhaps because the visual field has less to work on, but I don't think I would counsel shutting up somebody having a bad time on their own. Despite all this, the experience can indeed be as sublime as Hofmann eventually found it, and can lead to great deepening of affection between two or more already intimate friends. As to the relations with the rest of society, it may be that Siegel's neon tetras are instructive after all. People under the influence of LSD haven't the slightest desire to make contact with those not in the same state as themselves. Others look unfriendly, intimidating even, and—most chillingly—they all look as if they realize *exactly* what forbidden thing has been done.

FREEBASE COCAINE (crack \rocks)

Ecstasy and its analogues represented one type of designer drug in the 1980s, but freebase cocaine, which came universally to be known as crack, represented quite another. As so often when a new drug, or a newly synthesized batch of an established drug, comes onto the street market, its arrival is preceded by gruesome tales of the tragedies that have befallen its first users. This is particularly so when the drug has migrated, as the eighties designer drugs mostly did, from the USA to Europe. We are told that a lethal new substance has been introduced into a drug underground gullible enough to try anything, with consequences that have included, variously, appalling new conditions unfamiliar to medical science, ultrapsychotic behavior (the news media can always be relied on to come up with somebody who had a six-day session on the stuff and ended by killing and eating the neighbors' dog, later claiming they remember nothing of what happened) and another devastating crime wave.

The last arises because each new substance has to be described as being more rapaciously, instantaneously addictive than anything previously heard of. Thus is the drug's PR campaign assiduously mounted for free by tabloid crime correspondents more gullible than any seasoned drug-user would dare to be. The PR campaign for crack was a classic of the genre. One inhalation of it was said to addict the user for life, the obscene craving that it created making heroin withdrawal look like nothing more than a bit of a sniffle. Crack-smoking does indeed carry a high risk of addiction, and there are indeed dens of addicts ("crack houses") in New York and other cities full of degraded individuals reduced to theft and forced prostitution to fund their intake of the substance, although not now to the degree that there were. Already by 1987, when a recording artist now happy to be known once more as Prince wrote "Sign o' the Times," a bleak account of social meltdown in urban America, one of the specters contributing to the premillennial disaster was the dissolute adolescent whose only satisfaction in life was membership in a street gang in which, buzzing with crack and carrying an automatic weapon, he was able to terrorize his neighborhood.

Freebase cocaine came about probably because of a testing technique used in the 1970s by American dealers to establish the purity of batches of the drug. A small quantity was heated up until it released a vapor that was inhaled. This, it was found, had its own peculiarly pungent kick, and eventually the process was refined. Amateur freebasing carried out at home carried a high risk of causing explosion and injury, because a volatile material such as ether is needed to free the pure cocaine base from its salt (hydrochloride) element. The same technique has more recently been used on amphetamine to produce base speed, which is correspondingly cheaper on the streets but not as often encountered.

In the body, the effects of freebase drugs are appreciably similar to their antecedents, although the initial rush can be quite alarmingly violent. More in demand than base speed, after *Details* magazine published an article in 1997 in which users claimed variously to have bashed away on a drum kit for several hours or masturbated the top three layers of skin off their penises, is crystal meth (otherwise known as ice). This is the highly refined crystallized version of methylamphetamine, itself manufactured from a plant source of the naturally occurring stimulant ephedrine, and tenuously related to the Methedrine that was briefly prescribed to heroin addicts in the sixties. Cramming your system with as much crystal meth as your stomach and/or respiratory function would take was said to deliver just about the maximum psychophysical pleasure the brain was capable of bestowing on the human frame. A woman who was dealing the material in Britain at the time declined to make quite that claim for it, although a client of hers was seen dancing, fifteen minutes after snorting it, with a ferocity that made it seem as if he were trying to shake his limbs off. He felt hyperconfident, aggressive and ebulliently happy, but had admittedly boosted it with an E.

The appeal of these ultrarefined substances is rather similar to the appeal of riding the highest and fastest roller coaster in the world, wherever that now is. Just how much fear, fun or excitement can your body handle? The adrenaline of pushing oneself to the limits isn't solely the preserve of trainee Marines, mountaineers or marathon-runners, and it is both extraordinary as well as brazenly lazy to experience it by sitting in a room and smoking, swallowing or snorting your way to it. But the hit is the same, and the aura of dangerous addictiveness that the yellow press and the drugs tsars will insist on spinning about these substances only adds to their allure. If you can do crack and go back to work the next day, when all about you are pale and trembly, then you'll be a man, and the urge to tell everybody what you've achieved is irresistible. Contributors to a Greenwich University study of contemporary drug use in the UK examined the use of crack in Liverpool, and concluded that while some had undoubtedly become hooked on it, others did it as and when the opportunity arose and they could afford it: "Half the sample had been using crack occasionally for an average of 18 months, with many periods of abstinence—which conflicts with the theory of inevitable instant addiction."[14] Ian Penman, a journalist who has himself written a laudably candid account of his own period of heroin dependency, in 1994 had this to say about crack:

> The so-called crack epidemic remains a mystery awaiting real— journalistic and/or sociological—investigations. Everyone I know . . . has tried it, but not one person I know has become "hooked." Most have tried it a couple of times and concluded: what's all the fuss about?[15]

And then again, there is such a thing, albeit not one that the Drugs Tsar is prepared to concede, as *deciding* not to be addicted to something. A respondent who had taken virtually everything since his middle teens (and now, past 30, characteristically likes nothing more than a joint and a bit of wine in the evenings) described to me the crack rush he had experienced in 1994:

> "For a moment, nothing happens, and then you feel this great wave of massive, totally unhandleable energy rolling through you, until you feel you can't actually contain it, and it's about to burst through your finger-ends, and you know you won't ever do this again. Then you let out your breath and you feel *so* beautiful. For about ten minutes you feel like a king. And then you want to do it again."
> "And did you?"
> "I did it once more, and I've never touched it since."

INHALANTS

The range of substances that produce psychoactive effects when sniffed is wide and heterogeneous. Some leave the user in a hypnotic state, which can lead to dependency behavior. Glue-sniffing, which arose as an urban pastime in the United States in the 1970s, is the emblematic example of this, but the same sense of stoned displacement is available from inhaling the fumes of paint-stripper, paint itself, nail-varnish remover, typescript correction fluids and their thinners, dry-cleaning fluid, lighter fuel and petrol. Depending on the degree to which the habit is engaged in, the effects may range from pleasurable wooziness to full-on hallucinations. These substances are acutely toxic, which makes the fact that they are often the only intoxicants easily and economically available to young adolescents particularly dismaying. Fatalities from glue-sniffing and butane (lighter fuel) inhalation are a constant drip-drip in the medical statistics, certainly enough to shame the Drug Tsar, who is, as ever, more interested in anything that can be pinned on heroin. But the only media panic about inhalation addictions fizzled out many years ago, and it is interesting to ponder exactly why this is.

Accidental intoxication on the fumes of volatile substances used in various trades and in medical research was a familiar enough feature in the late eighteenth and nineteenth centuries. Sir Humphrey Davy, pioneer of nitrous oxide as an inhalable anesthetic and inventor of the miner's safety lamp, thought the experience delightful, and as well as demonstrating it to his students, used it several times recreationally with dramatic results, as he recounted in 1800 in a paper entitled "Researches, Chemical and Philosophical; Chiefly Concerning Nitrous Oxide, or Dephlogisticated Nitrous Air, and Its Respiration":

> I felt a physical and involuntary detachment that lifted me from my earthly cares and caused me to pass, through voluptuous transitions, into delicate sensations that, speaking candidly, were completely new to me. It seemed that, in my privileged condition, everything was performed spontaneously and instinctively. Time, in other words, existed only in my memory, and in a flash the most remote traditions were revived in all their splendour.[16]

Its capacity to bring on convulsive hilarity led to nitrous oxide being christened laughing gas, and it was for a time offered in West End theaters in London as an adjunct to the stage entertainment. Before laughing gas, there was ether, also an anesthetic agent, perhaps first formulated in rudimentary guise as early as the thirteenth century. It was so widely available by the early 1800s that it became an alternative intoxicant for those who abstained from alcohol, or on occasions when drinking was inappropriate. It was extensively used by the Irish peasantry of the nineteenth century, and was resorted to along with cannabis during the Prohibition era in America. In some circles, it was considered more ladylike than alcohol, the tittering giddiness it induced more becoming than the vulgarity of real drunkenness. The solvents used in the millinery profession in the Victorian era had such a marked effect on their users that anybody acting in a similarly unhinged manner was accused of being "as mad as a hatter."

Methods for maximizing the potential of inhalant intoxication have also maximized the risk of serious accidents and death. Breathing in the fumes of glue, which contain a neurologically ruinous compound called toluene, by burying the lower part of one's face in a plastic bag has led to suffocation. Inhaling the butane from lighter fuel is sometimes done, as is depicted in Larry Clark's 1996 film, *Kids,* by filling an inflated balloon with the vaporized fuel and letting the released air expel it in a rush down one's throat. Asphyxiation may be the price to pay for such a strong and violent hit. The technique is also used for inhaling the propellant gases in aerosol products, whereby it is presumed the other components—spray paint, hair spray, etc.—will be left on the inside surfaces of the balloon. Intoxication by these methods is, in the view of many (myself included), the most brain-damagingly hazardous and squalid way of getting high, but just as young people might be ready to turn away from the infantile obsession it represents into something more grown-up, they find the barriers have gone up. Cannabis is not permitted. Glue is. They may not sell it to minors on the high street, but it's in the cupboard at home anyway.

As well as commercial products, there is also a group of chemicals, nitrites, marketed through sex shops and bars as "room odorizers," intended theoretically to be left to volatilize on air contact with the top taken off. In fact, amyl, butyl and isobutyl nitrite are taken by inhalation straight from the bottle. First formulated in the mid-nineteenth century, amyl nitrite is used medically to dilate the blood vessels directly supplying the heart in angina patients. The massive kick it gives the blood pressure is so great that, in a normal circulatory system, it creates a pounding in the head and heart, complete disorientation, discolored vision and often a residual headache after repeated use. Known on the streets as "poppers" (the name derived from the little glass phials they originally came in, which had to be popped open), the nitrites are used to give a localized rush of energy to dancers in clubs. They are virtually universal on the gay scene, not least because the hypertensive stimulus the substance induces helps maintain a throbbing erection. Furthermore, many gay men enjoy taking a great sniff of poppers during sex just as they are coming to climax, for the extra sensual intensity and force it gives the ejaculation. The use of poppers has now become slightly classbound, even among gay clubbers. There is a feeling in some quarters that it is only a heartbeat away from glue-sniffing, enhanced by the fact that a bottle that has been open a long while, and not refrigerated, smells so pungently stale that its tenuous connection with exotic sensuality is rudely severed.

ALCOHOL

Legal intoxicants are all around us. They may not take immediately obvious forms in many cases, but from the caffeine brew that kick-starts the day through the nicotine breaks in the office toilets to the saffron in the risotto at lunch and the cocoa in the chocolate bar at teatime, they are there. No sanctioned intoxicant, however, is more unequivocally about altering the way reality is perceived and felt— in other words, is more self-evidently intoxicating—than alcohol. There are many who drink during the day, even in the course of work (the food and wine writing trade would be unthinkable without regular daylight libations of it), but for most it is the evening's first glass of wine, bottle of beer or G&T that most cheeringly announce the spiritual function of intoxication, its role, coeval with humanity itself, in displacing the given world by transformation of the way the brain works.

Fundamentally, no other official intoxicant is anywhere near as intoxicating as alcohol. If the criminalization program enthusiastically and disastrously embarked on by world governments in the twentieth century with regard to intoxication were ever to be extended, alcohol would be its next obvious target, as indeed it was during the Prohibition period in the United States. No matter how constrictively it has been hedged about with regulations—on who may drink it and when, and how much they should be allowed—it has survived because it is so ancient, because dodging the interdictions is even more absurdly straightforward than dodging the interdictions on synthesized drugs, and because, just perhaps, there is a recognition—everywhere unspoken if it does exist, of course—that one thoroughgoing intoxicant should be left in the daily pharmacopoeia if societies are not to buckle under the pressure of an unsatisfied secondary drive.

Nothing else works precisely like alcohol—not cannabis, not opiates, not gamma-hydroxy-butyrate—and yet its action, both physically and socioculturally, is formidably complex. This was recognized frankly by Richard Rudgley, who omits it from his *Encyclopedia of Psychoactive Substances* on the explicit grounds that "[s]o prevalent and multi-faceted is the human interaction with drinking that it requires a work to be dedicated to it alone."[17] The succeeding pages can't provide that, but we can take a magic-lantern view of some of the more diverting contexts and habiliments that alcohol has assumed in the course of its venerable history.

Martin Booth is of the certain opinion that opium is the oldest intoxicant in continuous human use (a view that I do not feel inclined to challenge), but alcohol has been and is more pervasive in human affairs than any other, and for the simple reason that all manner of plant species and their derivatives, from cereal grains to fruits, palm sap to honey, are capable of turning into it. Understanding this process is the nearest humankind has come to acquiring King Midas's mythological ability to turn everything he touched to gold. Not for nothing did its path cross, at one crucial stage in European history, with that of alchemy.

Distillation is much older than the Europeans for centuries told themselves it was. It has been established for around 40 years now that it had almost certainly been discovered in the East, probably China, during the first millennium B.C. The work of O. Prakash, an Indian food and drink historian, in 1961 furnished evidence that distillates of rice and barley beer were being made in India around 800 B.C., and the expertise may well have traveled there from China. Some centuries later, around 1100 A.D., the celebrated medical school at Salerno made the same breakthrough. The medical motivation for extracting the soul or "spirits" of wine was the notion that wine itself seemed to be a health-giving drink, and if it could be reduced to its active principle, alcohol, then its salving benefits might be the more enhanced. (This view, which to the Victorian era and the Prohibitionist caucus was a retarded and dangerous misconception, was fully rehabilitated by the 1990s, when the theory that red wine was actively good for health was gradually modified to take in all alcohol.) Aristotle had observed in Book 2 of his *Meteorology* that the distillation process was one that could be widely applied to any number of different liquids:

> Sea water, when it is converted into vapour, becomes drinkable, nor does it form sea water when it condenses again: this we say from experience. Other substances are influenced in this way. Wine and many liquids, when evaporated and condensed back into a liquid, become water.[18]

If the Greeks had only tasted enough of it, European science might have been advanced by fifteen centuries. The Salerno physicians came to believe, contra Aristotle, that this condensed "water," far from being an irrelevant by-product, was the very essence of the wine and, just as experimentation was being feverishly conducted to uncover the elixir or core element of metals in the hope of prolonging human life, so the attempt to separate the elixir of wine, already a medicinal standby, might just prove the Holy Grail of the alchemical enterprise. If the distillates so far tested had not yet yielded the hoped-for results in this regard, that may well be because the distillation had not been pursued to its ne plus ultra. The creation of stronger and stronger alcohols was the inevitable consequence of this endeavor, and when alchemy's quest was at last abandoned as futile, the bequest to European cultures was spirituous liquor, itself strongly promoted as medicinal until virtually the era of Hogarth.

It is difficult to grasp the precise moment at which drinking ceased to be part of humankind's natural estate, and began to be a social problem. The religions had had their more or less disapproving views of it, as we saw in chapter 3, but, with the exception of Islam, had not attempted to forbid it altogether. Before the rise of a nascent entrepreneurial capitalism in the early nineteenth century in Britain, drinking played a sanctified symbolic role in social relations, so much so that not to drink was to be seen as pretending to a cold aloofness that undervalued the community in which one lived. The Bacchanalian festivals of social inversion with which British pre-capitalist culture was colorfully endowed used drinking as the principal impetus for the entertaining and cathartic purpose of allowing the peasantry a vaguely political voice. That the humblest farm laborer could have his go at being lord of the manor, however theatrically, siphoned off much of his discontent at what was otherwise a bitterly hard life. Only drink—strong beer or cider, depending on the county—gave him the wherewithal to carry it off, and once the whole community was well oiled, the anarchy might prevail for days.

Versions of these festivals took place in one form or another all over Europe, and they are all crucially predicated on drinking as the strategic means of social release. Not unexpectedly, such carnivals could sometimes get quite out of hand, with looting and fornication breaking out, and just occasionally the distant whiff of more durable social rebellion creeping into the inebriated declamations. From as early as the mid-eighteenth century, cautionary voices were being raised against this form of recreation, and alcohol was implicated as the principal agent of the threatening lawlessness. Without it, the rural poor were docile, their discontents confined to inaudible mutterings in their cottages, but with ale inside them, their tongues were loosened and their inhibitions unshackled. The carnivals continued into the early nineteenth century but by then, the bourgeoisie—growing politically and economically powerful as a class but still uncertain of the security of its own power base among the under class—was becoming more vocal about the need to wean the lower orders off uncontrolled drinking. Thus were the temperance movements born, the Bacchanals killed off and drinking gradually—and with much injunctive effort—forced back to the margins of social existence. After the carnival was over, and the focal point of riotous drinking was gone, what was left was just drunkenness for its own sake, with concomitant effects on the health and welfare of the peasantry.

Marianna Adler has suggestively argued that the temperance movements played a significant role in the creation of the capitalist model of the new individual from the 1830s onward. Rather than spending his pittance on drink to wash away the drudgery of labor, the teetotalist-campaigners encouraged workers to save, thus investing in capitalism and reinventing themselves as prototypes of the modern consumer. They brought a sense of capitalist participation to the laborers that had previously only been found among those with the capital to be entrepreneurs, and inasmuch as they were successful, delivered up to the latter the precious gift of a labor force that, bound and gagged by abstinence, was a more efficient and productive player within the emerging economy.

The utilitarian concept of social order that gained ascendancy in this period, unmistakably Platonic in its dehumanizing sweep, saw no need for rowdy festivals to reassert a sense of everything being in its due place. A well-ordered society contained its own irresistible moral imperatives, among which were both the obligation to save money against one's future inability to provide and a more pressing sense of time and its prudent use. Intoxication has no clock other than the body's sheer physical capacity to withstand it, whereas the new work patterns the Victorian era ushered in required laborers to be available and fully functioning for a clearly defined major portion of their waking hours. Not only that, but as more and more extensive tracts of once common land came to be enclosed, the recreational spaces available outside the home were thereby reduced.

The home, I believe, is the crucial arena in which the dialectic of intoxication and abstinence is played out, beginning in the pre-Victorian period. Not for nothing was it the battleground of the Temperance movement. In their iconography, the home was ideally a tranquil refuge, returning to its maternal bosom the reward of a man's working day. It was ordained as such by the Christian vision of the family as the fulfillment of God's purpose, and by the immensely useful economic role it played in capitalism's dynamic. To stay out drinking was to subvert the proper harmony of the home, to neglect the obligations it embodied.

As working-class pub life became increasingly male-orientated after the decline of eighteenth-century public drinking habits, the case that the drinking man was cheating on his family became easier and easier for the temperance campaigners to put. They bustled into the pubs and tried to shame the laborers by pointing out that the money they were pouring down their throats was so much less spent on nourishing their offspring. That this was often undeniably true, especially at weekends when the greater part of the week's wages might be sunk in a night's inebriation, is what kept the teetotalers in business. Their campaigns may not have been finally decisive in converting the greater part of working-class society to abstinence, but they succeeded—perhaps forever—in wresting from the pub the status inscribed in its originally untruncated name, the "public house."

Pubs were not antithetical to the home. They were at first a more communal adjunct to it, in which working people mingled with their neighbors and colleagues more freely than any other form of socialization allowed. By demonizing the pubs as sinks of selfish excess, the temperance advocates ripped another plank away from the already half-demolished edifice of working-class sociality. Sitting in of an evening, meditating on the Bible, whittling away at a piece of wood or spinning yarn for knitting, was preferable to taking alcohol in groups. In this way, the campaign against intoxication succeeded in atomizing individuals, a move that many of the mass leisure pursuits of the twentieth century would reinforce by encouraging them to combine only in order to stare in ordered passivity at some entertainment spectacle, whether in the cinema, concert hall, football ground or in virtual reality, whereas intoxication had brought them together in interacting, dynamic gatherings. To the extent that it succeeded in placing the pubs beyond the pale of respectable social life, as the next best policy to inspiring the abstinence it really craved, teetotalism is what undermined society, not the Demon Drink.

When the temperance movements receded in failure in the UK (at about the time they were winning the day in the United States with the Volstead Act that brought in Prohibition), the pub as a legitimate social space was reaffirmed, but the practice of drinking had been hermetically compartmentalized. It had stopped being a seamless part of everyday behavior and had become one of the leisure activities, to which implicitly there were always more wholesome alternatives. Partly for this reason, the nineteenth century in both America and Britain saw the rise of drinking venues that were quite defiantly about intoxication, rather than being polite spaces where one might refresh oneself during an afternoon constitutional with a glass of light beer.

The transformation of the American tavern of the previous century into the later urban saloon is a fascinating development in itself, with the multiform social purposes of the former (that included eating and sleeping, finding work, exchanging news and debating political issues) undergoing mutation into the wholesale alternative society of the latter as the Temperance movement hacked away at the moral status of communal drinking. By the late 1800s, the saloons were full of prostitution and "crimping" (the practice of drugging clients unconscious so that they could be robbed and dumped in the street), illegal gambling and political graft. The philosophical disputations that Peter Thompson describes in a study of eighteenth-century tavern life in Philadelphia, and that helped to shape the tribunes of public debate in a newly emergent democracy, have become, by the 1890s, the backroom deals and bribe-paying of the Bowery saloons in Luc Sante's beautifully etched account in *Low Life,* a portrait of New York from the 1830s to the Great War. Public drinking in the Bowery saloons was as unembarrassably frank about itself as it was in the English gin-shops of the eighteenth century, or than it ever would be again in the USA. The very names of the bars shouted their defiance in the face of cultured Manhattan society: the Flea Bag, the Hell Hole, the Dump, the Morgue, the Inferno, the Slide (the last almost certainly New York's first gay bar). Nor was any conceivable section of society neglected, as Sante describes:

> Another feature of the time was the boys' dive. There were a number of these on Worth, Mott, Mulberry and Baxter Streets, catering to newsboys, bootblacks, and members of youth gangs. There they could purchase three-cent whiskies as well as the favors of little girls . . . There would be a lamp, a counter, maybe a bench. Chairs and tables would be discretionary. The floor would be wood, maybe, or maybe packed dirt. There might be chromos on the walls, but probably not. There would certainly be a peephole, a guard at the door. There would be nearly a zero level of amenity. Between poverty and drink, nobody would notice anyway.[19]

Some of the bars became notorious for suicides, the decrepit gloom of the ambience perfect for ending it all. One such was McGurk's, a four-story dive on Houston Street where in 1899, the half-dozen successful suicides included Blonde Madge Davenport, who swallowed carbolic acid there, although not her associate Big Mame, who in a dither of indecision spilled hers down her face. The resulting disfigurement was thought horrible enough to put other customers off, and she was barred for life.

To venture out to a dive where a headwaiter called Short-Change Charlie carried chloral hydrate for knocking the mug punters out cold might have sounded like a rather persuasive argument for staying at home after all, but the truth was that many of McGurk's customers had no homes. Then too, the squalor and the suicides made it a must-do stop on the tourist itinerary, and the lure of the underworld has never been confined to down-and-outs. The teetotalists could never quite agree among themselves on whether alcohol was a corrupting firewater that galvanized the weak-willed into lives of moral incontinence, or whether it was a stultifying anesthetic reducing all who got entangled with it to vegetative torpor. Inevitably, they tried to have it both ways, but in the model of the urban saloons, they saw their best chances of success. Temperance missions were set up throughout the Bowery, offering hot food and hymns to the destitute, as well as a bed for the night, and while their success rate in reforming dissolute characters may have been modest enough, the pastoral role they played is not to be impugned.

It was around the 1850s that another mode of drinking that was to have great cultural significance arose. A famous bartender named Jerry Thomas, who worked all over the city and had his own bar at one point, refined the art of mixing alcoholic drinks into enlivening new combinations as a novelty draw for his customers. One can't exactly say that he invented the cocktail, as such, but he is one of its patron saints. His two best-known recipes are very much snapshots of the era, in that they are hot concoctions for cold-weather drinking. (The hot toddy, an old folks' cold cure, appears to be just about the only survivor today of hot alcohol, unless one counts the lukewarm sake in the teppanyaki bar.) The Tom and Jerry, which bears his name, and after which the perpetually warring cartoon characters were named, is a mixture of sweetened, beaten, separated egg with brandy, rum and hot water. More spectacular was the Blue Blazer, a performance drink in which a mug each of flaming Scotch and boiled water were poured one into the other and back again several times, so that a cascade of liquid fire appeared before the patron's eyes. All cocktail barmen's theatricals are derived from this, even though the drink itself would not have been hugely inebriating, as much of the spirit would have burned off. Recipes for both are still going strong in the *Savoy Cocktail Book* of 1930, reverently credited to "Professor" Jerry Thomas, where it is noted in respect for the Tom and Jerry, that it hails from "the days when New York was the scene of the soundest drinking on earth."

The tone of wistful nostalgia indicates the fact that, by the time the Savoy book was published, America had been in the grip of Prohibition for eleven years. In the meantime, Americans fleeing the ban took the cocktail fashion with them to Europe. Relieved of its excess baggage of sordid desperation (one Bowery saloon that catered to terminal alcoholics served up "a punch composed of whiskey, hot rum, camphor, benzene and cocaine sweepings, for six cents a glass"), the mixed drink arrived in London, Paris, the Riviera, Berlin and Venice as the preferred tipple of the beau monde, a droll adjunct to the champers and coke that otherwise fueled a postwar generation with much too little to do. Cocktails of this era were nothing like the innocuously fruit-juiced long drinks of today. They were short, sharp, lethally potent drinks intended for knocking back as if there were no tomorrow—an intimation that the depredations of the Great War had instilled in the youth of the twenties.

Just as the bars of the Bowery were given cheerfully ungracious names, so the cocktails in their more playfully ironic way evoked sex, gambling, spiritual danger, even First World War munitions: Maiden's Blush, Casino, Hell, Little Devil, Whizzbang, Depth Bomb, Artillery. Whizzbang contained Scotch, dry vermouth, absinthe, grenadine and orange bitters, shaken with ice in the prescribed manner. The implicit challenge of the cocktail was "How many of me can you take?" It paradoxically combined both frivolousness and intimidation in the approach to strong drink, the attitude encapsulated in Savoy barman Harry Craddock's epigrammatic response to the inquiry as to how best to drink a cocktail. "Quickly," was his advice. "While it's laughing at you."

No form of drinking was more ruthlessly instrumental as that of the original cocktail era. When its heedless extravagance was blown away by the Depression years of the 1930s, it never really came back. Each decade sees a cocktail revival—that of the early 1980s was more assiduous in its researches than others have been—but the motivation for the style of drinking had gone, and in any case, pink frothy drinks were seen as hopelessly gender-specific. Shooters, those little shot-glasses of neat alcohol served in many American and European bars, recall something of the devil-may-care recklessness of the first cocktail age. (In the interest of not leaving any stone unturned, I swallowed a preparation called Kalashnikov in a back-street bar in Lisbon. It was virtually neat stone-cold vodka, with a dribble of absinthe poured over a sugared lemon slice on the side of the glass. You bite out the lemon flesh, then down the drink. This was followed by an Apocalypse Now, in which tequila, dry vermouth and Bailey's Irish Cream were mixed and served with a bit of burning lemon peel. Decorous pauses between shooters were the norm, allowing an almost druglike appreciation of the alcohol effect as it sank in.) Apart from shooters, there are the tequila slammers and Flaming Lamborghinis to which the die-hard British football star is drawn like any vicar to a Michelin-starred restaurant, and—cause of much earnest, class-based hand-wringing in the mid-1990s—alcopops, kids' fizzy drinks with the alcohol disguised beneath layers of fruit flavor and sweetening. (A respondent who had his whole life been one of those who couldn't take alcohol merely because the taste of it made him feel ill found a way of getting it down at last in the form of blackcurrant Hooch.)

There are beers and ciders made stronger by the ice method, in which the drink is partially frozen, and then the water that precipitates out of it, on account of its freezing at a higher temperature than alcohol, is removed as an icy slush, leaving a more concentrated brew behind. These in turn were the heirs of the Extra and Super brews that the lager and cider companies have always insisted are their premium products, but which became the beverage of choice among an unemployed 1980s underclass that hung around British shopping precincts with as little to do as their forebears in the twenties. In the Scott Fitzgerald epoch, they were Bright Young Things; in the eighties they were Lager Louts.

In 1999, a new fashion emerged among those drug-users who were cautiously ready to come back to alcohol, having comprehensively shunned it at the high-water mark of ecstasy. Vodka sniffing is a very druggy way of treating drink. Inhaled for long enough, the fumes of the neat spirit find their way in powerfully volatilized form to the brain, delivering a greater hammer-blow than the metabolized material swallowed in mingy pub measures with orange juice and ice could ever hope to do. Fears for the neurones of alcohol sniffers accompanied the first reports of the new method, with the confident expectation of stultifying brain damage becoming evident in heavy indulgers. To the sniffers themselves, it merely seemed more economical than knocking it back, but the habit does not appear to have become widespread.

Not all alcohol encounters, or by any means most of them, are about maximizing its throughput in the ruthless pursuit of intoxication. The ritualized ways of taking strong drink are simply indicative of its being the most intoxicating intoxicant permitted to us. But for such a potentially hazardous substance, we have found a limitlessly imaginative spectrum of polite ways to take it. Alcohol inebriation may have gone from sublime spiritual state with the Greeks to the stuff of feeble jokes on birthday cards, via the stage routines of generations of entertainers, but only neo-Prohibitionists and reformed alcoholics are really afraid of it even now. For every slothering deadbeat on the subway, there is a doctor tasting the Chablis in a bistro, a PR executive toasting her newly acquired account with champagne, a retired firefighter pouring a G&T at 3:30 in the afternoon, an office boy being treated to a lunchtime beer on his birthday, a former President unwinding with a Scotch, an evening-class reflectively sipping California Chardonnay, a widow in a ranch-house feeling the warmth of a Dubonnet go through her while the late-night news does its best to depress, an author half-guiltily opening a second bottle of wine toward midnight on an evening in . . .

Most intoxicants positively encourage social interaction for the precise reason that they make the users feel better than they would otherwise have done. The stimulants call forth in their clients a loquacious energy that their weekday routines might have utterly quashed; alcohol has the potential, up to a point, to achieve the same end. It may be that those drugs that encourage a slithering toward unconsciousness are not noticeably conducive to social exchanges, but that does not necessarily mean that their effects are in themselves disruptive of society. Only a drug that invariably caused its users to enter a murderous frenzy while under the influence could be said to be truly socially corrosive and, despite the best efforts of the prohibitionist brigades, no such recreational drug has come into being. (Candidates for it in the past have ranged from cannabis to crack, but as the froth of indignation has subsided in each case, the true picture has been revealed.) And even if it did, precisely who—apart from a psychopath looking for an excuse—would want it?

At the core of the panic over drugs, and the pleadings of the antialcohol lobby, lies a belief that intoxicants turn people into unrecognizable monsters. This is what we might term the Dr. Jekyll and Mr. Hyde philosophy, in honor of its progenitor Robert Louis Stevenson, whose tale of the urbane medic who becomes a hirsutely slobbering lunatic in his private life is seemingly intended as a paradigm about cocaine addiction among his colleagues. For the essential touch of realism, Stevenson wrote the novella in the fevered grip of a six-day cocaine splurge. Not even the major hallucinogenics, though, have the power to introduce psychic elements into a personality that were not already present. They may disturb previously repressed material, which may or may not be a good thing, but the last recourse of the scoundrel—it was drink/drugs/the smokes/that last cup of coffee what made me do it is less credible than ever in societies becoming gradually more familiar with the real effects of intoxicants. The teenage tabloid-reader anticipating with relish the drug-crazed orgies his rag has warned him of, as soon as he swallows that pill, is in for a mighty big disappointment.

None of this is to gloss over the indubitable fact that the use of certain intoxicants by certain sections of society has led to forlorn consequences. The opiates particularly, and in some circles crack too, are deeply implicated in the reduction of their clients' lives to appalling squalor, a far more soul-numbing social disengagement and anomie than wage labor ever manages to inflict. Depending on which authority one consults, the amount of crime said to be directly related to the search for drug money is variously put at anything between 30 percent and 70 percent, depending on which official spokesperson one is listening to. A man I spoke to in my researches was jostled into a shop doorway while walking home one night by a tightly choreographed mugging team, had three knives pressed to his throat and was told to keep quiet while he was relieved of the small amount of cash he had left on him. Did they look as if they might seriously hurt him? "They looked more embarrassed than anything else." Drugs? My own apartment was broken into by thieves who, in a fast and professional appraisal, sorted out those items with obvious resale value from among the tat. A dozen bottles of wine were left untouched while the bedroom was ransacked fruitlessly for valuables, the word processor, fax machine and video neatly decoupled from the mains and spirited away. Drugs? The police seemed to think so. If this is the result, then is society not right to be fearful of drug-taking? Is it not better that most intoxicants are illegal? But these things happen *precisely because* drugs are illegal, as we shall see in the next chapter.

As we have already noted, the very action of some drugs—specifically opiates and strong hallucinogenic materials—does have a socially disengaging impact upon the user, but we may fairly question whether that is in itself unhelpful. During the peak period of the Romantics' communion with nature, in certain highly valorized forms of religious introspection such as the monastic life or the votive gazing upon relics, even in the blinkered absorption in the Internet that is today's version of such abstracted states, the contemplative demeanor is generally found perfectly legitimate. If LSD produces something like the same breathless wonder that the Turin shroud might induce, or that reading the computerized rant of someone in a bedroom in Illinois might inspire in someone in a bedroom in Ipswich, why should we insist on only reading the abstraction represented by the drug experience as dangerously antisocial? The reason, I submit, lies not in some suggestion that we cannot tolerate the idea of desocialized solitude, but in the fact that our view of intoxication has been stained by its removal into the criminal realm. Withdrawal from society is emphatically not what is at issue here. When Wordsworth stumbled on the daffodils, after all, he was "lonely as a cloud."

In legitimately attempting to minimize the harm that ignorant overindulgence in some intoxicants can cause, world governments in the twentieth century landed themselves with the most baleful disaster in legislative history. The drug laws worldwide have created a whole new category of unstoppable crime, the effects of which have been more virulently toxic to social harmony than any pinch of dirty white powder or adulterated pill could ever be. To the origins of this impasse, we must now turn.

5

Living Outside the Law

Drugs can do strange things to the human brain. Darryl Gates, formerly head of the Los Angeles Police Department, testifying before the United States Senate Judiciary Committee in 1991, suggested that recreational users of cannabis "ought to be taken out and shot," as befitted the due prosecution of a war. William Bennett, one-time federal drug tsar, speaking on a live radio debate in 1990, suggested that those who offer drugs to juveniles should be decapitated: "Morally, I don't have any problem with that at all," he insisted. In China in the same decade, the hanging of 52 heroin dealers before a crowd of thousands was relayed on national television, the provincial governor superintending the executions announcing exultantly, "This is how we deal with drug traffickers!"

In this chapter, we shall look at how international law came to develop such a vituperative temper with regard to the mass of intoxicants. The movements that led to the enactment of Prohibition in the United States will be looked at, and the worst effects and most poignant lessons of that period will be examined. After an account of the origins of the modern drug laws, and a summary of some of the most recent arguments against them, I shall offer my own intervention in the legalization debate in the form of a critique of the work of a sociologist, Erich Goode, who has scrutinized the arguments for legalization more dispassionately than many, but nonetheless concluded that the status quo is the safer option.

The thirteen and a half years that national Prohibition was in force in the USA were, as has been repeatedly shown by historians of the period and through the testimony of those involved in its enforcement, an unbridled festival of lawbreaking. It began with smuggling and home distillation, and led on to the wholesale bribery of officials in the police departments and judiciaries. Eventually, it would spawn the gangland culture that gave rise to America's hero mobsters, Al Capone, Bugsy Siegel, Lucky Luciano and the rest, fondly celebrated in cinematic and televisual iconography ever since. The White House itself was awash with bootleg hooch, especially under the administration of Prohibition's first President, Warren Harding:

> Under Harding, visitors came in two categories: run-of-the-mill guests who were kept downstairs, and served fruit juice. Then Harding's cronies and other privileged guests, who were invited upstairs, where liquor flowed like water . . . [P]art of the Senate library had been curtained off, and had become "the best bar in town," well stocked thanks to regular visits from ingratiatingly subservient customs officials bringing with them confiscated liquor.[1]

While the political elite got away with systematic flouting of the law (at the 1924 Democratic Convention in Madison Square Garden, under the noses of enforcement officials, delegates openly swigged from bottles wrapped in paper bags, like panhandlers on a plaza), those without influence were pursued with gathering ferocity. Citing the cases of two Michigan individuals, one a mother of ten, each sentenced to life imprisonment for possession of a pint of gin, the *New York Herald Tribune* offered a waspish editorial on the climate of defiance in that state, suggesting: "Instead of sentencing to life imprisonment those of its citizens who insist on harboring pints of gin in their homes, let Michigan sentence them to the chair."

The rabidly vengeful impulse to persecute those who defy bans on intoxicating substances is a fascinating psychological phenomenon. Whenever some luckless smuggler is caught transporting heroin, either wittingly or unwittingly, through one of the Southeast Asian countries that have resorted to judicial killings in a futile attempt to choke off the international trade, even relatively liberal voices in the West are often heard to murmur that they are after all warned very clearly what the penalties are, so really it's hard to sympathize. A British man convicted of smuggling five kilograms of heroin into the Philippines in 1995 escaped a death sentence by entering a guilty plea, and was invited to consider himself lucky in only receiving thirty-five years' imprisonment.

In Saudi Arabia, the numbers of public decapitations prescribed for smugglers caught in possession of heroin in transit from Pakistan had amounted to such a backlog by 1995 that the days in the week earmarked for these spectacles were extended from two to four. Those who could barely get their fill of such entertainments could now see heads being lopped off in Jeddah from Thursday to Sunday inclusive. Sections of the tabloid press periodically work up a froth of indignation over drug-taking, suggesting that only hanging the evil pushers will begin to mitigate the terrible plague that has befallen a whole generation. When a current-affairs satire on the UK's Channel 4, *Brass Eye,* ran an item in 1997 on a horrifying new drug called "cake" that, among other frightening attributes, was rumored to make its victims cry their bodies into a state of dehydration, there was no shortage of reactionary MPs and TV personalities prepared to put their names, with no further questions asked, to a public campaign to denounce it.

A willingness to believe anything about drugs, allied to a bloodlust (often racially tinged) in hunting down those who trade in them, has characterized the entire public discourse about intoxication in the West, and is directly responsible for the paramilitary turn that overseas operations by America's Drug Enforcement Administration (DEA) have taken. DEA personnel working in over fifty foreign countries, particularly those where opium is produced, stalk around their offices in camouflage fatigues, the fancy-dress military gear and automatic weaponry reinforcing the point that the campaign against the drug trade is intended to be seen as a fully fledged war, but one that has assumed the lineaments of a multinational industry.

In one sense, the retributive desperation at work in all these instances is a figment of the law being seen not to work. If life sentences won't deter them, maybe electrocution will. When laws are contravened on such a massive and intractable scale, the laws themselves come to look ridiculous, the efforts of the enforcement industry a hapless farce compared to the resourcefulness of the traffickers and the dogged determination of the small-time users. When public revenues are allocated to advertising campaigns pleading with people not to break the law, then clearly one aspect of social consensus has broken down. What is peculiar to the prosecution of the War on Drugs, however, is that legislative authorities throughout the Western world have steeled themselves against the lessons of history in pursuing the retributive path.

In the period after World War Two, the United States tried the death penalty—by electricity or gas—against heroin dealers. There was, for perhaps the last time in its twentieth-century history, something of a public outcry that judicial killing was too severe a recourse, and the medical route (compulsory detoxification and psychiatric intervention) was explored instead. Just as salient an issue as public distaste, though, was the fact that execution didn't have the slightest effect on the numbers of heroin addicts, which continued to rise steadily. Now senior police personnel once more advocate killing even for recreational smokers of cannabis because they won't come to heel. Ayatollahs, it seems, do not have a monopoly on fanatical intolerance.

Banning intoxicants was initially the work of religions before civil society took over the task. The extermination of the Eleusinian Mysteries by the early Christian church, as we saw in chapter 2, was the first systematic program of interdiction to be enacted against the use of a particular intoxicant, although its primary motivation was the suppression of pagan polytheism. Ergot intoxication didn't come back on any significant scale, partly because the belief systems it sustained withered away with the onset of the Dark Ages, partly because the formula for the *kykeon* (or ergot brew) that induced it was never a matter of official record and partly because ergot came ineradicably to be associated with outbreaks of fatal mass toxicity. The witches of medieval Europe certainly used it, but their activities were hardly in the cultural mainstream, and in any case, ergot is a parasitic disease that affects a plant, rather than a cultivable plant in its own right. It was always too unreliable in its occurrence, and unpredictable in its effects, to continue to be the center of a historically enduring cultural practice. Christianity's first institutional victory over ritualized intoxicant use within a rival belief-system was to be far and away its easiest.

The next major religiously inspired prohibition came in the seventh century with the Prophet Mohammed's forbidding of alcohol to his followers after a fractious dinner party. Here the impulse is contrary to the Christian one. Rather than seeking to stamp out the existence of other theological practices in order to ensure the ascendancy of its own, the Mohammedan initiative is purely about reinforcing observant piety among its own devotees, thereby also incidentally creating a spiritual code that marked off the faith from those of its neighboring cultures. Christianity did not have to contend with pockets of defiant ergotism after the death of Eleusis, and so its punitive energies were initially diffused in other directions, but Islam did have to back up Mohammed's word with enforcement, in order that the Prophet's writ could be seen to run among those who claimed to be true believers. He himself set the example by prescribing forty lashes to the lawbreakers, a tariff his successor, Umar, briskly doubled.

The pattern that religion set with these impositions was to be carried on later in history by secular state legislatures, with varying degrees of barbarity. Because there was no prior tradition of abstinence among the worshipers of Allah, the artificially conceived one instituted by Mohammed carried only partial legitimacy, for all that the Prophet claimed to have had the policy delivered directly to him by the Creator. When an ordinance goes against the grain of established social custom, and especially where there is no obvious consensus that the custom was a problem in the first place, it can only seemingly be enforced by recourse to the lash. A faith reduced to inculcating the spiritual into its adherents by the merely physical means of common assault has surrendered its claim to be motivated purely by affairs of the soul, we might think, but the habit was by no means confined to Islam (although, as we see from events in postrevolutionary Iran, Saudi Arabia and Afghanistan during the Taliban period, Islam has been the last of the Western faiths to forfeit this method of indoctrination). The first Christian colonists in Latin America, on discovering a drug-rich pattern of indigenous religious practices, hardly knew where to start with the exemplary punishments.

The use of the hallucinogenic peyote cactus (*Lophophora williamsii*) among the Huichol, Toltec and Chichimeca Amerindian peoples of Mexico was first on the list because that is where the Conquest began, and where the first overseas outpost of the Spanish Inquisition was established in 1571. Peyote is a natural plant source of the hallucinogenic alkaloid mescaline, a potent intoxicant somewhat similar to LSD in its effects but with a strong stimulant edge underpinning the perceptual disturbances. It had been in ritual use for centuries among these tribal cultures, and was held to have multifarious functions, from divinations of the future to enabling direct contact with the deities in the realm of the spirits. At first, the Inquisition tried to claim that peyote functioned as a placebo, its so-called effects a mere matter of gullibility on the part of the ignorant savages who swallowed it. In which case, what was the problem?

> Inasmuch as the use of the herb or root called Peyote has been introduced into these Provinces for the purpose of detecting thefts, or divining other happenings, and of foretelling future events, it is an act of superstition condemned as opposed to the purity and integrity of our Holy Catholic Faith. This is certain because neither the said herb nor any other can possess the virtue or inherent quality of producing the effects claimed, nor can any cause the mental images, fantasies and hallucinations on which the above stated divinations are based. In these latter are plainly perceived the suggestion and intervention of the Devil, the real author of this vice, who first avails himself of the natural credulity of the Indians and their tendency to idolatry, and later strikes down many other persons too little disposed to fear God and of very little faith.[2]

This, the authentic voice of ecclesiastical persecution, was written in 1620 to justify the efforts the Catholic church was making to devalue and eliminate the sacraments of other religions. Note that it first has to condemn the suggestion that premonitory divination could be anything other than a superstition (a claim that would hold more water when advanced in the rationalist Enlightenment tradition than from a church steeped in the superstition of miraculous relics and weeping effigies), before then going on to insist that the hallucinogenic effects of the cactus, on which the claim to divination supposedly rests, are imagined anyway. If they are purely imaginary, then why would peyote have to be banned in order to stamp out the godless belief? In time, when the Indians had been weaned off such heresies and onto Catholicism, they could surely be safely allowed the consumption of plants that were as blandly inactive as all God's flora reportedly were. It seems unlikely that the Inquisition's officers on the ground actually believed the official line. They could see for themselves that the intoxicated state wasn't faked, but in any event, peyote proved uncontainable. Not only did the Indians cling tenaciously to it, the semiconverted among them managed— despite the depredations of the Inquisition—to effect a compromise in which peyote was incorporated pragmatically into Christian ceremonial. By the end of the seventeenth century, the Coahuila group of northern Mexico had successfully appropriated the concept of the patron saint for their own devotion to peyote. El Santo de Jesus Peyotes was his name, and both the nomenclature and the eucharistic practice of sanctifying the peyote cuttings at an altar were enough to persuade the Inquisitors that the Catholic God's influence had taken root. Sometimes the peyote Jesus, also known as El Santo Niño de Peyote, could be glimpsed hovering iridescently among the little cacti that he loved and cared for, quite like the Blessed Virgin making one of her many celebrated European apparitions in the centuries to come.

While peyote spread northward into Texas and the southern plains (it was to attract new aficionados among native peoples all the way up to western Canada), the conquistadores swept down into South America, their worst fears about the benighted continent confirmed as they encountered yet more examples of ecstatic rituals involving plant intoxicants. Where there wasn't peyote, there were exotic fungi, including the various members of the *Psilocybe* mushroom species, another powerful hallucinogen, and probably the fly-agaric, *Amanita muscaria*, too. (The latter was once thought native only to the northern part of the continent, but has now been discovered in Guatemala.) In what are now Bolivia, Peru, Ecuador and Colombia, the indigenous peoples chewed coca leaf, which wasn't hallucinogenic but was held in sacred esteem for its strengthening and energizing properties. Again, the first instinct of the colonists was to institute a ban, and again, they found themselves backtracking as they realized the productivity they could extract from their subject populations in the silver mines was considerably greater if they were fortified with coca.

Beyond the desire to suppress pagan habits, there is sometimes a pathos in the explorer's or missionary's encounter with native intoxication practices that suggests that, far from being repelled at the sight of unfathomable savagery, they distantly understood the emotional range and the spiritual resources these practices called forth in their participants. Bernardino de Sahagún, a Franciscan missionary who visited the Aztec people of Mexico in the sixteenth century, sounds mesmerized when he witnesses mass psilocybin intoxication among the Indians:

> At a banquet the first thing the Indians ate, was a black mushroom which they call nanácatl. These mushrooms caused them to become intoxicated, to see visions and also to be provoked to lust. They ate the mushrooms before dawn when they also drank cacao. They ate the mushrooms with honey and when they began to feel excited due to the effect of the mushrooms, the Indians started dancing, while some were singing and others weeping . . . Some Indians who did not care to sing, sat down in their rooms, remaining there as if to think. Others, however, saw in a vision that they died and thus cried . . .[3]

It seems quite likely that the intoxicant used here may have been *Stropharia cubensis*, the most potent psilocybin-bearing mushroom of them all. More than the other varieties, its effects resonate across the full emotional spectrum, so that only four or five dried specimens, reconstituted with saliva, were capable of inducing in me a six-hour trip that took in helpless hilarity, mild depression, surging love of life-altering profundity and exhilarating sexual hunger. This was behavior that Christian Europe, and particularly members of the monastic communities like Bernardino, had denied itself to the point of total alienation. It was not even a matter of denial as such. There was no cultural memory of it to repress as far as the colonists were concerned, and the sooner the red-skinned heathens they had been sent to civilize were separated from it, the sooner God's salvific work could begin. Still, it was hard not to find it oddly compelling, as Bernardino seems to have done.

Ritual hallucinogenic use closer to home came to light among the tribal peoples of Siberia, for some of whom the *Amanita* species was so highly prized, it was used as currency in a thriving barter economy. When the Russians first encountered these peoples in the seventeenth century, they were bemused by the strange behavior that the ingestion of the mushrooms, either dried or boiled in a sort of soup, caused in them. The most repulsive aspect of it to the Cossacks was that after the hallucinatory state began to fade, the tribesman would urinate into a vessel and then either drink his bladder's contents himself or offer them to another. (Urine-drinking was also encountered toward the end of the nineteenth century among the Coast Salish Indians of the northwestern tip of Washington State, distant descendants of the first eastward migration into the Americas from Siberia across the Bering Strait at about 10,000 B.C.) The explanation for this phenomenon was only provided in modern times, when it was shown that—alone among the hallucinogenic mushroom species—*Amanita* remains active in the urine, albeit at lower potency. Finding the whole spectacle deeply unedifying, the Russians attempted to suppress the mushroom trade, but failed. Even when they introduced distillation to the region, not all its inhabitants obediently turned to spirit-drinking instead. The Koryak of eastern Siberia, having learned to distill a kind of rudimentary eau-de-vie from bilberries, would steep the mushrooms in it, drink the resulting infusion and then go on to consume the urine it produced.

Throughout the nineteenth century, the gathering focus of prohibitionist efforts in Europe and America was on alcohol. The early years of the newly independent American republic in particular were marked by prodigious consumption, at least until the twin influences of entrepreneurial business culture and evangelical religion began to get a grip from the 1830s onward. To an extent all but unimaginable to today's unit-counting climate, being inebriated was seen in early American society as a sign of privilege. To have the time and resources to be "drunk as a lord" carried a plangent message about one's social station, even though public displays of rowdy drunkenness were relatively rare, largely because the habit of taking one's drink by little-and-often degrees meant that a certain level of habituation, or—as we would now put it—tolerance, had been developed.

Drinking was scarcely anywhere circumscribed within the boundaries that the Temperance campaigns would eventually impose upon it, whether by time of day, licensing hours, age, civil legislation or even gender. Starting first thing in the morning—sure indicator nowadays of dysfunctional alcohol use—was by no means uncommon. A gentleman might start the day with a bittered rum or whiskey upon rising to get the juices flowing, while factory workers would quite routinely go to work via the tavern, a nip of spirit conferring a modest glow on the bleary early dawn. Businessmen took a mid-morning break, eventually known by its hour as "the elevens," for another long spirit drink, perhaps a sweet hot toddy in the winter months. More drinks, in the shape of peach brandy juleps or gin slings with sugar and ice, might be taken at around 1 P.M., as aperitifs before the afternoon meal, which would itself be accompanied at the least by strong cider or perhaps watered spirits. A mid-afternoon work break to match the elevens was the occasion for a revivifying draught of iced spirits, and more strong cider was taken with early evening supper. Evenings were naturally the occasion for convivial gatherings by the fireside at home or at the tavern, the talk lubricated by copious quantities of whiskey, rum or gin.

A constant unobtrusive intake of alcohol was as innocuous a part of the daily regimen as bread, although its role was just as easily ceremonially inflated to become the festive libation at dances, country fairs, christenings and race meetings. It betokened the signing of contracts and the sealing of vows. It was passed from hand to hand among bidders at auction. It was dispensed by politicians to those they hoped would vote for them, and by defendants in court hearings to juries who had to decide their fates.

Children were given spirits, toddlers the dregs of their parents' glasses still sticky with undissolved sugar, perhaps a direct draught of rum or whiskey when a little older. Boys in early adolescence, for whom adulthood was a thing devoutly to be wished in an era before teen rebellion had been conceived, imitated their fathers by drinking in taverns as soon as they felt they could get away with it. Not only the ingestion of hard liquor, but the demeanor that went with it, made a boy of 12 feel as if his infancy were dropping off him like his first set of teeth as he swaggered into a bar around 11 A.M. and demanded a knee-trembling bittered brandy. That he was served without the raising of an eyebrow proved the point.

Women's drinking was considerably less visible in the taverns, but not so at other social gatherings. Mint juleps were served at the women's public baths in New York, and at society dinners and dances, the bottle was passed without regard for gender. In the home, virtually no restrictions were in force, and women sitting together to talk over sewing or picking the seeds from cotton drank whiskey as decorously and unremarkably as one now drinks tea. To decline was to refuse the hand of friendship, to offend against hospitality. This was alcohol's last, lost era of blameless innocence on the North American continent.

Excess was the mother of Prohibitionism, as it has been ever since. A glut of rum occasioned the first serious symptoms. American traders selling produce in the Caribbean islands accepted payment from British colonists in good local rum rather than molasses, seen as an ideal currency because it could withstand clumsy shipment and storage, and only improved with sitting in the cask. The American side of the triangular slave trade economy was devoted to distilling molasses. Slaves bought in West Africa with basic rum would be transported to the Caribbean, where they were sold on to the sugar plantations. The molasses that paid for them was then shipped to America and distilled into rum that would then finance the next voyage to Africa. Eventually, having cornered the African market with cheap rum, they squeezed the British out, meaning that more of the better Caribbean rum from the British islands had to be sold in America. Now awash with both its own inferior molasses product, and the better sugarcane rums of the Caribbean, the American market witnessed a spectacular price plunge. Despite the slave trade, Americans were drinking nearly 90 percent of the imported and home-produced rum themselves, and as the price tumbled, consumption went through the roof.

Most disturbing of all to the civil authorities, America's slaves—officially denied the opportunity of drinking spirits other than by their owners' consent—proved quite as resourceful in obtaining liquor as the underaged have done in other periods. Not every tavern refused them admission, either. In one North Carolina town, a local inhabitant complained that on Sunday afternoons, the streets were "infested with drunken negroes staggering from side to side." Something had to be done.

When the War of Independence led the British to blockade rum imports, the focus promptly switched to the intensive production of cheap grain whiskey to fill the gap. After the Revolution, in 1789, George Washington's Treasury Secretary, Alexander Hamilton, defying Congressional opposition from the southern states, brought in the Whiskey Tax as the first attempt to subject distilling to a federal impost. The tax was hated, and systematically evaded, until its repeal in 1802 under Thomas Jefferson's presidency. It had failed partly because it was seen as too harshly curbing the livelihoods of farmers who had no other means of income from surplus grain, but more pertinently because it was seen as embodying precisely the kind of patrician condescension toward the working classes that the War of Independence had been fought to defeat. Like today's sales tax in the USA, and value-added tax in the European Union, it fell disproportionately heavily on the poor. The propertied elite drank vintage Madeira anyway. With the abolition of the whiskey excise, the price again fell, consumption rose and whiskey came to be used, as rum had once been, as a form of currency. A social historian, W. J. Rorabaugh, cites the examples of a newspaper in Ohio that offered potential subscribers the chance of paying in whiskey, and of a Presbyterian minister's salary that was partly paid in 100 gallons of corn liquor. The constant intake of hard spirits began to occasion the kind of widespread public health crisis that Dr. Benjamin Rush and his moral thermometer had warned against in the 1780s, and so the stage was set for the entrance of the Temperance campaign.

It is important to recall that the one thing the Temperance movement was never about was temperance. From its very inception, it was a call to unequivocal abstinence, because it believed, contra Dr. Rush, that there was no such thing as restraint or moderation in the use of intoxicants. You may start out enjoying the odd julep in polite company, but several years down the line, you ended as an amoral wreck, corroding the neighborhood and society around you, and presenting a loathsome spectacle to your God.

The moral and health arguments ran dialectically together until, as Mariana Valverde has shown, the view came to preponderate in the USA by the end of the nineteenth century that medical professionals should not be wasting precious time on drunkards, who were suffering from a moral vice that could only really be cured by an exercise of their own will. Since, however, they appeared notoriously reluctant to exercise it, perhaps the temptation ought to be taken out of their hands altogether. Ridicule techniques, such as putting overindulgers in the public pillory, or parading them about town in hair shirts embroidered with the label "Drunkard," failed to stem the tide. If they were so far sunk in depravity, coercion into abstinence was the only merciful policy. As early as 1832, one General James Appleton, writing in his local newspaper, the *Salem Gazette,* became the Temperance movement's first advocate of total legal Prohibition. He embarked on a political career to that end, and four years later was sitting in the Massachusetts State Legislature, agitating tirelessly.

An energetic local campaign by Quaker businessman Neal Dow made Portland, Maine, America's first dry city in 1840, and Maine itself the first dry state in 1851. The full panoply of legal sanctions was applied to enforce the law: random searches, raids on venues suspected of serving alcohol, fines for first offenses, prison for recidivists. Scarcely a plank of the later Volstead Act, formulated in 1919, that outlawed the liquor trade nationwide, was overlooked. Eventually, Dow—dispirited by the Republicans' ambivalent stand on the issue of Prohibition—joined forces with a fringe group, the Prohibition Party, whose presidential candidate he was in the elections of 1880. Although other states followed Maine's example, they all rescinded their laws as the Civil War loomed. Only Maine kept the faith. Indeed, the state was responsible for creating the improbably popular Temperance Regiments (Dow himself commanded one) that guaranteed to the parents of boys who joined up that they would fight in a sober and dignified company, untainted by the dissolute ways of volunteers of Scots and Irish descent.

As the century turned, the various strands of Prohibition activism began to coalesce. They took in the Women's Christian Temperance Union and the Independent Order of Good Templars, as well as the maverick activities of campaigners such as Mother Thompson, who organized hymn-singing pickets outside liquor stores and saloons until their proprietors, tearful with remorse or just pig-sick of the hymn singing, agreed to find another trade to pursue.

No movement was big enough to contain the formidable Carry Nation, a WCTU activist who stumbled on her mission in life when in 1899, tired of the pussyfooting tactics of the Temperance Union, she walked into a drugstore in Medicine Lodge, Kansas, with a sledgehammer and proceeded to smash a keg of whiskey to bits. The owner looked on openmouthed, but—fatally—did nothing. It was a political epiphany. She smashed—or as she put it, "hatchetized"—her way through Kansas, engaging in acts of extraordinary violence, hurling billiard balls through saloon windows, first destroying casks of liquor and then, as nobody moved to stop her, reducing the bar furniture to splinters. She was an imposing, corpulent figure, over six feet tall with square shoulders and a huge square head, and her evidently genuine destructive rages were so intimidating, she was hardly ever challenged. When she did spend short periods in jail, she only emerged more determined than ever. She rapidly became a national media celebrity, smashing her way eastward through the bars of Missouri, Ohio, Philadelphia and New York, publishing a ranting newsletter, "The Smashers' Mail," and turning herself first into an industry by selling autographed postcards and even miniature sledgehammers, and then a stage attraction, in which she would act out her campaign on stage-set saloons, shrieking apoplectic poems amid the shivering glass. By now hot property, she acquired an agent, who was himself a drinker—a fact that seems not to have troubled her unduly—but her nemesis came when he booked her on a British tour. Londoners stayed away from her performances in droves, and when she tried to whip up interest by smashing a pub, she was arrested and fined. She was by now of course desperately unbalanced, but to her American audiences, the performances were a hoot.

In 1903, she turned up at a lavish New York ball hosted by Chuck Connors, an erstwhile boxer, bouncer and low-life overlord who became one of the stars of the Bowery saloon scene. After sweeping bottles and glasses off the tables, and knocking cigars out of the mouths of bemused guests, she proceeded to read out a plea from a woman who had asked her to find her daughter, believed to have fallen among hoodlums on the wrong side of the city. A game girl in the crowd lobbed a bottle at her, and Nation responded by pursuing her around the place with the famous hatchet. The whole venue erupted into a pandemonium of fistfights and shattered glass, until Connors himself did what hardly anybody had dared to do to her before, bodily throwing her out. All but disowned by the WCTU, she suffered a perhaps inevitable complete nervous collapse, and died in a mental institution in 1911, a few short years before her dream of a de-alcoholized America would come to official fruition.

One says "official" fruition because the effect of the Volstead Act, which became the law of the land on 17 January 1920, did anything but de-alcoholize the country. Chief among its sponsors was Wayne Wheeler of the Anti-Saloon League, an organization founded in 1893 on which all the most effective lobbying efforts on behalf of the cause were to devolve. Although he found his true vocation as a backstage fixer, lobbyist and media manipulator ("spin doctor" would be the contemporary equivalent), Wheeler had fancied himself as something of an orator and demagogue while still at college. He it was who drafted and tirelessly amended the bill that was eventually passed in Republican Congressman Andrew Volstead's name, and he it was who, eight years later, when the full scale of the public health tragedy and law enforcement fiasco that the Act had engendered became clear, maladroitly tried to defend it by saying that anybody who had died from drinking contaminated alcohol should be deemed to have committed suicide.

In the beginning, the ideals were a little loftier than that. "The evils of drink" had been a mandatory component of the schools curriculum since the Alcohol Education Act of 1886, but by the 1910s, the Prohibitionists were in no mood to allow adults to make their own informed decisions. The bottle had to be grappled out of their hands by force. A democratic patina had been painted onto the campaign by the local option arrangement, under which individual cities, counties and eventually whole states could decide, by referendum, to turn themselves dry. By the time Wheeler was lobbying President Woodrow Wilson for national legislation during the war in Europe, he was able to claim that 65 percent of the nation was already dry anyway.

A Worldwide Prohibition Congress at Columbus, Ohio, in November 1918, was marked by astonishing triumphalism. Despite all the well-known dangers of celebrating victory *avant la lettre,* the American delegates knew their battle was already effectively won. In a telling intimation of the logistical problems ahead, some speakers insisted—much as Lenin was simultaneously doing in the case of that other Revolution of the period—that the only way to safeguard the gains achieved by Prohibition would be to export it. William Jennings Bryan, erstwhile Democratic Secretary of State, urged the conference to reach out toward a more audacious goal than mere nationwide legislation, and "export the gift of Prohibition to other countries, turning the whole world dry." Speakers urged that Prohibition should be exacted as the price of assisting in the postwar reconstruction of Europe, and in the final communiqué of the conference, it was solemnly stated that "[t]he time has come for the formation of an international league for the extermination of the beverage traffic throughout the world."

We may wonder now at the infantility of believing such a thing possible, and yet to most of the delegates, the inevitable triumph of teetotalism was as much a sine qua non as the eventual victory of socialism was in other quarters. It would win in the end not by armed insurrection or guerrilla campaigns, but because the vision itself was so precisely, beautifully right that it would prove irresistible to the mass of humanity. When it did, the likes of Wayne Wheeler, Frances Willard of the WCTU, William Jennings Bryan, and—who knew?—even mad old Carry Nation the hatchet-wielder, would ascend to their rightful positions as humanity's redeemers. Not everybody in authority was swept along by the religion-driven hysteria of the campaign. The Volstead bill went to the Supreme Court to establish whether it was in fact a constitutional proposal, given that it appeared to represent a major incursion into the rights of the freeborn individual. Of the nine judges tasked with validating it, four decided against. It was finally adopted in the House of Representatives on October 10, 1919, by 321 votes to 70. To his lasting credit, President Wilson, in one of his last executive actions before his death in office, vetoed it. The veto was overturned by Congress the same day. All local option arrangements were deemed to have been replaced by what was now an article of the Constitution, the 18th Amendment. From 1920 onward, Americans were forbidden to "manufacture, sell, barter, transport, import, export, deliver, furnish or possess" alcoholic drink. The souls, and the livers, of the nation were pure.

The shambles began immediately. One of the Act's exemptions was for the medicinal use of alcohol, whereby those in possession of a bona fide prescription could obtain a pint of spirit every ten days as needed. Doctors did not, by and large, accede to demands for medicinal alcohol on a scale that would permit of widespread abuse by that means, but licensed manufacture was obviously allowable. Somewhere between the stroke of midnight and one o'clock on the morning that the 18th Amendment came into effect, a six-strong armed gang successfully seized a $100,000 consignment of whiskey that had been detailed for medical distribution. They were Prohibition's first criminals. The place was Chicago.

The thirteen and a half years that the Amendment took to die produced a criminal culture throughout America that was to become a cultural trope in later generations. Gangland rivalries, at their most picturesquely vicious in the Chicago of Al Capone, were only the most visible aspect of the illegal trade that flourished during the "dry" years. Speakeasies, the underground drinking dens to which formerly law-abiding citizens were constrained to flock if they didn't care to have abstinence thrust upon them, spawned their own vividly colorful subcultures, much as the Bowery saloons had in pre-Prohibition days, and the multifarious ruses Americans in all sectors of society found to evade a law that commanded so little general respect are in many ways a moving and pathetic tribute to human resourcefulness. People drank diluted industrial alcohol, as well as colognes and perfumes.

The more circumspect bought dried raisin cakes, which the Act permitted the vineyards of California to continue producing so that they didn't face total economic failure. Theoretically, the cakes were intended for the home production of sweet nonalcoholic grape juice. Sales representatives demonstrating the method to shoppers in the big department stores informed spectators, without even the suggestion of a knowing wink, that on no account must the jug of juice be left for 21 days in a warm place because it might ferment—and turn into wine. There was no need to put a stopper in it because that was only a necessity if the juice *fermented*—and turned into wine. To emphasize the point, the wrapper on the cakes cautioned purchasers that there was a risk that the contents, if not handled properly, might ferment—and turn into wine, by which time even Homer Simpson might have got the message.

Beringer Vineyards in the Napa Valley, still going strong today, was the trailblazer in exploiting this particular loophole. The other official options were to sell ready-made grape juice or sacramental wine for use in church services, neither of which was remotely as profitable as selling fermentable raisin cakes. Other vineyards soon imitated the Beringer initiative.

However much the raisin cakes were flouting the spirit of the law, though, even if not its letter, at least they weren't poisoning anybody. As existing stocks of whiskey from the pre-Prohibition period dwindled, alongside the reserves of vintage wine that wealthy individuals might have in their cellars, a booming underground distillation market came into being. Diethylene glycol (antifreeze), embalming fluid and foot ointment were all pressed into service for the production of something vaguely resembling spirits, the rank contamination of which would have to be disguised by additives such as juniper oil, iodine, caramel, perhaps (if you were lucky) steeped fruit. The proliferation of cocktail recipes in an era when alcohol was banned is explained largely by the need to find interesting and various ways of masking the fetid flavor of the filth they were based on.

It has been pointed out that the number of cases of cirrhosis and other alcohol-related conditions briefly dropped during Prohibition, as if in feeble insistence that the policy wasn't an absolute disaster, and yet the toll of fatalities from poisoned alcohol itself ran into the scores of thousands. Untold numbers were left blind or partially paralyzed. In 1925, the penalties for contravention of the Volstead Act were ratcheted up to five years' incarceration instead of two, with the maximum fine going up tenfold to $10,000, as if in frustrated acknowledgment that the Act was being systematically disregarded. A New Year celebration in New York at the beginning of 1927 left forty-one dead, and at last triggered a debate in the press about whether such tragedies were a price worth paying for Prohibition. Initially, the airing of doubts provoked only a backlash against the would-be reformers. Politicians who were inclined to question the wisdom of it all were subject to the full opprobrium of the Anti-Saloon League, with personal dirt being dug up wherever possible on those who favored repeal. Herbert Hoover, elected to the presidency in 1928, began his term by announcing

> I do not favor repeal of the 18th Amendment. I stand for efficient enforcement of the laws enacted thereunder . . . [It is a] great social and economic experiment, noble in motive and far-reaching in purpose.[4]

Efficient enforcement would certainly have been an experiment—the previous eight years had left a trail of corrupt commissioners, bribe-taking policemen, suborned judges and tooled-up street gangs in their wake—but the fact that Prohibition was now being referred to as a noble experiment (which may, by implication, be abandoned if it proved to have failed) marked a subtle modulation in its constitutional status.

The means of its termination were visible to those who cared to read the auguries as early as 1923, when a handful of states—namely, New York, New Jersey, Montana, Nevada and Wisconsin—began to make a policy point of not deploying state enforcement resources to police Prohibition, meaning that federal authorities could no longer rely on their cooperation in judicial proceedings. Instead, the entire cumbersome apparatus of the FBI, the Justice Department and the federal courts, not to mention the unsubtle ministrations of the Prohibition Bureau (itself now a sink of corruption, staffed at many levels by people who were themselves doing business with the bootleggers), was brought to bear. In 1929, the Volstead Act was dealt a severe blow by the publication of a book, *The Inside of Prohibition,* by Mabel Willebrandt, who had resigned the previous year as Deputy Attorney General with specific responsibility for Prohibition enforcement. Willebrandt argued cogently that the enforcement system was in widespread disarray, its public credibility undermined by the certain knowledge that evasion of the law was being practiced all the way up to the White House, and that corruption and bribery were endemic throughout it. The book had a coruscating effect, precisely because it was not dismissible as a piece of special pleading by the pro-alcohol lobby, but was the heartfelt lament of one who had drawn a public salary for eight years trying to uphold the Constitution. In it, she wrote of her enduring belief that "[w]ith the right kind of prosecutors the bootleggers will go out of business," but was moved to add that "during my eight years as Deputy Attorney General a large part of my time and energy was devoted to prosecuting prosecutors."

Some of the enforcement officials had financial interests in jointly owned illicit stills; others took protection money from the speak-easies, in return for which they would tip off the owners when a raid was about to be made. Then again, local courts in many instances saw the same proprietors coming up routinely before them every few weeks. Their derisory fines went into the community coffers, quite as if the licensing system of an earlier period were still being innocuously administered.

In the same year that Willebrandt's book appeared, the Wall Street stock market crashed, and the ensuing economic devastation sent unemployment soaring. As the federal government found itself deprived of income tax revenues, so the absence of tax from liquor sales began to be more and more sorely felt. Meanwhile, a rich business elite had been arguing for some years that the revenue flow from a relegalized alcohol industry might enable the government to consider the abolition of corporate, and even personal, income tax altogether. The obvious fact that the 18th Amendment was not being enforced to any constitutionally dignified degree meant that further resources would have to be allocated to it if America were not to become a laughingstock among its democratic allies. When Prohibition Commissioner James Doran coolly informed Congress that nothing short of $300 million would be needed for further recruitment, training and enforcement, the specter of soaring taxes to pay for it all sent a deep chill through the business lobby. Moreover, newspaper opinion polls were regularly showing that at least three-quarters of the population were now in favor of the Volstead Act's repeal. Against a background of searing privation, alcohol as a moral issue was rapidly dying.

In the wake of Franklin D. Roosevelt's presidential victory of 1932, a resolution to annul the 18th Amendment was placed before Congress. It achieved its majority in three days flat. Like the Volstead Act itself, it required ratification by two-thirds of the states in the Union, a process that was completed a year later, when the 21st Amendment was duly enacted. In practice, drinking was relegalized in stages, firstly by restoring the alcohol content in the widely despised "near beer" that Prohibition had brought in to something like an appreciable level, then by reintroducing sales of wine and spirits and later by relicensing the bars. The frail voices of protest raised by the dry lobby were almost inaudible by now. Most, surveying the moral and physical poison that Prohibition had disseminated throughout American society, had contritely lapsed into silence (a few may even have changed their minds), and those who did still propound the gospel, such as Senator Morris Sheppard of Texas, whose one-man filibuster ensured that the congressional debate took three days to conclude rather than two, knew perfectly well that the whole sorry enterprise was at last doomed. Prohibition died just in time to brighten up the Christmas of 1933, the only Amendment to the American Constitution ever to be struck out.

It is sometimes remarked that it is very easy to sneer at Prohibition, and that to do so is to overlook the stalwart efforts made by those who didn't succumb to corruption, the quiet heroism of Americans who chose to obey the law while not generally having seen the need for it, and the fact that some marginal impact on the incidence of alcohol-related liver diseases was initially made. But if it is easy to denigrate it, that is unavoidably because it is so concomitantly hard to find any positive enduring benefits in it. Edward Behr's history of the period concludes by suggesting persuasively that the farce that the Volstead Act made of law enforcement left in its wake a defeatist tolerance of both lawlessness and corruption at high levels that was to become deeply entrenched within the American psyche, so much so—one could argue by extension—that Prohibition itself will not quite die as an issue.

Even today, there are those who feel that if only it were enforced properly, with the full political and budgetary resources of an immensely more powerful state this time, it might profitably be tried again. The whole debate has been overshadowed since the 1980s by the drugs question, seen as an even more pressing social evil than enslavement to liquor, and yet the hysteria goes on. A social history of drink (both alcoholic and nonalcoholic) by British writer Andrew Barr was accused, on its US publication, by one press reviewer as having more sympathy for alcohol itself than for its victims. There is a whole stratum of opinion in the United States, reaching deep into the intelligentsia, that cannot tolerate any talk of alcohol that doesn't come hedged about with shrill, dissuasive moralisms. Neither the accumulated medical casualties nor the social degradation wrought by Prohibition have proved sufficient, in the recounting of modern American history, to mature this view. It remains stubbornly, defiantly impermeable to reason, like the article of religious faith that it almost always simultaneously is. And yet there are lessons to be absorbed from the Volstead era, lessons that would go some way to mitigating the present debacle if only the legislatures and judicatures of the developed world would hear them.

One of these began to be articulated in the 1920s while the drama was playing itself out. When the first tentative assertion was made by its critics, "Prohibition doesn't work," it threatened to have the disabusing impact of the little boy pointing out the emperor's nudity to the massed ranks of the gullible. The anti-saloon lobby that had invested so much capital and campaigning effort in seeing Prohibition enshrined on the statute retorted by saying that it could perfectly easily work if people would simply obey the law, to which the riposte could only be, then as now, that a law that falls so far short of public consensus will inevitably be widely flouted. In any event, the "people" of this simplistic prescription appeared not to include the custodians of the law themselves, so that a law that fewer and fewer citizens were able to respect was being intrusively and abusively enforced by agencies that considered themselves above it, a state of affairs more suited to a country where power has been usurped by a military goon-squad than to a mature democracy.

The 13 years of the 18th Amendment are in this sense a fascinating, if cumulatively tragic, illumination of how far the elastic of the legal apparatus can be stretched before it irreparably snaps. A pressure group dedicated to changing an unjust law in a constitutional state may succeed by dint of several years' petitioning and civil disobedience, but when an entire society holds the law in contempt, it may be rendered inoperable so quickly that its revocation becomes an executive formality, because the alternative is so fraught with embarrassments. The fiasco of the Volstead Act made this point luridly manifest.

The next point proved by the noble experiment is that simply declaring a substance off-limits does not automatically diminish the demand for it. Eventually the toxic garbage sold in the backstreets may have put off the more discerning souls, but those who felt a great gaping hole in their lives without a supply of their preferred intoxicant made a virtue of necessity by drinking it. That in turn created the climate in which a bootlegger who could supply uncontaminated liquor that had been seized on its way to other markets, or at worst whiskey that was merely watered down as opposed to having been boiled off from foot lotion and flavored with caramel, would be bound to make a killing—of the financial sort rather than the literal. The scarcity created by legal restrictions does not make a commodity undesirable, any more than natural scarcity does, otherwise there wouldn't be such a reliably bullish market for the *grand cru* wines of Burgundy's most highly ranked estates.

Most instructively of all, though, the lesson that reverberates down the decades from Prohibition is its analogy with the War on Drugs. It has to be conceded that the international drug laws do carry a rough-and-ready public consensus, with the result that appeals for their reassessment are still routinely brushed aside without creating widespread public disquiet. Each new generation of Western youth, however, finds itself more exposed to the everyday use of proscribed substances than the one before, with the result that more and more people have come to see the panoply of mystification and scare-mongering that has been used to keep the laws in place as having no basis in rational reality. Many of these individuals will go on to leave recreational drug use behind, for a variety of reasons, and may not therefore have anything to fear from the law, but they can't ever again believe that drugs are necessarily inimical to health, or that they represent a vicious spiral that can only be escaped, if at all, with the greatest difficulty, and with extensive collateral damage to one's relationships with others. Prohibition was repealed because Americans came to see that, while the legal presence of alcohol in society indubitably entailed a marginal risk in the form of those unable to control their intake of it, making such a staple substance illegal created far greater and costlier risks—and none greater or costlier than the criminal state of emergency that contravention produced from sea to shining sea.

• • •

Delegates to the Ohio Prohibition Congress of 1918, jubilating in advance at the hastening day of alcohol's demise, were right about two things. One was that they had won, by foul means and fair, the hearts and minds of enough members of the United States Congress to ensure their program would become law in the imminent future. The second, which the more circumspect among them did not choose to dwell on too lengthily, was that the law would not prevail if other countries—America's trading partners in particular—did not also move in the same direction. Not only was there the ever-present risk of smuggling via Canada, Mexico and the Caribbean, a trade that was to become enormously lucrative to those prepared to man the nocturnal boats and bribe the coast guards, but the government could hardly stop Americans from traveling abroad to countries where they were still able to drink.

If Prohibition was to work, not just the supply of alcohol, but the taste for it had to be progressively choked off. Wayne Wheeler even made an attempt at this time to have drinking banned among American soldiers serving in Europe during the Great War. France in particular he viewed as a cesspit of depravity. A country festooned with vineyards, where the local people drank wine at all hours of the day, and that had lived for far too long on the immoral earnings from selling its contaminating poisons internationally, could only represent a wilderness of spiritual hazards to the innocent Midwestern boy fresh off the troop carrier. The proposal was never implemented, and the war was in any case over by the time the Volstead Act became law, but as other countries declined to follow America into the tunnel of Prohibition, it was forced to retreat into a kind of Stalinist insularity, committed, in the absence of revolutionary zeal elsewhere, to building teetotalism in one country.

If Western authorities have learned anything at all from the failure of Prohibition, it is that it can't work unless everybody does it. It is this salient fact that has determined the tenor and scope of the international effort to suppress the drug trade, estimated in 1999 to be worth around $375 billion annually, or around 8 percent of world trade. Led by the DEA, a colossal global network of espionage, surveillance and policing activity is now devoted to trying to intercept the movements of narcotics around the world, to eradicate the production of intoxicant crops such as opium, coca and cannabis by making aid packages to impoverished governments conditional upon their agreeing to pursue the growers more vigorously, and to expropriating the profits of drug dealers for drug prevention programs within their own jurisdictions. Supporting this is a sporadically renewed effort to kill off the demand for drugs at source, so that it will cease to be profitable for Third World farmers to produce such commodities. Simultaneously, the demand goes on relentlessly increasing, as greater numbers within each new generation coming of age admit to having tried one or more of the proscribed substances at least once, and with greater numbers admitting to being regular, nonproblematic users.

Drugs are more available than ever before, more people are selling them than ever before, and their retail value on the streets has in most cases been inflation-proofed to a degree unthinkable in the legitimate market. The biggest single downward pressure on price, however—in this, as in other markets—is demand. Markets are often created by loss-leading initiatives, but fall away when the true cost of the commodity offered begins to be passed on. A smart restaurant offering lunch for $15 will get customers in, but either they will balk when lunch suddenly reverts to its traditional $40, or they will realize they are only eating plates of rocket and olive oil while the nondiscount patrons are luxuriating in sevruga and foie gras.

The economics of the drug trade are far more complex, and far more flexible, than this. Each material dealt in finds its natural economic level among its target constituency, and once the market is established, provision of it is largely determined by what customers pay. Moreover, a poor batch of pills, or a consignment of heavily adulterated coke, is absorbed with little or no adverse effect on consumer loyalty. It is insouciantly accepted that one will be sold short measures or substandard fare from time to time. Nobody asks for their money back, and given that the supply network in a particular locale may amount to a virtual monopoly, there may not be the chance of taking one's custom elsewhere. One may ask why suppliers near the top of the chain don't feel the urge to augment their profits with price hikes of the same order of inflationary regularity as consumers are habituated to in every other walk of life, to which the answer largely has to be because the client base is expanding so reliably, by word of mouth, by example and by the gradual unfettering of public discourse on the subject, that there isn't really the need. When the substances being dealt in are of high potential addictiveness, and especially where a dependent client is more or less mortgaged to one constant supplier, the above equation may well cease to apply.

Greater availability and stable prices have been the lethally effective supports of the drug trade's countercampaign against the enforcement industry. As growing demand ensures growing profitability, so the initiatives against it become more desperate. While they themselves shy away from hanging heroin smugglers, the Western democracies raise not a squeak of protest when such sentences are handed down in southeast Asia. This has always been the case. A British writer, E. G. Kemp, traveling in the Hunan province of China in 1920 observed that martial law under the imposition of a Christian Chinese, General Feng, had resulted in the closure of the opium dens and a steep decline in dealing in the town of Changde. Soldiers found selling opium were summarily executed, civilians were fined, flogged and then paraded about the town with shaming placards around their necks. This, to Kemp, constituted "a wonderful purification." She must have wondered why they didn't try it out at home in the East End of London on those coolies who entertained members of the theatrical profession in their dens of debauchery, unless of course she felt that such barbarities were fit for the native Chinese, albeit those at the mercy of a Christian teetotaler, but would be a little de trop when applied to naturalized British citizens.

A certain unease was felt in Britain in the 1990s when two teenage girls were sentenced to a program of daily whippings by a court in Singapore after they had been found in possession of a quantity of heroin. The girls claimed they had been used unwittingly as couriers, but that defense notoriously cuts no ice. Although clemency was eventually granted by means of diplomatic intercession, there was a strong body of opinion in the UK that believed their stupidity ought to be as severely punished as if they were the linchpins of an international cartel.

What are the antecedents of this infuriated, unforgiving attitude to intoxication in others? Can the old religious disapprovals still be spurring us on? Or is it that we find something deeply unsettling in the sight of others acting as if the apparatus of the law, and the forces ranged in its defense, were mere paper tigers? A Conservative member of the House of Lords is briefly suspended from the UK Parliament for purchasing a modest quantity of cocaine from a journalist within the confines of the Palace of Westminster—the lawgiver disregarding the law in the very site of its enactment. A teenage professional footballer, randomly tested after a training session, gives a positive result for cannabis, cocaine and ecstasy (and has his career summarily terminated). The son of the consort to the British heir-apparent confesses to an uncontrolled appetite for cocaine, while his own son takes up smoking at school. The daughter of the President and the British Prime Minister's son have both been publicly shamed in the press for being seen in a drunk and incapable state. The steady drip-drip of stories such as these has contributed hugely to demystifying the aura of unbridled maleficence that once surrounded drug use—they show that drugs are taken by people who, in the touching parlance of the high-school adventure yarns of another era, are theoretically supposed to "set an example"—and yet the moral bluster that always accompanies them in the conservative press suggests that, far from becoming inured to the fact that other people use drugs, we are expected to be repeatedly horrified by it.

What seems more likely to be the motivating force behind this concern, however, such as it is, is less a vindictive desire to see a disreputable body of law upheld than a conviction that drug-takers need to be saved from themselves, and from the sales pitches of the dealers, before they do themselves irredeemable damage. It is easy to forget, as we read of narcotics surveillance teams shot down by highly trained guerrillas over the jungles of Colombia, that it was that precise concern that led to the framing of the drug laws in the first place.

Until the later years of the nineteenth century, the concept of drug abuse barely existed. Great debates were joined in the late nineteenth century on how individuals suffering from alcohol dependency should be treated, with the European medical vanguard typically insisting that alcoholic behavior was a symptom of underlying psychological disturbance, a species of what the French termed monomania, rather than a purely physical condition in itself.

When the term "alcoholism" was deployed, it referred to the effects of heavy drinking, much as "morphinism" denoted the physical outcome of intravenous opiate use, rather than the addiction itself. The modern appropriation of the term to refer to chronic addiction to the substance, whether or not it could be exposed as having an obvious psychic antecedent, was in itself undermined when alcoholism was dropped, in the late 1970s, from the World Health Organization's International Classification of Diseases. What are now universally called "drugs" hardly entered into this dialectic. Substances such as opium, its derivative morphine, cocaine and later heroin and the barbiturates were classified purely as medicines, and were relatively freely available. Once a doctor sold a prescription for a particular ailment, it was deemed that it became the patient's property, so that repeat dispensations could be claimed on it ad infinitum.

It is worth remembering that the laudanum (opiated alcohol) that found such culturally iconic favour among English poets of the Romantic period was initially recommended to many of them, as it was to its most celebrated monographer, de Quincey, to relieve localized pain, in his case rheumatic pain brought on by bathing his head in icy water.

Martin Booth makes the point in his impeccably dispassionate history of the drug that, far from being an evil substance, opium and its derivatives have been among the very first rank of pharmacology's forces in the service of human comfort, still mitigating a hulking mass of suffering the world over even today. Other drugs, such as cocaine, were available without prescription, sold as linctuses and inhalant powders for topical relief from cold symptoms, with little other advice to the purchaser than to use them as required. It was only when it began to come to the attention of the medical profession that a minority of individuals was developing a ruinous fixation on certain substances that the idea of controlling them more strictly was first proposed.

The use of medical substances as entertainment was treated with a certain amount of levity in some contexts, as was shown by the

London theaters that offered the novelty of a hit of nitrous oxide to patrons in order to get them into the mood for the knockabout comedy to come. Laughing gas, to be sure, had enjoyed a career as sideshow attraction at carnivals and fairs since before it came to be used as an anesthetic, initially during dental extractions, in the mid-nineteenth century. It was Sir Humphrey Davy who had first proposed its use as a pain suppressant over forty years before, and who also enthusiastically commended its powers as an intoxicant. Unlike its fellow anesthetic, ether, nitrous oxide presents very little in the way of risk to the respiratory function, to blood pressure or the action of the heart or to the processes of the liver, kidneys or gastrointestinal tract, and while the quantity of ether inhaled by a patient undergoing surgery had to be administered in the presence of air to dilute it, raising the possibility of accidental overdosing if the proportions weren't right, nitrous oxide could be taken straight. When Davy introduced certain of his well-connected friends to the gas, they were so enthralled by the visionary effects a concentrated inhalation could deliver that they discussed the idea of founding an establishment along the lines of a genteel public house—a "nitrous oxide tavern"—where patrons would be piped with gas, rather than plied with vulgar drink. The 1840s were the great founding decade of anesthesia, with nitrous oxide, ether and chloroform all making their surgical debuts within three years of each other. After their success in mitigating the torture of tooth-pulling, they were widely used in other procedures, and came to be particularly commended during childbirth. (Queen Victoria, whom scarcely any nineteenth-century intoxicant appears to have bypassed, was delivered of Prince Leopold with the aid of chloroform in 1853, barely six years after its experimental introduction.)

The gases came to replace such crude presurgical administrations as alcohol or opium, or—in cases where the patient wasn't deemed to be of sufficient standing to warrant the expense of brandy—a blow to the head, or else partial asphyxiation. A procedure like amputation had been carried out to a descant of screaming agony, with the thrashing patient pinioned to the table by muscular surgeons' assistants. In that context, it was perhaps hardly surprising that a substance like nitrous oxide should be seen not merely as an ameliorative adjunct to the medical armory, but as a more general boon to humankind. That is, in taking away pain, it delivered the fullness of sensory pleasure that the negation of acute suffering always brings.

With the example of eminent scientists before them, first the beau monde and then the generality derived much harmless (and, in the case of ether, occasionally toxic) pleasure from the recreational use of anesthetic gas. Scarcely a decade after its introduction, the hypodermic syringe was invented, and anesthesia took another revolutionary turn, so that gassing came to be seen as more and more antiquated. Inasmuch as the gases bequeathed a cultural as well as medical legacy, though, they left in the popular mind an intimation that pharmacological substances could well have a ludic face on the obverse of the prescriptive one, particularly where they involved the easing of pain. Spirituous alcohol had once been medical, of course, but became unalterably recreational. Wine was used in classical times to assist in the rudimentary sterilization of wounds, but that application was a helpful supplement to what was firstly a hedonistic substance. Anesthetic gas was a recreational material that, in becoming fully medicalized, came to enjoy both statuses simultaneously. While nitrous oxide transformed the operating table from a place of medieval torment into one of sweet relief, it also licitly dispensed its benison at country fairs and urban theaters, pop concerts and student parties.

When the substance being used for fun was as relatively innocuous as laughing gas, it posed no problems to society. What began to turn the tide was the sportive use of items such as cocaine hydrochloride, morphine and later heroin. Even in these instances, official concern was not immediate. As early as 1857, when the Sale of Poisons Bill was laid before the British Parliament to try to limit the distribution of opiates, the point was made during the debate and in the public hearings that control would inevitably prove unenforceable owing to the sheer pervasiveness of laudanum and opium use. The Bill suggested that chemists be required to keep such substances under lock and key, but how would that be practicable, asked one of the magistrates giving evidence, when something in the region of a hundred transactions a day were quite typical at a busy city pharmacy? People believed in opium as a cure-all, and hedging about its availability with an adventitious bureaucratic pantomime was hardly likely to prove popular. The Bill died a natural death.

Possibly as a result of reports from China made topical by the Opium Wars, however, the subject itself refused to die, and in 1868, Parliament passed the Poisons and Pharmacy Act. This established the first serious restrictive framework for regulating how and by whom opium, and a range of other substances, could be sold. The maximum penalty for contravention was set at a very modest £5. Whilst the numbers of convictions under the Act were extremely low, it did have one measurable effect in that it substantially reduced the incidence of infant opium mortality, caused by nursing mothers and nannies overdosing howling babies on opium preparations to get them off to sleep. There the matter rested legislatively until the cocaine panic of the Great War, as discussed in chapter 4, persuaded legislators that the 1868 Act was impotent to deal with the upsurge in popularity of the drug.

Several factors lie behind the formulation in 1916 of the emergency wartime regulations codified as the Defence of the Realm Act, section 40B. Firstly, there were the luridly publicized fatalities, such as those of the Yeoland sisters, actresses whose grisly double suicide by cocaine overdose highlighted the dangers of allowing such a substance to be used recreationally in a world as louche and amoral as the West End theater reportedly was. Secondly, there was the prosecution of a war that was grinding attritionally on, seemingly without prospect of early resolution, to consider. Anything seen as likely to undermine further the will to fight of men who had already survived the carnage of Mons, Arras and the Somme had to be held in check, and the myth got about—largely through the efforts of trouble-seeking newspaper reports—that actresses and prostitutes were plying soldiers on furlough with cocaine during wild West End nights out. Thirdly, the apparent involvement of members of the immigrant communities—both Chinese and West Indian—in controlling the distribution of drugs, and the unseemly associations that many of these men had lured vulnerable white girls into, fomented a paranoid fear that racial contamination may be the outcome of uncontrolled drug use. There were white girls on the arms of black men in the underground dives of the West End, and more white girls lying stupefied on the divans in the opium dens of Limehouse.

Inevitably, it wasn't just their bloodstreams that the politicians wanted to protect. They were seen as sexually vulnerable to their black- and yellow-skinned companions, on the one hand to the carnal rapacity of the obscenely endowed Negro, and on the other to the vile, hyperimaginative sadism of the Chinaman. In this context, dope—then the all-embracing colloquialism for recreational drugs—could easily wear down the resistance of feebleminded women, and at worst, might be capable of lashing them into a venereal frenzy, with all the ghastly consequences of syphilis, amateur abortions and miscegenation that would entail.

None of these reasons, however, would alone have enabled DORA 40B to solidify into permanent legislation, and then withstand the verdict of history. Their patronizing view of women and insulting racial stereotyping belong to an all but vanished era, or at least could not now be made explicitly the motivation for any lawmaking. What changed the world forever was the realization that controlling the recreational use of pharmaceutical drugs was not simply a matter of regulating the pharmacists. Increasingly, these drugs were being bought on the streets and in the bars, by people who would not have had the slightest clue how to convince a chemist that they needed a bottle of cocaine. When the police arrested Willy Johnson in central London in 1916 and brought him to trial, he was acquitted because, although he wasn't a registered pharmacist (he had an established criminal record and lived with a prostitute), he hadn't been seen actually selling the cocaine he had in his possession, only attempting to. The Poisons and Pharmacy Act only referred to the unlicensed sale of drugs. Thus did the legislative occasion arise for proscribing unauthorized possession of them. In future, the cocaine in Johnson's bag would be enough in itself to convict others caught as he was, whether they had managed to sell any of it or not, and whether indeed they intended to sell it at all. This simple, radical, but fatally flawed principle was the Achilles' heel of the new law, and was to set the stage—did Parliament but know it—for the century of human misery and legislative disaster that was to follow.

With the exception of the Misuse of Drugs Act of 1971, which established the A, B and C classification system of relative seriousness for the controlled substances, all subsequent British drug legislation has amounted to little more than updating the law by adding new substances to it—all of which, mysteriously, tend to fall under Class A, attracting the severest penalties. Legislation coming into effect under the New Labour government in 1998 handed local councils the power to close down any establishment in which drug use was found to be taking place. This, it was hoped, would transfer the onus onto the proprietors to act as unpaid police officers, an honor that surprisingly few seem enthusiastic to assume. None of that would have been possible without the 1916 regulations. The aim of earlier legislation had been to regulate the sale of certain substances that, it was felt, posed a significant hazard to public health by being too freely available. When the law was made to look impotent in controlling the situation of a man who may or may not have obtained cocaine legally from a registered pharmacist offering to sell it to passersby, it was decided that it had to control the likes of him as well as unscrupulous shopkeepers, but it could think of no more precise means of doing that than to criminalize mere possession of the drug. In this, it criminalized not just the unauthorized dealer of cocaine, but everybody who took it as well. By needlessly wielding such a sledgehammer against a whole stratum of society, it invented a criminal class where previously there had been none.

It is difficult to think of another legislative move of comparable magnitude that, instead of responding in the usual way to an antisocial activity by making it illegal, turned a hitherto blameless pursuit into a crime. The example of American Prohibition was not yet before the world, and so the model of outlawing possession and private use of drugs was adopted everywhere. Even when Prohibition showed what happened to society when criminal classes were created ex nihilo by an act of government, the sledgehammer was not relinquished, because it was felt that the use of other intoxicants than alcohol was of sufficiently recent provenance to be susceptible to being stamped out again. Moreover, the point was made once and for all that ordinary people had no right of access to certain substances, which were henceforward to be made the exclusive preserve of the medical profession. They could fool about with nitrous oxide if they must, but cocaine and the rest were strictly out-of-bounds to them. Every contravention of the drug laws since has been nothing more than a presumption to differ with that asinine diktat.

In the United States, the same progressive accretion of bad law as has been the case in Britain made the smoking of opium illegal in

1909, and introduced the Harrison Narcotic Act of 1914, under which cocaine and the opiates were made subject to stringent controls. Alcohol was prohibited in 1920, heroin finally banned altogether (even on prescription) in 1924, and in 1937 a labyrinth of specious tax regulations was used to close off access to cannabis. There was even less informed debate before substances were expropriated from its citizens than there had been in Europe. We have already seen the fate of alcohol Prohibition, but the Marijuana Tax Act was eventually buried in the 1960s when the Supreme Court ruled it unconstitutional.

In order to tie up the straggling ends, the Comprehensive Drug Abuse Prevention and Control Act was passed in 1970, in which the tabulation approach was formally enshrined in law. This permitted for five classes of drugs, "depending on the potential for abuse and dependency and the accepted medical use of each drug." At the lowest level—Schedule Five—are noncritical levels of narcotics such as codeine in painkillers, while at the top are substances that are thought so toxic and hazardous that neither private citizens nor the medical profession may handle them. These include heroin and LSD, but also cannabis, so Schedule One is not precisely comparable to Britain's Class A. Nonetheless, it was an attempt at a taxonomic system aimed at making the laws against drugs appear scientifically founded that the UK was to copy when it introduced its own version the following year.

It will be seen that the American legislation posits that drugs that are available for doctors to prescribe, such as morphine, amphetamine and cocaine, should attract milder censure than those that are deemed to have no medical use, whereas the British rank them according to their perceived levels of toxicity regardless of their roles in medicine. This is why cannabis and cocaine, for example, find themselves in opposite categories on either side of the Atlantic: in the USA, cannabis is Schedule One and cocaine is Schedule Two, while Britain has classified cocaine as Class A and has recently downgraded cannabis from Class B to Class C. These variant positions are of course irreconcilable, but that does not stop the enforcement industries in each country from claiming to be making common cause. (Notwithstanding that, the DEA is at a loss to understand why heroin retains its place in the British National Formulary, the index of all pharmaceutical materials available to the health service.)

As David Lenson has argued, these legislative moves toward codification had the effect not of making the law more precise in its operations, but of streamlining it by dealing with all proscribed substances within the same narrow bands, thus paving the way for the ruthlessly simplistic antidrug crusades of the 1980s and 1990s, in which all niceties such as which drugs one was taking, in what concentrations and frequencies and so forth, were all subsumed under the querulous imperative not to be on anything called Drugs at all. The effect is not accidental. It was a deliberate function of the need to deal with the burgeoning numbers of drug offenders as swiftly and as retributively as possible.

The 1970 US Act and the 1971 Misuse of Drugs Act in the UK are as umbilically related as their legal approaches and historical proximity would suggest. They were the responses of legal systems in panic at the widespread contempt that existing laws were being shown, specifically arising as a result of the explosion in drug use— particularly that of hallucinogenics—that the late sixties had seen. Not even a fivefold increase in the maximum fine for possession of cannabis in the UK, instituted by a moribund ultraconservative regime in 1994, and at first enthusiastically retained by its officially centrist successor, has had any measurable effect on the incidence of use. But then, with any passing doctor who is asked for his or her opinion on the subject declaring the stuff to be substantially harmless, and juries unanimously acquitting those arraigned for growing and supplying it for medical application, how can it? With each accumulation of retributive severity in the matter of illegal intoxicants, the law only renders itself more preposterous as it leaves reality further and further behind.

The Frankfurt philosopher Theodor Adorno remarked, in one of his darkest late meditations on the course of modern history, that whereas no universal story of general human progress could convincingly be written, there was nonetheless one that led from the slingshot to the megaton bomb. In the development of destructive capacity, at least, our species has been formidably resourceful. A rumor persisted for many years that Albert Einstein destroyed the drafts of his last major theoretical breakthrough after he saw the apocalypse that political authorities were preparing to draw down upon humanity with the aid of atomic fission. The history of intoxication is blighted by just such an indomitably contradictory impulse. As the numbers of intoxicants known to humanity have multiplied, so the repertoire of sanctions against them has grown more invasive and more prohibitive.

Christianity banned the Eleusinian celebrations in order to establish its own spiritual hegemony, Islam banned all intoxication, and then the civil powers stepped in to curtail and repress practices they found inconvenient among their client populations in the colonies (whose ancestors had virtually invented most of the forms of intoxication banned today), and finally their own citizens at home were, by degrees, denied nearly everything.

The use of intoxicants in their multifarious forms is as old as humanity itself, and yet the last hundred years have seen legislatures all over the world claiming for themselves the right to dispossess their populations of part of their true biological inheritance. This could only be achieved by malevolently denying the genetic imprint of that inheritance, by improbably—and, in the event, tragically—seeking to pretend that intoxication was a late, decadent development of a Western culture gone rank with immorality. But a biological predisposition cannot be wished away by legislative fiat, any more than gay people could be rendered celibate because the law came to revile them. The impulse persists, which is why supplying it has become such a lucrative worldwide business. Freed from any licensing system, trade agreements, price fixing and—what is worst—from any obligation to guarantee quality, the international drug trade conducts its affairs in ostentatious defiance of American policemen in their soldier costumes. And faced with the final couple of intoxicants still begrudgingly allowed to them, increasing numbers of individuals who thought they were born freer than that are ushered into the embrace of gunrunners, money-launderers and backstreet chemists of every level of ability and scruple.

It is against this baleful impasse that some commentators, intoxicology specialists and social analysts, but also representatives of the enforcement industry, legislators and teachers, have begun to question whether a way back can be found from the disaster before complete anarchy takes hold.

The debate over legalization or decriminalization of banned substances is motivated by an immediate and overwhelming fact: that bans don't work. That is to say, while they undoubtedly deter some, they can never be—and never have been—wholly effective, and bans on intoxicants, as compared to bans on publications or forms of political activity, are the very least effective of all prohibitions.

There are two chief reasons for this. One is that dealing in illicit intoxicants is much less visible than organizing and participating in a march or protest rally, which can be beaten back with batons, water cannon and ultimately guns and tanks in a regime hell-bent on repression, and considerably less detectable than underground pamphlets and books, which can be seized and pulped. Drugs are not about advertising defiance as in the case of the former activity, nor do they remain in circulation as with the latter, because they are intended, at the end of the commercial chain, to be consumed. In transit along that chain, they are readily concealable. A woman arrested in Pakistan while about to board a flight to Amsterdam in July 1999 was allegedly found to have 2.7 kilograms of heroin in her luggage, but such stories are, as the enforcement industry well knows, only the high-profile successes in a campaign that is being defeated by overwhelming odds. It is widely estimated that about 90 percent of drugs carried across international borders like this reach their intended destinations without interference.

The second reason for the ineffectuality of law enforcement is the sheer quantity and variety of contravention. A banned trade union movement must be sparing in its enterprises, for fear of its numbers being critically reduced by arrests and killings. Underground printing presses can only put out so much literature without running an unacceptable risk of detection. Somebody somewhere, by contrast, is buying, selling or taking drugs every minute of the day. Contravention of the drug laws, certainly at the level of personal consumption, is a continuous, literally unstoppable activity.

During the 1990s, the police attempt in the UK to stop ecstasy use—as distinct from dealing in it—fizzled down to virtually nothing. Arresting everybody queuing to get into a nightclub who turned out to have one or two pills in their pockets is simply not worth the bother. Occasionally, one would see a balding middle-aged man improbably tapping his foot to the pounding Techno music, beadily watching the activities of everybody around him and perhaps asking a copiously sweating dancer taking a break to slug at a bottle of water, "Do you know where you can get pills?" One of my respondents, who acted for a while as a club dealer's runner, was approached one night by a young woman who asked her, "Do you know anybody here who might be selling drugs?"—phraseology that only needed the courtesy of a final "madam" to give the game away conclusively. The tacit understanding seemed to be that they were mainly interested in the dealers themselves, not the bottom-end purchasers who mostly arrived at and left the clubs empty-handed, whatever might happen to slip through their fingers while they were in there.

The volume of global drug use would not in itself be an argument for legalization. Many other forms of lawbreaking, such as negligent environmental pollution by large companies, are so extensive as to be virtually unpoliceable, and yet the effort to prevent it is a constructive and worthwhile one, for the reason that its effects will damage our habitat for ourselves and for succeeding generations. But drug-taking is only tenuously a crime in the traditional sense of the word, because it does not involve an individual or group victimizing another individual or group. One may, in the long term and depending on the circumstances, do lasting damage to one's own physical or mental health by taking drugs in an uncontrolled and chaotic fashion, but even that worst-case scenario, which is not in any event the greater part of the picture, is not in other respects illegal. Slashing one's arms in a fit of attention-seeking is not illegal. Nor is starving oneself silly in the interest of looking like a supermodel. Nor is becoming irretrievably addicted to cigarettes, or slithering into alcoholism—assuming medical theoreticians have made up their minds yet as to whether that latter condition exists or not.

And yet smoking cannabis in the privacy of one's apartment is enough, theoretically, to earn one an entry on the police computers as a criminal. If the political and judicial authorities were to say (which they don't, the universal formula being that it would "send out the wrong message") that the efforts of the enforcement agencies were only being targeted at the importers and dealers of prohibited substances, there would still be a logical lacuna in the argument, but they might at least be reflecting the desire of the legislators of the early twentieth century to impede the activities of unauthorized traffickers. They are stuck, however, with the flawed legislation of the time that made possession itself illegal, and so they must also continue to fine and imprison those who only ever buy small quantities for personal use, and who might even wish that in a better world they wouldn't have to consort with the criminal classes in order to do so. (An intriguing aspect of legislation on both sides of the Atlantic is that while manufacturing, trading in and possessing banned substances is against the law, actually consuming them isn't, technically. The challenge would perhaps be to find a way of taking drugs that didn't involve possessing them. Claiming that you hadn't yet paid for them, and that they therefore remained the property of the dealer, won't work because the mere fact of having them about your person counts as possession. Whether having a pill placed directly onto your tongue by somebody else could conceivably count as possession might make an interesting test case, but who can be bothered with a rigmarole like that when there isn't seemingly anybody around to stop them anyway?)

Arguments for reform of the law, spanning the range from constructive decriminalization (accompanied by compulsory treatment programs) to blanket relegalization, are outlined in the works of many of the intoxication writers discussed in chapter 1. Terence McKenna's idiosyncratic manifesto, which endorses the use of economic blackmail against countries producing so-called "hard drugs" whilst enshrining the right of Americans to grow what they please, has already been mentioned. It is flawed to the degree that it accepts the doctrine of the inherent moral valencies of drugs—i.e., that some drugs such as LSD are beneficial, while others like alcohol are responsible for the corruption of the human soul—and thus replicates the spurious distinctions already embodied in the very laws it seeks to overturn. In essence, this is Timothy Leary stuff, but backed up with a little more academic gravitas than Dr. Leary was generally capable of mustering, fatally tying its case to a belief that something called the Archaic Revival is afoot, in which growing numbers are turning away from the sickly spectacle of consumerist capitalism in favor of a thoroughly Americanized version of spiritual freedom:

> A new global consensus appears to be building . . . The collapse of the Marxist alternative to media-dense, high-tech democratic consumerism has been swift and complete. For the first time in planetary history, a defined, albeit dimly defined, consensus exists for "democratic values" . . . It is a phenomenon of expanded consciousness driven by the information explosion. Democracy is an articulation of the Archaic notion of the nomadic egalitarian group. In its purest expression it is thoroughly psychedelic and its triumph seems ultimately certain.[5]

If this sounds by now a little like Francis Fukuyama on psilocybin ("The Cold War is over. We won. Get blitzed."), the resemblance is not wholly inexplicable. A symptomatic analysis of the fault lines in the McKenna doctrine might question whether there is necessarily anything egalitarian about the ascendant version of democracy now apparently advocated everywhere from Tripoli and Kabul to Brazzaville and Pyongyang. That "purest expression" of democracy is of course the one that political authorities in even the most enlightened regimes have told us is the only one we can't have, and if the desirability of those "democratic values" is a matter of such overweening global consent, why the need for scare quotes? If this is a commodity so "dimly defined" that we scarcely know what it is we are talking about, or how to name it, how can we know that we all want it, or indeed that this thing we all so elusively want is the same indivisible thing at all? That this is an ideology separated at birth from that of Professor Fukuyama's conservative triumphalism, but otherwise springing from the same North American womb, may be noted from the weedy exhalation that accompanies the "collapse of the Marxist alternative," and that we may safely take to be a sigh of relief. Notwithstanding its author's affecting descriptions of the mental liberations on offer from the drugs it chooses to valorize, this is an argument that hasn't a hope of being heeded by the enforcement industry, long attuned to sniffing out rancid hippieisms ever since Dr. Leary was sacked and ignored.

David Lenson offers a more realistic assessment of the factors at work in the legalization arguments, pointing out that it isn't just lawbreakers and enlightened politicians who may have an interest in seeing reform come about:

> The addition of products like Rogaine and Prozac to the pre-scription lists reinforces the notion that the pharmaceutical companies are trying to invade the markets previously served by quacks and outlaw dealers . . . [T]he new and expanded medical corporations are calling on the state to help them get their share of the interdicted markets. This would be the effect of "legaliza-tion," which is little more than a recognition that there is a lot of money to be made in euphorics and herbal remedies, and that the "legitimate" health-care establishment wants its share.[6]

The price to pay for relaxation of the statutes may be the wholesale medicalization of drug use, as the now officially tolerated substances became a matter of doctors' maintenance prescriptions. Surrender to treatment programs will be the stick that follows the carrot of decriminalization, with the implied aim being that although you won't now be fined or imprisoned for taking your preferred intoxi-cant, you will be expected to make a solemn pledge to come off it. Here is the gaping hole in the "free market" argument of someone like the Friedmanite theoretician Thomas Szasz efficiently exposed. Since the manufacture and, to some extent, the dispensation of most of the relegalized substances will be in the hands of the giant phar-maceutical companies, the market will be anything but free. In fact, it is arguably freer now than it would be under a prescription sys-tem. Illicit production would therefore inevitably continue.

Perhaps the most tantalizing case in point in this context is that of cannabis. Given that it is such a significant cash crop in the United States, legalization would provide a major boost for agriculture, particularly if the market for tobacco continues to decline world-wide. As far as America at least was concerned, the money currently spent on cannabis would all continue to be spent within the national economy, and partakers would not be patronizing the crime syndi-cates. Utopia? Alas, no:

The trouble is, of course, that the plant is so easy to cultivate that no one would need the synthetic alternatives that the drug companies would like to sell . . . Nor would it be possible to collect taxes on this trade; it would be like trying to tax crabgrass or dandelions. It is this escape from the macroeconomy that makes legal cannabis too subversive to be considered seriously . . .[7]

Lenson goes on to advocate, like McKenna, an immediate general amnesty for cannabis offenders serving jail terms (provided their felonies did not also involve weapons), as well as federal repeal of the ban on cultivation, sale and possession of the drug. With luck, that action would then create the context in which a wider public debate about the drug laws could take place. But he is not especially optimistic:

This proposal has the virtue of realism, but probably has little chance of adoption, since there is no money and power to be accrued by police, National Guard, hospitals, or drug companies if people are allowed to grow a weed and do what they please with it.[8]

The revocation of the ban could only seriously be advanced purely and simply as a blow for civil liberties—an argument not likely to curry much favor in an enforcement culture degraded to the level of deploying the United States military against American citizens.

For Alexander Shulgin too, the issue is one of individual liberty. In the case of the drug compounds that he and his experimental group of volunteers tested on themselves over fifteen years, the psychedelic phenethylamines and tryptamines, their potential for offering the user profound and beneficial insights is too great to be expropriated by law:

Every drug, legal or illegal, provides some reward. Every drug presents some risk. And every drug can be abused. Ultimately, in my opinion, it is up to each of us to measure the reward against the risk and decide which outweighs the other . . . My philosophy can be distilled into four words: be informed, then choose.[9]

But it is precisely the privatisation of risk assessment that is denied us in the matter of intoxicants. We are so little trusted by political authorities to make our own judgments about the likely harm or gratification we may receive from the use of certain substances that it is thought better if they don't fall into our hands. Shulgin's work falls squarely within that pioneering tradition of alternative pharmacology that argues for the merits of hallucinogenic materials in particular as revelatory sacraments that can immeasurably enhance the lives of those who take them, and holds that it is an offense to try to deny them to a humanity more alienated from its own nature—at least in the developed world—than at any previous time in its history. "Our generation," he comments, "is the first, ever, to have made the search for self-awareness a crime."[10]

In the face of the conventional wisdom that one grows out of drug-taking as one slips into maturity, Shulgin insists that the urge to self-awareness becomes more intense as one grows older, which helps to explain why, in his seventies, he was happily still ingesting these substances—and writing about the resulting experiences with a positively evangelistic fervor. Rediscovering a hallucinogenic compound called DOM (2,5-dimethoxy-4-methylamphetamine), which was evidently distributed free in incautiously large doses throughout the Haight-Ashbury district of San Francisco in the summer of 1967, when it was known as STP, after a motor-oil additive to which it was not in fact related, he says of the effects of taking 4mg of it, "It is a beautiful experience. Of all past joys, LSD, mescaline, cannabis, peyote, this ranks number one." On 5mg, "I felt I knew what it was like to look across the brink towards insanity." On 10mg, "It is true that DOM has the glory and the doom sealed up in it . . . all the dark things are made clear." On 12mg, he tells us, "The music was exceptional, the erotic was exceptional, the fantasy was exceptional. Liszt's 'A Christmas Cantata No 1,' part 1, with eyes closed was an experience without precedent. There were some residual effects still noted the next day." The closing comment is a wistful sigh: "This may be a bit much for me."[11] All the twitching of eyeballs, grinding of teeth, the tremors, nauseous attacks and frank panics are meticulously catalogued, as are the flat disappointments, in a body of work that, while it does share some philosophical territory with the likes of McKenna, nonetheless carries greater authority because it is so rigorously grounded in scientific practice.

The greatest subversive impact any intervention can have against the forbidding bulwark of the drug laws is to see or read of somebody having a thoroughly rewarding time on the substances in question. Many take illegal drugs in the first place because they see their friends doing them and coming to no harm. In the propaganda of government drug "education" can be read the frustrated attempt to neutralize peer-group example as one of the motivating factors for embarking on a life of what they call "substance abuse," but the effort will always fail because what one sees with one's own eyes is a more powerful testament to reality than the tendentious alarums of authority, as everyone since St. Thomas can readily vouch. The Shulgins' two massive volumes are an extended refutation of the affected ignorance of the law, an ignorance that it does not itself labour under, but that it seeks to instill in its client populations by the evil of misinformation.

Kevin Williamson's work is more a straightforward polemic against the drug laws, in which he seeks to prioritize his proposed measures, so that the argument is not reducible to a simplistic "legalize everything" plea. He says the first two candidates for relegalization ought to be cannabis (because it is relatively harmless, and because the vast majority of drug convictions—around four-fifths—are for mere possession of this drug alone, so that a major dent would be made in the crime statistics for drugs if it ceased to be part of the equation) and heroin (because the medical consequences of heroin dependency need to be addressed free of the atmosphere of criminal taint that its victims now incur, and because the dependencies that it creates are largely responsible for the burgeoning property crime that represents a far more acute social malaise than simply getting high can ever do). The argument draws productively on the Dutch example, where licensed coffee shops are permitted to sell cannabis either loose or in pre-rolled joints despite the fact that the drug is still technically illegal. Williamson goes on to suggest that perhaps "drug-specific" establishments might flourish in the wake of the decriminalizations of cannabis and heroin, so that a cocaine bar might sit across the street from an ecstasy club. Small amounts of the drugs for personal use only would be dispensed, along with advice on safe procedure and an explanation of the effects for the uninitiated.

One of the most valuable assets of his book is a richly entertaining account of the adventures of a UK government propaganda campaign of the late 1990s called Scotland Against Drugs (with an acronym made in satirical heaven). Ninety percent of its budget of £1 million was wasted on an advertising campaign of negative publicity—the kind that doesn't exist—and when that failed, the committee of incompetents running it could come up with no more imaginative a ruse than to mount another lavish advertising campaign of negative publicity. As an illustration of official fatheadedness, it remains hard to better, not just because we can all laugh at the spectacle of government ministers donning sweatshirts and reversed baseball caps to show that it is perfectly possible to have a good old ravey time without mind-altering substances, but because it demonstrates that both the economics and the psychology of such disasters as these are faulty through and through.

Williamson ends by arguing, persuasively enough, that the benefits of repeal of the Misuse of Drugs Act would be such that society would come to ask itself why such a move was not made many years earlier. He also notes, however, that a supposedly more reform-minded British government, overturning a generation of finally moribund conservative retrenchment in May 1997, initially chose to stick doggedly to the same outworn mantras on drugs that its predecessor had done. The Home Secretary, a man whose brother smoked cannabis in the hippie sixties, and whose son was cautioned for offering to supply it to an undercover reporter in a pub, staked out the old Conservative territory once more by proclaiming soon after his government came to power that the arguments for cannabis legalization were "so irresponsible" because it was well known that smoking dope led on to harder drugs, which would destroy people's futures. After 18 years in opposition, this dog-eared superstition looked for a time about as new as New Labour thinking on drugs was likely to get. Reelection in 2001, however, brought fresh thinking to the Home Office, and although it is much too early to be generally optimistic, the reclassifying of cannabis and the recommendation to doctors to go back to prescribing heroin to patients who are addicted to it should duly be acknowledged as courageous and constructive measures.

Clearly, then, there will be no shortage of voices in the years to come calling for reform of the laws governing intoxicants, and given that the utter disarray that the enforcement industry finds itself in is only likely to worsen with time, it may be that one or two of the more modest proposals do stand a chance of being adopted. The sanctioning of cannabis preparations for medical treatment looks inevitable, as perhaps does a wholesale return to the maintenance philosophy in treating intravenous opiate addicts, if only to alleviate the spiraling social costs of the crime that many of them are responsible for. Whether the coffee shops of Amsterdam will ever arrive in London seems a little harder to postulate (although one called The Dutch Experience opened in the northwestern town of Stockport in 2001 after an initial false start bedeviled by police interference), and the chances of them coming to Washington, DC, are nil. Then again, as governments in need of revenue enviously eye the global value of the drug trade, it is harder still to imagine them continuing to forgo the potential takings to be made from it, if only they were brave enough to decide to mount a takeover bid. Representatives of successive Dutch governments and the police service have said, on and off the record, that they could conceivably countenance blanket decriminalization without worry, given the example that decriminalized cannabis has set, but that they are prevented—as all governments are—from relegalizing any drug by United Nations treaty agreements that specifically forbid any member state from doing so. When the United States, international linchpin of the enforcement industry, calls such a major part of the financial tune at the UN, any hope of renegotiating the relevant accords seems forlorn indeed.

In the light of the growing pressure from interested and informed parties on this question, it seems as well to conclude our interrogation of the drug laws by examining the arguments against legalization, not as they proceed from the mouths of conservative politicians, but from an informed source who has considered the arguments from an objective point of view, and concedes honestly enough that the present system is far from ideal. Erich Goode's contribution to the debate, published in the USA in the same year as Kevin Williamson's book was published in Britain, is the work of a sociologist who takes a rigorous content-analysis approach to the attitudes of all sides in the debate, before offering his own closely argued conclusions. If there is to be a cogent argument against reform of the existing statutes, this will probably be as articulate and persuasive as it will get.

Goode begins by acknowledging that the War on Drugs, renewed on such a spectacular scale in America by the Reagans in 1986, was driven more by outrage that drug-using individuals were flouting civil authority than by any palpable concern for the medical or social consequences of their actions. "Drug use," Nancy declared, "is a repudiation of everything that America is." Thus did the military come to be enlisted in the struggle against this unpatriotic internal element, making it harder than ever to perceive the issues that surround serious physical addiction, and all but impossible to discern the factors driving the occasional, nonproblematic use of drugs by so many American citizens. With regard to the latter, Goode attempts to fill in the gaps, citing "unconventionality, a desire for adventure, curiosity for a 'forbidden fruit,' hedonism, willingness to take risks, sociability, and subcultural involvement."[12] Beyond that suspiciously loaded designation "hedonism," there is otherwise no acknowledgment of the biggest factor of all: namely, the fact that the user happens to enjoy taking the substance concerned. Perhaps Goode feels this is addressed by hedonism, but this would imply that every pleasurable experience consciously opted for marks its practitioner out as a self-obsessed, card-carrying Aristippean. Under this definition, every glass of wine drunk with dinner would have to go down as hedonism, which seems a very milk-and-water version of the sensual life, to say the least, but the point is anyway well made that very few of these types of users will go on to present a problem to society, "except for the fact that they are often *targeted* as a problem" [his emphasis].[13]

In an analysis of prohibition as a legislative mechanism, it is accepted that there are two gradations of the punitive approach. One holds that criminalization can eradicate drug use altogether (to which we may with conviction put the question, "Then what is taking it so long?"); the other, more realistically, suggests that criminalization, in being at least marginally effective, is better than no criminalization at all. This latter view, it will emerge, is Goode's own preferred nostrum. He argues that the Volstead Act did bring about an initial drop in alcohol-related diseases, and appears not to be aware that they had begun to rise again before repeal, or to be unduly concerned that the incidences of people poisoned and killed by illegal alcohol soon made up for the shortfall.

Chapter 5 of his book offers a taxonomy of the five distinct sociopolitical types that attitudes to drugs shake down to. The first three of these are familiar enough: the cultural conservative (who might be an old-school right-wing tabloid reader) who believes that drug-taking is immoral, and that people should be severely dealt with for contravening the law of the land, as well as the consensual wishes of the majority; the free-market libertarian, à la Thomas Szasz, who holds that there is too much government interference in everyday life, and that we should be free to pursue our own pleasures, including drug-taking; and the radical constructionist (whom we might less honorifically dub the conspiracy theorist) who believes the War on Drugs is an attempt to scapegoat certain groups within society in order to deflect attention from the true institutional causes of social disaffection. That last position, superficially attractive to a socially critical or Marxist inclination, is still in itself a reactionary posture because it won't relinquish the idea that intoxication is a negative phenomenon. It still categorizes drug use as, in Goode's words, "an expression . . . of hopelessness brought on by urban decay."[14] But why precisely would economic empowerment, seen as the response to drug use on this analysis, "bring about a defeat of drug abuse as a major problem in American society?"[15] The colossal salaries being paid to futures traders in the 1980s in both America and Britain didn't cure many of them of a fondness for cocaine. This argument also fails to explain why any rock-industry plutocrat or squillionaire basketball-player would ever acquire a drug habit. Again, there is no acknowledgment that drug use may be motivated by enjoyment, and so we may—along with Goode himself—lay this inadequate argument to rest.

The remaining two types are of more recent vintage. The progressive legalizer is in favor of a rolling program of decriminalization because intoxicants should be seen as a matter of individual conscience and liberty, and in any event criminalizing otherwise socially respectful individuals in this way is wholly counterproductive.

Perhaps with certain press commentators specifically in mind, he states that these polemicists are usually in favor of more stringent controls on the legal intoxicants, and then administers what is intended to be the coup de grâce by saying that they naively argue that legalization will reduce drug use, presumably because the "forbidden fruit" factor will no longer obtain. His final type, the progressive prohibitionist, is a category fit for Professor Goode himself, a prescriptive theorist who holds that the health of the community must take precedence over the rights of the individual. Nobody has the right to harm himself if the health of society may thereby suffer. The progressive prohibitionists easily trump the arguments of the progressive legalizers, thinks Goode, because while the former are concerned with the intrinsic pharmacological harm that drugs can do, the latter's emphasis is only ever on the secondary harms caused by their illegality.

The legalizers also stand accused of failing to delineate precisely how legalization would work in practice, and of gleefully indicting the baleful consequences of prohibition without paying any concomitant attention to whatever unwanted by-products of legalization there might be. This point has some force, it must be conceded, although it is not universally true as a summation of the relegalization case, and it should also be admitted that there is indeed a strangely persistent belief among many legalizers (Williamson is a case in point) that the numbers of drug users would go down rather than up if the controls were lifted. My own expectation is that consumption of all drugs would increase after relegalization, slightly so in the case of opiates and major hallucinogenics, exponentially so with regard to cannabis, cocaine, ecstasy and amphetamines. Pretending it wouldn't is too much like dishonestly sugaring the pill of a radical proposal. But in any case, if drugs were being declared generally accessible once more, why would the fact that taxpayers were now exercising a right that was being restored to them need to be seen as undesirable? It would be rather like extending the licensing hours, and then bemoaning the fact that there were people in the pubs at midnight. If an act of public policy is right, why would its enactment be accompanied by the hope that as few people as possible would be seen to benefit from it? Legalizers must be brave enough to acknowledge that, in the short term at least, more problematic use and more addiction would arise from relegalization, and that the intensiveness of use among currently dysfunctional users would go through the roof.

The point is that all of this would be vastly outweighed by the reduction in both organized and opportunistic crime, by the more enlightened management of addiction than is currently on offer in the Western world (despite the Dutch and Swiss examples), and by the simple constitutional benefit to be gained from declining to classify whole swathes of society as criminal. At the close of this chapter, Goode asserts that there is anyway greater overlap between these last two positions than there is between any other two positions in the debate, which sounds to me a little like hoping that some of the genuine radicalism of the legalizers' position will rub off, by association, on the more ideologically timid progressive prohibitionism.

Goode identifies the five main proposals for law reform as follows: *legalization,* under which the sale of currently banned substances would be subjected to state licensing; *decriminalization,* here defined not (as it tends to be on the British side of the debate) as removing the threat of criminal sanctions surrounding drug use while the substances themselves remained technically illegal, but as a complete laissez-faire system, under which the distribution of drugs "would no more be the concern of the government than, say, selling tomatoes or undershirts is";[16] *partial decriminalization* in the Dutch sense, where the partiality may refer to the intermediate legal status now enjoyed by cannabis there, or indeed to the fact that only certain drugs, but not others, are affected; the *medical approach,* which treats some drug users as patients and assumes their basic motivation is maintenance of a dependency state, rather than recreation, and will clearly only apply to some drugs while the rest remain officially unavailable; and *harm reduction,* now vigorously in force throughout the Netherlands, Switzerland and parts of the UK, such as Liverpool, in which a combined medical and social-services strategy produces a drug-specific, and highly pragmatic, response to each local context, while arguments about changing the law take a backseat.

Harm reduction, of which Goode himself is an apostle, is summarized in the following desiderata:

> Stress treatment and rehabilitation; underplay the punitive, penal or police approach, and explore nonpenal alternatives to trivial drug offenses. Expand drug maintenance, especially

methadone programs; experiment with or study the feasibility
of heroin maintenance programs; expand drug education programs; permit heroin and marijuana to be used by prescription
for medical treatment. Consider ways of controlling the legal
drugs, alcohol and tobacco. Be flexible and pragmatic: Think
about new programs that might reduce harm from drug abuse,
and if one aspect of the program fails, scuttle it, and try something else. Remember: Drugs are not the enemy; harm to society
and its constituent members is the enemy. Whatever reduces
harm by whatever means necessary is all to the good.[17]

Except, of course, removing people from the police criminal computers by declaring that drug use is a blameless activity. Goode
acknowledges candidly that the harm-reduction argument is full
of internal dilemmas and inconsistencies, but avers—with fingers
crossed—that "reliable information and good common sense" will
save the day. Thus does the policy end not with the bang of a cell
door, but with a whimpering plea for everybody to be sensible. It
seems an act of almost superstitious wise-monkeyism to suggest
"nonpenal alternatives to trivial drug offenses" without seeing that
ceasing to consider them offenses altogether would be immaculately
nonpenal. Methadone as a solution to heroin is a flush that was
busted long ago, as was amply demonstrated by the findings of a
homelessness charity in the UK in August 1999, which surveyed 561
opiate addicts in the north of England on methadone maintenance,
and found fully 80 percent of them still using street heroin alongside
it. Heroin maintenance should not just be experimented with or
studied; it should be implemented forthwith in all jurisdictions. An
expansion of drug education programs sounds suspiciously like
more costly negative propaganda, shown time and again to be a
waste of public funds and yet still advocated as an article of faith
across the spectrum from liberal harm reductionists to hang-'em-
and-flog-'em conservatives, and will presumably be predicated yet
again on the assumption that the fewer people who take anything,
the better. Heroin is already permitted for medical treatment in
Europe, and cannabis may well follow, but the USA seems likely to
continue to lag behind in this while it is so obsessed with enforcement the world over. And the offer to consider any proposal that

reduces harm to society *except* the withdrawal of legal sanctions hobbles the entire otherwise rigorously fair-minded apparatus of harm reduction from the start. Calling every dope smoker and coke snorter a criminal is itself harmful, and no amount of Professor Goode's trusted "common sense"—a chimerical commodity once banished from the vocabulary of analytical sociology—can salve the harm done by the raids, the arraignments, the fines and jail terms that prohibition brings in its train.

In a chapter entitled "Business as Usual?" Goode addresses the question of whether current legislation is having, or can hope to have, any measurable impact on the incidence of drug consumption. Referring to successive attempts in the USA to eliminate the supply of cannabis, heroin and cocaine, he describes what he calls the "push-down/pop-up" syndrome, whereby the cutting off of one source in a targeted district only leads to another springing readily into its place. The aim of the DEA is now, of course, to try to stamp out the supply at its source by means of crop eradication in the producer countries, but the logistics of this are formidable and its chances of success can be contemplated in the light of some sobering statistics. The world's heroin supply could be grown in less than 50 square miles of field. The total worldwide area of land under coca cultivation is currently estimated at less than 1,000 square miles, while something in the region of 2.5 million square miles in South America alone is climatically suitable for it, having sufficient rainfall but no risk of frosts. A profit of about $250,000 per annum could be derived from a cannabis patch no larger than a pool table. Crop eradication will clearly never work. Exercises in massively intrusive surveillance could therefore be the next weapon in the enforcement industry's armory.

In 1969, the US authorities mounted Operation Intercept along the border with Mexico, in an effort to prevent cannabis importation into the States. Every single vehicle and person crossing into America was stopped and searched. The colossal tailbacks that resulted, with waits of three hours quite typical, caused immense ill will and turned out to be completely futile. The amount of cannabis seized was no higher than that impounded under the random process. What did happen was that importers looked to other sources as a backup just in case the experiment was repeated and

met with more success, while a major boost was given to home cultivation. It isn't clear how long the customs authorities thought they
could sustain a daily monumental traffic jam in the interests of drug
control, but the operation was abandoned anyway after twenty
days, and has not been repeated since.

Quite how long it would have been before the universal presumption of criminality among returning American citizens began to be a
cause of serious resentment is hard to say, but public pressure would
surely in any event have led to the policy being rescinded. Neither
will the economics of increased seizures be likely to prove critical, in
the sense that price-fixing is tuned to a far greater degree of sophisti-
cation than legitimate industry can manage. It is estimated, for
example, that even if half of all the cocaine entering the USA were
seized, it would only add about 5 percent to the street price of what
did get through.

Against these brutally insuperable odds, the best suggestion the
progressive prohibitionists can make is that saturation arrests in targeted areas can have some noticeable temporary effect, but even
Goode concedes that the business will simply move to other areas
(push down/pop up), and relocate to the original area when the
street-sweeping operation cools off.

A chapter on the links between drugs and crime begins by assert-
ing that crime would increase under legalization because the incidences of being drugged and disorderly or of driving while under the
influence would go up, as if the net gain in reduced criminality on
the scale of organized, violent gangland crime counted for nothing.
In an unfathomable lacuna, Goode argues that the Dutch de facto
policy of decriminalizing cannabis hasn't worked because there is
still a 30 percent proportion of drug offenders among the prison
population, although he simultaneously acknowledges that only a
minority of those are there for cannabis dealing. The point is that
the Dutch policy *has* worked inasmuch as it addresses cannabis, and
hasn't inasmuch as it doesn't address the other drugs.

Plunging into ever murkier waters, he goes on to assert that
people who use drugs are the types who are predisposed to crime
anyway, perhaps for the very reason that the laws in this instance do
not appear to deter them. On the one hand, he insists that violence
goes hand in hand with a drug-using lifestyle, but on the other, he

claims that this can't be just because drugs are illegal because most of the violence among the most serious offenders is not drug- but alcohol-derived, in which case legalization couldn't have any impact on it anyway. He cites the findings of Goldstein et al (1991), which showed that "Among cocaine abusers, the drug that was most intimately connected with violence was alcohol, not cocaine, and that the more they used cocaine, the less that cocaine played a role in their violence."[18] He points out correctly that more crime is committed by users of alcohol and tobacco than by users of illegal drugs (excepting the drug use itself, of course), but then says this shows that if illegal drugs were moved into the legal category, that would correspondingly increase criminality.

On the other hand, he insists that the crime that most drinkers and smokers commit is not typically the serious kind involving custodial sentences, the implication being that that means we can be relaxed about those drugs being legal. If this latter point is true, though, then the destigmatizing of illegal drugs might be held to be an improvement, but no: Goldstein et al are no sooner cited than summarily disowned, as a rise in overall criminality is deemed likely to follow the relegalization of substances such as cocaine. From here it is but a short step to a piece of straightforward tabloid slander: drug users are no better than criminals because each group displays low self-esteem. "[D]rug users and criminals are essentially the same people . . . [T]hese two denizens are cut from the same cloth . . . [T]hey are, in fact, motivated by the same impulse."[19]

These equations, he grants, only hold true for crime and drug-taking at a certain high level of frequency and seriousness, but still the ontological link is deemed to have been established. There is a criminal essence in illegal drugs that makes them attractive to people who are drawn to crime. (Indeed there is. It consists of nothing other than the fact that they are illegal.) Legalization can't change the behavior of those who are violent and antisocial anyway, he thinks, so there is no point in doing it, which admission of defeat condemns every addict and even recreational user to keep consorting with these unrecuperable misfits in order to get what they need or want.

In a shameless display of having it both ways, the Summary to this chapter claims that legalization will leave the crime rate unaffected, because drug users are criminal types anyway (in which case, why not risk it, since it will bring down drug-related crime at least?), but also that legalization may increase the crime rate because, as use went up with legal availability, so predisposition to crime would increase. He should, if he could find the courage of his polemical convictions, be arguing that legalization would cause a massive increase in crime because drug use apparently turns people into hedonistic, thrill-seeking criminals by its very nature. In fact, he is forced to walk, eyes wide open, into his own trap, by insisting that it won't materially change because nearly all the criminals must already be doing drugs anyway, because that is what criminals do, and therefore we may conclude with satisfaction—even if he can't bring himself to do so—that his argument does not finally stand in the way of legalization, at least on the grounds of its possible impact on crime.

The final chapter of Goode's book addresses an aspect of the debate on intoxication that has been a constant in the literature for a large part of the period that drugs have been illegal. This classic move involves comparing the official attitude taken toward banned substances to that prevailing with regard to alcohol and tobacco. In many of the legalizers' arguments, the point is put that it can only be a matter of supreme hypocrisy that society tolerates the use of these arguably more inimical substances while ring-fencing the others off with ever more forbidding thickets of legislative barbed wire. There was always at least a slight suggestion of thin ice about this argument, not least because—since two wrongs have never yet made a right—the logical corollary of it would be to wrap the barbed wire around drinking and smoking as well. Or perhaps to relegalize cannabis and whatever else the legalizers wanted to see on the menu, and then ban alcohol and tobacco instead, thus shifting the focus of coordinated criminality onto these latter commodities. It has thus left the enforcement industry in indisputable possession of the easy riposte that the law may not be perfect, but at least *some* harm is being prevented, and to reform it would be to add many heroin addicts, amphetamine psychotics and acid casualties to the already dismal roll call of alcoholics and lung-cancer victims. It has nonetheless come to be a much intoned article of faith among reform campaigners to adopt a censorious stance on alcohol and tobacco as a way of showing that, although they are proposing a major policy shift toward substances the law regards as too dangerous to trust its subjects with, they are not nonetheless seen to stand accused of a Szaszian compact with pharmaceutical anarchy in which everybody would be free to wreck their health, and to hell with the social consequences.

Goode's polemic intriguingly attempts to untwist this double bind by using an intensely restrictive set of proposals on alcohol and tobacco—tentatively indicted as "The Real Dangerous Drugs?" in the chapter's subtitle—to buttress what has turned out to be an argument for the legislative status quo on the illegal drugs. In other words, he is offering the enforcement industry the fig leaf of a sort of consistency as a way of concealing the shame of its drug policy, urging it to tighten up its act by getting heavier with drinkers and smokers, so that its exposed flank on banned drugs need not be so relentlessly peppered by the reform campaigners. The chapter thus begins with a facile travesty of the reform case:

> Legalizers claim that the legal drugs, alcohol and tobacco, are more dangerous than has been acknowledged and, in fact, more dangerous than the illegal drugs—heroin, cocaine, marijuana, LSD, methedrine ("ice"), PCP (Scrnyl, or "angel dust"), and the prescription drugs (when used for the purpose of intoxication rather than medication).[20]

If every argument for legalization were as myopic as this, then the case could indeed easily be brushed aside as misinformed wittering. But it won't wash. Terence McKenna may feel that alcohol was responsible for the Cold War, which wouldn't have happened if we'd all been drinking psilocybin tea instead, but no writer with at least one foot in the rationalist camp has seriously suggested that swallowing *anything* else at all—from PCP pig tranquilizer to phenobarbital—would be better than a bottle of Chablis.

From this unpromising opener, the text then goes on to make a handful of fair and valid points in comparing the total harm caused to individuals by legal and illegal drugs. Accepting that premature deaths among needle addicts may well decline under legalization (partly because purity of the drug itself will not be so unguessable, and partly because legalized needle exchange will drastically reduce the incidence of HIV infection), he goes on to make the obvious case that other chronic medical problems would increase as they survived. Furthermore, one takes his point that fatality figures have to be given as a coefficient of the number of participants and episodes of use.

Of course there is an absolutely greater figure for deaths from alcohol and tobacco because many more people use those drugs than use the illegal ones. Also, many more doses of the legal drugs are consumed than are those of the illegal, because nothing is quite as addictive as tobacco and a vast proportion of social life revolves around drinking alcohol in some form. However, even allowing for these considerations, Goode can do no more than suggest that there is proportional parity between the two classes, whereas the prohibitionist position might have hoped for a proportional holocaust to emerge from the data on the illegal side. Even when the relative harm is considered as "years of life lost"—i.e., at what age the various substances kill their problem users, rather than the bald fact of fatality itself—the statistics he refers to for years lost to illegal drugs scarcely begin to approach parity with those lost to cirrhosis and lung cancer. In any event, the legalizing argument isn't intent on ignoring these grisly tallies, merely on pointing out that the premature deaths arise largely from preventable HIV and AIDS infection, and uncertainty about the purity of any given batch of street material, which factors are in turn a function of its illegality. In defiance of this, Goode, without a blush for tautology, offers the assertion that "[I]t is *heroin* that causes addicts to overdose if they take too much. It is not legal policy by itself that causes the medical problem addicts experience" [his emphasis].[21]

Throughout the argument, Goode insists that changing the law on banned drugs will activate a deadly chain reaction: "Legalise them, and more people will use them—and more will become sick and die as a result."[22] But why? The point is that dosages and quality will be controlled, and the risk of mishap thereby reduced. Certainly those who are currently killing themselves may well kill themselves more quickly, but that doesn't mean that noncritical users will be drawn into this medical nightmare. It has long been evident that campaigning to restrict alcohol intake, insofar as it affects anyone, leads only those whose consumption is not problematic anyway to cut down, while alcoholics carry on as before. Ending the relentless campaign of antialcohol propaganda in the USA, from the Surgeon General's health warnings to the ranting of the idiot press, would not instantly produce more alcoholics, any more than freeing users of the other drugs from the lowering threat of the enforcement industry will unleash the fettered death-wishes of millions of needle addicts waiting for the chance to take a fatal overdose. And then he keeps making the point that, to the extent that there would still be some restrictions on availability under a legalization program, there would still be a black market. Of course there would, but it would be a much smaller black market, and in any case, if a black market is wrong, how can a socially concerned commentator defend the present system, which guarantees a much wider, and seemingly unstoppable, black market?

Somebody has persuaded Professor Goode that the UK would make a useful example of a "far more liberal and flexible" approach to heroin addiction these days than is operated in the USA, and that given that the rate of premature fatality among addicts is proportionately the same as in America (at about 2 percent a year), Britain may therefore be adduced as proof that the legalization paradigm is likely to fail. To anybody who has ever presented themselves voluntarily to the British medical system as an intravenous opiate addict in the last 30 years, this comparison is absolutely risible. True, harm reduction has been tried (and found wanting) in areas of high addiction such as Liverpool and Glasgow, but to suggest that the system is more liberal because an addict is allowed to swallow a beaker of methadone at the dispensary at prescribed times, and then only to a calendar that assumes that addicts have a break over a bank-holiday weekend like everybody else, is lamentably short of the truth. The British system is in fact considerably less flexible and more punitive than it was up to 1967, when heroin maintenance was officially outlawed as a treatment policy by an otherwise left-liberal government.

Our only chance in recent years to compare the maintenance system against Goode's preferred model of criminalization-plus-methadone came when it was briefly tried again at a unit in Widnes on Merseyside in the northwest of England. Under the tutelage of the pioneering Dr. John Marks, opiate addicts were prescribed not methadone but pharmaceutical diamorphine—i.e., real heroin.

Cocaine users were given cocaine, and amphetamine users amphetamine. Between 1985 and 1990, the experiment yielded extraordinary, but—to the legalization advocate—unsurprising, results. In this severely deprived area of England, plagued with property crime and structural unemployment, where generations are turned out of the schools undereducated, unqualified and without a shred of visible motivation for constructing a productive life, use of mind-numbing narcotics, and the crime and violence their illegality generates, is endemic. Within the five years that Dr. Marks's invaluable work was allowed to continue unmolested, Widnes enjoyed a 96 percent reduction in thefts and break-ins, a 92 percent reduction in new cases of addiction, a reduction in the incidence of drug-related HIV acquisition to zero, and a reduction in the numbers of premature deaths from heroin overdose to zero. To the prohibitionist, Goodean progressive or unevolved Neanderthal, this could theoretically never happen. On their analysis, the Widnes experiment should have resembled the innermost circle of Hades, with the hospitals full to bursting with new casualties, the mortuaries overflowing soon after and sociology professors working through the night balefully computing the galloping tally of "years of life lost."

The Widnes clinic was forced to backtrack on its initiative in 1990 when a commercial TV documentary questioned whether it was not flying in the face of Prime Minister Thatcher's avowed opposition to legalization, and then abandoned altogether in 1995 when the methadone that was being phased back in alongside heroin finally supplanted it altogether on the spurious grounds of cost. A more sympathetic American TV documentary screened just as President George Bush Sr. was emptying federal coffers to boost the latest skirmish in America's global War on Drugs struck such a discordant note that diplomatic pressure was brought to bear on the British government to trample Dr. Marks's findings into the dust. In this as in much else, the British did as they were told by the Americans, and the program's death warrant was obediently signed. The streets of Widnes are once again safe for dealers to ply their contaminated heroin, drug-related HIV infection—throttled to the point of submission by Dr. Marks—is rallying back to something like its former vigor, and deaths from heroin and methadone overdoses once more adorn the coroners' certificates. Order has been restored.

Turning back to the cases of alcohol and tobacco, Goode notes that the direct, chronic medical effects of the legal drugs are considerably more virulent than those caused by heroin and other narcotics. "Incredibly," he gasps, "overdosing aside, narcotics cause no life-threatening medical pathologies of any kind," but whereas we might expect to see such a point given prominence in the audit of comparative harm occasioned by intoxicants, it is typically relegated to a shifty parenthesis. The question of whether the criminalization of some drugs may be unjust or unfair while others are permitted is, he feels, "essentially unanswerable"; at least, it must apparently render a sociologist, as opposed to a moral philosopher or ideologist, dumbstruck. Getting to grips with the problems caused by use of the legal intoxicants, he strongly advocates the policy of increased taxation to discourage their use, while acknowledging frankly that, as per historical precedent, that would have the effect of creating another of these black markets he professes to detest, in addition to bearing most heavily—like all indirect taxation—on those least able to afford it. His manifesto goes on to incorporate the following policy points:

Ban all cigarette vending machines.
Enforce the law against cigarette sales to minors.
Increase negative advertising.
Ban the export of American cigarette products abroad.
Enact legislation outlawing the *use* of tobacco by minors.
Enact legislation further restricting public smoking.
Enforce the drunk-driving laws.
Restrict the sale of alcoholic beverages.[23]

Under point 2, he makes a reasonable enough case for licensing tobacco retailers like liquor-sellers, so that if they were found selling cigarettes to children, they would have a license to lose. This at least would have the virtue of consistency, and might indeed discourage sales to underage smokers to some modest extent, thereby postponing the age at which the habit is acquired. Point 3 advocates making the alcohol and tobacco manufacturers donate some of their profits to a continued federal campaign to persuade consumers not to buy their products, while a larger share continues to be disbursed on their own campaigns to maximize sales through advertising. The hypocrisy of this approach has long been a source of the utmost contempt among both drinkers and smokers in all the jurisdictions where it is practiced. While the health warnings get more starkly lurid with each new revision, so that the brute assurance these days is simply that "SMOKING KILLS," the national treasuries increase the tax take from sales of cigarettes by a hyperinflationary factor each year, as if the loss of revenue from any decline in the habit has to be offset by squeezing more out of those who do persist.

Under point 4, the search for other markets to replace declining domestic consumption of the tobacco companies' products is condemned, on the grounds that creating the cigarette habit in Third World countries will result in "the premature death of substantial segments of their populations."[24] This argument comes from the same Professor Goode who had earlier assured us, when comparing tobacco to the illegal drugs, that tobacco smokers died later in life even than heavy drinkers, and that premature death on a critical scale was the preserve of heroin addicts. Point 5 would create an interesting new category of offense (not to mention set a dangerous precedent), and enforcing the sanctions would make a challenging enterprise for the law, since these would evidently consist of fines (to twelve-year-olds?), community service and that last redoubt of punitive enforcement regimes the world over, "meaningful reeducation." We may permit ourselves a shudder in imagining precisely what that might consist of.

With point 8, we arrive at the pulsing heart of repression at the center of Professor Goode's entire prospectus. Here is the complete paragraph:

> Should beer and wine be sold in supermarkets? In fact, perhaps the sale of all alcoholic beverages could be restricted to a small number of state-run Alcoholic Beverage Control or "package" stores. Abolish all "happy hours" and all other special occasions in bars during which large discounts are offered to customers. Abolish all sale and use of alcoholic beverages at sporting events, on college and university campuses, on public transportation, and at all government functions. While none of these,

by themselves, is likely to have a measurable impact on drinking, they send a message and set a climate that may signal a move to greater moderation in drinking.[25]

That this miserable farrago could emerge from the only country in the non-Islamic world ever to embark on the disaster of Prohibition is enough to shake one's faith in sociology. It is a standing indictment of its author's pretension to evenhanded reportage, given that he insists earlier in the chapter that he isn't necessarily putting these arguments himself, only considering them hypothetically. Disingenuously enough, the chapter's conclusion says that enforcement of this draconian new code would not be "vindictive," and that citizens should take these initiatives themselves so as to ward off the ghastly specter of government intervention, but that government intervention should be enforced anyway if "it becomes clear either that private citizens do not have certain powers or that they are unwilling to exercise them"[26]—in other words, even where they don't want them. He then grants that these strategies have next to no chance of implementation, but outlines them with moralistic urgency nonetheless, even though the unlikelihood factor has been allowed to dismiss legalization arguments earlier in the book. It is then a short step down to the Unimaginability Fallacy, that just because nobody could imagine the imminent collapse of the USSR the year before it happened (ask President Gorbachev), then anything else currently unimaginable could equally well come to pass—a feeble syllogism beloved of those science-fiction fans eagerly anticipating the real-life invention of time travel. Looking forward to his manifesto being adopted during the twenty-first century, he concludes, "If not, it is our loss."[27] So much for the dispassionate hypothesizing. It only remains to point out that an entirely different complexion would have been cast on the arguments about illegal drugs in his work, had this chapter appeared up front. Only then, Goode might have seemed to bear a discomfiting resemblance to an old-time, illiberal control freak, which wouldn't have done at all.

The days when it was possible to conceive of drugs as a purely generational issue are now past. Time was when a brief flirtation with dope, and perhaps something a little more hectic for party nights, was succeeded, as one slithered into one's thirties, by a lifetime of controlled drinking and intermittent attempts to give up smoking. One of my respondents was shown by her mother how to use a "bong" (for drawing cannabis smoke through water) so as to avoid social embarrassments later on, quite as she would once have been told how to turn down a boy's request for a foxtrot. Another was initiated into the hallucinogenic mushroom experience by hers. These were bonding scenarios of the same degree of significance as being bought one's first bra, or being sustained through the transforming induction into menstruation. The sixties generation that was the first to make a political stance out of conspicuous drug consumption may in most cases have grown away from drug-taking, but many retained the sense of perspective that the period bequeathed them, and refused to see anything wrong, as their own children grew up, in their discovery of recreational intoxication.

When ecstasy became the drug of choice in the 1990s, the traffic was often reversed: I met one pair of sixties veterans who had been introduced to the drug by their son, and now varied their weekly intake of wine and dope by taking half a pill each on Saturday nights. (One imagined him stumbling out of bed at 3 A.M., yelling at them from the top of the stairs to turn the Pink Floyd down.) What will continue to motivate defiance of the drug laws, as the DEA does it damnedest around the world, is not old-time civil disobedience so much as experiences like these. Personal involvement with banned substances tears away the veil of ignorance the enforcement industry keeps trying to pull down over intoxication, and once torn, it can't ever be patched up again.

In 1998, the UK government appointed Keith Hellawell, formerly chief constable of West Yorkshire, as Britain's first antidrugs coordinator, after the model of the American Drug Tsar. His brief was to launch education programs and set annually reviewed targets for drug-use reduction. A drug prevention agency that encourages the public to snitch on each other as a support service for a police effort at full ineffectual stretch was set up. It was decided that the seized assets of drug dealers would be redirected into the fight against drugs, in contrast to an earlier stance when the UK rejected an American attempt to force such a policy on it with regard to seized

assets from international enforcement operations. Class A drug traffickers arraigned for a third offense would now face a minimum
seven-year jail term. To pay for it all, an extra £217 ($325) million
of public funds was to be spent over a two-year period.

At the end of the first year's work, after Mr. Hellawell had tirelessly toured the country spouting negative publicity in school-
rooms, youth clubs and to whoever else would have him, his first
annual report—launched on 25 May 1999—declared that, far from
having the slightest impact on the drug culture in Britain, the whole
circus had been completely ignored. Drugs were more plentifully
available at better retail rates, and at generally more reliable levels of
purity, than at any time in recent experience. The despairing Mr.
Hellawell called it "a new epidemic."

If the law were a small infant, the destructive rage that it is now
displaying over drugs would be classed as a tantrum occasioned by
its not getting its own way. A wise parent may choose to ignore it
until the child had had its fill of screaming, but ornaments are being
smashed and furniture is being gouged, so to stand idly by seems a
little rash. Dr. Spock advises hugging. Similarly, calling our politicians Nazis and carrying on regardless is not going to get our societies out of the present squalor. We need to swallow our pride, and
try to help the law out of the traumatic fracas it has got itself and its
subjects into.

Law reform is urgently needed —to cut crime, make drugs safer,
reduce the risk of illness and infection and restore a sense of civic
dignity to those who wish to use a wider range of intoxicants than
just booze and cigarettes. It is absolutely pointless declaring a substance to be in itself illegal. The thinking of the First World War era
must be outgrown, and a frank acknowledgment arrived at that a
policy that doesn't work, however much utopia had been fantasized
into its formulation, has to be dropped. We pay our governments to
find workable solutions to society's dilemmas, not to keep banging
their heads against the same brick wall. The Widnes experiment in
treating addicted patients should be adopted wholesale. We may
confidently predict that some of the heroin being prescribed to
clients of the clinics will find its way into the black market, but
the condition of addiction itself is manageable, and nobody—given
a genuine (and so far unprecedented) choice—*wants* to use dirty

needles, or buy adulterated junk in back alleys. They didn't in Widnes until the British government, doing the bidding of the White House, brought the black market back to that town. As to non-addictive substances, exactly the same licensing could be made to apply to distribution of these intoxicants as applies to alcohol. The age of adult responsibility for intoxication should be standardized at sixteen, the age at which (in the UK) one may have straight or gay sex, get married, pay taxes and die for Queen and Country.

It would be prudent, as Kevin Williamson suggests, to confine the relegalized intoxicants to specific retail outlets where specialized advice can be given, but in time, as people are at last trusted to be grown-up enough to manage their own bodies, more general distribution will no doubt be tolerable. If the new Cocaine Club retail chain proved to be a runaway commercial success, opening franchised branches in record stores, cafés and bars throughout the country, it is hard to imagine that the supermarket chains—who can't see a thriving market in anything without trying to monopolize it—will sit and watch from the sidelines. Restrictions on the disruptive use of intoxicants would naturally remain, so that driving under the influence, for example, would be severely punishable. Anything smokable would be subject to the same restrictions as tobacco smoking now is. Bespoke venues for the use of strong hallucinogenic materials could offer the support of practiced users for those on their initiatory trips, as well as offering all manner of up-to-the-minute digital and virtual-reality effects to make the experience more rewarding than sitting at home or lounging about the town center would be. Theme parks, fairgrounds and nightclubs are doing their technological best now to create sensual environments of this nature, while nobody actually mentions drugs, much as advertisers sell bottles of fizzy drink containing guarana, ginseng and so forth as if they are speaking (as they know they are) to a constituency already far better versed than the Drug Tsar in the effects of psychotropic drugs. And against this background, governments could conduct research to their hearts' content into the physical and mental effects of the various substances in order to make value-free, intelligent advice available to the public, instead of treating everybody as though they were retarded.

More than any of these practical points, however, one overarching issue transcends the whole debate. It is the point that Professor Goode, in a dither of academic indecision, abdicates responsibility for, claiming to find it "essentially unanswerable," and yet that will not just be wished away at the invocation of sociological rigor. It is the matter of who intoxicants actually belong to. I do not believe that any government has, or ever had, the right to act as if it were an ecclesiastical authority in this respect, locking away the powders and pills out of harm's way with a booming "Thou shalt not." Indeed, no secular government seriously tried it on a comprehensive scale until the dawn of the twentieth century. It is sometimes said that just because a practice was once legal and has now been outlawed is not in itself a reason to bring it back again, otherwise we could happily send children down coal mines again. The point has undeniable logical force, but one isn't suggesting that drugs should be relegalized *just because* they were once legal, but because the criminalization initiative has in itself been such a fiasco.

There is nothing untoward in withdrawing a body of bad law if it hasn't commanded popular support, and has been rendered unworkable. The licensing laws, once formulated to keep workers in the munitions factories on the job for longer at a time of national emergency, are at long last beginning to be unpicked. So too must the drug laws, like an unexploded bomb, be carefully taken apart. Intoxication is a universal human yearning, and its forms of expression will not be circumscribed even by the global intimidation of the enforcement industry. They might as well try to forbid nonreproductive sex. In a moving peroration at the end of his own keynote work in this field, Ronald K. Siegel has this to say of what he calls the "fourth drive," after eating, drinking and sex:

> [O]ur society must find a place in its thinking for intoxication. We must recognize the drive to get there, then pursue safe paths . . . We need not fear the street sorcerers who can change spices like nutmeg into enchanting but imperfect elixirs like Ecstasy; we can master their art of designer chemistry and do better. Though our every step is challenged by plants with thorns and bittersweet chemicals, though voices cry out for us to come

back, we can no more turn back than climb down the evolutionary ladder. We must learn from these encounters and move on.
To say No is to deny all that we are and all that we could be.[28]

And yet the chant the governments lead is "Just Say No." This is a
destructive and wasteful impasse. To begin to survive it will involve
telling the truth about what we do in an atmosphere free of the
threat of police harassment. Such forums will come into being by
negotiation, and inevitably through a certain amount of defiance. If
one were asked to suggest a T-shirt slogan for such a campaign, it
would have to read INTOXICATION IS A HUMAN RIGHT.

6

Out of It

It was the medicalizing of intoxication in the latter half of the nine-teenth century that led to its eventual criminalization. After the doctors had mopped up the wasted remains of the overindulgent, politicians moved in to try to prevent their numbers from multiply-ing. As all intoxicants are in some sense poisons, a notion the prohi-bitionists have gleefully loaded with moral baggage wherever they have sought to intervene in the private practices of others, there was clearly a critical mass—variant from one individual to another—that would hasten a medical alert. In not knowing when to stop, or in not being able to when crisis loomed, a society hostess with her jeweled syringe, or a working man resorting to the pub every evening, became the emblems of what intoxication was thought to lead to: helpless excess.

We are still living under the rule of that model today, still talking the language of restrained gentility when we refer to intoxication, both in others and in ourselves. The uncle at the wedding who ill-advisedly essays a spot of fifties jive with the bridesmaid when the DJ plays Bill Haley has obviously had "a little too much to drink," we feel, despite the fact that the occasion seems to be tempting us to just such abandon. To be drunk and disorderly in public is an arrestable offense in Britain, but so too is merely being drunk, no matter how impeccable the state of one's dress or the unteetering sta-bility of one's carriage. A respondent tells of a friend who had the astonishing bad fortune to be arrested in central London in the

1980s for precisely this infraction, in an anachronistic enactment of a Bateman cartoon—"The Man Who Got Drunk in Soho."

What has happened since the drug laws and the licensing regulations came into being is that the medicalized version of altered consciousness has been allowed to stand, metonymously, for the whole field of experience that intoxication refers to. That this remains a highly dubious postulate can be seen in the fact that histories of medicine do not generally encompass any reference to intoxication practices in themselves. If a person swallows LSD, succumbs to a hallucinogenic episode of several hours and then drifts out at the other end quite safe and sound, in what sense is there some clinical implication in what he has done? Would a doctor on hand feel duty-bound to administer an antidote injection, now that there is one available? In order to find intoxicants in the medical histories, we have to look up "addiction" or "alcoholism," but these references obviously only apply to intoxication carried on at a critical and chronic level, and yet that is where the motivation for the legal controls on altered states of consciousness has come from. And excess is the rubric that guides not only the law but all medical advice on the subject, so that—at least until the advent of the red-wine-is-good-for-you gospel promulgated by the findings of Lyon cardiologist Dr. Serge Renaud's team in the early 1990s—doctors were constantly enjoining their patients to cut down on everything that might lead to ruinous consequences if taken in surfeit.

The concept of moderation is a slippery, and yet remarkably hardy, cultural theme in Western history. It is a function of the development of social etiquette in European societies, particularly Britain, in the late eighteenth century, an era in which the world of the drawing room began to assert an affected superiority over the life of the street and the public spaces. Along with the codification of table manners, and polite modes of address, came a growing taste for disguising the appetites, whether gustatory or sexual. Public shows of inebriation, part of the very fabric of social life until the early part of that century, came to be seen as evidence of having surrendered basely to animal instincts. Drunkenness undermined the elegant exchanges of genteel conversation, it encouraged licentiousness and shambolic déshabille, qualities best left as the preserve of the lower orders, of those who knew no better, who had no brains to befuddle in the first place.

As the new gentility was refined to a state of costive excruciation in the Victorian period, euphemistic ways of taking intoxicants had to be found. A lady partaking of a glass of gin referred to it as "white wine," in case anybody confused it with the stuff the undeserving poor were throwing down themselves in such corrosive quantities in the London stews. Not even the social upheaval of the 1920s has quite cured us of this euphemizing, guilt-encrusted attitude to intoxication practices, so that any reference to what is for most the principal purpose of drinking is necessarily hedged about with disclaimers and dissociations. (A consumer book on spirits and liqueurs I wrote in 1997 contained the following passage: "The Benedictine monks may have been a little shocked to hear that their revered creation [the liqueur Bénédictine] was being mixed with English gin, American applejack, apricot brandy and maple syrup, shaken to within an inch of its life and then rechristened the Mule's Hind Leg, but at least it was drunk—as were the giggling flappers after knocking back three or four of them." When a subsequent edition of the book appeared, this had been doctored by the publisher so that the last part of the sentence read, "as were any giggling flappers unwise enough to knock back three or four of them."[1] But what would be unwise about that? This was ostensibly a book about enjoying alcohol. Why would anybody buying a reference work on distilled drinks, bristling with cocktail recipes, wish to be told that becoming drunk in the course of trying them out would be an act of folly? Because moderation is the totem before which all, even those mixing up a shakerful of Mule's Hind Leg for an enterprising bunch of bravos, must genuflect, and no mention of getting drunk must be allowed to stand without the voice of responsibility intervening with a tut-tut-tut of disapproval.)

To fall under the influence of intoxicants, even more so when it becomes a regularly willed experience, is thought to be a halfway house to addiction to them, which is why we instinctively feel we must keep up the extraordinary charade of being impervious to their effects. Thus does the swaying, slurring bar habitué insist, at the end of his nightly intake of beers, that—despite the external evidence—

he is not actually drunk, merely a little loosened up. This burgeoning vocabulary of understatement in the English-speaking world has included descriptives such as "merry," which has an air of blameless festivity about it, or such tittering twenties Lewis Carrollisms as "squiffy" or "blotto." Interestingly, drug subcultures since the 1960s have produced coinages that have moved inexorably in the opposite direction, as if to assert their liberation from the infantile decorums of legal intoxication. From being "totally out of it"—of one's skull, that is, or of the game—we have progressed to being blitzed, mashed, wrecked, twatted, annihilated and thoroughly bombed out. One girl told me she ended a weekend of partying "starfished," a yogalike name for the prone, scattered position of the drug-ravaged body, while the current locution in Brighton, as I write, is to say that you got absolutely "wankered," that is, reduced by prolonged intake to the indignity of talking and behaving like a complete wanker. This discourse doesn't contain much that's likely to change the minds of prohibitionists, although it does reassert the limitless neologizing capacity of English.

As addiction, or monomania, came to be seen as the nucleus at the center of all intoxication behavior, medical science managed in the late Victorian era to annex the field as its own. Not only were the foundations laid for the construction of alcoholism as a disease, but addiction generally—as well as the search for cures for it—was of particular interest to the early psychoanalysts. Morphine had been tried and found wanting as a potential cure for habituation to opium, and now cocaine was tried, most famously by Freud, as a specific against morphine addiction. This created the first cocaine-dependent patients, and in many cases, the first to be simultaneously dependent on morphine and cocaine. The formulation of heroin led some doctors to have a go at curing morphine addiction with it, until finally it was accepted that addiction to a substance was not likely to be treatable by administration of an even more addictive one.

It is perhaps easier to understand the motivation behind searching for a pharmaceutical cure for drug dependency if we bear in mind the fact that the only available alternative to it was the rest cure offered by the sanatorium system. These privately run homes were generally rural retreats, advertised both in the medical journals and in gentlemen's periodicals. Some of these, such as the chain of Keeley homes (or "institutes," as they were styled) in the USA, administered a proprietary remedy as part of the treatment. Dr. Keeley employed gold chloride, although at least one authority of the period (1907) disputed whether anything at all was given, since as a doctor, Keeley could have been presumed to know—in accordance with the prevailing medical orthodoxy of the time—that alcoholism was not susceptible to pharmaceutical cures, being rather the consequence of an etiolated will. Perhaps hypnosis was responsible for whatever successes the Keeley empire could boast.

Mainly, though, the private sanatoriums offered the kinds of panaceas against eroded moral will that the nineteenth and early twentieth centuries held dear. Periods of rest were interspersed with bracing walks in the country air, plenty of meat and fish in the diet and cups of weak beef stock instead of the nerve-rattling caffeine of coffee and tea. An extensively detailed portrait of the life of such institutions as these is painted in Thomas Mann's novel *The Magic Mountain*. Mann's inmates are there because they are suffering from nervous exhaustion, but this is precisely how alcoholism too was thought to arise, the difference being that those in the throes of the alcohol habit would not be permitted the Château Gruaud-Larose or the G. H. Mumm champagne served on the magic mountain. The gentlemen's retreats that catered for members of the aristocracy and the professional classes in the UK offered a rudimentary form of counseling supplemented by a range of leisure activities. Not only alcoholics, but victims of "the morphia habit" or other forms of "narcomania," were accepted. One establishment near Fife in Scotland was able to provide facilities for game shooting and trout fishing, as well as tennis and badminton courts, a golf course, a cricket pitch, a skating rink, billiard tables and, should the sporting instinct falter, a photographic darkroom. The fees charged were routinely astronomical since only the better class of drunkard was wanted, and the sanatoriums in turn treated their inmates like the paying customers they were. As Mariana Valverde has pointed out in a meticulous study of the changing approaches to alcoholism, they were the antecedents of today's health clubs rather than specifically medical concerns, although many were run by qualified physicians.

The legislation that formalized the process of committal to the retreats in the UK was the Habitual Drunkards Act of 1879. For the lower orders, inebriate reformatories, as provided for by the more overtly criminological Habitual Inebriates Act of 1898, were the judicial response. The earlier Act established a singular mechanism, soon supplanted, under which a well-to-do drunkard appearing before the courts would be committed to a retreat, but only with his consent. He may have been pressured by his family to seek treatment, or he may have volunteered himself to the JP, but he could only be referred by the court for treatment if he wished it. Valverde correctly notes that this approach implicitly acknowledged the abiding wisdom that alcoholics can only be reformed if they want to be, although the legislation all but collapsed under the weight of its own internal contradictions. Inebriety was defined in the Act as rendering its victim "incapable of managing himself or herself and his or her affairs," and yet what was the self-committal process other than the managing of one's affairs? By 1898, the legislation had become distinctly more punitive and was now to be used against persistent offenders lower down the social scale. These people were not to be trusted to make decisions about self-committal, and so the later Act provided for compulsory incarceration in a reformatory for a statutory three years for each offender who appeared before the courts at least four times in the space of a year.

Tellingly, the 1898 Act was used disproportionately against female inebriates, those fallen women who had perhaps incurred the wrath of the law through prostitution, but for whom the Inebriates Act established a ready method for their removal from society. Others were categorized as neglectful mothers, neglectful of their children or indeed of their duty to bear children for the propagation of the Empire. The twin-track, class-based approach was chaotic and ultimately unworkable. Occasionally, inebriates from better-off families would find themselves convicted under the 1898 Act, and would later be hastily transferred from urban reformatory to rural retreat where their recuperation could proceed amid the skating rinks and croquet lawns that were inappropriate for the criminalized poor. What scientific study there was of the efficacy of treatment techniques was entirely concentrated on the reformatories. Apart from the bureaucratic entanglements the two-tier system created, it was in any case to be undermined—in London, particularly—by a pitched battle over whether the local authority or central government should finance the three-year incarcerations the later Act made mandatory. The issue was never resolved, and by the time the Great War broke upon Britain, the legislation had been rendered impotent. Although it was never enforced again, and the reformatories were eventually superseded by institutions devoted to more obviously pastoral care along the lines of the Salvation Army hostels, the Inebriates Acts sat anachronistically on the statutes until 1976.

Valverde refuses the point made by other historians of the period that the Habitual Inebriates laws marked another stage in "the relentless medicalisation of deviance" by arguing that committals under the Acts did not require medical ratification. Doctors were welcome to offer testimony in the courts but it was never considered necessary. This seems a spurious nicety at best. The legislation itself was driven by the medical profession, as she grants, and established a licensing system for the private retreats. When the doctors vociferously opposed the principle of self-committal written into the 1879 Act, the later Act duly bowed to their demand for more coercive measures. Most significantly of all, perhaps, the 1879 Act was formulated by a physician MP, Dr. Dalrymple, who—not entirely by chance—ran a gentlemen's retreat himself, the first to be licensed under the new law. In steering his bill onto the statute, Dalrymple not only augmented the potential earning power of his own institution, but helped to drive unlicensed rival establishments to the wall. These two laws set the stage for the monopolization of inebriety treatment by the medical profession, a point it seems perverse of Valverde to deny. True, "the Acts did not even attempt to construct a homogeneous population of medicalised inebriates,"[2] but that would simply come later as the concept of the alcoholic was elaborated.

Although the Acts did, I believe, issue from the medicalizing of intoxication, that is not to say that the medicalization process has enjoyed an uninterrupted ascendancy since. There has always been an irresolvable tension at work between the latter-day physiological treatment of alcohol dependency, in which certain individuals are just presumed to be incapable of handling potentially habit-forming drugs such as alcohol without inexorably becoming medical cases, and the psychiatric approach, in which the dependency is one symptom of a complex of neurotic factors, but not in itself an autonomous illness. It was this tension that led to the fraying of alcoholism as a medical idea in the 1970s, when its status on the World Health Organization's roll call of official diseases was revoked.

The problematic use of alcohol had obvious medical implications, but the notion that a patient could be pathologized as an alcoholic, in the same way that another could turn out to be a multiple sclerosis sufferer, was thrown into serious doubt. The origins of this more pragmatic attitude may be seen in the fact that, after referrals under the Inebriates Acts ceased in 1914, hope for reform of habitual drunkards was invested in the hugely more restrictive licensing laws brought in by the war effort. If the temptation wasn't there, maybe consumption would drop. The same thinking lay behind the emergency drug laws also enacted in this period, which then ossified into permanent statute, as we saw in the last chapter. Once medicalization of these issues had laid the groundwork for the legislative authorities to intervene, the latter then occupied the whole field, leaving in their wake a thoroughly humbled medical sector, and one that has since undergone a fascinating rite of passage over the whole question of intoxication.

Having concluded by the 1980s that governmental initiatives were sorely lacking to cope with what it insisted was an emergent national crisis over alcohol, the British medical profession launched a coordinated campaign to reduce overall consumption levels. A flurry of reports around this time emerged from the Royal Colleges of Psychiatrists, of Physicians, of General Practitioners and the British Psychological Society that purported to document the vertiginous decline the nation's health was in for if alcohol intake was not much more rigorously controlled. The British Medical Association lobbied tirelessly for prohibitive excise rates to be applied to drink, particularly spirits, in the way that tobacco by then routinely attracted, but in the absence of these, public campaigns to curb excessive drinking were undertaken by the doctors themselves, mainly under the auspices of the Health Education Authority.

This is the era in which the widely used unit system came into effect. An honest enough attempt to address the question of how much was too much, units supposedly represented a handily straightforward way of measuring your intake, in the way that weight watchers counted their calories. One unit, it was pronounced, was a half pint of beer, a glass of wine, a small glass of fortified wine or a standard pub measure (then one-sixth of a gill, now 25 milliliters) of spirit. Twenty-one of these units was the recommended maximum weekly intake for men, and 14 for women. These were the agreed calculations of the reports that were published by the Psychiatrists in 1986 ("Alcohol: Our Favourite Drug") and the Physicians in 1987 ("A Great and Growing Evil"). Only four years before publication of their contribution, however, the Psychiatrists had been assuring the nation that 56 units a week constituted a reasonable guideline at the upper end, while the BMA itself declared that 42 units a week for men and 21 for women were "safe" levels. Between 1982 and 1986, the Psychiatrists, showing the classic symptoms of guilt-induced repression, were claiming that the safe male drinking limit was a mere 37.5 percent of what they had originally advised was reasonable. Since then, the government—having originally swallowed the 1986 figures whole—has revised the advice yet again, and we are now told that men may take up to 28 units a week, and women 21. This witless chopping and changing initially produced confusion, and then understandable cynicism as to the merits of these guidelines.

Most people remain blissfully ignorant of what's in a unit, let alone how many of them they are officially permitted to drink according to this year's estimates. Nonetheless, booklets full of handy hints on cutting down drinking are foisted upon patients who may have turned up at the surgery to discuss the removal of an unsightly wart, and however much one says one drinks is, in certain general practices, a potential problem that must be stamped on before it becomes a medical tragedy and, perhaps more pertinently, a drain on Health Service funds. Not merely the sum total of intake, but its frequency was also to be taken into account. I have personally been told by one health professional that a little a day is a deceptively dangerous way of drinking because the liver never has a chance to rest, while another has said precisely the opposite, that having days off leads to concentrating one's weekly intake in what is now universally referred to as a "binge." One may wonder what dispiriting Romper-Room purgatory these latter doctors must have grown up in that counted a bottle of wine on a Saturday night as a "binge," with all its associations of ruinous superfluity, until one actually encounters such people off duty, and discovers that their own habits may well bear no relation whatsoever to the advice they are doling out, unsolicited, to their patients. (A "binge," in use to mean a drinking spree since the mid-nineteenth century, is probably derived from a dialect verb meaning "to soak," the implication clearly being that one's system is well and truly soused, sluiced, sopping with alcohol after engaging in one.)

When the world-changing investigations of Dr. Serge Renaud into the so-called "French paradox" were released, offering an explanation as to why the southern French had the lowest incidence of coronary heart disease in Europe, despite their formidably high intake of animal fats, the unit-rationing system was rather stopped in its tracks. Counting the half pints always contained an implication that total abstinence would be the happiest and healthiest estate of all, and now here were findings—soon to be replicated by other research teams beyond refutation—that not only did the antioxidants in red wines in particular break down the low-density lipoproteins that can obstruct the arteries and result in clot formation and heart disease, but that they were, for example, twenty times more efficient in the matter than vitamin E. Furthermore, it was found by a team in Denmark that ethyl alcohol itself, C_2H_5OH, has a protective effect on the heart. While the BMA and those American pressure groups that had been consistently lobbying government for greater restrictions on the availability of alcohol retired to lick their wounds, the alcohol-is-good-for-you message penetrated the popular consciousness rather more speedily than their unit system had. The airing of Renaud's findings on TV's 60 Minutes in 1992 led almost overnight to a fourfold rise in the demand for red wine, so that California's market-leading producers suddenly found they couldn't turn out the stuff fast enough. (Even E & J Gallo, no less—largest wine-producing combine on the planet—was forced to put sales of their basic generic red, "Hearty Burgundy," on allocation, so indomitable was the stampede.)

The unit is in fact an utterly spurious attempt to give some sort of quantification to concepts like "moderation" and "balance." When told to drink only in moderation, it didn't require an unduly pedantic patient to question how many drinks that translated into. But there is no international consistency on the matter. A UK alcohol unit at 8g turns out to be only two-thirds of the American designation of 12g, and less than half that of Japan, where a rather festive 17g prevails. The system is doomed to irrelevance not merely because each individual has his or her own general tolerance of alcohol, but that tolerance is moreover affected by a number of physiological variables, such as blood pressure, stomach contents, the overall state of the immune system, the stage of the menstrual cycle and so forth. When it emerged that some health-insurance companies were beginning to set higher premiums for abstainers than for drinkers, on the grounds that forgoing wine altogether now looked like a risk factor for cardiovascular fitness, a return to unit counting might have seemed unlikely.

Renaud's discoveries, however, have not been able to address one remaining salutary factor. The French may indeed have less heart trouble than any other Europeans, but they also have dolefully high levels of liver disease, from fatty liver through alcohol hepatitis to full-blown cirrhosis. In all the publicity about the links between wine and health, understandably seized on by the wine trade and given a thorough airing by wine journalists in the 1990s, hardly anybody seems to want to talk about livers. If the health authorities had irresponsibly raised the ante by fomenting a sense of alarm in hundreds of thousands of people whose drinking never has been, and never will be, problematic to their health, then the wine industry has read the runes in what can at best be described as a disingenuously selective manner.

The breach has to some extent been filled by the rise of the sensible-drinking guru, the imago of whom is Dr. Thomas Stuttaford of *The Times*. In a book dedicated "to all moderate drinkers," Stuttaford gently upbraids his medical colleagues for some of their more alarmist pronouncements, and vouchsafes that "[t]here is mounting evidence worldwide that the recommendations [for maximum weekly unit intake] for both men and women are still more restrictive than they need be."[3] If so, this is a message still being doughtily resisted by the BMA, which greets every relaxation of the licensing laws, or failure to ratchet up the excise on alcohol in the annual budget, with ululations of disapproval, while the campaign to have health warnings printed on bottles and cans, as in the States, continues unabated.

And yet far from dismantling the moderate-drinking model, Stuttaford's whole project is to reinforce it by enjoining such improbable practicalities as "Set yourself a limit before you start an evening's drinking," and "Try to keep track of when and what you drink."[4] All such advice, however well intentioned, falls at the final hurdle of failing to recognize that, for most, drinking is a social activity, not a solipsistic indulgence. The descriptions of alcohol use contained in the urgings of alcohol pressure-groups often make it sound as though drinking were an experience akin to taking LSD, something that one did purely for its own sake, in order to enjoy its range of effects, whereas in the majority of scenarios—in pubs, restaurants and in the home—it is encompassed by the forms of social interaction in which it takes place. Imagine announcing as the port was being passed, "I would love to, but I am afraid I reached the limit I had set myself for this evening halfway through that last glass of Shiraz," or entering every sip meticulously on one's personal organizer. And with what aim? So that one might permit oneself an admonitory shake of the head at the week's accumulated tally? Meanwhile, as the doctors disagree with each other about where the safe limits should be pegged, the terms are fraught with useless nebulosity. On page 5 of his book, Stuttaford cautions that "it is considered unwise [by the Department of Health] to take all of one's weekly ration in one or two binges," while later on, we are warned that cases of sudden fatal cardiac collapse "are particularly likely to happen if the drinker has been bingeing."[5] Presumably, the reader is not seriously being asked to believe that saving up one's unit ration until the weekend is likely to kill him, and yet for every abruptly crumpling fatality, an ill-advised binge might have been the cause. Perhaps we should insist on knowing once and for all how much alcohol constitutes one of these binges, if only as an interlude in the bickering over what the correct daily limit should be.

What all of this ignores is that intoxication is its own justification. We overlook the deleterious effect that drinking may cumulatively have on our livers to the same degree that we might think it nicely reassuring, but no more, to hear that our low-density cholesterol is being kicked into touch by it. Whatever other physiological processes are going on while we drink, our brains are experiencing intoxication symptoms, and the pleasure, satisfaction and relief that that affords were the reasons we scrabbled through the drawer for the corkscrew in the first place. Andrew Barr, in a paper delivered to an international seminar on Wine and Health in London in 1999, put it thus:

> [T]he principal reason that drinking wine helps people to live longer is not to be found in the manner it affects certain substances in the blood but in the fact that it enables the people who drink it to enjoy life more. The most important medicinal benefits of wine lie in its potential to reduce stress and to make people feel happier. If wine is good for us, it is because it gives us pleasure.[6]

This is the most forceful argument it is possible to offer against the unit-counting, binge-policing mentality. Its only problem (and Barr is a writer who certainly nails his colors to the sensible-drinking mast) is that it is also a most beguiling instinctual argument against moderation. Even were we to be able to agree on a definition of what moderation consisted in, which would mean answering the eternally undecidable question of how much was too much, we would then be confronted with the even thornier issue of just why moderation is seen as such a self-recommending virtue, and we might also be moved to reflect on the fact that what exactly constitutes a breach of moderation always seems to be somebody else's decision ("Don't you think you've had enough?").

Moderation is not, in fact, an ideal that finds much house room within the domain of intoxication. Indeed, intoxication is in itself the opportunity for a temporary escape from the moderation that the rest of life is necessarily mortgaged to. It is the one aspect of our daily lives, even more than sex, that allows us radically to question the point of moderation as a desirable goal in itself, and it achieves this precisely because it makes us wonder what the opposite of moderation would be. Excess? Greed? Gluttony? And here we become embroiled in another great conundrum. What exactly is morally objectionable about excess? We avert our eyes from the sight of others cramming their faces with free food at a reception, but if nobody else is going without, and the culprit is not eating in an offensively noisy or messy manner, but just simply refusing to stop, why is that particularly disgusting? It is perhaps because we feel that eating should be about the assuaging of appetite alone, and that, once sated, we ought to desist. Thus, we may find it stomach-turning to read the sort of restaurant review where the critic, masticating his way remorselessly through the seven-course *menu gastronomique* in a grand hotel dining room, complains that by the time the second dessert course arrives, his waistband is beginning to groan in protest at the surfeit of it all. And indeed the principle of moderation, etymologically, contains within it not a *staying within* reasonable bounds, but a *scaling back down* to them, the Latin verb *"moderare"* meaning to reduce, to abate, to track back and tone down. How, in any case, are we to know what moderation is unless we have at some point exceeded its limits? To believe in moderation, one has to have dwelt in the realms of excess, to have gone the whole giddy hog, before returning to a state of seemly proportion. In short, it isn't *necessary* to overindulge, for all that it may be necessary to eat.

Intoxication, however, hovers in an uncharted space between necessity and indulgence. It is, I believe, a biological necessity, otherwise it wouldn't be so continuously prevalent in all human societies, but it is one we can do without if we have to (and assuming we are not physically habituated in some way). The occasions for it have therefore become the moments of our lives given over to the ludic, the celebratory, the digressive and the recreational, and it is just these holiday moods that the dutiful, conscientious, ordering and prioritizing sides of our natures find it hard to contend with. If a night on the town is happier than a day at the office, we come to feel we have a right to more of this kind of happiness, and thus the specter of excess announces itself. A company solicitor still drinking in the hotel bar at 3 A.M. when she is giving a presentation to the Board at 9:30 the following morning is not making her leisure time commensurate with her professional duties, it is felt (and if she is very unlucky, her employers may be the sort who like to audit the blood alcohol levels of their staff). Within this impulse to express disapprobation of, and even try to prevent, the immoderate appetites of others is written not just the unrequested advice of doctors, but the drug legislation itself. The brick wall one often collides with in discussing law reform with those who broadly favor the current dispensation is that, although they can't explain specifically what it is that makes them not want other people to smoke cannabis, they just *know* they don't want them to be able to.

Is this a form of jealousy, a self-loathing at the lack of one's own adventurousness, or just a feeling that people shouldn't give over parts of their lives to enjoyment while others suffer, as if intoxication were not in itself partly a response to the everyday suffering of a life full of disappointments? Then again, the desire to prevent others from doing themselves harm tends to be a strong factor, fueled as often as not by serious misapprehension of the actual risk being taken. Here too is a dilemma. Do we have the right to stop others from doing themselves harm if they so wish? To try to kill oneself is no longer illegal in the UK, and nor indeed can any authority stop somebody from destroying their health with tobacco or alcohol. A 65-year-old with emphysema may be begged by her doctor, by friends and family, to stop smoking. Her life insurance premiums will be rapaciously high. The government's health warnings will yell from billboard and packet, and yet nobody can constitutionally stop her. In the event of her being wheeled into the corner store on a ventilator, the shopkeeper has committed no crime if he sells her another pack of 20 cool, filter-tipped, smooth-tasting Dromedaries. Ultimately, government can live with this (even if the health authorities wish it wouldn't). But it is not an easy coexistence, and the idea of other more obviously intoxicating materials being generally available alarms it unutterably.

The disputed zone between individuals and intoxicants is a crowded border area where institutional forces are massed uncomfortably close. Among the hostile legions of the law-enforcement industry, the more pacific battalions of social services personnel, pressure groups, the anointed bhagwans of the self-help movement and the chieftains of the medical profession less menacingly mingle. Though they may fight amongst themselves as to whose responsibility intoxicated persons ought to be, and though their tactics may differ accordingly, all march behind the same tattered standard of prevention, dissuasion and interdiction. The liberal doctor tries to wrest the heroin addict away from the clutches of the arresting officer, while the local government drug project coordinator attempts, unheard, to convince them both that, left to his own devices, the user of intoxicants will tone down his intake by responding to dispassionate information. But why should their efforts be so fruitless? Can it simply be that just because these intermixed voices continue to compete with each other in futile dissonance, they thereby cancel each other out? Or is there really some deeper impulse toward intoxicated states at work within us that keeps deleting the messages these voices transmit? If we are biologically predisposed to intoxication, how can we ever be talked out of it?

Drugs appeal to us because they deliver a variety of moods and states not immediately available from our surrounding realities: these may take in complete relaxation, ecstatic happiness, the negation of suffering, radically transformed perceptions or just a sense of being alert and full of potential energy. What unites these disparate effects is what is most important of all, however: namely, that they make us feel *different*. They reorientate our sense of being in the world, either disruptively, in the case of strong hallucinogens, or else by just mildly sharpening (as with cocaine, for example) or softening (as with alcohol) the lineaments of that world. It isn't merely a question of doing something else, otherwise switching off the TV and going out for a swim would be more obviously therapeutic than it tends to be. What is sought is the changing of one's own relationship to the external world by means of the way one experiences it. Swimming may well produce a modest elevation in the mood in the sense that physical exercise stimulates the body's production of the antidepressant norepinephrine. Compare that with the much more instrumental uprush of amphetamine, or the pseudo-electrical tingling of cocaine, or the comet trails of serotonin unleashed by MDMA, and there seems no contest. Ronald K. Siegel makes an important philosophical point in this regard:

These statements of motives, of what people say they seek with drugs—and there could be an endless catalogue of such motives—is also what they say they seek without drugs. They are the same internal urges, wishes, wants, and aspirations that give rise to much of our behaviour.[7]

But that the circumstances of our lives do not readily fulfill. This isn't to suggest that it is always the ache of existential angst that drives us to drugs (although that remains a powerful impetus for many), only that there is an unquenchable ambition in most of us to have more of whatever it is about life that makes it feel dynamic.

Siegel separates intoxication from the primary drives on which our survival as a species depends—those of hunger, thirst and reproduction—but argues that, simply because intoxication is not a physiological imperative, neither is it any less indispensable to our existences.

> We are not born with acquired motivations [as distinct from innate ones] yet they are not unnatural—they are simply an expression of what we strive to be. The pursuit of intoxication is no more abnormal than the pursuit of love . . .[8]

The concept of "pursuit" is a key one. Indeed, it is what ties the acquired drive for intoxication within us to the innate drives for food and water. Having demonstrated experimentally that mammals, fish, reptiles and insects will all go after intoxicants with the same determination as they seek out sustenance, Siegel has repeatedly observed the same behaviors in humans. He suggests that, as an acquired drive, intoxication is unique in this respect. We may lust after glamorous social attachments, the thrills of dangerous sports or fairground rides, the sensuality of power and authority that may be derived from leading a gang, chairing a committee or captaining a rowing eight, but only intoxication is pursued with the same sense of imperative as we feel the need to feed ourselves:

> Unlike other acquired motives, intoxication functions with the strength of a primary drive in its ability to steer the behaviour of individuals, societies, and species. Like sex, hunger, and thirst, the fourth drive, to pursue intoxication, can never be repressed. It is biologically inevitable.[9]

Those spinning games of earliest infancy mentioned in chapter 1 are about inducing what is almost certainly the ur-intoxication state, dizziness. Later fairground rides, inhalants perhaps, and then alcohol, will deliver the same feeling of weightless disorientation, but a child possessing neither materials nor special equipment has already discovered the principle of altered consciousness in spinning round on the spot, and discovered that it is possible to enjoy it and yet still evade the attentions of the proscriptive adult world. Vigorous whirling actions are common to tribal rituals across the Americas, Africa and Asia. Not only the Sufi dervishes, but aboriginal peoples in the rain forests of the Amazon basin, in the deserts of southern Africa, in the island cultures of the South Pacific, perform spinning dances that induce trance states bordering on the hallucinogenic. Without this sacramental element, dizziness recommends itself to a child because it is funny—in both senses of the word. It can be self-administered, unlike tickling, and can be relied on to induce a fit of that deliciously irresponsible giggling that adults appear only to have a very limited capacity for. In fact, to adults too, part of the appeal of certain intoxicants lies in the pointless merriment they can provoke. Drunken tittering is familiar enough, but hallucinogenic experiences—notably psilocybin and mescaline—often incorporate an ecstatically funny phase, in which paroxysms of hilarity accompany the realization that all the things one is used to having to take seriously are in fact patently absurd, and are topped with a layer of sheer joy so pure that laughter seems the only bodily response to it. We are used to grinning with delight when things turn out well, but not actually laughing uncontrollably. In these ecstatic hallucinatory states, true laughter—freed from its compromising association with derision—is restored to us. In the nineteenth century, it was nitrous oxide that delivered the guffaws.

In addition to the disorientation and the hilarity, though, there is a third component of dizziness that attracts the young child, as well as the mature adult, to it. That is the just-under-control feeling of danger that lurks at the heart of it. For a moment, the child—dropping to the ground and closing her eyes—feels as though her moorings to the safe, known world have been loosed. She floats free in a perilous limbo, unable to think or see in the normal way, and then reality repossesses her senses, insistently bringing the focus back to what, a moment ago, was a liquefied blur. Her mind had gone somewhere else, and then come back. A popular pastime among the adventurous in later childhood is the hyperventilation fainting game, in which the subject gulps in lungfuls of air until, giddy with oxygenation, he signals to his friend to constrict his chest in a sudden bear-hug from behind. The blood flow to the brain is momentarily drastically reduced, and the subject crumples to the ground in a blackout. Sometimes the action is judged so that a near-faint state is produced, avoidance of total unconsciousness meaning that the effect can be appreciated all the way through—the helpless rubberized limbs, the rushing in the ears, the prickle of cold sweat on the brow. After hyperventilation, flirting with asphyxiation may well be the next stage.

The appalling death in February 1999 of a fifteen-year-old boy at Eton College revealed that recreational asphyxiation had been all the rage in one of the houses of Berkshire's famous public school. Boys were inducing blackouts in each other by tightening dressing-gown cords around each other's necks until they collapsed. So obsessive had the game become that it was practiced virtually every evening over a period of four months. At the victim's inquest, one of his housemates, when asked what the attraction of such a dangerous activity was, explained, "The attraction was that it was something different. It made you feel abnormal." Six or seven episodes an evening were not uncommon, and the tragedy occurred because the boy who died couldn't persuade anybody else to give him another go. Left alone, he tied his cord to a peg on the door and effectively hanged himself, his body being found the next morning after he failed to turn up at breakfast. Did he imagine that his head would be jerked out of the cord as he collapsed, or was he simply so blindly hell-bent on the experience that he forgot that what made the game safer before was precisely the fact that his pal would let go when he lost consciousness? Another boy told the inquest, "We got a slight buzz when we came round." But was the point not rather the passing out more than the coming round, and to hell with the consequences afterward? Passing unhesitatingly over the possibility of suicide, the coroner, in recording the only proper verdict of Death by

Misadventure, announced that he had tried to reconstruct for himself what must be going through the mind of a young man actively wishing oblivion on himself for its own sweet sake:

> The fainting game was taking place between boys who are some of the cream of our society, who are probably also of above average intelligence. Why? What words spring to mind? Crazy? Mad? Stupid?[10]

Try "human."

Danger is the price we accept we pay for the use of certain intoxicants, or perhaps for the continued use of intoxicants that were previously relatively harmless but whose compulsive use has become critical. Inuring ourselves to situations of apparent peril, and then voluntarily undergoing them again, is a way of showing ourselves that we have mastered something intimidating in life. Some go through life avoiding such unnecessary risk as they can; others court it. That first-ever parachute jump is reportedly a leap into extreme terror until repeat experience produces something like euphoria, a thrill that persists long after the landing. The world-famous Pepsi-Max Big One roller-coaster at Blackpool Pleasure Beach in northwest England offers a more contained version of the same phenomenon. The carriage mounts a seemingly endless vertiginous incline into the buffeting wind off the Irish Sea until, having breathlessly attained the summit, it pauses for a sickening few seconds before twisting to the right and plummeting through the near-perpendicular at two and a half times the force of gravity. The severity of the drop is such that you cannot, unless you are sitting right at the front, see the track below you, and so for a moment you are hurtling sightlessly downward in a semiconscious limbo. It is difficult to recount the state of paralytic fear that flooded me the first time I rode on it, and yet when the ride is finished, all you want out of life is to do it again. The question of whether the experience is good or bad is an irrelevant one, what classical philosophical inquiry would have termed a category error. Its point is that it isn't the same as the life those people on the biliously distant ground are living while you crash through a vortex of supergravity. This is also what intoxication is about, in a more practically convenient form.

As Siegel puts it, "The fourth drive is not just motivating people to feel good or bad—it is a desire to feel different, to achieve a rapid change in one's state."[11] More even than the cheerfulness produced by stimulants, the hypnotic bliss of cannabis or the psychic fascination of hallucinogenic drugs, the appeal of intoxicants lies in their transformative impact on the brain. This is the way the world is one minute—and the next it isn't.

Such is the power exerted by the intoxication drive that, throughout human history, it has presented many individuals with a dilemma. At its heart is a fundamental instinctual hiatus between physical safety and the lure of mental euphoria. How can it be that the latter can repeatedly override our biological programming to protect the former? To leave aside for the moment the obvious explanation of acute physical dependency in the case of opiates and refined synthetics such as crystal meth, what, for example, makes the boy who hasn't been able to shake off a chill for the last month, and has a faceful of spots to boot, go out for yet another weekend on E, and what makes his mother open another bottle of Chardonnay when she is wincing from a grumbling liver? If a suspect frozen prawn gives us a three-day bout of food poisoning, it often sets up a potently aversive reaction within us, so that the mere sight of another prawn sandwich is enough to induce nausea. To be able to eat one again involves a mighty mustering of willpower to overcome the irrational fear that every specimen may now contain within it the means to strike us down.

And yet this overprotective psychosomatic reaction does not appear to translate itself to the use of intoxicants. Or at least it does, but it is disregarded with a seemingly more effortless act of will than the prawn sandwich requires. I have seen people having difficulty controlling a retching reaction for long enough to get another tiny pill down. A man at a chill-out vomited one straight back up again, retrieved it from the sink, rinsed it and swallowed it again. If the stomach simply says no, it may be inserted into the rectum like a suppository, or else crushed and snorted instead. The only explanation for this singularly dogged behavior is that the intoxication effect is too devoutly wished to be denied, whereas there are nearly always alternatives to the prawn sandwich that will have quite the same effect on the appetite. To the detached observer, this form of compulsion is often mistaken for the symptoms of physical addiction, when it is nothing other than the determination to achieve a goal against whatever impracticalities the body throws in the way. Similarly, users of some nonaddictive drugs are often challenged to go for a prescribed period without them in order to prove that they are not dependent on them. This is a challenge that may be honorably resisted on the grounds that there is no point in it. To quote an old but good analogy, a man may agree to go about without trousers on for a week and experience a certain amount of psychological discomfort in doing so, only to fall upon his 501s again gratefully when the test week is over, but the experiment will not have proved that he is therefore addicted to trousers, and that they are something he ought to wean himself off. The aversion reaction is held up by those who are selectively hostile to intoxicant use as a demonstration that ultimately the body is trying to warn us off it, and that we should heed this message. On this analysis, the aversion is accorded privilege over the unquenchable desire of the brain for the effect of it, but why should the churning stomach be the arbiter of the matter more than the hopeful brain?

In the nineteenth century, the notion of the will was mobilized to address the matter of physical dependency. People had fallen into alcoholism or "the morphia habit" because their wills had been weakened by nervous debilities, for which the catchall term "neurasthenia" was usually deployed, or else—as in the case of women—they were presumed to be genetically weak-willed to begin with. (Valverde highlights the glaring contradiction in the thinking of medical personnel who commented on the fact that some headstrong working-class women doughtily resisted institutionalization in alcohol reformatories in no uncertain terms, despite the fact that it was precisely their lack of will and self-possession that was thought to have brought them to the brink of it.) The same analysis has returned in latter-day professional attitudes to intoxication, especially given that alcoholism and the other addictions are no longer classified as pathological conditions in themselves. Alcoholism makes you sick, but it is not in itself a sickness. Therefore, those who lapse into it are suffering from debilitated willpower. In the case, however, of the individual overcoming aversive responses in order to continue taking an intoxicant, exactly the opposite is the case. It can't be a feeble will that makes the woman with obstructed and streaming nasal passages take another line of cocaine, because she is having to muster reserves of volition in order to do something she knows is a bad idea. When prohibitionists are constrained to acknowledge this point, they fall back on the argument that there must then be some physical dependency at work—anything rather than accept the fact that the desire for altered states is a powerful constant in human life.

The discomfort that the prohibitionist argument feels over the matter is nowhere more acute than when it is confronted with the proposition that knowing of the physiological harm that is being incurred appears not to have a decisive effect on some people. The attitude of medical authorities has always been that if people only understood what they were doing to themselves, they would desist from using intoxicants. Hence the posters that used to plaster the doctors' waiting rooms that showed Petri dishes of malevolent black gunge with the message to smokers that this was what they were putting into their lungs. A particular brand of cigarettes was once held (mythically, I think) to make the lungs bleed with each one smoked, but when student colleagues lighting them up were apprised of the theory, the reaction was only ever the most perfunctory muted indignation. Nobody switched to another brand. The late food-writer and broadcaster Jennifer Paterson smoked openly and unrepentantly on the BBC cookery show she copresented. As she turned 70, she responded to the many people who suggested that she ought to stop, by declaring, "Thousands die from smoking each year, but knowing this I continue to smoke myself. It is my informed decision." She was admitted to hospital with lung cancer at the age of 71, told her doctors that it was far too late for her to stop now and died within a few weeks. W. C. Fields, patron-saint of heedless boozers, drank himself to death, wondering only why the process was taking so inordinately long. The one thing above all prohibitionism cannot comprehend or tolerate is when its warnings to drug-takers that they will destroy themselves are met with an unconcerned shrug, even when for once the prognosis may be right. And yet this is not necessarily the sign of an entropic will crumbling to dust: it can be the last luminescence of a life-force that has burned brighter than prohibitionism, even in the fervor of its despair at the world, knows how to.

If we are to have a chance of explaining where the often self-destructive bravado of intoxication comes from, it will be necessary to look at what the various classes of intoxicant actually chemically do to us, and decide why the resulting states might be psychologically valuable. To suggest, as some authorities do, that altering one's consciousness is just a habit-forming, but ultimately meaningless, end in itself—as if intoxication were a mere matter of irrational routine, on a par with preferring to get out of the right side of the bed rather than the left—seems an insufficient way of accounting for such a persistent human impulse. There must be something at work in the chemical principles of these various substances that animates our desire for them, and that, inasmuch as they possess different properties and classes of action within the body, answers a range of different needs. I am dealing here purely with the onset effects and peak action of these substances, the elements that provide the motivation each time for embarking on another ingestion of them, and not the bodily consequences of overuse, which are the principal focus of all medical advice on the subject.

STIMULANTS

Drugs such as amphetamine and cocaine, and their more powerful superrefined analogues crystal meth, ice and crack, have the most readily comprehensible effect on the brain. It derives largely from stimulation of the central nervous system, which is accompanied by a repertoire of other sympathetic physical responses. The psychomotor function of the brain is aroused, resulting in a feeling of potential energy, so that the stimulated body wants to move restlessly about, whether by dancing, running, pacing about or even—in some predisposed individuals—fighting. The whole body is sent into a state of alert, much as it is in response to production of the body's own natural chemical stimulant norepinephrine. Blood pressure rises with an increase in the heart rate as the circulatory system copes with the narrowing of blood vessels near the skin, but a widening of those that go into the muscles. (Not the least reason for the diminishing-returns aspect of snorting stimulants is that the blood vessels into which the powders are absorbed become progressively constricted as the stimulant effects set in.) What is classically referred to as the fight-or-flight mechanism takes over, in which the body, responding to the brain's assessment of a dangerous situation, prepares itself either for physical defense or for running away. The bronchioles, tubes in the lungs through which inhaled oxygen passes, dilate to allow for deeper and more rapid breathing, and the sugar level in the blood starts climbing. Sugar is delivered more rapidly than usual to muscle tissue, resulting in greater muscular capacity and endurance, while the metabolic system breaks down accumulated fats to extract the energy potential from them.

What the drugs have done is fool the body into thinking that a state of emergency is upon it. When energy does begin to be burned up in frantic dancing, the system raids its reserves—those stocks that it would normally only call on if one were stuck halfway up a mountain without immediate help to hand—which is why there is no exhaustion quite like the abject deflation that follows a night on speed. The body may need a whole day or more to replenish itself. These effects are maximized in the case of crack-smoking because the material is most readily and immediately absorbed into the system in the vaporous form of smoke. Snorting is in turn a more rapid method of administration than swallowing, after which the drugs are more immediately metabolized and thus neutralized. Any means of introduction that initially bypasses the filtering function of the liver, such as smoking, snorting and intravenous injection, will lead to a more direct impact on the brain than swallowing does.

Three chemicals that are naturally produced within the body are key to the effects produced by stimulant drugs. These are norepinephrine, which is manufactured during bouts of strenuous physical exercise, serotonin and dopamine. All have marked antidepressive properties, and production of all is considerably enhanced when stimulants are introduced into the body. Research has shown that one particular complex of nerves where dopamine is produced appears to play a central role in the brain's apperception of pleasure. These nerves are typically richer in dopamine during the pleasurable experiences in life, in sexual activity or in eating good food. When cocaine and amphetamine hit the brain, this function is hugely stimulated, so that the neural pathways are flooded with dopamine, far more so than can be delivered by all but the most singularly life-transforming orgasm. Cocaine also has the ability to inhibit the conduction of physical impulses along the nerves, which is what has made it historically such an important local anesthetic. (High priests of the Inca people administered it to their human sacrifices as a final tender mercy before their chests were hewn open and their hearts removed.)

As the effect subsides, which takes considerably longer in the case of amphetamine than it does with cocaine, the depleted substances are voided in the urine. Elimination of amphetamine occurs at a greater rate, the lower the pH balance of the urine is, which is why bumping up its acid level by taking on plenty of vitamin C hastens the climb-down period at the end of a speed session. By the same token, orange juice is not a particularly efficient thing to drink when just getting going.

It isn't hard to see where the attraction of stimulant drugs lies. Even before the action of dopamine began to be understood, the connection between physical stimulation and the elevation of mood was obvious, and it holds good not just for cocaine and speed, but for the considerably milder caffeine present in coffee, tea, chocolate and such recently commercialized products as guarana. The most appealing aspect of stimulant intoxication, for the sake of which one could often quite well do without the augmented energy and endurance, is that it makes its participants feel cheerier, chattier, more convivial. The immediate circumstances of life assume a more radiant luster, enjoyable activities are more keenly anticipated, and a sense of scarcely containable excitement accompanies what might ordinarily be a perfectly routine, banal agenda. Self-help manuals and deep breathing might aim at the same state, but fall some way short of the uprush delivered by strong doses of stimulant.

CANNABIS

It has very recently been established that cannabis too stimulates the dopamine nerve-cells, although at less frenetic a rate than do the stimulant drugs. The most provocative finding to have emerged in recent years, however, has been the discovery of a specific receptor in the brain for d-9-tetrahydrocannabinol (THC), the plant's active constituent. That there is a receptor for the opiate drugs, that facilitates their analgesic and calming effects, has long been known to medical science, and stands in the clear light of evolutionary logic. Why there should be a THC receptor in there as well remains as mysterious for the time being as the purpose of the pineal gland once was. Or perhaps it doesn't. Perhaps our brains evolved, in conjunction with the broad geographical spread of the cannabis plant, to be hospitable toward a naturally occurring substance that offered the sedating qualities of other tranquilizers without their acutely narcotic effects. More likely, it indicates that the brain produces its own cannabinoids for the purpose so that cannabis is able to latch itself on to these receptors in the same way that morphine and the other opiates exploit the brain's ability to manufacture pain-suppressing endorphins.

However that may be decided, THC is transported into the brain when the smoke from cannabis is absorbed through the bronchioles into the pulmonary bloodstream, from whence it passes directly to the brain. Inhaling smoke that has been trapped in a bottle, by ensuring that none escapes into the surrounding atmosphere, delivers higher concentrations of THC into the bloodstream. Higher concentrations still will be obtained by swallowing the resin. The substance is only cleared from the system rather slowly compared to other drugs, so that residual THC from an evening's prolonged smoke—or from oral ingestion of a hearty lump of the stuff—may be present in the bloodstream for several days. Cannabis resin is slightly higher in THC than grass (about 10–15 percent by weight, compared to less than 10 percent). While the drug goes to work more or less immediately on the brain, the effects on the rest of the body are very modest. There is an increase in heart rate, and perhaps a slight diminution in body temperature. A part of the brain called the hippocampus is where the cannabinoid receptors are most heavily concentrated; it is responsible for dealing with memory and the process of learning. It has been suggested that overloading this part of the brain with THC is what leads to short-term memory loss in heavy users of cannabis, and that while recall of existing knowledge is not noticeably impaired, the ability to learn and absorb new material is inhibited by high concentrations of cannabinoids.

Cannabis is valued for its sedative and relaxant properties, qualities that may be so profoundly appreciated as an antidote to the normal doses of low-level stress that everyday life delivers that the drug effect may produce fits of innocently irresponsible giggling. On the other hand, a heightened sense of awareness often accompanies the initial onset, so that everything from the food being eaten, the music heard and the sociability of the occasion are experienced at a more sensuously intense pitch. Being stoned appears to make things feel entertainingly larger than life for a while, before the demotivated stupor of deeper intoxication with the drug takes over. The sedative effect may be had from alcohol, of course, but nothing quite like the feeling of drifting free of one's perceptual moorings is available at comparably low doses from drinking. For an explanation of the attraction of swallowing cannabis, we must look at the highly complex actions of hallucinogenic substances.

HALLUCINOGENS

The nature and extent of the actions of hallucinogenic drugs in the brain is still only very partially understood. There is a vast array of botanical specimens covering virtually all regions of the earth that offer these effects to human (and animal) use, and all may have their own peculiar attributes depending on what the active alkaloid is in each case. Some plants contain a complex of psychoactive alkaloids that are all capable of altering the cognitive functions of the brain, as well as inducing visual, auditory, olfactory, tactile and gustatory sense-illusions, and playing upon the emotional faculties of the partaker. Many have been incorporated into religious rituals among aboriginal peoples in the Americas, Africa, Australasia and the South Pacific, while some have been proposed for therapeutic use in Western medicine, although without much chance of take-up owing to their legal status. What follows is only a highly simplified account of what would appear to be the case as regards the more widely experienced substances, both natural and synthetic. Should the tryptamine snuffs of the Amazon basin, made from such sources as the beans of the anadenanthera tree or the bark of the virola, find their way in due course into Western recreational use on a significant scale, systematic research will have to be extended accordingly, but for the time being, it has been concerned mainly with LSD and MDMA.

In the case of the psychedelic compounds that form the basis of lysergic acid diethylamide (LSD), their nuclear structure bears a striking resemblance to that of the brain's principal neurotransmitters serotonin, dopamine and norepinephrine. These are the naturally produced chemicals that influence and modulate mood, together with functions such as sleep and the appetite. It was established by research in the early years of the twentieth century that electrical pulses caused the brain's neurons, or nerve fibers, to release these chemicals and, in so doing, carry messages across the gaps—or synapses—that exist between them in the brain. What is now understood is that the psychoactive alkaloids in hallucinogenic drugs, when introduced to the brain via the bloodstream, bind tightly to the receptors for serotonin especially (and possibly to those for dopamine too, in the case of LSD) and trigger not only alterations in mood but profound disturbances in sensory consciousness too. It has been found that there are at least a dozen types of serotonin (or 5-HT) receptors in the brain, of which one particular group, 5-HT_2, are crucially susceptible to the intervention of psychedelic drugs. 5-HT_{2C}, for example, is thought to be the neurotransmitter responsible for producing feelings of anxiety. Overstimulation of that receptor may be what leads to bad trips and panic attacks during certain episodes of hallucinogenic intoxication. It has further been established that newly developed antipsychotic drugs, such as clozapine and risperidone, by blocking the interaction of other compounds with the main serotonin receptor, 5-HT_{2A}, can act as antidotes to LSD by displacing it from the relevant neurons. The bad trip can at last be cured, although the binding action of LSD on the receptors is so strong that the antidotes may take up to half an hour to work (as compared with a mere 30 seconds for the opiate antidote naloxone in the case of heroin overdose). Much research was done in the 1950s and early 1960s on the possible therapeutic use of LSD in the treatment of mental conditions such as depression and obsessive-compulsive disorder, and even dependency states such as alcoholism or other drug addiction, but the illegalizing of these drugs stifled all such efforts, and there was fairly compelling evidence that individuals with a history of schizophrenia could be done nothing but harm by them. For the time being, all bets are off, particularly as a significant amount of research effort is now going into studying the effects of MDMA on the neurons of the brain.

Ecstasy is not technically a pure hallucinogen, but rather a modified amphetamine, and its hallucinogenic potency is relatively mild compared with that of LSD. As an amphetamine-based drug, it has some effect on dopamine receptors, thus elevating mood, but its principal, and dramatic, impact is on serotonin terminals. By detonating a huge release of 5-HT across the synapses, it vastly raises overall serotonin levels in the brain, not least because it appears to get inside the receptor and vacuum out every last drop of the stuff. What has begun to worry research pharmacologists, and thus the public-health authorities, is that it has now been established beyond doubt that the impact of the drug results in progressive degeneration of serotonin nerve fibers. That degeneration peaks at about 24–36 hours after an episode of use. The question is: Will this cause long-term harm? So far the scientific answer has been a cautious shrug. It may be that we can survive perfectly well with depleted serotonin, and without falling victim to the vicious depressions that some commentators are warning may be the consequence in later life of repeated, heavy use of MDMA. It would also seem to be the case that, to some extent, neurons do regenerate (i.e., they simply grow back), but—inexplicably so far—only in some parts of the brain and not in others. One more cheering finding, courtesy of Mark Molliver, a neurology professor at Johns Hopkins University at Baltimore, Maryland, is that the antidepressant drug fluoxetine (widely marketed and prescribed as Prozac) has the power to displace MDMA in the nerve terminals. This means that if a dose is taken between the end of an ecstasy session, but before 24 hours have elapsed, the neurological degeneration can be prevented. It also helps to explain why individuals on a continuous course of Prozac are rendered partially or wholly immune to ecstasy.

The interaction of antidepressant drugs and hallucinogenics has provided another fascinating field of study. While drugs in the Prozac class (selective serotonin reuptake inhibitors, or SSRIs) blunt or completely neutralize the effects of psychotropic drugs—with the intriguing exception of psilocybin—drugs in the tricyclic antidepressant class (imipramine, desipramine, clomipramine) and lithium seem to magnify susceptibility to them, and can result in gruesomely heightened sensory disturbances occasioning serious panic and terror. Even worse, the remaining class of antidepressants, the monoamine oxidase inhibitors, MAOIs, such as phenelzine, are *absolutely con-*

traindicated in combination with ecstasy, as indeed they are with
other stimulants. Hypertensive crisis through rocketing blood pressure will be the result, and it seems likely that at least a handful of
the fatalities attributed to ecstasy have arisen through combining
it with phenelzine. (An LSD-MAOI juxtaposition is not harmful,
but the antidepressant will mute the effects of the trip, rather as
Prozac does.)

As to other sudden deaths following ecstasy use, and where one
can be sure that the cause is not massive overingestion of water as in
the tragic case of the British schoolgirl Leah Betts, whose avoidable
death became something of a cause célèbre in the annals of antidrug
propaganda in the 1990s, it may be that some individuals are critically susceptible to the hypertensive effects of the drug, and that the
upsurge in body temperature that results in certain conditions (overcrowded clubs with inadequate air-conditioning) proves fatal. While
one would not wish in any way to minimize the gravity of untimely
deaths in any circumstances, it should be stressed that these outcomes represent a tiny proportion of all MDMA usage, and that all
official and media interpretations of these tragedies as deriving from
batches of poisoned pills are to be resisted strenuously. There are no
instances of multiple deaths among groups of people who had taken
the same pills, for all that such a calamity would, one suspects, be a
godsend to certain tabloid editors.

Flooding the brain with serotonin results in an almost indescrib-
ably beautiful feeling of weightless happiness, in which one is blown
along (especially so in the case of ecstasy) on currents of amphetamine excitation. There is a concomitant comedown effect, to be
sure, but it can be mitigated to some modest extent by application of
Prozac or of 5-HTP (hydroxy-tryptophan), a plant-derived serotonin replacement medicine available in health stores. What is less
immediately apprehensible is why the sensory disturbances offered
by strong hallucinogenics like LSD, psilocybin and mescaline, and
which do not typically prompt concentrated regular use on the scale
that ecstasy does, should be so attractive. It is at this point that textbooks on the subject start invoking religion, spirituality and cosmology, and it is certainly the case that hallucinogenic tripping can have
a mystical dimension to those so disposed. Perhaps more interestingly, it can feel powerfully self-revealing, so that a lot of repressed

psychic material might be liberated, with accompanying emotional descant, during the sluggishly passing hours of a trip. Given the possibility of these consequences, I was not surprised to be told by the man in the psychedelic shop in Amsterdam that he didn't counsel using the psilocybin-containing *Stropharia* mushrooms he was selling more than about three or four times a year. That said, I have met people who take low doses of LSD quite regularly, and don't feel as though they have gone through a Wagnerian cataclysm every time, and so it seems certain that habituation is an issue here too.

OPIATES

The key advance in the understanding of the action of opiates in the brain came in 1975 when a class of protein chemicals, or peptides, was discovered. These substances, which came collectively to be termed the endorphins, play a crucial role in regulating the activity of the neurotransmitters we have already encountered. They are activated whenever the body is subject to physical pain or discomfort, and they assist in modifying its perception. What the opiate/opioid drugs (such as heroin, morphine or their various analogues such as hydromorphone, meperidine, buprenorphine, methadone, etc.) do in the brain is bind to the nerve receptors where the endorphins are active, and influence them to initiate that neurotransmission, resulting in a feeling of soothing calm being dispensed as if in response to stress. The effect is precisely the opposite of that prompted by the stimulant drugs. The so-called fight-or-flight mechanism is neutralized as feelings of anxiety, tension or panic are washed away. Breathing becomes lighter and shallower, the heart rate slows to a plod and body temperature is lowered. Muscles become loose and rubbery, with the exception of the sphincter muscle, which goes into a state of suspended tension, which is why prolonged opiate use causes constipation. With a sufficient dose, consciousness at the most basic level is turned off, and the subject drifts into sleep.

Opiate drugs exercise their greatest appeal to individuals who have difficulty coping with the multiple tiny traumas that day-to-day living throws up. Even more than alcohol, and to a considerably more effective degree than benzodiazepine tranquilizers such as Valium and Librium, the anesthetic haze they cloud the world over with is its own irresistible argument. And whereas barbiturates may put you to sleep, the beauty of opiates is that the user doesn't have to withdraw altogether from sentient consciousness, but has the satisfaction of seeing a hurtful, hard reality diffused into soft focus. For some (a minority), however, the use of opiates goes on to create chronic physical dependency or addiction. When this happens, the desire for a dose of the drug becomes more a matter of avoiding the acute discomfort of not having it, rather than a yearning to experience its beatific effects again. Why should this be so? What is it about the action of these drugs that causes this obsessive behavior, and—in the paradigm beloved of all antidrug campaigners—leads to loss of engagement with reality, a squalid, miserable pseudo-life, and very likely a lapse into crime?

Here again we must turn to the neural circuits of the brain. Just as the endorphins govern the body's response to pain, so the system that produces the neurotransmitter dopamine influences our responses to pleasurable stimulants. The pleasure-giving or hedonic circuits in the brain are not there simply as a gift from an all-bountiful nature; they play an essential part in ensuring the survival and propagation of a species. The pleasure to be had from eating when hungry is designed to encourage us to nourish the body thoroughly, just as the erogenous bliss of sexual activity prompts the reproductive urge in most. Drinking a glass of water is all the more relishable after physical exercise on a hot day because that is when the system most needs rehydrating, and so forth. This mechanism has been given the name of the reward circuit, because it rewards the individual with a feeling of pleasure for doing something that turns out to be good for it. Opiate drugs activate this circuit to a peculiarly intense degree. (Other drugs do too, but not to the same extent, which may be why we are still arguing over whether somebody who uses cocaine every day or another who drinks several bottles of beer every night is technically addicted to their drug of choice, but why nobody really doubts that an individual reduced to smashing his way into a parked car in pursuit of funds for the next dose is a drug addict.)

Laboratory rats trained to hit levers that deliver them drug doses as an alternative to food or water quickly discover they would rather have smack than snacks. This is so even when the injection of the drug requires up to 300 hits on the lever where food may only require one. Administer a modest dose of heroin to them before the experiment starts, and pursuit of the drug is all the more frenetic. Neutralize their neural reward circuits electrically, though, and they suddenly don't give a damn. They can eat, drink, engage in sexual activity or help themselves to another whoosh of the drug, but they just don't care to. Now sunk in anomic stupor, they gaze glassy-eyed at their handlers with all the élan vital of a bored teenager awakening at noon.

Why, though, do some individuals become drug dependent, while others appear to be able to use their substances in a more or less functional manner? Answering that question has inevitably led some researchers to posit that there may be some genetic factor, possibly a hereditary feature, in the brains of a minority of people that causes them to carry on overriding the warning signals that accompany sustained overuse of any intoxicant. Perhaps removing that gene somehow may be the eventual medical answer to addiction. Then again, if it is so deeply implanted in the pleasure circuits, might such an intervention create a lobotomized, amotivational individual on a par with those radically apathetic rats? Should the gene theory be disproved, it could be that addiction studies will be forced back onto the personality-prototype model that insists that some people—risk-takers, thrill-seekers, as they are known in the laboratories—just are driven to seek out more exciting forms of experience than the consolidators and safety-seekers would be seen dead near. Perhaps most persuasive of all is the postulate that some people are simply more neurochemically receptive to drug experiences than others. All drug-users have tales to tell of friends who simply looked on in bafflement while they, having taken one of the same batch of pills, went off at the supersensual deep end. Some are intriguingly resistant to the effects of cannabis. If susceptibility to intoxicants is a continuum, then there will inevitably be those whose dopamine readings will practically go off the scale on receipt of heroin. Are these the future addicts?

A group of behavioral pharmacologists writing in *Nature* magazine in July 1999 reported that they had synthesized a substance, given the laboratory reference BP 897, that might hold the key to regulating addiction responses in humans. In tests on rats that had been trained to self-administer cocaine, they found that BP 897 had the potentially groundbreaking effect of suppressing the craving for cocaine in the presence of certain associative stimuli. One of the reasons for the high rate of relapse among reformed cocaine addicts is that environmental and contextual triggers, such as being in a particular room where a lot of cocaine was taken, seeing a small mirror or razor blade, or even overhearing somebody talking about the drug can set off an intense desire to take it again. Not only did BP 897 render equivalent associative triggers inactive in the rats, but it had no reinforcing activity of its own in the brain, meaning that it carries no danger of simply replacing cocaine addiction with a serious BP 897 habit. It would appear that it works by weakly stimulating the dopamine receptors that normally go into overdrive at the prospect of taking more cocaine. However, if cocaine is taken again, the new substance appears to have little effect in blunting its reward mechanism in the brain, so if clinical trials do eventually lead to BP 897 becoming a prescribable medication in the treatment of addiction, it seems likely that it will only be useful to those patients who genuinely want to give it up. This study did, moreover, limit itself to cocaine, and so what implications it might have for opiate addiction remains unclear, and—like all laboratory rat tests—it will be confined to the status of a tantalizing hypothesis until such time as human studies are carried out.

ALCOHOL

When alcohol is swallowed, it passes into the bloodstream initially by means of blood vessels in the stomach wall, although only about a quarter of what is ingested is absorbed this way. The remainder is discharged into the small intestine, which is also copiously furnished with blood vessels. It is then distributed to all organs of the body, but its predominant effects are registered in the brain because that is where the fatty matter takes it up most readily. Alcohol is highly soluble in both fat and water. Generally speaking, the higher the concentration of alcohol in the drink being taken, the more rapidly it will seem to take effect, but some studies have shown that there is an optimum level for absorption of alcohol at about 30 percent by volume, which is why anybody who claims to feel slightly tipsier slightly more quickly on a Scotch and soda, compared to the spirit taken neat at 40 percent, is not necessarily fooling himself. Other factors that influence the rate of absorption are the speed at which one drinks, and the contents of the stomach. If food is being taken simultaneously, then the alcohol has to wait in line behind it, whereas if the drinking is happening on an empty stomach, it enjoys a free passage. Thus, if that aperitif looks like turning into three, it is a sensible idea to avail oneself of the salty nibbles and canapés in order to avoid feeling too far gone before sitting down to dinner.

Many other differentials often cited with regard to alcohol capacity, such as that larger people take longer to get drunk because they have a greater volume of body fluids in which to disperse it, or that women are more susceptible than men because a proportionally larger percentage of their bodies are made up of fatty tissue, seem to permit so many exceptions that one may wonder how useful they are. (A Hong Kong brothel-keeper of the Victorian era, Maude Jones, routinely used to down eight or nine glasses of a proprietary mixture known as Hong Kong Fizz as a prelude to lunch every day. It consisted of gin, vodka, green and yellow Chartreuse, Bénédictine and a splash of lemon juice, all bubbled up with soda—enough to produce lethal hypertension in today's health professionals.) Sparkling drinks seem to carry alcohol into the bloodstream more rapidly because the carbon dioxide acts to open up the valve between the stomach and small intestine.

When it reaches the brain, alcohol has a disinhibiting effect on the higher cerebral functions. The drinker becomes more chatty and more articulate, and readier to interact with others. This is a temporary inaugural phase in intoxication with alcohol, however, as more of the drug begins to alter the functioning of the centers that control memory, mental alertness and speech. Despite its initially animating effect, it is a depressant of the central nervous system, which is why critical levels eventually induce decelerated, slurring speech, lack of motor coordination, sleep and—in extremis—complete blackout. Because of its loosening influence on social inhibitions, it has been used throughout human history to fortify the nerves against trepidation (the famous "Dutch courage") or to excite sexual response (for which purpose "candy is dandy," to cite Ogden Nash, "but liquor is quicker"). The liver metabolizes alcohol at the rate of about one of the famous units every hour, and so if drink is taken at a faster rate than that, as it almost always is, the quantity of alcohol in the system awaiting metabolism backs up, which is what creates the feeling of intoxication. Some of it is voided in the urine, but 90 percent or more has to await the attention of the liver. Particularly heavy drinkers—those who take in around eight pints of beer, two bottles of wine or about 16 shots of spirit every night—will essentially never have alcohol out of their systems, and will always fail a breath test.

Alcohol, like most other drugs, causes a release of dopamine in the brain, at least while the level of alcohol in the system is rising. That action is halted once peak concentrations have been reached, which is why the period after drinking is often accompanied by a sense of listless ennui, particularly noticeable in the afternoon to those who have drunk at lunchtime, but mostly disguised by sleep for evening drinkers. Alcohol also activates two other important neurotransmitters, namely glutamate and gamma-aminobutyric acid (GABA). The latter is the principal inhibitory neurotransmitter, meaning that it slows down the firing of the neural circuits, one of the results of which is to suppress the memory function. This explains not only why people are apt to forget some piece of information that has been relayed to them while under the influence, but also why some people appear to be affected by the blackout syndrome—not loss of consciousness, but inability to remember whole phases of the previous evening. (That may not entirely be a handicap: it may be quite enough simply to be *told* that one was dancing on the table at the Hilton, without the need to relive the full horror of the averted gazes, the smashed glassware, the furious father-in-law, the bloody-nosed maître-d' and the arrival of the constabulary.) Sleep patterns are also disrupted, especially in the second phase, so that, although one may sink very readily into deep slumber, repeated awakening from about 4 A.M. onward is a dully familiar phenomenon for daily drinkers.

Excessive intake of alcohol without precautionary measures results in a hangover, the more severe examples of which may be among the very worst postintoxicant experiences available. Dehydration, arising from the acute diuretic effect of heavy drinking, results in a sand-dry mouth and headache, the latter exacerbated by dilation of the cranial blood vessels. As compensation reactions set in, other symptoms become apparent. The central nervous system, in recovering from its subdued state, overallows for sensory awareness, meaning that light seems hideously brighter and sounds more clangorously pronounced. Excess alkalinity in the tissues is the body's attempt to cope with the nausea-producing higher acidity alcohol has burdened them with, but it contributes in itself to the overall feeling of enfeebled malaise.

Certain drinks, such as the darker spirits, red wines and port, contain higher levels of substances called congeners, which have a more powerful narcotic effect on the brain cells, and will result in a more purgatorial hangover than that caused by colorless spirits or white wines. Drinking plenty of water to rehydrate the system, swallowing a gram of either aspirin or acetaminophen and perhaps coffee or tea to narrow those distended blood vessels with caffeine are the remedies, together of course with lying perfectly still in a darkened room assailed by intimations of mortality. Low blood sugar can be repaired by eating starchy carbohydrates.

The "hair-of-the-dog" solution, which involves taking on a little more alcohol to mitigate the effects of what is basically a withdrawal process, can also work, but may well seem about as enticing as the prospect of throwing up—which, however, also makes the world look a little more appealing than it did. All of these recourses may be rendered unnecessary if precautionary measures are taken before, during or immediately after a drinking spree: lining the stomach with lactic fat by drinking whole milk beforehand, using alcohol as an accompaniment to food, drinking plenty of water before sleeping, and taking a preemptive analgesic either before retiring or even—in the case of those who suffer particularly from the congeners in red wine—before embarking on the first glass.

To understand the physical actions of intoxicants within the body is simultaneously to appreciate that we are not machines, that there are parameters governing our ability to absorb, metabolize and expel them that can only be stretched so far, no matter what the differentials are between our constitutions as individuals. This, after all, is what sensible drinking advice and (far less honestly) government drug education are supposedly about. Nonetheless, it is a common cross-cultural experience to find out, at some initiatory stage and perhaps later on in life too, where the boundaries are. An overdose is not exclusively a matter of untimely death or lingering coma. It is also the name of the rupture that is marked by overadministration of intoxicant substances, whether through ignorance of one's own limits, ignorance of the purity or precise content of a particular drug or disinclination to call a halt. It may well represent an important rite of passage among many groups in both tribal and postindustrial milieus, in the sense that being humbled by the power of intoxicants at an early age may be seen as the only certain way to acquire a fit measure of respect for them. Some will indeed abjure alcohol after an early flirtation with projectile vomiting and thumping hangover, but most will simply learn how to avoid such a disastrous outcome precisely because they have put their heads in the lion's mouth and not after all been decapitated.

Initiation rituals in the many tribal cultures in which intoxicants are a form of sacrament often deliberately incorporate an element of going too far, so that the youngsters are made transformatively aware of the potency of the divinity locked within them, or into whose presence the intoxicant ushers them. A particularly graphic example is provided by anthropologist Fitz Poole, who visited the Bimin-Kuskusmin tribe of Papua New Guinea, and reported on a meticulously ordered hierarchical society in which the social stratification among males is determined by a progressive series of intoxication episodes, each with its own specific degree of intensity. A kind of inverted twelve-step program brings male members of the tribe to the eventual status of elders, which only the eleventh and twelfth stages of the process can deliver.

In preparation for the cycle, the initiate absents himself from the company of women, children and any other males who are still on a lower grade than he is. Against a background of chanting and drumming, he paints the symbols of his current rank and his ancestral lineage on his face. For the first three stages of the initiation process, the sacred substance turns out, somewhat surprisingly, to be ginger. He will sit by a ceremonial fire through the night, and at first light, he receives the sacrament. Fragments of the stem are eaten, and he snorts the ground leaves of the plant. At the first level, he will have had to fast for one day and had one sleepless night; at the second and third, he must fast for two days, have one sleepless night and refrain from taking water on the day before the ritual. (Rudgley, in citing this work, suggests that if we are puzzled as to the possible psychoactive potential of ginger, we must bear in mind these preparatory privations as well as the profound psychological antici- pation unleashed in the candidates. Their systolic heart-rates shoot up, they sweat out copiously and the ordeal is augmented by the application of a stinging-nettle frottage to their inner thighs. Initia- tion is not meant to be easy.)

For the next six levels, the sacrament is the tobacco genus, *Nico- tiana tabacum*. It is smoked throughout the night, beginning at the fall of darkness, and takes place within the sacred ancestral ossuary of the initiate's clan. In between bouts of smoking, he will wander about outside in the nocturnal cold and damp until the pain of expo- sure brings him back to the fire. For the fourth and fifth grades, a day's fasting and two sleep-deprived nights are required, with a day free of water intake added for the sixth stage. At the seventh and eighth, the fasting period doubles, and for the ninth, two days with- out food or water and two nights without sleep are the preparation. In the final three ranks, the ritual centers on hallucinogenic mush- rooms, but of what precise species, Poole was unable to ascertain. Here, the candidates go up into the mountains to remove themselves completely from the life they have known hitherto. At the tenth level, having denied themselves food and water for a day and gone three nights without sleep, they experience, at the mouth of a cave in which bones of their ancestors have been laid, a hallucinogenic state that takes them into the underworld in which the arcane knowledge guarded by their tribe's elders begins to be revealed to them. The eleventh level is the first, or junior, rank of eldership. To attain this, the initiate must go higher into the mountains, where he is given another, more potent kind of mushroom. This he swallows after two days' fasting without water and three successive sleepless nights.

The twelfth and final stage of the process, in which the tribesman becomes a senior elder, takes place on the mountaintop. He may not take food for three days or sleep for three nights, and for two of the days, he is not permitted water. Only the excreta of the sacred cassowary bird is given to him to eat, in the belief that it will help him fumble his way toward enlightenment. A mushroom almost certainly of the *Psilocybe* species is administered, an intensely toxic item that would easily prove fatal under other circumstances. The final ritual takes place at night in the lashing of a thunderstorm, in which the initiate is left to face his tribal god, Afek, alone. Revelations of rarefied cognitive power come tumbling over him, and at the end of the ordeal, he has attained a state of entitlement in which he is empowered from now on to contribute his own insights to his clan's stock of knowledge. The stages of initiation have altered not only the dimensions of his own consciousness, but also his entire objective status within his community. He is allowed a period of reorientation to everyday awareness before he comes back down the mountain to rejoin them.

The profound mental transformation that intoxication rituals always involve is typically characterized by an emblematic loss of consciousness to mark a crossing of the boundary from one state to the other. Among the Chukchi people of eastern Siberia, the ritual use of tobacco to achieve a condition of intense intoxication was often accompanied by physical collapse, while fainting is a widely noted aspect of initiation to the peyote cactus among Mexican Indians. In some cultures, the alarming or distressing nature of introduction to a powerfully hallucinogenic intoxicant is used as a form of social control. Native peoples of the upper Amazon use a preparation of the datura plant, a malodorous, spiny-fruited shrub, to initiate their boys into manhood. The celebrated early intoxicologist Louis Lewin reports that the Jíbaros of the river Upano area prepare a drink, *maikoa,* by pressing juice from the bark of the plant as an initiatory sacrament, but also notes that "[b]adly behaved boys are made to drink *maikoa* while fasting. This is considered a radical cure."[12]

Something of this motivation lingered on in the once-fashionable disciplinary practice of forcing cigarettes on adolescents caught smoking until they were biliously revolted by them. That too was no doubt considered a radical cure. But the faculty for disregarding the alarm warnings of toxic substances is a very deeply rooted one, and comes to be overridden as tolerance of them develops. At the beginning of the first century A.D., the Roman satirical poet Martial depicts an obdurate drinker laughing off medical cautions:

> *Phryx, the worthy drinker, was blind*
> *In one eye, and the other was running.*
> *To him said Heras, the doctor: Avoid wine!*
> *If you continue like this you will see nothing.*
> *Phryx smilingly answered: Goodbye to thee, my eye!*
> *And on the spot he had many glasses mixed.*
> *Do you want to know the end?*
> *Phryx drank wine and his eye poison.*[13]

Another model of defiance observed by Lewin in a Florentine tomb inscription shows this imperviousness to the counsel of moderation still going strong within the Christian tradition:

> *Wine, which gives life, to me gave death.*
> *Sober I never saw the dawn—*
> *Now my very bones are thirsty!*
> *Wanderer! Besprinkle the tomb with wine,*
> *Empty the cup, and go!*
> *Farewell, ye drinkers!*[14]

The welfare culture of modern Western society has tended to make bravado of this nature more circumspect in the last two centuries, but it lives on in somewhat apologetic form in the addiction confessional, that literary form instigated by de Quincey but still doing a roaring trade in our own day. We shall look more closely at this in the next chapter, but what de Quincey's unflinching narrative of his own dissolution indicated was that what might, in the more rollicking atmosphere of the literary eighteenth century, have been a picaresque tale of a rake's demise can now be recast as a mea culpa, but with all the ghoulish details intact for a reading public that had lost none of its prurience even at the very threshold of Victorian mannerliness. Tottering around the West End of London half-starved and woozy with laudanum in the company of Ann, a fifteen-year-old prostitute, he recounts an incident of touching kindness that she showed to him upon his sinking in exhaustion on to the front steps of a house on Soho Square:

> Suddenly, as we sate, I grew much worse: I had been leaning my head against her bosom; and all at once I sank from her arms and fell backwards on the steps. From the sensations I then had, I felt an inner conviction of the liveliest kind that without some powerful and reviving stimulus, I should either have died on the spot—or should at least have sunk to a point of exhaustion from which all reascent under my friendless circumstances would soon have become hopeless. Then it was, at this crisis of my fate, that my poor orphan companion—who had herself met with little but injuries in this world—stretched out a saving hand to me. Uttering a cry of terror, but without a moment's delay, she ran off into Oxford Street, and in less time than could be imagined, returned to me with a glass of port wine and spices, that acted upon my empty stomach (which at that time would have rejected all solid food) with an instantaneous power of restoration . . .[15]

At the extreme end of intoxicant dependency, the stories of the depths to which human beings will sink in order to be satiated with their drug of choice are legion, and are often finely balanced in tone between cold-eyed, steady-voiced admission and reckless swagger. Here is TV writer Jerry Stahl in the labor ward:

> March 31, 1989, I found myself in the sterile confines of the Cedars-Sinai OB/GYN toilet, injecting a bomb-size hit of Mexican heroin while, twenty feet away, my baby daughter inched her way south in my screaming wife's uterine canal. Somehow, cross-eyed and bloody-armed, I managed to scuffle back in time to witness the sweetest thing in life shoot out of the womb and into Los Angeles. Not, however, before I saw the sheer, unfettered loathsomeness of my being reflected in the eyes of the man delivering my daughter . . . And who could blame him? It doesn't take Jonas Salk to surmise the future of a newborn whose daddy slimes into the delivery room oozing from the arms.[16]

When intravenous drug-use runs the risk not merely of physical addiction and critical overdose, but also of the transmission of HIV through shared hypodermics, then the adept has truly learned, if not to laugh at, then at least to return a gaze of blank indifference to, the face of death. And, much as we may be given pause by the insouciance of tribal societies administering strong hallucinogenic materials to their young, age has frequently proved to be only a very feeble barrier against the imperatives of intoxication behavior. Lewin cites the case of a German boy who, at the age of ten, had acquired a daily ether habit—he doesn't tell us how—that amounted to drinking around 50 grams a day, with the same quantity inhaled at night in the form of vapor. The child claimed it enhanced his intellectual capabilities at school, and indeed he appeared to have no difficulty solving complex mathematical problems immediately after reviving from an etherated sleep. He fueled the habit by stealing money from his parents and breaking into pharmacies. (By 19, we are told, he had succumbed to subcutaneous morphine injections too, but Lewin diagnoses his death from heart failure as owing to ether poisoning.) Similarly, a chemist's apprentice who inhaled chloroform every day died when, in the course of an especially greedy session, he collapsed across the counter with his face buried in the towel he had drenched with it. In the ten minutes it took for someone to discover him, his pulse had virtually ceased to beat, and efforts to resuscitate him came to nothing.

Fatal mishaps such as these, though, are everywhere counterbalanced in intoxication history by the kind of ingenuity that not only discovers the psychoactive properties of various botanical specimens, but learns also by trial and error what the safe, controlled dosage ought to be. Ethnobotanists throughout the past century have constantly had cause to wonder what on earth the primary route must have been by which primitive societies learned the use of certain plant hallucinogens to the extent that they could be incorporated into shamanistic practices and religious ritual, and thus come to define the earliest systematic cosmologies. Some materials require not only elaborate preparation of particular parts of the plant, in the form of drying, crushing and perhaps prolonged mastication, but a further additive may be called for to free the alkaloids that constitute its active principle. There are numerous examples of these, but pituri—in use since ancient times by the Aboriginal peoples of Australia—is a typical instance. It is derived from a shrub, *Duboisia hopwoodii,* from which the tops and leaves are gathered when it blossoms. These are then wind-dried and ground until a lumpy brown mass is obtained. It is either chewed or smoked. Chewing is a communal enterprise, the gobbet passed from mouth to mouth and then stuck behind the ear until needed, or else it is rolled into the rough shape of a cigar and smoked. In both cases, charcoal is mixed with it, its alkalinity liberating the potent psychoactive element, scopolamine.

The alkalizing of plant intoxicants is a practice that may also be observed among the coca-leaf chewers of South America and wherever tobacco is chewed among native peoples. How this principle was stumbled on in the first place may forever remain unknown, but it has been found out all over the world, and in the case of pituri (which can trigger a dissociative, hallucinogenic state at concentrations of one-tenth of a milligram), it has been identified in the face of the substance's evident toxicity. Not only does it announce its inimical nature by severely irritating the mucous membranes of the nose and mouth, but the Aboriginal people have also used it as a poison in trapping emus and kangaroos. Notwithstanding this, pituri plays a central role as an intoxicant in ceremonial occasions and gatherings of tribal elders.

Australian anthropologist Pamela Watson has suggested that the high degree of refinement to be observed in pituri use suggests that both its preparation and the principle of alkalizing it—for which purpose the indigenous peoples have isolated the most efficient medium available in their landscape, namely a variety of acacia—were painstakingly arrived at in antiquity by an impeccably scientific process. Reflecting on this development, she became one of the first commentators to postulate, as others have done in relation to tobacco, that the cultivation of intoxicants was the spur to the development of agriculture. It has always been assumed that food crops were the earliest agricultural enterprise, but given that they initiate no significant ergonomic or dietetic improvements in the lives of Paleolithic peoples, it seems more likely that the urge to ensure a ready supply of their discovered intoxicant was what marked the end of the hunter-gatherer way of life.

An even more extraordinary example of human triumph over the pharmacology of a dangerous material was to arise in the modern era in central Europe. It is not precisely clear when the taking of arsenic originated among the people of the Tyrol in southern Austria, but Lewin suggests that it may have arisen among horse dealers as early as the sixteenth century. Certainly, the drug was traditionally being given to workhorses against exhaustion at this time; it supposedly helped them to get their food down more easily and generally kept them in good shape. Experiments have shown that it can have a short-term growth-promoting effect in laboratory mammals, and assist in cell formation. At some stage before the mid-eighteenth century, at any rate, it had passed into human use. Tiny doses were taken and were found to improve skin quality, promote sexual vigor, bestow energy and endurance and facilitate breathing at high altitude. It was also discovered that tolerance developed, and that the dose had to be increased, but the degrees by which it was increased had to be infinitesimally small. A sudden, incautious augmentation of the dose could be fatal.

Writing in the 1920s, Lewin finds its use still quite widespread among workers in the Styrian forests, and finds medical references furthermore to a Halle student who, in 1750, had habituated himself to tolerating considerable quantities of it by eating it with bacon. A tiny pellet might suffice as a weekly dose to begin with, but may build up to a daily dose the size of a pea, perhaps the better part of half a gram. It was still being eaten with bacon in Lewin's day, or else it was spread on bread or dissolved in spirits. Among some villagers, a sidereal consumption system had developed, so that arsenic-eating was suspended at the new moon, but gradually increased again as the moon rounded out. Some took the drug in the form of arsenious acid, others as orpiment, a manufactured compound (arsenic trisulphide) that was also used as a yellow dyestuff. For a while, it was in use among southern Baptists in the USA who took it in coffee, and Lewin insists that some European girls' boarding-schools used to add it to their pupils' food under medical supervision in order to ensure that the girls always looked fresh-faced and shiny-haired. Certain Italian mineral waters contained traces of it, and were thirstily sought-after when medical provision of arsenic proved hard to secure. The tolerance that developed to it was attested by the fact that it tended to cause withdrawal symptoms on discontinuance, and in rising doses, it led eventually to gastro-intestinal disorders, discolored skin, nerve damage and final collapse.

If arsenic seems a rather reckless remedy, even with the promise of radiant skin tone, it will perhaps strike us as even more unfathomable that people living on the Baltic coast of Lithuania in what is now Klaipeda used to be avid consumers of mercury, having discovered that if it is dispersed quickly through the intestine in plenty of fluid, it can pass harmlessly out of the system again. Their adolescent boys, here as elsewhere the unsuspecting initiates of radical intoxicology, were inducted with doses of about five grams, which would gradually mount with maturity to six times that. Those accustomed to the habit would thriftily recover whatever was voided in the feces for future use. It is said that George, Prince-Elector of Brandenburg, heroically swallowed a bottle of mercury on the eve of his wedding, and lived to tell the tale because it was flushed through by the voluminous quantity of alcohol he had drunk. It has also been established that the mercury compound sub-limate (mercuric bichloride)—known as a violent poison at least since the Renaissance—was traditionally taken in conjunction with opium among Turkish smokers because it was found to have the remarkable effect of sustaining the hypnotic effects of the drug. When high tolerance had developed through prolonged use, an admixture of sublimate refortified its opiating potential in the brain. Reports that sublimate could then be tolerated without opium, and produce alone "an intense feeling of well-being" at concentrations that should theoretically have been fatal only serve to reinforce one's sense of wonder at what the body is capable of accepting if the will is sufficiently strong.

Accounts of physical mortification, extreme feats of endurance and sensory deprivation—whether the motivation for them be religion, alternative lifestyles or plain vanity—have been a fashionable cultural theme in recent decades, and yet in focusing on these visible instances of the urge to self-modification, we have possibly overlooked the often equally pioneering *internal* investigations that human beings have been conducting for considerably longer. If, peering over the garden wall from mainstream society, we may wonder what makes people discover in themselves a desire to be hung by the flesh of their backs from meat-hooks, it might make just as searching a call on our rational faculties to comprehend why anybody, knowing full well what contortions it unleashed in its unwitting victims, first voluntarily swallowed sublimated mercury.

Evelyn Waugh's debut novel, *Decline and Fall,* concludes with its central character, Paul Pennyfeather—a hapless ingenue who has stumbled from teaching at a minor public school to going to prison to enrolling at Oxford to study theology without quite understanding why anything in particular happens to him—being apprised of the meaning of life by an avant-garde architect, the self-styled "Professor" Otto Silenus. He is told that life is like the big wheel at Paris' Luna Park fairground, a revolving disk of polished wood with tiers of seats all round. Some people try to cling on to it and are flung centrifugally off, some inch their way to the center, where the rotation is less violent, while still others simply sit in the seats and spectate:

> There's generally someone in the centre who stands up and sometimes does a sort of dance . . . Lots of people just enjoy scrambling on and being whisked off and scrambling on again. How they all shriek and giggle! Then there are others . . . who sit as far out as they can and hold on for dear life and enjoy that. But the whole point about the wheel is that you needn't get on it at all, if you don't want to. People get hold of ideas about life, and that makes them think they've got to join in the game, even if they don't enjoy it. It doesn't suit everyone.[17]

And neither does LSD. What cannot be written out of human development, however, is that we all have the intoxication instinct within us. In some, it may have evolved to the point where it is evanescently faint, and quite satiated with herbal tea or a festive sip of champagne. These will be Silenus' spectators. Others, perhaps a tiny minority, have so ordered their lives that they take exactly what they want when they want, know when to stop, and manage to avoid hangovers, comedowns and periods of ill health as a result of their intake. These are the dancers at the center. But for the great majority, intoxication is a case of clambering on to the wheel and being flung off again in continually renewed hilarity. There may be injuries, outbreaks of nausea, an occasional feeling that it might be nice to go on the carousel for once instead, but the wheel goes on spinning nonetheless.

To the cringing worldview of prohibitionism, intoxication is only ever a question of taking desperate measures to displace a grim reality. It is never allowed to be a celebration, an adventure or a laugh, and yet through the ages, it is almost exclusively this that has called us forth into that exterior space where domesticity and duty's straitjacket hold no sway. After all obeisant lip-services have been paid to the specters of alcoholism, social disruption and the baleful neglect of responsibility, the inescapable fact is that being drunk can be supremely funny, as the comic archetype of the driveling inebriate has long attested—funnier than TV comedy certainly, and perhaps even funnier than sex—and thus profoundly psychologically therapeutic.

At the center of intoxication is a joy. It whispers its imminence in the warmth of the first couple of drinks, the beautiful serenity of heroin's uncoiling across the synapses or the preliminary abdominal tingling of MDMA. That some of our more demonstrative social rituals should have evolved around the taking of intoxicants, especially those we are allowed, is no surprise, and may be witnessed in the likes of tequila-slamming, yard-of-ale competitions, Happy Hour with its iridescent drinks full of miniature parasols and tropical fruit, champagne fountains and those pyrotechnic cocktails (Flaming Lamborghinis) that once visited shame upon the England soccer team on the eve of a major tournament. These affirmations of life are the antithesis of desperation.

A combination of moral strictures, legal circumscription and medical admonition has reduced the experience of intoxication, our organic birthright, to the status of guilt material in an ego assailed on all sides by neurosis. We have allowed ourselves to be persuaded that there is a tragic irresolvable antagonism between the fleeting pleasures of intoxicated states and the permanently elusive goal of a genuine and lasting happiness. To be high is a waste of time, this morbid tradition has convinced us. It is too much of a temptation to excess. It is selfish, irresponsible and will make you ill. Just say "No." But we make a fundamental mistake in seeing intoxication as a sad substitute for real fulfillment, instead of what it simply and irreducibly is—an integral component of a life fully lived. There may be higher things to dwell on, in the way of fine art or true love or transports of the soul, but they are not defeated by intoxication, and anyway they don't show their faces half often enough.

In the early years of the century, a South African naturalist, Eugene Marais, who lived among a colony of baboons, both wild and captive, observed their use of the tobacco plant. The wild primates tended to ignore it, even where it was plentifully available, while the captive creatures pleaded obsessively for it and appeared to have developed fully fledged dependency. His conclusion was that it was the mental torment brought on by lack of freedom that induced the psychological predisposition in the captive animal to crave a stimulating intoxicant. Theories like these have been much extrapolated to provide fuel for the argument that intoxication in humans is similarly a cry of protest against the world. Whether the fact that Marais was a chronically depressed morphine addict who eventually killed himself contributed to the development of this postulate is a topic for some deliberation.

Siegel lends succor to his theory by citing a laboratory experiment in which caged squirrel monkeys that had turned up their noses at the offer of a drink of nicotine solution suddenly preferred it to water when they were stressed with electrocution. But that finding rather jostles Marais out of the picture altogether. For him, the caged state alone should have been enough to tempt the monkeys to the nicotine without the need for electrical torture. The question is nonetheless raised, though, and we must finally dutifully ponder it: Would humans living in a free and nonantagonistic society any longer need intoxicants?

For Nietzsche in the 1880s, at least, the question was perfectly clear-cut. In the course of lambasting those tired souls whose lives are so devoid of dynamic action that they have to wash away the tedium of the working day by spending the evening in the theater, where they are treated to depictions of individuals whose lives consist of nothing but dynamic action, he indicts this function of high art as being no nobler than the befuddling function of alcohol:

> This [theatre] is designed for those everyday souls who in the evening are not like victors on their triumphal chariots but rather like tired mules who have been whipped too much by life.

What would men of this type know of "higher moods" if there
were no intoxicants and idealistic whips? Hence they have those
who enthuse them even as they have their wines. But what are
their drinks and their intoxication to me? Does he that is enthusiastic need wine?[18]

But why not? This is Nietzsche at his most infuriatingly idealistic,
the scarlet-faced Plato of the Alps heaping scorn on the drones who
can't be Faust but, incriminatingly, don't even *want* to be. If the
working day has indeed delivered you home spent and deflated,
your triumphal chariot having overheated in a snarl-up on the inter-
state highway, recourse to a glass of Graacher Himmelreich Riesling
Kabinett might indeed seem like easy relief.

Nietzsche's argument against the kind of drama and music that
manipulates the emotions is a forceful one (and would doubtless be
extended, were he living at this hour, to encompass TV, the Internet
and advertising) but in reaching for the example of intoxication, he
allows himself a jaded, exclamatory metaphor not entirely worthy
of the case:

The strongest ideas and passions brought before those who are
not capable of ideas and passions but only of intoxication! And
here they are employed as a means to produce intoxication!
Theatre and music as the hashish-smoking and betel-chewing of
the European! Who will ever relate the whole history of narcot-
ica?—It is almost the history of "culture," of our so-called
higher culture.[19]

I think it probably is, but to view that culture as merely narcotizing,
and by extension to view all intoxication as a matter of being
drugged senseless, is both an insufficiently complex account of the
social dimension of aesthetics, as well as a shallow misapprehension
of the multiform valencies of altered consciousness. At least Marx
was scrupulous enough to specify *opium* as the drug to which the
comfortable, stultifying effect of religion could be compared.

Nonetheless, Nietzsche's antipathy to the relevance of intoxication
in the life of his prototype *Übermensch* has found plenty of respon-
sive echoes in the century and more since his work was published.

The post-structuralist psychologist Jacques Lacan expounds the proposition that in the development of higher-order consciousness, or rationality, early human beings found their deeper instinctual desires alienated. Language, in symbolically constructing the external world, became the stuff that defined us as social beings (which is advantageous from an evolutionary point of view), but thereby forced us to live a life of objectivized symbolic representations, rather than one that was truly, unmediatedly expressive of our inner urges—which can now only ever, at best, be partially addressed, never wholly fulfilled. On this reading, drug and alcohol use are motivated by the desire to achieve a more pervasive satisfaction of those urges. The lapsarian conceptual currency has barely moved on from Nietzsche, though. By contrast, when Adorno, in his late work *Aesthetic Theory*, acknowledges the strength of the comparison between art and intoxicants, he allows that the impact of some works can indeed be intoxicating (and in a positive sense, moreover), but that the feeling is nothing compared to the pleasure of actual drunkenness.

The use of intoxication both as an analogue for, and as a literal consequence of, the strategies we employ to conceal the inadequacy of what life delivers to most of us is, I believe, a culturally specific trope whose time has gone. It arose in the post-Romantic period when advances in the understanding of the actions of intoxicants began to be made, and altered consciousness was duly wrested away from its poetic implication in heavenly delirium, to be exposed as a squalid chemical business, artificial through and through, or at its noblest, an accidental by-product of medical procedures. It speaks stridently through Jung's dictum, "Every form of addiction is bad, no matter whether the narcotic be alcohol or morphine or idealism."

Much expository energy has been expended in the century just finished on what the post-antagonistic society envisioned in the polemical tradition inaugurated by Marx might look like. There may be an end of the economic relations that define individuals by their value in an exchange system. There ought to be an end of armed conflict. It may even be that the self-deluding notion of romantic love will wither away, but intoxication? Don't bet the house on it. If the alteration of consciousness is indeed a purely consolatory operation, then human life in its unstoppable contingency will still furnish us with the need for that—to cope with every accident, personal dilemma and untimely loss of a loved one. If, on the other hand, it is primarily a reinforcement practice, as deeply imprinted in us as the desire for exquisite food and sexual pleasure, then one can only imagine that such a well-ordered society will provide more time for it. In fact, to be tiresomely dialectical about it, it is an intricately meshed compound of the two, and thus—at the very least—doubly indispensable.

Sociologist David Wagner concludes his study of the resurgence of moral repression in the USA, a phenomenon he terms the New Temperance, with a heartening analysis of the ways in which even the most intolerant societies can't police our personal behavior all the time. The Muslim cleric Ayatollah Khalkhali traveled Iran soon after the Shi'ite revolution of 1979 with the apparent authority personally to execute on the spot any individual found in possession of drugs. He reportedly shot 176 people over the course of seven weeks before he began to weary of the killing. When asked why there were nonetheless still drug-users, he replied that to kill absolutely everybody caught in possession might have made that figure of 176 something more like 5,000. "This would be difficult," he demurred. It is precisely because the effort to stamp out intoxication runs up against its near-universality that it proves both impractical, and morally revolting, to keep trying. We don't even have to subscribe to the last-gasp hint at a conspiracy theory with which Wagner concludes: namely, that governments may one day license the dispensing of some new palliative drug in the interests of political relief. If they did, it still wouldn't displace all the others available, both legally and illegally, that go on supplying our need, established already as we emerged from the caves, to change our experience of the world.

A piece of American doggerel published in a temperance almanac of 1831 manages, despite itself, to blurt out in its rattling sardonic quatrains at least some of the attraction of intoxication:

> O come let us all to the grog-shop:
> The tempest is gathering fast—
> There surely is nought like the grog-shop
> To shield from the turbulent blast . . .

And there will be tippling and talk
And fuddling and fun to the life,
And swaggering, swearing, and smoke,
And shuffling and scuffling and strife.

And there will be swapping of horses,
And betting, and beating, and blows,
And laughter, and lewdness, and losses,
And winning, and wounding, and woes.

O then let us off to the grog-shop;
Come, father, come, Jonathan, come;
Far drearier far than a Sunday
Is a storm in the dullness of home.[20]

This Jonathan that the Temperance movement fixed in its sights from this period on was supposed to be shamed by being caught hanging around the grog shop. He was mortgaging his soul and wrecking his health by frequenting it. But notwithstanding their best efforts, its convivial uproar of scuffling, horse-dealing and laughter, its tippling and talk, exercised too great a pull on his heart. The alternative, after all, was to succumb to the dreary Sundays of a lifetime of staying at home—and that really is dull.

7

Hitting the Bottle
for Inspiration

On a visit to the UK late in her poignantly brief career, the iconic Janis Joplin gave a short, shambolic press conference to publicize some live appearances. During the course of a question-and-answer session with reporters from the music press and the daily papers, she drank an entire half bottle of Southern Comfort, punctuating her hazily burbled responses with thirsty swigs. As the last drops disappeared down her parched boozer's throat, she noticed a tabloid journalist gaping in slack-jawed disbelief at the ostentation of it. "Didn't ya know?" she cackled. "I'm a juicer."

Only one profession permits more or less open engagement in the practices of intoxication, in a zone relatively unpoliced by the moral sanctions that everybody else must submit to: that of the artist. The lives of writers and musicians, painters and actors, may be held up as salutary warnings of the perils of unrestrained indulgence, didactic parables that teach, as classical Greek tragedy once did, that the uneventful life the rest of us have to lead is really the privileged one, if we could but see it. Nevertheless, to a great extent, artists are allowed to get on with it, partly because—in some enduring neo-Romantic way—we haven't quite given up the belief that they are driven by implacable demons, which must be plied with inebriating potions that would be hazardous to anybody not so possessed. To be sure, this Sturm-und-Drang account of the creative life, rescued from classical antiquity by the self-dramatizing of nineteenth-century aesthetics, seems a little ill-fitting when applied to the life of an Elizabeth Bowen or an Arnold Bennett. But we are prepared to accept that there are some tormented individuals for whom the struggle with genius is a titanic contest with forces that will eventually consume them, and that if they were not so prepared to immolate themselves on this Dionysian altar, we should have been deprived of their most transcendent productions. Why, in short, are there so many piss artists and drug fiends in the Western creative pantheon? Can it be, as writers like McKenna insist, that intoxication can have a galvanizing effect on creativity, or is it just the last resort of the burnt-out case? In this chapter, we'll look at a few symptomatic case studies, and ask what the true relationship was in each between the creative faculty and immersion in the life of altered consciousness.

Perhaps the most likely explanation for the highly charged connections that are held to exist between intoxicated states and the aesthetic faculty is that they both involve looking at the world at one or more removes from everyday consciousness. This is a metaphorical shift that just about holds good in the light of hallucinogenic drugs, but can't really serve for the transparently excitatory states offered by stimulants or the brain-muffling impact of alcohol, the intoxicant of first choice for artists as for the rest of society. Alcohol retards the pace of intellectual processes as the metabolic system fills up with it, so it is hard to imagine that it could stand in as the ignition key to the imagination. On the other hand, the jumpy exhilaration of amphetamine or cocaine may make the user feel capable of anything, but are not in the event particularly conducive to the concentrated attention to detail that writing or painting generally require. With regard to the visionary states delivered by LSD, psilocybin or mescaline, their roles as triggers to the imaginative arts remain, it seems to me, deeply ambivalent. Nineteenth-century literature furnishes us with a handful of elegant descriptions of visionary drug-induced experiences, such as the opium dreams of de Quincey and a strikingly lyrical account of the same drug state in Dickens' last work, *The Mystery of Edwin Drood*, but these are reconstituted after the fact.

The same point applies to Aldous Huxley's celebrated 1954 text, *The Doors of Perception*, a piece of overblown philosophical journalese about the author's encounter with mescaline. It functions as the reportage it simply is, its crabbed, scholarly ruminations apparently untouched by the life-changing perceptual shifts the narrator

tells us he has experienced. If we were expecting the literary equivalent of a Dali or Ernst canvas, a dance of the febrile unconscious
made manifest by the heady psychic gusts unleashed by a little pinch
of powder, we are to remain forever disappointed. What we get is
the voice of pre-mescaline Huxley, but now assuring us that his
fondness for Eastern mysticism is plumbed more deeply than ever.
He can now see the point of previously nonsensical Zen parables
(those linguistic twists whose antirational force was once beaten
into novices in the temples by masters wielding clubs), and we are
assured that everything appears more radiantly itself than it does to
the unseeing eyes of ordinary perception. In attempting to tell us
how pungently uncanny the world now looks to him, the text veers
close to parodic bathos:

> . . . I looked down by chance, and went on passionately staring
> by choice, at my own crossed legs. Those folds in the trousers—
> what a labyrinth of endlessly significant complexity! And the
> texture of the grey flannel—how rich, how deeply, mysteriously
> sumptuous![1]

The ruffled trousers seem to echo the gorgeous detail of Botticelli's
rendering of folded cloth in his painting *Judith*, seen in a book of art
reproductions, but their significance goes deeper than that. " 'This is
how one ought to see,' I kept saying as I looked down at my
trousers . . . 'One ought to be able,' I said, 'to see these trousers as
infinitely important . . .' "[2] A nondrugged accomplice hands him a
Cézanne self-portrait to contemplate, but the image is troubling and,
after a brief digression in which it is compared to a photograph of
Arnold Bennett in the Dolomites, his portly frame bulging, as it
appears, like a Brighton bow-fronted façade, we are back again with
the trousers:

> For relief I turned back to the folds in my trousers. "This is how
> one ought to see," I repeated yet again. And I might have added,
> "These are the sort of things one ought to look at."[3]

In my own amphetamine-fueled teen cynicism, I contented myself
with imagining that the hallucinogenic state that friends went into
on acid seemed to amount to nothing more profound than staring,

rapt, at something like a tea strainer and whispering a "Wow!" of suspended wonderment at its previously unobserved singularity. What on earth was the point of that? Years later, on my first nightmare encounter with fly-agaric intoxication, I was to discover that this was not a million miles from the truth of the matter, but that its pile-driving impact on one's cognitive functions deserved something a little more articulate than "Wow!"

Huxley's account of the psychedelic state, all West Coast–Oxbridge in its erudite broad-mindedness, is ultimately one long "Wow!" Fixated on the draperies in Botticelli's picture, he announces that "[w]hat the rest of us see only under the influence of mescalin, the artist is congenitally equipped to see all the time."[4] This remained the hope of those who wished to excavate untapped strata of the creative function by use of hallucinogenic substances of all kinds, but it doesn't appear yet to have produced a single, undisputed aesthetic triumph. In his crisply forensic way, Huxley may have grasped at the lineaments of what trippy drugs feel like, but they haven't changed the way he writes, only induced him to venture ever further into the thickets of oriental theosophy, finally owning at the conclusion that the "unfathomable Mystery" of existence may not be apprehended by the straight "systematic reasoning" that is the Western intellectual inheritance.

If one were to look for more convincing instances of hallucinogenic substances in the service of the literary arts, one would have to turn to the writings of the American Beat Generation, which sprouted soon after Huxley's text appeared and came to full efflorescence in the 1960s. Much has already been written on such central texts of the period as William S. Burroughs' admonitory junk novel, *The Naked Lunch,* a sustained imaginative excursion into the horrors of heroin withdrawal, and Allen Ginsberg's long poem "Howl," his cri de coeur against the degenerate conformism of American society—both of which appeared in the late 1950s, something of a watershed era in American letters. *The Naked Lunch,* in particular, deserves to be read. It isn't an easy ride, because it is an explication of the diseased consciousness of heroin dependency, not a celebration of it. There is a smell of the detox clinic rising off every page, but the first-person confessional is confined to the preface; the main text is one long nightmare from which one waits in vain for the narrator to awake. In the 1990s, David Cronenberg essayed a state-of-the-art cinematic adaptation of it, a foolhardy venture that—in its tricksy but labored special-effects morphing—fell a long way short of conveying the Force 10 impact of Burroughs' feverish prose.

My point is that in this, and in some of the late work of Jack Kerouac (especially *Desolation Angels* of 1966), the experiences of intoxicated states inform the writing stylistically. Kerouac's mature style, admittedly, was already off and running before hallucinogenics came into his world, but the use of drugs brought even greater liberation to what was already a radically unfettered idiom. Somewhat surprisingly for a writer so inextricably associated with the hippie sixties (for all that he came to revile the stoned apathy of longhaired layabouts as irascibly as befitted the bibulous, bloated old fart he unhappily turned into), interest in Kerouac's work has endured. Bookshops report that he is the most shoplifted author in the world, and the undying fascination with him has meant that, as the biographies pile up, every last bit of screwed-up paper in his wastebasket is now finding its way into print. This is *Old Angel Midnight*, jigsawed together from scattered late-fifties notebooks, a stream of altered consciousness made up of interior meditation and ambient sound:

> and what talents it takes to bail boats out you'd never flank till flail pipe throwed howdy who was it out the bar of the seven seas and all the Italians of 7th Street in Sausalcety slit sleet with parting knives that were used in the ream kitchens to cut the innards of gizzards out on a board, wa, twa, wow, why, shit, Ow, man, I'm telling you—[5]

Distantly, one hears the babble of Joyce, but the references that flicker and disappear in Kerouac's aimless rambling are to phenomena that have come and gone in his fields of vision and hearing where he sits typing, rather than to the deep structures of classical myth. Much of this feels like the authentic voice of stoned synapses, momentarily diverting but as tiresome over sixty pages as listening to hours of dope drivel when you aren't partaking.

Burroughs, as much to his own surprise as anyone else's, outlived all the principal Beat writers, even though he probably took more drugs more recklessly than any of them over the decades. In his seventies and early eighties, he had become a rather engaging patrician figure, full of punctilious, stern gentility and yet still unable, on a late visit to the UK, to face the prospect of a press interview without getting a trifle high on some good blow beforehand.

It was not just dope and hallucinogenic cacti that fueled the incendiary writing of the Beats. Benzedrine (amphetamine) pills played a crucial role too. The best of Kerouac's work displays the high-octane, staccato jitteriness of a man on speed with so much to say, he'll probably never get it all out. The surface may look the same as the more obviously stoned pieces, but the underlying textures are richer and denser, and his gift for lyrical description can be sublime. *Desolation Angels* is his great achievement in this style. The prose technique, he insisted, was an attempt to replicate the improvisatory flux of a bebop jazz soloist, the sentences released from the constrictions of classical grammar to become phrases in the musical sense, the dashes that hold them apart (and that have supplanted that signifier of ends and finality, the full stop) equating to the indrawn breath of the sax player, filling his lungs with fuel for the next set of aural squiggles. Naming the method "action writing," he sought an explicit analogy with the action painting of Jackson Pollock then fascinating the American intelligentsia, and just as Pollock had himself filmed slopping and dribbling paint onto his huge horizontal canvases, lest anybody should be in any doubt about the electrified pace that the new art mandated, so Kerouac ought also to have been filmed clattering away at his typewriter. He famously wrote his great early masterpiece, *On the Road*, in three furious weeks, tearing off one sweat-soaked T-shirt after another as the work spewed out before him on a single scroll of paper forty yards long. His final decline into a vile-tempered bourbon stupor, reflected in the fuzzy mawkishness of his late texts, was to some degree the price that all this frenetic creative energy later extracted from him. Robert Louis Stevenson may have written *The Strange Case of Dr. Jekyll and Mr. Hyde* in a six-day cocaine run, but he didn't attempt to make it the modus operandi for all his work.

Kerouac's decline into alcoholism blunted and then completely neutralized his creative impetus. It is in the nature of alcohol dependency that it casts a veil of sozzled apathy over everything the drinker contemplates. Nothing seems particularly worth doing, and the chronically inebriated state provides its own justification for not bothering to try. Even thinking about day-to-day practicalities such as washing and dressing is a tiresome exhaustion. Having to think in a sufficiently structured way to write would therefore seem unimaginable. And yet some writers have managed it, and produced, under the most inauspicious of conditions, works of memorable power. Again, it took the twentieth century—the era in which the medical concept of alcoholism has been chiefly elaborated—to produce its classic text, Malcolm Lowry's *Under the Volcano* (1947), the hypertensive tale of a drunken former British Consul in Mexico, Geoffrey Firmin, on the festival of the Day of the Dead. We follow his stumbling peregrinations about the town of Quauhnahuac, from cantina to cantina, where his preferred tincture—and the means of his final doom—is mescal, the fiery cactus spirit that once had gruesomely hallucinogenic properties. The novel is an extended meditation on a life that has ended in failure, contained nothing of heroism and is a source of heartbreak to those around it.

It is, like all Lowry's work, intensely personal, gazing unflinchingly on aspects of the alcoholic's life that are drawn from his own bitter experience. Not just the permanently blitzed state, but the shabby subterfuges that alcoholics resort to, are displayed (having awoken in a "horripilating hangover" on the porch, Firmin lurches off down the garden, where he falls upon a bottle of tequila he has hidden behind a bush). The horrible squalor of constant drunkenness is the novel's central motif, and yet there are also rhapsodic flights in which Firmin recalls, with something bordering on gastronomic delight, his passionate devotion to the bottle. Here is the boozy philosophizing ("Is there anything in the world worse than an empty bottle?" he asks himself, and supplies the instant answer, "Yes—an empty glass"), and also the celebration of drink's protean variety, its riotous excitement, and that mystical component as old as distillation itself that seems to be concentrated within the ethyl alcohol—solace. The strange fiesta going on all around Firmin, in which dancing ghouls and chocolate death's-heads take part in an uproarious celebration, accurately mirrors the dual nature of the liquid sustenance that drives him on. It is at once comforter and killer, poison and sacrament, a disgorging cornucopia of ruin:

> ... and now he saw them, smelt them, all, from the very begin-ning—bottles, bottles, bottles, and glasses, glasses, glasses, of bitter, of Dubonnet, of Falstaff, Rye, Johnny Walker, Vieux Whisky, *blanc* Canadien, the apéritifs, the digestifs, the demis, the dobles, the *noch ein* Herr Obers, the *et glas* Araks, the *tusen taks,* the bottles, the bottles, the beautiful bottles of tequila, and the gourds, gourds, gourds, the millions of gourds of beautiful mescal ... How indeed could he hope to find himself to begin again when, somewhere, perhaps, in one of those lost or broken bottles, in one of those glasses, lay, for ever, the solitary clue to his identity?[6]

Even after Joyce, work of this kind was only very uneasily received. The original manuscript of the book was rejected by Lowry's Lon-don publisher, Jonathan Cape. He spent a fortnight writing an impassioned defense of the work as it stood, a tormented exercise during the course of which he made a low-level attempt to kill him-self by cutting his wrists. What we have, thankfully, is essentially the text as Lowry intended it to appear. His mental state was such that he hardly ever regarded any piece of writing as truly finished, and his corpus contains a tellingly large quotient of fragments, out-lines and sketches. He was remorselessly self-obsessed, quite likely incapable of writing about anything other than himself, and the exasperations and wrong-turnings that his life seemed exclusively composed of.

And yet the evidence in *Under the Volcano* of a formidably accomplished literary sensibility is too great to ignore. One of the commentators on his work remarks that he was "a drunk of gargan-tuan proportions, yet a man who seems never to have let go an almost preternatural degree of self-awareness, even when face down on the floor of a pub or a cantina,"[7] and it is this indeed that makes him so valuable. The story of the drunken ex-Consul is told with quite brutal objectivity, and without relapse into instant pathos. It is a common trope of addiction confessionals that they ask us not to waste our sympathy on the author's plight—a luxury that can usually be dispensed with by the time the book is written, because it is nearly always the reformed character who is writing it. Lowry's magnum opus, in its novelistic way, assumes such alienation on the reader's part to be axiomatic, and its searing energy is all the fiercer for it. Not only is this a great text on the subject of alcoholism, but it took a great alcoholic to write it.

Writing, even the free-form stylings of fifties Beat, requires a level of conceptual control that the performing arts have no need of. For musicians, singers and actors, the creative function issues from more instinctual zones than the process of literary composition does. A writer may undergo a dissociative trance after swallowing hashish, as Walter Benjamin did in Marseilles in 1928. Knowing that he will write about the experience later, he tries to provide himself with *aides-mémoire* for that task by jotting down periodically the insights that come flashing through. As he attempts to recapture the lustrous happiness that came over him at one point, he discovers that he has scribbled on his newspaper, "One should scoop sameness from reality with a spoon."[8] Peering down onto a dark evening square from the upper floor of a restaurant, where he is now enjoying a half bottle of the local white wine, he notes down, "From century to century things grow more estranged."[9] Another stoned aphorism reads, "How things withstand the gaze."[10] Expatiating on what it might all mean, Benjamin tries to fit these insights into the stream of his philosophizing, and exclaims

> The certainty of unrolling an artfully wound skein—is that not the joy of all productivity, at least in prose? And under hashish we are enraptured prose-beings in the highest power.[11]

The notion is kin to Huxley's insistence that the mescaline trip gives him the chance to see the world as painters see it. But the aporias in Benjamin's little monograph between the thoughts that have come to him under the influence of hashish and the interpretative efforts he makes to grasp their meaning in the essay itself mark the gap that must inevitably yawn between drugged consciousness and the literary enterprise. You do have to wait until you've come back down to earth before you can begin to make written sense of it all. At least Benjamin sets out to do more than simply offer us reportage; he wants to know whether hashish can offer the chance of enhancing the reflective potential of his philosophy. Perhaps it can, but he didn't have the chance to repeat the experiment systematically. For the performer, however, the condition of being on drugs doesn't necessarily preclude the enactment of the art.

Not all performers who took drugs have advertised the fact. Despite the fact that pop history since the sixties has been clogged solid with examples of a songwriting genre one might call the drug eulogy—whether the substance of choice be LSD, cannabis or heroin—many have seen no particular need to let the world know what they were on, at least partly, of course, because it was illegal. Marianne Faithfull may, in this regard, have surprised many who remembered admiring her luminous Ophelia in a London stage production of *Hamlet* in the 1960s by revealing in a TV retrospective of her career that she habitually shot up with heroin in the interval, lending her second-half performance a dreamy luster. Her singing career has been a document of heroin addiction and—since the mid-1980s—of recovery, a trajectory that ran from her first winsome vocal at the age of 17 for the Rolling Stones ("As Tears Go By"), through the disillusioned "Sister Morphine" lyric that Jagger and Richards subsequently wrote for her, to the flat croak in which her work since the eighties has been delivered. The lyric of a recent song, "Vagabond Ways," finds her still publicly acknowledging that she is famous first and foremost for being a drug addict who once had an affair with Mick Jagger.

The demise of Janis Joplin through alcohol and heroin dependency left a gaping hole in rock culture at the end of the sixties, although it had been fairly easy to see which way her appetites were likely to take her as early as 1965, the year in which the San Francisco entrepreneur Chet Helms effectively discovered her. After about five minutes on the West Coast folk scene, she got hooked on methedrine, and Helms quickly delivered her back to her native Texas. The house band he had conceived for his regular venue, the Longshoreman's Hall, needed a singer, and it wasn't long before Joplin was lured back to California to front Big Brother and the Holding Company. It was as a result of her appearances at the Monterey pop festival in June 1967—the same event that transformed the career of Jimi Hendrix—that the band was signed to Columbia

Records. Joplin's vocal style matured quickly. While she tends to be remembered more for the straight-ahead rock idiom of the outfit she created in 1970, the Full Tilt Boogie Band, in which she hollered over a lead-heavy backing of blues-based white rock, she came to prominence as a supremely gifted soul singer.

A 1969 album, *I Got Dem Ol' Kozmic Blues Again Mama!*, is her finest hour. On "Maybe," "Kozmic Blues" and "To Love Somebody," she is in immaculate vocal form, the disarming power of her voice reinforced by the total control she has over its tonal hues. On "Kozmic Blues," she sings the introductory line in a subdued murmur that gives no hint of the opening of the throttle immediately to follow on the first word—"Friends"—of the next line. It is a startling crescendo that blooms out of nowhere, ending in full, effortless vibrato, an imperfectible piece of pyrotechnics that has burst upon you before she has barely got into the lyric. "To Love Somebody" is a Gibb Brothers composition that, in Joplin's throat, becomes a furnace of rage, the whingey resentment of the hook line now ablaze with righteous indignation, and emphasized with the extemporizing liberty that the soul singer can take with a lyric. Here, her voice possesses the full emotional charge of Aretha Franklin's best recordings of the early to mid-sixties. She may not have had Franklin's range, but Janis Joplin's interpretative powers with a lyric were never better than on this album.

The summit is reached on "Little Girl Blue," a Rodgers and Hart song that had been memorably covered by Nina Simone. The lyric addresses a girl in a state of melancholy resignation, offering a sympathetic voice as she sits alone and contemplates the rain for want of anything better to do. Joplin reads it as a slow crescendo, exactly as Aretha Franklin does on a number such as "Sweet Bitter Love," so that what begins in soothing, almost lullaby mode has accreted, by the third verse, the tones of angry, vicarious despair at what the world has done to the girl. It is that anger, just barely suppressed beneath the flood of pity, that churns up something like the same emotional turmoil in the listener. No white vocalist before or since has sung soul with such authentic conviction.

From there, it was a vertiginous decline into the smack-racked ghost-voice of her final recordings. The passion is still there, but the openness of the vocal tone is now reduced to a guttural squawk, the sound emerging only from the throat rather than the lungs. In live appearances, the ruination is inevitably even more apparent. One of the side-effects of heroin is to leave the throat permanently dry, and the voice takes on a correspondingly husky quality, which is sometimes thought to lend a kind of ravaged character to a singer's voice. This may or may not be a good thing, depending on the type of material. In Joplin's case, it robbed her of the ability to replicate the soulful performances of the *Kozmic Blues* album, and confined her exclusively to the relatively humdrum heavy rock idiom. Tracks such as "Move Over" and "Half Moon" from her final album, *Pearl,* indicate how much has been lost.

Pearl was still a work in progress when Joplin died. She was found alone in her room at the Landmark Hotel in Hollywood on 4 October 1970, just two and a half weeks after the barbiturate death in London of Jimi Hendrix. She had drunk heroic quantities of tequila, and had for a long time been taking Valium as though it were going out of fashion. Although she had been free of heroin for around six months, she had decided to take a fix that night and would appear to have administered the kind of quantity that would have sustained her during full-blown addiction. Now having lost a certain level of tolerance through being off it for several months, the dose—combined with alcohol—carried her off. She was just twenty-seven, but could easily have passed for fifty. Although her death was sorely felt among the West Coast rock community at the time, nobody could claim to be in the least surprised that this is the way she went. When the chips were down, she simply didn't care to be careful.

It was a trail that had already been well blazed, in any case. Not much more than a decade earlier, the jazz singer Billie Holiday had destroyed herself in much the same way, although she took somewhat longer about it. Her life had seemingly never been anything other than chaos and pain, and when she blagged her way into the club scene in the Harlem of 1933 as a chubby teenager who could sing a bit, it must have seemed to her as though the tragedies of her childhood and adolescent years might be behind her. In fact, she was to fall prey to a malevolent cast of commercial exploiters and violent sexual partners, eventually spending a year in a reformatory for possession of heroin, to which she had been introduced in the mid-1940s. Her appetite for drugs and alcohol was almost insatiable, and although she had regular spells off heroin, she basically turned to drinking to help her through the periods of craving. When admitted to hospital in May 1959, she had collapsed from alcohol hepatitis, complicated by a potentially life-threatening heart condition. No sooner had her liver begun to stabilize than an infection broke out in her kidneys, followed by fluid congestion on the lungs. Her arms and legs were covered with injection sites. During her confinement, she was found to have taken delivery of a quantity of cocaine, which a nurse discovered in a tissue box on the bedside table. She still had traces of the powder under her nostrils, which led to her being arrested in her sickbed. A personal companion brought her some beer to keep her spirits up. After six weeks in hospital, during which she appeared to have at best only a partial understanding of the severity of her condition, she died as peacefully as could be expected, leaving a lingering sense of an era's end behind her.

The vicissitudes of Billie Holiday's personal life are acutely marked in the bountiful catalogue of work she left. In the 1930s, she recorded with small swing bands, most notably the Teddy Wilson Orchestra, rendering clever-twee throwaway hit songs of the day. Here she sounds spry, cheeky and—despite her high little voice—ineffably knowing too, as she quickly gained a reputation for a vocal technique that was all her own. On even the most uptempo numbers, she sings intriguingly behind the beat, letting the accompanists carry the melody while she seems to tag on behind. The ne plus ultra of this style is her reading of "When You're Smiling (The Whole World Smiles With You)," recorded with Wilson's ensemble in 1938, in which she drawls the lyric out so elastically that one wonders whether she will even finish on time. Recording for Decca in the 1940s, she was given lush string arrangements, and the extraordinary emotional resonance she was capable of evoking with what was essentially quite a limited vocal range came to full bloom. This is the era in which some of the performances most indelibly associated with her, including "Lover Man," "That Ole Devil Called Love" and her own compositions "God Bless the Child" and "Don't Explain," were recorded. On a track like "I'll Look Around," made in 1946, in which she is backed only by piano and trio, the sense of resigned tristesse she evokes through a foursquare, simple lyric is breathtaking.

After her spell of incarceration, she emerged grittier, throatier and a lot less in control of her vocal resources. Nonetheless, between 1951 and 1957, she recorded a compendious volume of work for Verve Records, fronting six- and seven-piece groups, her deliveries of popular show tunes and jazz standards, as well as her own songs, punctuated by some fine solo work from leading jazz musicians of the day. The highlights are legion, and include a reading of "One for My Baby (And One More for the Road)" that—whisper it—is better than Sinatra's. There is a convivial, frankly slightly pissed feeling to many of the renditions that makes this one of the warmest and most listener-friendly vocal jazz portfolios of the period. Her voice is very shot, as is evidenced particularly by the live recordings and jam sessions that survive from the fifties, but the impression of raw, unmediated feeling that radiates from her at this incipiently disastrous time is what puts this work beyond reproach.

Only with her last two albums for Columbia—*Lady in Satin* (1958) and *Billie Holiday* (1959)—does the disintegration become at last unbearable to hear. Backed by the Ray Ellis Orchestra, she somehow gets through a collection of uniformly downbeat songs, the rasping, pickled voice floating disembodied in an echo chamber above the rather schmaltzy cinematic strings. It seems necessary to extend the greatest benefit of the doubt to the performances on *Lady in Satin* in particular. Nobody previously unfamiliar with Billie's work could conceivably want to investigate further after hearing these tranquilized laments. The mood is so low, you feel you may never come up again (I once made the grave mistake of listening to this album in the predawn despair of amphetamine comedown—not to be repeated) and the sepulchral tone of it doesn't vary. And yet it is also somehow the dog-eared masterpiece she herself believed it to be. On songs such as "I'm a Fool to Want You," "Glad to Be Unhappy" and the closing "I'll Be Around," the aura of utter dejection is a philosophical lesson all its own, the whimpering self-delusion of the lyric to that last—you just wait till she's blown you out, buddy, and then you'll see you should have stuck with me all along—accentuated by the voice that keeps catching and tearing on the higher notes.

Stuart Nicholson's 1995 biography reveals that on the three sessions for the 1959 album, two of which were recorded in the middle of the night, she is being held upright on her stool by her companion, Alice Vrbsky. This we might have inferred without being told. The selections are not without a certain deliberate irony: "I'll Never Smile Again" is a sentiment that rings all too true, "Don't Worry 'Bout Me," with its improbable assurance that she'll get along, takes a little more swallowing. When we hear these performances in the light of what we know about her life, and her pitiful physical condition, we can acknowledge the inextinguishable artistry at work in them, despite the wreckage that is all that is left of her technique. More than any other twentieth-century recording star, Billie Holiday possessed the ability to turn her personal plight to the service of her art. In this at least, nobody else came close to her.

Since the first studios were constructed in the Los Angeles suburb of Hollywood, the entertainment industry has been plagued with stories of stars who have succumbed not merely to the taking of illegal intoxicants, which may be no more remarkable than it is among mainstream society, but to spectacularly dysfunctional behavior that seems quite resistant to any natural instinct for caution. The roll call of casualties in both cinema and popular music is a long one, and it is hard to see it ever being brought to a halt, no matter what provision the contracts may come to have written into them in future for the pastoral care of the young and the impressionable. To some extent, this is because the drug dealer is a constant éminence grise in these surroundings. If dealers know they can clean up among the underpaid and unemployed in a city nightclub at the weekends, how much more tempting to the big operator must the potential takings be among those who have the resources never to need to stop? A shadowy dealer known as the Count patrolled the Mack Sennett lot in Hollywood's infancy, and is thought to have turned several young wide-eyed starlets on to heroin. Barbara La Marr was one who succumbed to his blandishments and was soon dead of addiction. Similarly, today's pop icons, whatever their initial intentions were, may find themselves fighting a losing battle against the drug-taking culture that encloses them on all sides as soon as their careers are in the ascendant. I have been told of a man whose job it is to test drugs on behalf of various rock-group clients: he spikes himself with a quantity of whatever has been delivered, and if he is still alive after half an hour or so, the band takes it as well.

Marc Almond, whose rise in the early 1980s with the hugely successful Soft Cell was soon supported by indiscriminate drug use, documents his personal decline into dependence on tranquilizers in a more than usually cogent pop autobiography. He told me that his approach to drugs in the end consisted of little more than consuming whatever appeared in front of him, often in shudder-inducing combinations. Afflicted with a lifelong squeamishness about injections, he nonetheless came to cross that particular Rubicon too, self-administering intravenous cocaine. I wondered if he had ever asked himself where it would end. The response, perhaps predictably, was that you don't really give it a thought. This attitude, the shrug of indifference to harm that I discussed in chapter 6, is not unconnected with a phenomenon cited by Carl Jung in a television interview he gave toward the end of his life. From his observations of terminally ill patients, he had discovered that as long as the brain is functioning normally, it largely dissociates itself from any sympathetic involvement with the deteriorating body. Faced with the physical entropy it can do nothing about, it simply disregards it. Perhaps the drugged-out pop star, on a hiding to nothing, takes much the same view of the developing physical consequences of his or her own excesses. Almond recalls that, semi-paralyzed in bed at home in a state of severe toxicity brought on by ketamine and hallucinogens in combination, he found himself deciding that he would have the room painted red if he was ever able to move again.

Most of this behavior is usually hidden from public view, although stories of it leak out from time to time in the more salacious organs of the music press. As drugs have become more pervasive in the rest of society, though, a feeling has arisen that the stars themselves can afford to be less secretive about it all. A fascinating public froth developed in 1996 in the UK after a flurry of incautious statements to this effect led to angry exchanges in the House of Commons. When a disillusioned young celebrity with more money than discretion, East 17's Brian Harvey, said that taking ecstasy could "increase the love between people," a Conservative back-bencher raised the matter later that day at Prime Minister's Questions. Would the Prime Minister (John Major) condemn such an irresponsible outrage? The Prime Minister would, repeating the old discredited mantra: soft drugs led to hard drugs and hard drugs led to tragedy. In this case, the tragedy was only too graphically illustrated. The culprit's colleagues in the band adopted a united front against him, and drummed him out of their ranks. To wolf down a dozen Es, as Harvey reported he had done, in one uncommonly eventful night might itself have been overlooked, but to blab it to a journalist was an iniquity punishable only by summary dismissal. In the interval between firing off his views and being fired for them, Harvey became the lightning conductor for a nation's opprobrium. Radio switchboards struggled to cope with the incoming tide of condemnation, while a DJ at a regional station ritually smashed the group's disks on-air. The fact that Harvey was encouraged to withdraw his comments cut no ice with the moral majority. Withdrawal is always the toughest challenge a drug-user has to face, and Harvey's robotic disavowal of his earlier opinions carried about the same degree of conviction as the televised mea culpas of captured POWs on Iraqi TV during the Gulf War. Expelled from the group anyway, he must have been sorely tempted to retract his retraction by saying something like: "In the last couple of days, I have made stupid, ill-informed statements about drugs that I now regret. When I said that all drugs were dangerous, I was willfully ignoring the whopping great heap of fun I have had on them in the last few years. They say 'One pill can kill'—so just think of the well wicked time you could have on twelve!"

Scarcely was the ink dry on Harvey's signed confession, though, than Noel Gallagher, founding member of the then highly prominent Oasis, entered his own contribution to the debate. Gallagher attacked Members of Parliament for their hypocrisy, claiming that it was a well-known fact that some of them weren't averse to the odd snifter of coke or skag, and that to most people, taking drugs was as unremarkable as having a cup of tea in the morning. This appeared to be an invocation of the emblematic cup of tea that pop stars often cite when reflecting upon their personal lives. (It is the self-same comforting beverage that Boy George once pronounced more rewarding than a sex life.) Whether a slob pop singer took cocaine was neither here nor there to most legislators, but Gallagher's fanciful tip-off about substance abuse within the Palace of Westminster caused apoplexy. One Member suggested that the coauthor of "Cig-arettes and Alcohol" be arraigned before the Bar of the House and forced to apologize. Here, public concern did seem to have dried up, though. When MPs start fulminating against rock icons with suffi-cient disposable income to support a life of uninterrupted sensory stimulation, they merely end up sounding like envious old ratbags. This is the sort of expostulation that gives politicians a bad name among the young, and makes them disinclined to vote. In an era of monetary scandals and serial sex exposés in British politics, the proposition that Honourable Members might be anything other than paragons of virtuous restraint was low comedy, which is per-haps why the proposal to summon Gallagher wasn't taken up. In their half-articulate way, he and Harvey had begun to tell the truth about drugs and, in the latter case at least, had duly paid the price. For every hopeless addict and petty criminal, there are scores of upstanding citizens who do drugs and whose lives are not in any way ruined, chaotic or sad.

If drugs and drinking expand to fill the lives of the stars to the point of dependency and breakdown, this may be partly owing to their having too much time available, especially in cases where the lucky break has suddenly cut somebody adrift from nine-to-five employment patterns. There may be ferocious schedules in the recording studio or at rehearsals, and then the treadmill of touring to promote an album, with its banal imperative to give a suitably impassioned account of oneself five nights out of seven, whether it be for the benefit of Dallas, Des Moines or Sacramento. The rest of life may be felt as empty time stumbling past, an afternoon frittering on even more dully than it used to do in the office, shop or factory, or as uselessly as it did when—eking out an existence on benefits—you colonized the daytime hours with the driveling of TV and called that living.

What intoxicants do, in these circumstances, is add a sense of structure, of being alive in the dead spaces between soundchecks. During those times of the year when there are neither performing nor recording contracts to fulfill, intoxication provides life with an agenda. If the practice becomes a matter of physical need, as it did in the self-destructive cases of Kurt Cobain or Sid Vicious, then the emphasis is even greater. There is now something that has to be done, just as there might once have been a production quota to achieve. It is little wonder that certain dinosaur survivors from the earliest eon of rock music (one thinks of the Rolling Stones or Bob Dylan) have addressed the problem, as they have hurtled toward sixty, by touring virtually nonstop. What else is there to do?

The same network of connections between the use of intoxicants by artists and writers and the habitual practices of the public at large is to be found in the nineteenth century. Despite the cultural ideology that placed the artist on a special plinth as a different type of human being from the generality, it was only in the matter of interpretation—supported by the resource of articulacy—that responses to the effects of intoxicants differed, a point candidly noted by de Quincey. He announces at the opening of his *Confessions* his hope that the work might stand as a salutary document for the benefit of "the whole class of opium-eaters." In case we should be surprised that a whole class of such dissolutes might exist, he leaves us in no doubt by submitting to our scrutiny a not altogether helpful list of discreetly blanked names. These are people who, to his personal knowledge, have indulged the opium habit, and include

> the eloquent and benevolent———; the late dean of———; Lord———; Mr.———, the philosopher; a late under-secretary of state (who described to me the sensation which first drove him to the use of opium, in the very same words as the dean of   , viz. "that he felt as though rats were gnawing and abrading the coats of his stomach"); Mr.———; and many others, hardly less known, whom it would be tedious to mention.[12]

Not that he has really mentioned even these for the time being. These courteous elisions, however, have been filled in by the time the 1856 edition of the work appeared, the intervening gap of thirty-five years now deemed sufficient to have dimmed our prurience. The unmasked ciphers turn out to be William Wilberforce, parliamentary campaigner for the abolition of the slave trade; Isaac Milner, dean of Carlisle; Lord Erskine; a mysterious philosopher whom de Quincey insists he genuinely can't recall; Foreign Office Under-Secretary Henry Addington, and Mr. Coleridge—the last of whom,

as de Quincey assures us in a gossiping footnote on the previous
page, has certainly taken more gigantic quantities of opium than
even him. But lest we should run away with the idea that opium
must be the decadent habit of intellectuals, church officials and
politicians, he tells us of conversations he had with cotton manufacturers on passing through Manchester some years before, in which
he learned that opium use was spreading like wildfire among their
mill-workers—

> so much so, that on a Saturday afternoon the counters of the
> druggists were strewed with pills of one, two, or three grains, in
> preparation for the known demand of the evening. The immedi-
> ate occasion of this practice was the lowness of wages, which, at
> that time, would not allow them to indulge in ale or spirits: and,
> wages rising, it may be thought that this practice would cease:
> but . . . I do not readily believe that any man, having once tasted
> the divine luxuries of opium, will afterwards descend to the
> gross and mortal enjoyments of alcohol . . .[13]

Some hope. Nonetheless, de Quincey acknowledges to us that there
is nothing particularly privileged about the mental state bestowed by
opium. If it is more readily available to the Lancashire cotton workers than beer, then no white-gloved aesthete could claim exclusive
rights to it as the mystic source of creativity. That said, both de
Quincey and that "Mr. Coleridge" who appears on the charge-sheet
of indulgers began by seeing the resplendent visions produced by the
drug as a trigger for poetic inspiration, indeed even perhaps a superior replacement for it.

Charles Lamb's beautifully understated description of the poet
Samuel Coleridge's face in later life—when reading his poetry, he
looked like "an Archangel a little damaged"—hints, with the decorum of the nineteenth century, at the ravages that had in fact over-
whelmed it. It had all begun with his visionary poem "Kubla Khan,"
inspired, as he tells us in his preface to it, by the shimmering dreams
he experienced after taking medicinal opium. He is at pains to point
out, however, that writing phantasmagoric poetry under its influence is not a mere matter of the hand taking dictation from the illu-
minated brain. The poet's own facility with the poetic muse must be

taken as given. Although there is no "sensation or consciousness of effort" in composing in this way, it is nonetheless that poetic imagination that the pyrotechnic trails of the opium trance need to be able to play on. The images that arise are then suffused with a psychedelic vividness denied to ordinary versifiers. From a wild, enchanted chasm in Kubla's luxuriant gardens, a mighty fountain abruptly gushes forth,

> Amid whose swift half-intermitted burst
> Huge fragments vaulted like rebounding hail,
> Or chaffy grain beneath the thresher's flail:
> And mid these dancing rocks at once and ever
> It flung up momently the sacred river.

Before we know it, we are listening to an Abyssinian maid singing of Mount Abora to a dulcimer, and the tenuous, associative thread leads us back to the poet's insistence that if he could only hear the African girl's song again, it would inspire him to re-create the Xanadu pleasure-dome himself out of thin air. At the poem's end, a peremptory warning is sounded about the transformation that the altered state has wrought in the poet, and that recommends him for an almost superstitious ostracism from the remainder of society:

> And all should cry, Beware! Beware!
> His flashing eyes, his floating hair!
> Weave a circle round him thrice,
> And close your eyes with holy dread,
> For he on honey-dew hath fed,
> And drunk the milk of Paradise.

Coleridge was just 24 when he wrote this poem and, while it exists officially as a mere "fragment" only (his creative stream is dammed up by the interruption of somebody arriving at the door to transact some bothersome bit of business that ends up taking over an hour), we can still discern within it the spirit of youthful thirst for the new that had led him and others to support the ideals of the French Revolution a few years earlier. The deliberately ambivalent tone of the closing admonition is what launched the whole genre of drug-induced visionary literature. A century later, and that preface would have been a manifesto.

The theme was to run through the fevered writings of the French aestheticists and symbolists (with Théophile Gautier and Charles Baudelaire in the vanguard) and even in the automatic-writing experiments of the Parisian surrealists. Alethea Hayter's key text on the links between opium and creativity in the Romantic period says of de Quincey (and it applies equally to the Coleridge of "Kubla Khan"):

> It was his belief that opium dreams and reveries could be in themselves a creative process both analogous to, and leading to, literary creation. He used dreams in his writing not as decoration, not as allegory, not as a device to create atmosphere or to forestall and help on the plot (although he believed that they were that) but as a form of art in themselves.[14]

Only a few years into the development of the new genre, though, the grisly truth about its personal implications was coming to light. Somewhere just offstage from these dreams of gorgeous architecture, the Ottoman palaces, cantilevered balustrades and torrents of jewels that furnish the intoxicated imagination so exquisitely, we come upon the figure of a man embroiled in the squalid labors of trying, vainly and shamefully, to shit. Coleridge embarked on a Mediterranean cruise in the spring of 1804, during which he underwent the humiliating agony of acute constipation, recording the details for us so that, by disgusting some imagined reader, he might perhaps disgust himself enough to break his habit. His ship pulls alongside another, from where a doctor is summoned to apply an enema:

> The Surgeon instantly came, went back for Pipe & Syringe & returned & with extreme difficulty & the exertion of his utmost strength injected the latter. Good God!—What a sensation when the obstruction suddenly shot up! . . . O what a time!—equal in pain to any before. Anguish took away all disgust, & I picked out the hardened matter & after awhile was completely relieved. The poor mate who stood by me all this while had the tears running down his face.[15]

It turns out, though, that opium has lost none of its power to ignite the imagination with uncommonly powerful images:

> To weep & sweat & moan & scream for parturience of an excrement with such pangs and such convulsions as a woman with an Infant heir of Immortality: for Sleep a pandemonium of all the shames and miseries of the past Life from earliest child-hood all huddled together, and bronzed with one stormy Light of Terror and Self-torture. O this is hard, hard, hard.[16]

But whatever the obscene indignity of manual evacuation, the ghastliness of addiction not only failed to tarnish the ideal of opium as an elixir, but had a further incidental consequence.

When Thomas de Quincey published his laudanum confessional in 1821, long before Coleridge's scatological parturitions saw the light of day, he inaugurated a literary genre that still shows no signs of exhaustion. But his work is noteworthy for establishing an even more pervasive cultural archetype: that of the self-destructive genius, fueled by forces within that can only be unleashed by chemical combustion. It is perhaps to de Quincey's eternal handicap that he is remembered for scarcely nothing other than a piece of piercingly objective journalese the size of a novella, but he was the first among that prodigious literary group of the early nineteenth century to write about the negative effects of the opium tincture. The *Confessions,* like many of the my-drug-hell narratives ghostwritten for today's sport and pop celebrities, are an account of peering over the rim of the abyss and pulling back, and yet the greatest source of fascination in the work resides now in its descriptions of the opium trances that proved an aesthetic catalyst for almost his entire circle. We are intended to rejoice at the prodigal's safe return to pious sobriety, but what really thrills us is sharing his excursion into states of hallucinatory limbo that are presented as soaring bliss one moment and grim depravity the next.

After *Confessions,* Western aesthetics would forever refuse to do without this archetype. It may have germinated in the stony ground of the literary craft, with its inevitable solipsism and isolation, but it found in the mass entertainment forms of the twentieth century its most prolifically fertile soils. To be sure, the romance of untimely death has not always depended on substance abuse. When physical frailty carries off great artists in their prime (Nijinsky's writhing innovations mutating into terminal nervous collapse) or, worse, when they had barely got going (the Brontës going down like skittles), their reputations as paradigms of precious fragility are sealed. When they appear to have destroyed themselves unnecessarily through some heedless inner compulsion, the sense of awe is only deepened. It is as though there were some critically ambivalent quality in the creative gift that may dispense exemplary talent, but at the cost of an inability to live proportionately and with restraint. In some, the self-annihilating urge leads to quiet, meticulous suicides. In others, it is a drawn-out sequence of collapses, arrests and detoxing, ending in the final Coleridgean ignominy of death in a hotel bathroom, in blood and vomit and diarrhea. And still others avoid either fate, cutting down or giving up just as the trap was about to snap. These are the ones who may well go on to write abuse confessionals, and each is a distant descendant of de Quincey.

It is only with the suppression of intoxication by religious morality and, eventually, the law that the idea of creating under the influence could possibly be conceived as a groundbreaking innovation. In earlier times, drinking and thinking went together as uncontroversially as walking and talking, as may be witnessed in the Greek symposia. The great Socrates, who like Christ never produced a written work, was an enthusiastic exponent of the notion that knowledge arises from human social interaction. Not for him the Olympian abstentionism of a Nietzsche, retreating to a mountain and refusing all human society in order to think great thoughts unhindered. Socrates is reported to have said that wandering through idyllic forests was a pointless pursuit because the trees had nothing to say to him. He is, however, very largely dependent on his pupil and most energetic publicist Plato for whatever intellectual presence he enjoys in posterity. As may be recalled from chapter 2, Plato's thought developed into a high-toned refusal of sensory stimulation, other than for basic physical necessity, in the interests of a more purely contemplative ideology, and so we may fear that his verbal picture of the master will be a fastidiously airbrushed pinup. In fact, he rises above his own proclivities in the matter by giving us what we may confidently take to be the real Socrates, most at home when in the thick of the verbal jousting, disputations and carousing.

Toward the end of *Symposium,* when the inebriated Alcibiades turns up in the mood for flirting and further drinking, Socrates has just finished his disquisition on Eros. The newcomer scorns the rather abstemious intake the symposiasts appear to have confined themselves to and, spotting a capacious ice-bucket, calls for it to be filled with wine. Having drained the first bucket himself, he orders it to be replenished for his sometime lover Socrates, assuring the others, "It doesn't matter how much you give him to drink, he'll drink it and be none the worse for wear."[17] The slave boy duly obliges, and Socrates now knocks it back, perhaps two liters or more of watered wine, and the elegant dialogues continue. Even following the arrival of another group on their way back from a party, the reflective discourse is uninterrupted. The narrator confesses to having fallen into an alcohol sleep, but on waking near dawn discovers the tragedian Agathon, Aristophanes the comic dramatist and Socrates still at it, the last apparently prevailing by force of argument in a dispute about whether the arts of comedy and tragedy should be mutually exclusive. As the others finally go spark out with the arrival of daylight, Socrates touchingly tucks them up, and lets himself out. He goes for a bath at the Lyceum, gets through a normal day's business and finally goes home to his own bed toward evening. Whatever fictional embroidery there is in a narrative like this, it is clear that Plato, who might most have been at pains to gloss over the fact, is happy to present the founding father of dialectical reasoning as a seasoned and capacious drinker. Indeed, the Greek philosophical tradition, to which Socrates gave the revolutionary turn of hard, analytic rationality, is unthinkable without alcohol.

For apparently casting doubt on the old gods, fomenting social upheaval and leading Athenian youth into dangerously liberal intellectual habits, Socrates was tried and condemned to death in 399 B.C. at the age of seventy. A five-hundred-strong jury of his fellow citizens voted him guilty as charged by a wafer-thin margin. Although he could have appealed against the sentence, or simply quit Athens to save his skin, he chose not to. His self-defense is faithfully set down by Plato, whose account of the execution is one of classical literature's most affecting death scenes. He was given a lethally sedative draught thought to be hemlock, ground leaves of the toxic plant *Conium maculatum* infused in a drink. The sight of him draining this final cup sends his friends into paroxysms of grief but Socrates, pillar of scholarly equanimity to the last, reproaches them for their unmanliness. As the poison begins to take effect, he starts going numb from the feet upward. He lies down to accept the inevitable and covers his face, only revealing it again to call on his friend Crito to make a sacrifice to one of the minor Athenian deities once he is departed: "We owe a cock to Asclepios. See that you discharge my debt. Don't forget." These turn out to be his last words, for when asked if he has any final piece of wisdom to impart, he makes no effort at reply. With the world swimming out of focus before him, he is making ready to embark on the greatest alteration of consciousness of them all.

If we have become more reluctant to buy the myth of the intoxicated artist as privileged communicant with the muses these days, it may be because there are so damn many of them. At a certain level, what we are witnessing is nothing more sublimated than an individual's helpless greed driven by total boredom. It is a fairly steep descent after all from Coleridge's phantasms to the smacked-out vacancy of Sid Vicious lying prone on a disheveled bed, mumbling fatuities at an uncommonly patient interviewer who scarcely emits an "Ahem" when he passes out in the middle of a sentence. And it is precisely that proliferation that has reconfigured the correspondences between the artists and the artisans in the matter of intoxication, for while de Quincey can acknowledge that the working masses also had recourse to opium, it remains the case that they had no cultural access to the sphere of poets with classical educations and aesthetic theories.

Today, mass entertainment—what the Frankfurt School philosophers called the "culture industry"—has disseminated these stories of addiction and excess to general consciousness, and they now serve a different function. Any suggestion that cocaine or cannabis might be important creative tools is greeted with skeptical derision because people know that their own use of such drugs is purely recreational. A rock star stuffed with coke is now accorded no greater admiration for the habit than is the workmate who has blown his overtime payment on a couple of Gs of Charlie. In the case of sports stars, only unmitigated contempt may attend the revelation that the captain of the team you support was underperforming on the pitch because he was in a state of sluggish collapse after a night on the powders, or else just monstrously hung over. (A work like English soccer star Tony Adams's booze confessional, *Addicted*, might stand, in that sense, as a rather braver act of self-disclosure than a pop singer's tearful recollections. We can take the singer having to be propped up at the microphone, but Tony was expected to be the backbone of both his club's and his country's defensive lines when he was drinking himself into a blackout on peach schnapps.) Although I take issue, then, with some of its modulations, an argument put by Harry Shapiro in *Waiting for the Man* makes an important central point:

> It's almost part of the pop star job description to be bad on our behalf, so that we can carry on as normal when the show is over . . . But . . . surely young people look up to these glamorous ne'er-do-wells and actually ape the worst indulgences of stardom?[18]

Not so, he says, although he tries to support the contention by pointing out that nobody, asked by researchers why they take drugs, answers, "Because pop stars do," which seems a touch simplistic. The trappings of fame in any case weave an alienating web around the lives of the idols:

> It is stretching the imagination to think that a remote pop star living in a world of limousines, first class travel and bodyguards has anything to say to a kid living in an inner-city housing estate or in some of our less obviously impoverished rural areas. Given the widespread use of drugs by young people these days, it is almost tempting to suggest that when a rock star goes public on drugs, he . . . is actually trying to establish street cred by declaring, "Hey, kids, I take drugs too. Please buy the record."[19]

That at least has the ring of credibility. But I shall suggest that another unwitting message is going out to this housing-estate kid (the Unknown Soldier of the drug wars)— one that also informs the way the lives of less outwardly loutish celebrities are read by those of nondeprived backgrounds.

The exemplary physical ruination of certain stars of cinema and pop has allowed us to project, via the mass media, the etiology of conspicuous drink and drug consumption onto the lives of spectacular individuals, so that Liz's or Liza's battle with the booze, the pills, the powders, the bullshit and so on becomes a magnified and mythically exteriorized version of our own habits. As long as somebody famous is being stretchered, mascara-streaked and sobbing, into the Betty Ford Clinic (as we imagine it), we can reassure ourselves that our own bibulous nights in the Pig and Corkscrew are free of moral taint. It is the aestheticization of altered states—that is, their externalization to the status of an aesthetic theme in the lives of emblematic others—that, more than any other phenomenon, makes them safe and cautiously permissible to us down here on earth. The point should not be confused with the way legislative authorities view this relationship. To them, we are all little Minnellis and Gallaghers in the making, and must be beaten back with the full repressive armor of the licensing and enforcement agencies if we look like getting too near the medicine cupboard. My point is about the ways in which we represent intoxication practices to ourselves. Just as no amount of aversive propaganda can undermine the evidence of our own eyes and the testimony of others that drugs do not inevitably and immediately lead to tragedy, so the evidence that one British rock star in American tax exile in the 1970s kept a goldfish bowl full of cocaine in the bathroom, into which ironic trough the snouts of household names would nightly snuffle, forbids believing that our own shared-out Friday-night gram will lead to blasted sinuses and destitution.

Taking a step back, we might see this projective relationship with the profligacy of the celebrities come to resemble, through the curvature of historical relativity, that other such relationship between the great and the obscure in classical times. It is the self-comforting homily of the Greek choruses in the tragedies, most notably in the opening act of Sophocles' *Antigone,* that it is better to be a law-abiding nobody-in-particular than to be one of these hubristic individuals who upsets the gods in some way and promptly crashes to a salutary ruin. As we saw in chapter 2, the fate of the misguided King Pentheus in *The Bacchae* of Euripides is to be torn apart by the followers of Dionysos—principally his own nearest and dearest—for foolishly attempting to suppress the orgiastic rites consecrated to the god. The decapitated head and dismembered body are milked for all the didactic force they contain. Similarly, when the tabloid press brings us scandalous news of the stars' shenanigans, such as Johnny Depp splashing £11,000 ($16,500) on a bottle of 20-year-old Burgundy in a London restaurant and then emerging to belabor waiting photographers with a lump of wood, the dauntless cameras that capture the moment of his arrest intend to evoke in us a sense of there-but-for-the-grace-of-God. The abuse confessional then becomes the star's own spin on the shameful events, replete with every exhibit we fill the public gallery to gawp at—the jeans soaked in incontinent urine, the silver nasal plate that replaces the corroded septum, the track marks up the arms, the vandalized hotel rooms, the police mugshots. It is an absorbing story, and one that is as old as the theater itself. And its representation in the arts was still going strong in 1999, when among the work of the British artist Tracey Emin shortlisted for the annual Turner Prize for contemporary art was a soiled bed surrounded by a detritus of cigarette packets, pills and empty vodka bottles. Emin has declared herself to be alcoholic, and this installation, which many commentators professed to find nauseous and gratuitous, functioned intriguingly as both self-indictment and shrine. Smell my shame, it offered, as you do me homage.

Euripides has Dionysos coming over all pompous and Athenian at the end of the play, justifying the cruel sentence of exile pronounced on Pentheus' grandfather Cadmus, for not recognizing him when he appeared in mortal guise, by saying that it is the price for insulting a god. When Cadmus vainly upbraids him for stooping to the vindictiveness of mortals, Dionysos wearily retorts that it is all preordained anyway, so there's no point in arguing: the festival god evolved at the last from merry prankster to stone-faced bureaucrat. Agauë, the mother who has slaughtered her son in the service of the wine god, is left ruing the day she ever got sucked into the Dionysiac cult:

> I have had my fill
> Of mountain-ecstasy; now take who will
> My holy ivy-wreath, my thyrsus-rod,
> All that reminds me how I served this god.[20]

If we too are tempted into such renunciations by drug-addled hang-overs on Monday mornings, we will often find ourselves at it again by Friday night. If good intentions pave the road to hell anyway, per-haps we should just accept it. On the other hand, the moral tales the tabloids tell remind us that there are disasters far greater than ours lying in wait for the rich and shameless, and it is they—more than the urgings of the medical establishment and our political represen-tatives—that exercise the strongest dissuasive force on us. Mean-while, as Shapiro suggests, the contract may not work quite so benevolently in the reverse direction, since the stars may be all too aware that their followers look to them to provide the exemplars of grungy excess:

> That's partly why so many of those with the worst reputations don't survive; they transfer those audience expectations into their own private lives and play out their own mythology.[21]

Is there aesthetic or philosophical inspiration at the bottom of the bottle? Socrates might not have demurred at the thought, but today we are more likely to avert our gazes from the conceptual artist rant-ing drunkenly on live TV, and wheeling her bed into the gallery to show us the minutiae of her personal disintegration. What's interest-ing is to see what certain artists, writers and thinkers have made of the fact of intoxication in their lives, how they have managed to negotiate a space for creativity within its demands, or have turned it into a motif, or how, notoriously, it has overcome them.

The initiative represented by "Kubla Khan" was, at the moment of its instigation, an undoubted striking-out into new territory. Yet it seems not altogether accidental—apposite, anyway—that the endeavor itself should be struck out by Coleridge's infuriating visitor from the neighboring village, the "person on business from Porlock" who manages to thwart the remainder of what should have been a much larger composition by detaining him with some nameless trivia, making the detail of the opium visions melt into air. Specula-tion as to the precise identity of the person from Porlock has gone on ever since Coleridge's death, and there is a tendency now, exempli-fied by his recent biographer, Richard Holmes, to lean toward the notion that there was no such person, and that the exasperating intruder is simply a device by which the poet, he who (like Malcolm Lowry) left so much unfinished, marked the limits of his inspiration. This of course suits the arguments of those less subtle interpreters than Holmes who will claim that intoxication is always corrosive to the creative impulse. For what it's worth, I incline to believe that a writer not much known for his circumspection would hardly have needed such a raggy excuse. It may be belittling for the artist to acknowledge that the muse has deserted him (although Wordsworth turns just such a dilemma to productive poetic account in *The Prelude,* and it didn't much bother Philip Larkin), but the blunt, banal fact of life is that sometimes the doorbell does ring and somebody is standing there wanting to sell you cable TV just as you had hit full flow. Or just as you had started coming up on magic mushrooms.

Intoxicants, finally, have no power to confer on any intellect capabilities that it did not already possess, a point Coleridge is at pains to make in the "Kubla Khan" preface, any more than they can promote murderous or other criminal behavior in those not so predisposed. Each individual must make of them what he or she will, even if that amounts to nothing more than having a good laugh. When all is said and written, the attempt to portray intoxication as a mystical element of the creative process was just another way of skirting our refusal to grant it independent validity in our lives.

As I hope to have shown, intoxication has been coerced to hide its head before religions, and to stand in the dock as an agent of social unrest. It has been branded with the sign of criminality, and been pilloried mercilessly by the guardians of our health. It has not been defeated by any of these forces, and so it scarcely needs a rescue squad of intoxicated artists to save it. Intoxication belongs to all of us. It is our birthright, our inheritance and our saving grace.

Conclusion

Coming Round

Of course, to be intoxicated is not the be-all and end-all of life, nor should it, or could it, ever be. At the end of Pulp's briefly infamous lyric "Sorted for Es and Wizz," singer Jarvis Cocker poses the question as to what a life of never coming down might be like. The song is about going to a rave, plentifully supplied with the drugs of the title, and aroused a short-lived flutter of indignation in the UK when it was released as a single in the year of the death of teenager Leah Betts. It doesn't make the adventure sound an especially rewarding one, it has to be said. Reminiscing about it afterward, the narrator reveals to his mother that he might have left an important part of his brain in a field somewhere outside London. What was missed, as radio DJs forbore to utter the song's title on air for fear of reminding listeners that ecstasy and amphetamines existed, was the ironic commentary on the rave experience the lyric offered in the middle of a dance culture reverberant with thinly disguised celebrations of ecstasy. A pleasantly forgettable painting-by-numbers instrumental tune of the same year, "Coming Up" by Chemical Heaven, showed just how brazenly drug references were being appropriated by anything that could technically be classified as dance music, whether it was sufficiently hectic or trancey to have been given house room at a rave or not. When Pulp was invited to perform a song at the Brit Awards ceremony that year, they defiantly chose to do "Sorted for Es and Wizz" rather than their much bigger hit "Common People," and the rhetorical query at the end was elevated to pure pantomime as Cocker was hoisted above the stage on a safety rope, where he swung helplessly about, plaintively bleating the question that has always already answered itself. What *if* you never come down?

There is no such thing as never coming down, and so the hypothesis doesn't have to be addressed. On the other hand, to posit that coming down means returning to a state of drug-free purity, of disintoxication as with some sort of reality antidote, won't serve either. "I believe that words like 'sober' and 'drug-free' are meaningless," writes David Lenson in *On Drugs*,

> and that "sobriety" is a cultural construction created for the furtherance of a political and economic agenda. The fact that the legal history shows a cumulative and piecemeal process strongly suggests that the present-day notion of sobriety, far from being "natural" or intuitive, is the result of nearly a century of social engineering.[1]

We may accept the point being made here that there is no idealized state of noninvolvement with which all intoxicated states may be unfavorably compared, and yet there is an exit state of coming off, or coming down, or coming round, that marks an often troubled reentry into the condition that preceded them. Lenson's analysis of the way we subjectively construct our hangovers and comedowns as retributive visitations of normality upon the overindulgent body is suggestive, but tinged with more than a dash of hope:

> Is a hangover really retributive? Must it be thought of as punishment, or can it be considered a sequential development of the high? . . . A strong speed high can reassert itself uninvited the following day. It might be as delightful as the original dose if it were allowed to be, if it weren't smothered in the proper regret. In LSD hangovers, stationary objects appear to be smoking, and moving objects leave visual trails behind them. There would be some interest in all this, if we let there be.[2]

Perhaps. But if we do construct the aftermath of an intoxication as chastisement, it is often because it is felt to be a kind of critical surplus, something more than we had bargained for, and that has arisen through our own lack of judgment. The nervy post-amphetamine state that goes on crackling away like static electricity the day after being up all night feels wrong because the body is now so exhausted that it needs precisely the chance to recuperate that these residues seem intent on denying it. Several hours of hallucinogenic intoxication can leave the mind in a condition of psychic exhaustion, in which the return to perceptual stability is what would now make the whole experience completely rewarding, but where smoking lampposts and cars that go by leaving color trails only induce a sort of cognitive seasickness. These reparations that the body appears to exact after being flooded with intoxicants don't have to be accompanied by naive contrition—"Never again!"—but that is not to say that they can't, or shouldn't, be construed as the obverse face of intoxication's enjoyment, the price you pay, the chance you take.

To many of my respondents, they fulfill an importantly self-regulating function in warning the user that that will be quite enough for the time being. To some, they are part and parcel of the experience itself. Short of falling into total constant dependency, we are given the opportunity, if we would but listen to what our bodies are saying to us in the aftermath, to measure these episodes out in a manageable way, one that minimizes the overall level of harm and ensures future enjoyment is not compromised by mindless repetition. It is not at all fanciful to suggest that part of the reason some people take an array of different substances, depending on mood and context, is that to be limited to just the one (alcohol being the only radical intoxicant we are allowed) is to be confined within the dullest regimen, as if *every* night's supper had to be lobster thermidor. There is such a thing as satiety, as having stuffed oneself, having drained the cup, burned oneself out and danced oneself to a standstill. At the end of the line, a sense of sickly dejection may be entirely to be expected. It may well be the best thing for us. Like the filicidal mother in *The Bacchae,* we may now have had our fill of mountain ecstasy.

To acknowledge that there is a time for coming down is emphatically not, however, to postulate the necessity of eventual abstinence as some kind of Holy Grail. It is not incumbent upon us to forswear all intoxicants in order to be better human beings. Who, apart from the furious imams and the official guardians of our health, can say anyway whether we would be better? Nor is it essential for the good of society. The nineteenth-century view of an overheated Baudelaire, exercised mightily by the transmogrifications of hashish, does not lack for modern believers: "Hashish, like all other solitary delights, makes the individual useless to mankind, and also makes society unnecessary to the individual."[3]

Cannabis now, however, enjoys a considerably wider currency in Western societies (the British police typically make around 80,000 seizures a year of the drug) than it did when you could form a Club des Haschischins, as Baudelaire did in consort with Delacroix, Gautier, Gérard de Nerval and others, and imagine that you were the privileged elite, a Brahmin caste aloof from the hoi polloi with their *vin ordinaire* and pastis. It should therefore be that much more difficult these days to get away with such sepulchral condescension. Dope is rarely ever a solitary delight, and in the sharing of its intoxication, it makes the user more than useful to her associates. Why should solitary delights, in any case, be socially useless, as Baudelaire insists? Why might they not reequip the individual psychically for her further participation in society? And why, to pick up the other half of his maxim, would that society be unwelcome to the smoker? Would not her loved ones still be valuable to her, even more so perhaps? What, we may wonder with a slight shiver, is to become of those deemed useless to mankind by the use of intoxication? In the latter half of the twentieth century, a verdict like that could no longer be wielded with such careless insouciance. And, at the risk of laboring the point, what alien beings make up this impeccably utilitarian mankind anyway, from whom all solitariness has been banished, along with all interest in altering consciousness? If not hashish, then what are *they* on?

It is interesting to notice the discomfiting ambivalence of institutional authority, in the century that made most of the intoxicants illegal, on the question of whether their use is disruptive or tranquilizing. For Terence McKenna, in *Food of the Gods,* the question is not in doubt. The state's invisible agents used the international drug trade of the nineteenth century as an instrument of national policy, both in order to quell victim nations and to make them play an obeisant role in the trade structures the dominant states profited from. Then, after the drugs themselves were made illegal, television became the instrument of control:

> Flattening, editing, and simplifying, television did its job and created a postwar American culture of the Ken-and-Barbie variety. The children of Ken and Barbie briefly broke out of the television intoxication in the mid-sixties through the use of hallucinogens. "Oops," responded the dominators, and they quickly made psychedelics illegal and halted all research. A double dose of TV therapy plus cocaine was ordered up for the errant hippies, and they were quickly cured and turned into consumption-oriented yuppies. Only a recalcitrant few escaped this levelling of values.[4]

I imagine we can safely presume this plucky, rebellious, undeceivable few included Terence McKenna, in whom the baleful entrancements of television appear to have met their match. This, of course, is paranoia run riot, right up to the suggestion that these dominators were in the slightest degree perturbed at the antics of white hippies blowing fairy bubbles in the quagmire of Woodstock. Quite the opposite conclusion is drawn by Sadie Plant in *Writing on Drugs*. Having consulted the same reference as McKenna—Martin A. Lee and Bruce Shlain's *Acid Dreams*, a minutely detailed analysis of the CIA's experiments with LSD during the so-called countercultural period of the 1960s in the United States—Plant observes that

> there were many suggestions, not so improbable, that the drug had been deliberately popularised by the CIA in an effort to depoliticise its 1960s users and undermine their ability to organise, co-ordinate or even simply think straight.[5]

In her next paragraph, she credits it with having "inspired Vietnam War protests," so if the CIA had used it as a deliberate means of disorientating these politically active hippies, it must have been left kicking itself over such a spectacular own goal.

No conspiracy theory along these lines can be granted much in the way of credibility for the compelling reason that the effects of intoxicants, and the uses to which they are put, are never so securely predictable as this. This is not to deny that the CIA carried out nefarious research on hallucinogenics and many other classes of drug in the 1950s and 1960s, in the hopes of finding either a truth serum for use on captured spies, a scrambling agent to prevent CIA spies captured by the Soviets from blurting under torture or some substance that could productively be processed into chemical weaponry to raise the stakes in the Cold War. (On this last point, nobody can seriously doubt that, had LSD fallen into the hands of Nazi Germany, it would have been put to horrendous use in the occupied territories or in the medical experiment camps.) Amphetamine was extravagantly prescribed in the postwar years because it was thought it would cheer everybody up and increase their productive capacity, but it simply succeeded in fueling confrontational aggression among the disadvantaged, creating cases of severe malnourishment through its appetite-suppressant qualities, and, most traumatically in Japan, increasing the incidence of psychoses. In any case, if one thinks oneself momentarily into the role of Commissar for Mind Control, exactly what class of substance would be best suited to the task? A brain-shredding hallucinogen or stupefying sedative (in which case, how will the production targets ever be met)? Or a brutal stimulant that might run the risk of creating a restless populace with not enough to occupy it? The dangers of any of these courses of action outweigh the benefits when considered on a socially prescriptive scale. Surely, it would be safer to keep people off them altogether, which is exactly the policy we now have before us in the shape of the globe-encircling network of proscriptions orchestrated by the enforcement industry. If we are looking for conspiracy theories, this will do nicely. The greatest conspiracy ever mounted against the mass of humanity—greatest because so enormously ambitious in its reach—is the effort to close off access to alternative mental states completely.

Our desire for intoxicants, and our capacity for them, arise early and, other than by a major exercise of will, do not die. Three gulps of razor-sharp Chilean Sauvignon Blanc did not at all faze my four-year-old nephew when he tried it. A boy of about twelve who was pestering passengers on the bus for a cigarette was challenged as to whether he was old enough to be smoking, but was already unanswerably well versed in the niceties of the law: "I can smoke, I just can't buy them." Almost the very last thing to make my grand-mother, helpless with Alzheimer's in a nursing home in her nineties, light up with the laughter of rational recognition was the sweet brown sherry that was lifted to her lips on her birthday.

When our path to them is blocked, or strewn with obstacles, we may find ourselves in the most indelicately compromising circum-stances. That was certainly the case when a man with a severely restrictive religious upbringing, and a responsible job in the property sector, found himself being dragged hanging from the door of a Lon-don cab, and then punched unconscious in the road, in an effort to secure a quantity of cocaine he had paid for. When there are no alternative substances, new ways of administering the old familiar ones may be tried. Thus was vodka sniffing born, and thus did I see a boy with an ambiguously addictive love affair with needles inject himself with Scotch and even Pernod to obviate the tiresome longueurs of metabolism. Deprived of everything in an isolation cell, we could still—and probably would—try hyperventilating.

In a public debate in London in December 1997 on the question of whether cannabis should be decriminalized, Nigel Evans, Conser-vative MP for Ribble Valley in the northwest of England, stated that "alcohol and tobacco are two eggs that have been scrambled. You can't unscramble those particular eggs."[6] In less gnomic terminol-ogy, the point was that society just had to shrug off the general avail-ability of the substances mentioned because they were already in common currency, but that was no reason to let anything else, specifically cannabis, become available. (Evans owns a retail outlet in south Wales that sells cigarettes, and had been accused of hypocrisy.) As an argument for the status quo, this is wholly self-defeating. The drug laws of the twentieth century were nothing other than an attempt to unscramble numerous eggs, since every intoxicant begins its career by being available. If it were not avail-able, where would the need for legislation come from? And if it continues to be available anyway, as cannabis and all the rest are, why has the law convinced itself that these particular eggs are unscrambleable, while the other two aren't? As an argument for the dysfunctionality of the drug laws, by contrast, this little metaphoric flight is unimpeachable. There will be no unscrambling—ever—of cannabis, or ecstasy, or cocaine, or heroin, or anything else that anybody has tried, liked and wants to buy, for the very good reason that no substance springs into being fully formed as a "controlled" substance. That is only the status it incurs once people have started using it. It only needs one person to use it, talk about it or write about it, and it has entered human consciousness as another intoxicant. It has already been scrambled and can't be unscrambled, even if only the Shulgins have taken it.

In October 1994, the DEA arrived mob-handed at the home of Alexander and Ann Shulgin in Lafayette, California. Thirty agents in eight vehicles, including a phalanx of police cars and a fire engine, had dropped in to carry out a random check-up. After nosing around the laboratory, they claimed to have identified a number of technical infringements of the terms of Shulgin's license to work with controlled substances. He was fined $25,000, a sum that rose to $40,000 with legal fees, which had to be raided from their pension funds. As a salient part of the final bargain, Shulgin surrendered his license. The federal authorities had neutralized a prominent dissident, but his written work continues to circulate and his later career was not in vain, because Shulgin's bloodstream had already played host to a multitude of phenethylamines and tryptamines before the DEA had barely had time to look them up. We have since had the chance to read about them. There is no unscrambling these eggs either.

Somewhere in the middle of Werner Herzog's massive film *Fitzcarraldo* (1982), a parable is told. It is the story of the first team of French explorers to venture into the Canadian hinterland. One day, one of their members separates from the group, wandering away by himself. In the course of his lonely meanderings, he comes across the most heart-stopping sight he has ever seen, a mighty waterfall crashing over a precipice in the middle of nowhere known to civilization. By the time he rejoins the others, he can hardly gasp out the news in his wild excitement. Believing him to have become deranged while wandering alone, his companions treat his claim with friendly skepticism. But he won't relinquish the story. Finally, one of the explorers, intending to play the trump card of Western rationalism against him, demands of him, "If you insist this waterfall exists, then prove it!" to which the man's reply is, "The proof is—that I've seen it."

It may be protested that the word of one man won't suffice. He has to be *seen* to have seen it, otherwise we are entitled to the same exercise of doubt we would extend to one who claimed to have seen Elvis in the laundromat. But this is to miss the point. This isn't the skeptics' tale, it is his, and its pathos lies in the fact that we now know the Niagara Falls do indeed exist, but that there was once a time when only one European pair of eyes had seen them, and that to that solitary soul, who knew he wasn't lying or hallucinating, his testimony demanded to be heard. The same is true of Shulgin's compounds, and of any individual's own encounter with whatever it is he or she has taken. Nobody else has the precise experience you have when you take ecstasy or cannabis or Sancerre, and nobody should have presumed to tell you—not even for the very best altruistic motives—that that experience was wrong when you knew it wasn't. Intoxication is so uncontrollable because it is lustrously colored with the deepest dyes of subjectivity. It reminds you gloriously that you exist, that you are capable of quite different forms of consciousness from the one you wake up in each morning and that your serotonin reserves are after all your own to manage.

The proof is—that you've seen it.

Notes

INTRODUCTION: COMING UP

1. Hugh Johnson, *Vintage: The Story of Wine* (Mitchell Beazley, 1989), p. 10.
2. Louis Lewin, *Phantastica: Narcotic and Stimulating Drugs,* trans. P. H. A. Wirth (Park Street Press, Rochester, Vermont, 1998), pp. 124, 158, 264.
3. Peter Conrad, *Modern Times, Modern Places: Life and Art in the 20th Century* (Thames & Hudson, 1998), p. 697.
4. Slavoj Zizek, *For They Know Not What They Do: Enjoyment as a Political Factor* (Verso, 1991), p. 239.
5. Ibid.

CHAPTER 1: INTOXICOLOGY

1. Andrew Weil, *The Natural Mind* (Jonathan Cape, 1973), p. 17.
2. David Lenson, *On Drugs* (Minneapolis, MN: University of Minnesota Press, 1995), p. xviii.
3. Terence McKenna, *Food of the Gods: The Search for the Original Tree of Knowledge* (Rider, 1992), p. 237.
4. Ibid., p. 166.
5. Ibid., p. 258.
6. Martin Heidegger, *Being and Time,* trans. John Macquarrie and Edward Robinson (New York: Harper & Row, 1962), p. 195.
7. Op. cit., pp. 31–2.
8. Ibid., p. 256.
9. Avital Ronell, *Crack Wars: Literature, Addiction, Mania* (Lincoln, NE: University of Nebraska Press, 1992), p. 13.
10. Richard Rudgley, *The Alchemy of Culture: Intoxicants in Society* (British Museum Press, 1993), p. 146.
11. Op. cit., p. 269.
12. Op. cit., p. 3.
13. Ibid., p. 6.
14. Ibid., p. 190.

CHAPTER 2: THE RIDICULOUS AND THE SUBLIME

1. Euripides, *The Bacchae and Other Plays,* trans. Philip Vellacott (Penguin, 1973), p. 196.
2. Ibid., p. 218.
3. James Davidson, *Courtesans and Fishcakes: The Consuming Passions of Classical Athens* (Fontana, 1998), pp. 65–6.
4. Robert Turcan, *The Cults of the Roman Empire,* trans. Antonia Nevill (Blackwell, 1996), p. 305.
5. Ibid., p. 324.
6. Plato, *Symposium and the Death of Socrates,* trans. Tom Griffith (Wordsworth Editions, 1997), p. 146.
7. Andrew Dalby, *Siren Feasts: A History of Food and Gastronomy in Greece* (Routledge, 1997), p. 120.
8. Epicurus, *The Epicurus Reader: Selected Writings and Testimonia,* trans. Brad Inwood and L. P. Gerson (Indianapolis, IN: Hackett, 1994), p. 31.

9. Ibid., p. 28.
10. Theodor W. Adorno, *The Stars Down to Earth, and Other Essays on the Irrational in Culture* (Routledge, 1994), p. 60.
11. Op. cit., pp. 44–5.

CHAPTER 3: THE FOURTH DEADLY SIN

1. Peggy Morgan and Clive Lawton (eds.), *Ethical Issues in Six Religious Traditions* (Edinburgh University Press, 1996), p. 193.
2. Ibid.
3. Ibid., p. 194.
4. Christopher Hibbert, *The English: A Social History 1066–1945* (Harper-Collins, 1994), p. 45.
5. The Qur'an, trans. N.J. Dawood, 1974.
6. *Ethical Issues in Six Religious Traditions,* p. 243.
7. *The Alchemy of Culture,* p. 101.
8. Ninian Smart, *The World's Religions* (Cambridge University Press, 1998), p. 301.
9. Cited in *Ethical Issues in Six Religious Traditions,* p. 243.
10. Cited in Susanna Barrows and Robin Room (eds.), *Drinking: Behavior and Belief in Modern History* (Berkley, CA: University of California Press, 1991), p. 191.

CHAPTER 4: FROM GIN LANE TO CRACK CITY

1. Ronald K. Siegel, *Intoxication: Life in Pursuit of Artificial Paradise* (New York: E.P. Dutton, 1989), p. 199.
2. Ibid., p. 195.
3. Ibid., p. 204.
4. Andrew Tyler, *Street Drugs* (Hodder and Stoughton, 1995), pp. 269–70.
5. Cited in Harold McGee, *On Food and Cooking: The Science and Lore of the Kitchen* (Allen & Unwin, 1984), p. 220.
6. Cited in Richard Rudgley, *The Encyclopedia of Psychoactive Substances* (Little, Brown, 1998), p. 248.
7. Cited in *The Alchemy of Culture,* p. 35.
8. Julie Burchill and Tony Parsons, *The Boy Looked at Johnny: The Obituary of Rock and Roll* (Pluto Press, 1978), p. 84.
9. *Food of the Gods,* pp. 165–6.
10. Cited in Marek Kohn, *Dope Girls: The Birth of the British Drug Underground* (Lawrence & Wishart, 1992), p. 179.
11. Thomas de Quincey, *Confessions of an English Opium-Eater* (New York: Dover Publications, 1995), p. 54.
12. Alexander and Ann Shulgin, *PIHKAL: A Chemical Love Story* (Berkeley, CA: Transform Press, 1995), p. 737.
13. Ibid., p. 736.
14. Russell Newcombe and Lyn Matthews, "Crack in Liverpool," in Ross Coomber (ed.), *Drugs and Drug Use in Society: A Critical Reader* (Greenwich University Press, 1994), p. 4.
15. Ian Penman, *Vital Signs: Music, Movies and Other Manias* (Serpent's Tail, 1998), p. 12.
16. Cited in Rudgley, *The Encyclopaedia of Psychoactive Substances,* pp. 138–9.
17. Ibid., p. xvii.
18. Cited in McGee, *On Food and Cooking,* p. 432.
19. Luc Sante, *Low Life: Lures and Snares of Old New York* (Granta, 1998), p. 113.

CHAPTER 5: LIVING OUTSIDE THE LAW
1. Edward Behr, *Prohibition: Thirteen Years That Changed America* (BBC Books/Penguin, 1997), p. 118.
2. Cited in Rudgley, *The Alchemy of Culture*, p. 75.
3. Ibid., p. 73.
4. Cited in Behr, p. 227.
5. *Food of the Gods*, p. 268.
6. *On Drugs*, p. 193.
7. Ibid., p. 196.
8. Ibid., p. 197.
9. *PIHKAL*, pp. xiv–xv.
10. Ibid., p. xvi.
11. Ibid., pp. 639–40.
12. Erich Goode, *Between Politics and Reason: The Drug Legalization Debate* (New York: St Martin's Press, 1997), p. 36.
13. Ibid.
14. Ibid., p. 65.
15. Ibid.
16. Ibid., p. 78.
17. Ibid., p. 82.
18. Ibid., p. 129.
19. Ibid., p. 131.
20. Ibid., p. 135.
21. Ibid., p. 140.
22. Ibid., p. 141.
23. Ibid., pp. 146–8.
24. Ibid., p. 147.
25. Ibid., p. 148.
26. Ibid., p. 149.
27. Ibid.
28. *Intoxication*, pp. 316–7.

CHAPTER 6: OUT OF IT
1. Stuart Walton and Brian Glover, *The Ultimate Encyclopedia of Wine, Beer, Spirits and Liqueurs* (Hermes House, 1998), p. 9.
2. Mariana Valverde, *Diseases of the Will: Alcohol and the Dilemmas of Freedom* (Cambridge University Press, 1998), p. 76.
3. Dr. Thomas Stuttaford, *To Your Good Health! The Wise Drinker's Guide* (Faber and Faber, 1997), p. 5.
4. Ibid., p. 30.
5. Ibid., p. 50.
6. Andrew Barr, "Are We Ready for the Truth?" paper delivered to the Safeway Wine and Health Seminar, London, 22 April 1999.
7. *Intoxication*, p. 209.
8. Ibid.
9. Ibid., p. 210.
10. "Eton Boy Died After 'Fainting Game,' " *Guardian*, 17 March 1999.
11. *Intoxication*, p. 217.
12. *Phantastica*, p. 114.
13. Cited in *Phantastica*, p. 130.
14. Ibid., p. 136.
15. *Confessions of an English Opium-Eater*, pp. 19–20.
16. Jerry Stahl, *Permanent Midnight* (Abacus, 1996), pp. 4–5.
17. Evelyn Waugh, *Decline and Fall* (Penguin, 1937), p. 208.

18. Friedrich Nietzsche, *The Gay Science*, trans. Walter Kaufmann (Vintage, 1974), pp. 141–2.
19. Ibid., p. 142.
20. Cited in W. J. Rorabaugh, *The Alcoholic Republic: An American Tradition* (Oxford University Press, 1981), p. vii.

CHAPTER 7: HITTING THE BOTTLE FOR INSPIRATION
1. Aldous Huxley, *The Doors of Perception* (Flamingo, 1994), p. 17.
2. Ibid., p. 21.
3. Ibid., p. 23.
4. Ibid., pp. 19–20.
5. Jack Kerouac, *Old Angel Midnight* (San Francisco, CA: Grey Fox Press, 1995), p. 2.
6. Malcolm Lowry, *Under the Volcano* (Penguin, 1984), p. 294.
7. Douglas Day, Preface to Malcolm Lowry, *Dark as the Grave Wherein My Friend Is Laid* (Penguin, 1972), p. 5.
8. Walter Benjamin, *One-Way Street, and Other Writings*, trans. Edmund Jephcott (Verso, 1985), p. 220.
9. Ibid., p. 219.
10. Ibid., p. 222.
11. Ibid., p. 220.
12. *Confessions of an English Opium-Eater*, p. 3.
13. Ibid.
14. Alethea Hayter, *Opium and the Romantic Imagination* (Berkeley, CA: University of California Press, 1968), p. 103.
15. Cited in Richard Holmes, *Coleridge: Darker Reflections* (HarperCollins, 1998), p. 14.
16. Ibid.
17. *Symposium*, p. 48.
18. Harry Shapiro, *Waiting for the Man: The Story of Drugs and Popular Music* (Helter Skelter, 1999), p. 163.
19. Ibid.
20. *The Bacchae*, p. 244.
21. Op. cit.

CONCLUSION: COMING ROUND
1. *On Drugs*, p. 6.
2. Ibid., pp. 180–1.
3. Cited in Sadie Plant, *Writing on Drugs* (Faber and Faber, 1999), p. 37.
4. *Food of the Gods*, p. 220.
5. *Writing on Drugs*, p. 126.
6. "Cannabis: Should It Be Decriminalised?" public debate, London, 11 December 1997.

Bibliography

The following is a list of works referred to in the text, together with other consulted works and titles of related interest.

Adams, Tony with Ian Ridley, *Addicted* (CollinsWillow), 1998.

Adorno, Theodor W, *The Stars Down to Earth, and Other Essays on the Irrational Culture* (Routledge), 1994.

Almond, Marc, *Tainted Life: The Autobiography* (Sidgwick & Jackson), 1999.

Barr, Andrew, *Drink: A Social History* (Pimlico), 1998.

Barrows, Susanna and Robin Room (eds.), *Drinking: Behavior and Belief in Modern History* (University of California Press, Berkeley, CA), 1991.

Behr, Edward, *Prohibition: Thirteen Years That Changed America* (Penguin/ BBC Books), 1998.

Benjamin, Walter, *One-Way Street and Other Writings* (Verso), 1985.

Booth, Martin, *Opium: A History* (Pocket Books), 1997.

Burchill, Julie and Tony Parsons, *"The Boy Looked at Johnny": The Obituary of Rock and Roll* (Pluto Press), 1978.

Clarke, Donald, *Wishing on the Moon: The Life and Times of Billie Holiday* (Viking), 1994.

Coleridge, Samuel Taylor, *Selected Poetry* (Oxford University Press), 1999.

Conrad, Peter, *Modern Times, Modern Places: Life and Art in the 20th Century* (Thames & Hudson), 1998.

Coomber, Ross (ed.), *Drugs and Drug Use in Society: A Critical Reader*, in the series Greenwich Readers (Greenwich University Press), 1994.

Dalby, Andrew, *Siren Feasts: A History of Food and Gastronomy in Greece* (Routledge), 1997.

Davidson, James, *Courtesans and Fishcakes: The Consuming Passions of Classical Athens* (Fontana), 1998.

Davidson, Toni (ed.), *Intoxication: An Anthology of Stimulant-Based Writing* (Serpent's Tail), 1998.

Dean, Alan, *Chaos and Intoxication: Complexity and Adaptation in the Structure of Human Nature* (Routledge), 1997.

de Quincey, Thomas, *Confessions of an English Opium-Eater* (Dover Publications, Mineola, NY), 1995.

Devereux, Paul, *The Long Trip: A Prehistory of Psychedelia* (Penguin), 1997.

Euripides, *The Bacchae and Other Plays*, trans. Philip Vellacott (Penguin), 1973.

Fisher, M. F. K., *The Art of Eating* (PAPERMAC), 1991.

Fletcher, Richard, *The Conversion of Europe: From Paganism to Christianity 371–1386 A.D.* (Fontana), 1998.

Goode, Erich, *Between Politics and Reason: The Drug Legalization Debate* (St. Martin's Press, New York, NY), 1997.

Gottlieb, Adam, *The Pleasures of Cocaine* (20th Century Alchemist, Manhattan Beach, CA), 1976.

Harrison, Jane Ellen, *Prolegomena to the Study of Greek Religion* (Princeton University Press, Princeton, NJ), 1991.

Heather, Nick, Alex Wodak, Ethan Nadelmann and Pat O'Hare (eds.), *Psychoactive Drugs and Harm Reduction: From Faith to Science* (Whurr), 1993.

Hibbert, Christopher, *The English: A Social History 1066–1945* (Harper-Collins), 1994.

Hollands, Robert G., *Friday Night, Saturday Night: Youth-Cultural Identification in the Post-industrial City* (Department of Social Policy, University of Newcastle), 1995.

Holmes, Richard, *Coleridge: Darker Reflections* (HarperCollins), 1998.

Huxley, Aldous, *The Doors of Perception* (Flamingo), 1994.

Inwood, Brad and L. P. Gerson (eds. and trans.), *The Epicurus Reader: Selected Writings and Testimonia* (Hackett, Indianapolis, IN), 1994.

Johnson, Hugh, *Vintage: The Story of Wine* (Mitchell Beazley), 1989.

Kerouac, Jack, *Old Angel Midnight* (Grey Fox Press, San Francisco, CA), 1995.

Kohn, Marek, *Dope Girls: The Birth of the British Drug Underground* (Lawrence & Wishart), 1992.

Kuhn, Cynthia, Scott Swartzwelder and Wilkie Wilson, *Buzzed: The Straight Facts About the Most Used and Abused Drugs from Alcohol to Ecstasy* (W. W. Norton, New York, NY), 1998.

Lenson, David, *On Drugs* (University of Minnesota Press, Minneapolis, MN), 1995.

Lewin, Louis, *Phantastica: Narcotic and Stimulating Drugs* (Park Street Press, Rochester, VT), 1998.

Low, Donald A., *The Regency Underworld* (Sutton), 1982.

Lowry, Malcolm, *Dark as the Grave Wherein My Friend Is Laid* (Penguin), 1972.

Lowry, Malcolm, *Under the Volcano* (Penguin), 1984.

Mann, Thomas, *The Magic Mountain,* trans. H. T. Lowe-Porter (Penguin), 1987.

Matthews, Patrick, *Cannabis Culture: A Journey Through Disputed Territory* (Bloomsbury), 1999.

McAllister, William B., *Drug Diplomacy in the Twentieth Century: An International History* (Routledge), 2000.

McDonald, J. Ian H., *The Crucible of Christian Morality* (Routledge), 1998.

McGee, Harold, *On Food and Cooking: The Science and Lore of the Kitchen* (Allen & Unwin), 1984.

McKenna, Terence, *Food of the Gods: The Search for the Original Tree of Knowledge* (Rider), 1992.

Morgan, Peggy and Clive Lawton, *Ethical Issues in Six Religious Traditions* (Edinburgh University Press), 1996.

Nicholson, Stuart, *Billie Holiday* (Victor Gollancz), 1995.

Nietzsche, Friedrich, *The Gay Science,* trans. Walter Kaufmann (Vintage), 1974.

Pellerin, Cheryl, *Trips: How Hallucinogens Work in Your Brain* (Seven Stories Press, New York, NY), 1998.

Penman, Ian, *Vital Signs: Music, Movies and Other Manias* (Serpent's Tail), 1998.

Plant, Sadie, *Writing on Drugs* (Faber and Faber), 1999.

Plato, *Symposium and the Death of Socrates* (Wordsworth Editions), 1997.

Public debate transcript, London, 11 December 1997: "Cannabis: Should It Be Decriminalised?" (Rooted Media).

Robinson, Jancis, *The Demon Drink* (Mandarin), 1989.

Robson, Philip, *Forbidden Drugs: Understanding Drugs and Why People Take Them* (Oxford University Press), 1994.

Ronell, Avital, *Crack Wars: Literature, Addiction, Mania* (University of Nebraska Press, Lincoln, NE), 1992.

Rorabaugh, W. J., *The Alcoholic Republic: An American Tradition* (Oxford University Press), 1979.

Rudgley, Richard, *The Alchemy of Culture: Intoxicants in Society* (British Museum Press), 1993.

Rudgley, Richard, *The Encyclopedia of Psychoactive Substances* (Little, Brown), 1998.

Sante, Luc, *Low Life: Lures and Snares of Old New York* (Granta), 1998.

Saunders, Nicholas, *Ecstasy Reconsidered* (Nicholas Saunders), 1997.

Seminar papers, London, 22 April 1999: "Wine and Health."

Shapiro, Harry, *Waiting for the Man: The Story of Drugs and Popular Music* (Helter Skelter), 1999.

Shulgin, Alexander and Ann Shulgin, *PIHKAL: A Chemical Love Story* (Transform Press, Berkeley, CA), 1995.

Shulgin, Alexander and Ann Shulgin, *TIHKAL: The Continuation* (Transform Press, Berkeley, CA), 1997.

Siegel, Ronald K., *Intoxication: Life in Pursuit of Artificial Paradise* (E. P. Dutton, New York, NY), 1989.

Simon, André, *Drink* (Burke), 1948.

Smart, Ninian, *The World's Religions* (Cambridge University Press), 1998.

Stahl, Jerry, *Permanent Midnight* (Abacus), 1996.

Stuttaford, Dr. Thomas, *To Your Good Health! The Wise Drinker's Guide* (Faber and Faber), 1997.

Tannahill, Reay, *Food in History* (Penguin), 1988.

Thompson, Peter, *Rum Punch & Revolution: Taverngoing & Public Life in Eighteenth-Century Philadelphia* (University of Pennsylvania Press, Philadelphia, PA), 1999.

Turcan, Robert, *The Cults of the Roman Empire*, trans. Antonia Nevill (Blackwell), 1996.

Tyler, Andrew, *Street Drugs* (Hodder and Stoughton), 1995.

Valverde, Mariana, *Diseases of the Will: Alcohol and the Dilemmas of Freedom* (Cambridge University Press), 1998.

Veyne, Paul (ed.), *A History of Private Life: From Pagan Rome to Byzantium*, trans. Arthur Goldhammer (Harvard University Press), 1992.

Wagner, David, *The New Temperance: The American Obsession with Sin and Vice* (Westview Press, Boulder, CO), 1997.

Walton, Stuart and Brian Glover, *The Ultimate Encyclopedia of Wine, Beer, Spirits and Liqueurs* (Hermes House), 1998.

Waugh, Evelyn, *Decline and Fall* (Penguin), 1937.

Weil, Andrew, *The Natural Mind* (Jonathan Cape), 1973.

Williamson, Kevin, *Drugs and the Party Line* (Rebel Inc.), 1997.

Zizek, Slavoj, *For They Know Not What They Do: Enjoyment as a Political Factor* (Verso), 1991.

Index

About the Author

Stuart Walton has written for the *Observer* and the *Sunday Telegraph* as well as for numerous magazines in the United Kingdom. He is the author of *The World Encyclopedia of Wine* and *You Heard It Through the Grapevine*. He lives in Brighton, England.